SWEDEN

THEATRE OF CONFLICT
1804-1814

openhagen

Tilsit

Königsberg

Lauenbourg

Eylau

Friedland

Stralsund

Allenstein

Grodno

PRUSSIA

Bialystok

RUSSIA

R. Oder

Stettin

Thorn

R. Vistula

Pultusk

Berlin

R. Spree

Posen

Warsaw

Brest-Litovsk

runswick

Magdeburg

Potsdam

Halle

POLAND

R. Bug

Leipzig

Dresden

Breslau

Erfurt

SAXONY

SILESIA

Krakow

Lemberg

BOHEMIA

Nuremberg

Olmütz

GALICIA

MORAVIA

Austerlitz

AUSTRIA

Augsburg

Linz

R. Danube

Pressburg

Munich

Vienna

HUNGARY

Salzburg

Wagram

Essling

Buda

Pest

Innsbruck

Leoben

TRANSYLVANIA

Trent

R. Drave

Trieste

R. Danube

Venice

GDOM
TALY

RURIA

OTTOMAN EMPIRE

0   100 miles

PAPAL STATES

How far from Austerlitz?

Napoleon 1805–1815

ALISTAIR HORNE

How far from Austerlitz?

NAPOLEON 1805–1815

St. Martin's Press
New York

A THOMAS DUNNE BOOK.
An imprint of St. Martin's Press.

HOW FAR FROM AUSTERLITZ? Copyright © 1996 by Alistair
Horne. Maps copyright © 1996 by Macmillan Publishers Ltd.
All rights reserved. Printed in the United States of America.
No part of this book may be used or reproduced in any manner
whatsoever without written permission except in the case of
brief quotations embodied in critical articles or reviews. For
information, address St. Martin's Press, 175 Fifth Avenue,
New York, N.Y. 10010.

Parts of this book were originally published 1979 by
William Morrow and Company Inc., New York, as
Napoleon, Master of Europe 1805–1807,
copyright © Alistair Horne 1979.

ISBN 0-312-15548-4

First published in Great Britain by Macmillan, an imprint of
Macmillan Publishers Ltd.

First U.S. Edition: May 1996

10 9 8 7 6 5 4 3 2 1

For Nancy

A St Helena Lullaby

'How far is St Helena from a little child at play?'
What makes you want to wander there with all the world between?
Oh, Mother, call your son again or else he'll run away.
(*No one thinks of winter when the grass is green!*)

'How far is St Helena from a fight in Paris Street?'
I haven't time to answer now — the men are falling fast.
The guns begin to thunder, and the drums begin to beat.
(*If you take the first step, you will take the last!*)

'How far is St Helena from the field of Austerlitz?'
You couldn't hear me if I told — so loud the cannon roar.
But not so far for people who are living by their wits.
(*'Gay go up' means 'Gay go down' the wide world o'er!*)

'How far is St Helena from an Emperor of France?'
I cannot see — I cannot tell — the Crowns they dazzle so.
The Kings sit down to dinner, and the Queens stand up to dance.
(*After open weather you may look for snow!*)

'How far is St Helena from the Capes of Trafalgar?'
A longish way — a longish way — with ten year more to run.
It's south across the water underneath a falling star.
(*What you cannot finish you must leave undone!*)

'How far is St Helena from the Beresina ice?'
An ill way — a chill way — the ice begins to crack.
But not so far for gentlemen who never took advice.
(*When you can't go forward you must e'en come back!*)

'How far is St Helena from the field of Waterloo?'
A near way — a clear way — the ship will take you soon.
A pleasant place for gentlemen with little left to do.
(*Morning never tries you till the afternoon!*)

'How far from St Helena to the Gate of Heaven's Grace?'
That no one knows — that no one knows — and no one ever will.
But fold your hands across your heart and cover up your face.
And after all your trapesings, child, lie still!

Rudyard Kipling

Contents

List of Maps

The maps in this book, drawn by ML Design, have been based on those included in the author's earlier book *Napoleon, Master of Europe 1805–1807*, and due acknowledgement to the cartographer Peter White is made with thanks.

List of Illustrations

The author and publishers wish to record their thanks to the owners and copyright holders of the illustrations used in this book for permission to reproduce them.

Sources and photograph credits are set out in brackets after each illustration.

in the text

in the plate section

Napoleon at Fontainebleau, brooding after defeat in 1814
  (Sotheby's)

Josephine in 1797 (Mary Evans Picture Library)

Marie Walewska at Versailles, 1812 (Lauros–Giraudon)

Fouché, a deceptively benevolent painting from Versailles,
  c. 1813 (Lauros–Giraudon)

Talleyrand in 1828 (Lauros–Giraudon)

'The Arch Duchess Maria Louisa going to take her Nap' (Private
  Collection/Bridgeman Art Library, London)

Triumph at Austerlitz, 1805 (Château de Versailles, France/
  Giraudon/Bridgeman Art Library, London)

Napoleon I receives Tsar Alexander I, Queen Louise and King
  Frederick William III of Prussia at Tilsit, 1807 (Musée de
  Versailles/E.T.Archive)

The Duke of Wellington in 1834 (Wallace Collection, London/
  Bridgeman Art Library, London)

Pitt the Younger (Rafael Valls Gallery, London/Bridgeman Art
  Library, London)

Blücher (Wellington Museum/E.T.Archive)

Kutuzov (State Historical Museum, Moscow/Bridgeman Art
  Library, London; Novosti/Bridgeman Art Library)

Wagram, 1809: Napoleon's Passage of the Danube (Wellington
  Museum/E.T.Archive)

Waterloo, 1815. Marshal Ney rallying his troops with a broken
  sword (Private Collection/Bridgeman Art Library, London)

Chronology

1769	Napoleon and Wellington born
1789	French Revolution begins
1792–1801	Revolutionary Wars; First Coalition (1792–7)
1793	Louis XVI guillotined
1792–5	The National Convention
1793	Napoleon at Siege of Toulon
1795	'Whiff of Grapeshot'; The Directory formed (1795–99)
1796–7	First Italian Campaigns
1798–9	Egyptian Campaign
1799	*Brumaire* coup; Napoleon becomes First Consul
1799–1804	The Consulate; Second Coalition (1799–1802)
1800	Battle of Marengo
1802	Peace of Amiens
1803–5	Plans to invade England
1804	Napoleon crowned Emperor
1805–6	Third Coalition
1805	Battles of Ulm and Austerlitz
1806–7	Fourth Coalition
1806	Creation of Confederation of the Rhine; Battle of Jena
1807	Battles of Eylau and Friedland; Peace of Tilsit
1808–14	Peninsular War
1809	Fifth Coalition; Battle of Wagram
1810	Napoleon marries Marie Louise
1812–14	Sixth Coalition
1812	Invasion of Russia; War of 1812, Britain versus USA
1813	Leipzig Campaign
1814	'La Patrie en Danger!' Campaign; First Abdication
1814–15	Congress of Vienna
1815	'The Hundred Days'; Seventh Coalition; Waterloo; Second Abdication
1821	Napoleon dies on St Helena

Preface

My argument is that War makes rattling good history; but
Peace is poor reading. So I back Bonaparte for the reason
that he will give pleasure to posterity.

'Spirit Sinister' from *The Dynasts* by Thomas Hardy, Act II, scene V

THE YEARS 1996 AND 1997 mark the 200th anniversary
of twenty-seven-year-old General Bonaparte's first outstanding
successes in the Italian Campaign against Austria. It was the
campaign that launched his star into orbit in France. Nearly
twenty years ago I wrote my earliest book on Napoleon and his
wars, entitled *Napoleon, Master of Europe, 1805–1807.** It was
what was known as a coffee-table book, heavily illustrated but
with a relatively concise text, written at a time of debunking and
revisionism. From Florence Nightingale and General Gordon to
Montgomery and Churchill, from Alexander Hamilton to General
Douglas MacArthur, reputations once unassailable had come
under attack – even the great Bonaparte. Approaching it, I
hoped, with a fresh and open mind, I wondered, Did he deserve
it? How did his reputation look, nearly two centuries later?

Curiosity is, or ought to be, what motivates most historians.
Most of my previous books on French history and conflicts had
been about the century from 1870 (the Franco-Prussian War)[1]
onward to the Algerian War of the 1950s.[2] So when I started out
on Napoleon in the 1970s, my ignorance was considerable and I

---

* Published in 1979 by Weidenfeld & Nicolson, London, and William Morrow,
New York.

was unashamedly driven by desire for self-education. Why, how, could this little Corsican nobody have climbed from nowhere to the top of the world and have achieved so much? Since then, Napoleon, the epoch so rich in drama and romance which he dominated, his larger-than-life contemporaries, have never quite left me. So now, twenty years and five books later, I found myself wanting to re-explore what finally destroyed the Giant, or the 'Ogre' as many Europeans had come to call him by the first decade of the nineteenth century. What paths led him to his final, wretched exile? 'How far is St Helena?' as Kipling asked.

During the First World War, when sorely tried by his Anglo-Saxon allies, Marshal Ferdinand Foch made a classic remark: 'Now I know about coalitions, I respect Napoleon rather less!' Certainly – as this book tries to show – the coalition leaders who confronted Napoleon were not, right to the very end in 1815, always marked with the highest distinction. Also, as successive Israeli governments have learnt to their cost since 1967, it is easier to win wars than peace. Unfortunately for France, Napoleon's unbounded military genius was in no way matched by his political and diplomatic sensitivity. He had Talleyrand for that; and, once he and Talleyrand had parted after Tilsit, his star was set in its downward trajectory. Nonetheless, the fact remains that in an astoundingly short space of time Napoleon had chalked up a career of military conquests almost unparalleled in the modern world. His physical empire may have proved hardly more durable than Hitler's, but the legacy of his civil and social works endures to this day. Few institutions or monuments in modern France do not bear some relation to his name. There are no memorials to the *Kultur* of Adolf Hitler.

Apart from the irresistible and eternal allure of the subject, an additional excuse for adding yet another title to those 300,000 already existing can always be found in Thomas Hardy's remark in *The Dynasts*. 'War', he wrote, 'makes rattling good history' – and the Napoleonic saga which gripped Hardy certainly rattled along at a pace comparable with that with which the Emperor sped from one battlefield to another. There is about Napoleon's campaigns a constant relevance, particularly with regard to his notions of space and movement. It is easy to forget over what a vast geographical canvas his wars were waged: from the West Indies to Egypt and Syria, from Scandinavia to Sicily, from Lisbon to Moscow. Even India and the Far East were not outside the schemes of his grand strategy, and those two decades culminating in Waterloo deserve more appropriately to be labelled the 'First World War' than the briefer struggle of a hundred years later. In the course of that century following Napoleon, weaponry may have progressed considerably more than during the previous one, but the style of warfare showed relatively little advance until the 'mass' battle *à la* Leipzig reached its apotheosis in the hideous stalemate bloodbaths of Flanders, the Somme and Verdun. The battles of the American Civil War owed much to the lessons inherited from Napoleon; while in terms of mobility, and what Liddell Hart dubbed 'the indirect approach', the Napoleonic battles bear an even closer affinity to the mechanized techniques of 1939–45, to the subsequent Israeli wars and to the Gulf War of 1990–1, than to the trench warfare of 1914–18. Finally, the elements of guerrilla and irregular warfare called forth by Napoleon in Spain, in Russia and in the battles of national liberation, to his enormous cost from 1808 onwards, have an even more modern ring about them.

In *Napoleon, Master of Europe*, I concentrated on the Battle of Austerlitz in 1805, and the campaigns which followed it until the conclusion of peace at Tilsit two years later. It was the period in which the *Grande Armée* reached its apogee of excellence, winning its most brilliant succession of victories. Austerlitz, which has been called 'the first great battle of modern history', was the brightest gem of them all in Napoleon's martial diadem, and it was also his first 'big' battle. There was of course the small matter of Trafalgar in 1805, the news of which reached him *en route* for Austerlitz. It seemed insignificant by comparison with the great land triumph that was imminent, but it was to cost him forever any hope of control of the seas — and it thereby put final victory beyond his reach. Nevertheless, it was the peace treaty he dictated after the 1805–7 campaigns that came closest to granting Napoleon unchallenged, and unchallengeable, dominion over the mainland of Europe. After Tilsit he looked, at least temporarily, unbeatable. Yet, from Tilsit onwards — like Hitler after Alamein and Stalingrad — he found himself strategically on the defensive, fighting to hang on to the vast territories he had already subjugated.

Uncle Matthew, Nancy Mitford's legendary creation based on her father, once admitted that he had found *White Fang* such a superlative novel that he had never read another. The student of military history could almost feel the same about Austerlitz. Napoleon's mastery of the battlefield was at its peak; again and again in the years that followed, he would use tactics that had stood him in such good stead there — until, eventually, the Allies learnt how to parry them, and apply them to his ruin. Without apologies, I have redeployed here much of what I wrote about Austerlitz twenty years ago, amplified and qualified in the light of experience and new knowledge.

While writing *The Fall of Paris*, I travelled all round the old *enceinte* that girdled 1870 Paris, getting to know corners of the city few ever visit. For *The Price of Glory*, I plodded for many days round the battered forts and crater-fields of Verdun. Sometimes the sadness of it all reduced me to tears. I followed from the Ardennes to the Channel coast the deadly route of Guderian's and Rommel's Panzers in that terrifyingly swift campaign of 1940, for the third leg of my Franco-German battle trilogy, *To Lose a Battle*. In Algeria, my researches for *A Savage War of Peace* took me for hundreds of miles round the *bled*, and on vertiginous leaps from roof to overhanging roof of the houses huddled in the Casbah of Algiers, trying to piece together the course of that complicated, bitter struggle which dragged on from 1954 to 1962. While writing in 1992 *The Lonely Leader*, an account of Montgomery's conduct of the Normandy Campaign of 1944, his

son David and I were able to take his victorious route —
discovering all twenty-seven of the little Field-Marshal's TAC
HQs, each one revealing much about the course of the campaign.
We travelled from Portsmouth to Lüneburg Heath, where Monty
had received the German surrender in May 1945. But, in the
1970s, coming so soon after the tragic suppression of the so-
called Prague Spring by the Russians, the Cold War was at its
peak and, because of my earlier association with British Intelligence I was strongly advised by the late Sir Maurice Oldfield
(then head of MI6) not to try to get to Austerlitz, which lies
close to the Czech city of Brno. It was a source of lasting regret.
I felt I could describe the battle only at one remove, without
properly being able to visualize it, and having to rely upon such
masterly descriptions as Tolstoy's in *War and Peace*, rather than
on my own eyes and instincts.

At last, in November 1995, when I was working on this new
study of Napoleon, the opportunity came for me to visit the field
of Austerlitz — within days of the 190th anniversary of the battle.
I had the great good fortune to have as my travelling companion
David Mynett, a Napoleonic buff and a wonderful artist, who
came to sketch the battlefield. Arriving at Napoleon's vantage
point on the Turan (now, in Czech, called the Žuran) at precisely
the right time, we had the miraculous good fortune to find the
weather perform just as it did on the morning of 2 December
1805 — and as Napoleon had anticipated it would. There was snow
on the ground, and a hard frost. At 8 a.m. the Pratzen Heights
were beginning to emerge from the thick fog in the valley of the
Goldbach, where Soult's troops had waited, hidden, for their
charge up the slopes of the Pratzen which would determine the
outcome of this decisive battle. Then, exactly as it had in Napoleon's day, the sun came out — 'Le beau soleil d'Austerlitz' — as
depicted in David Mynett's illustration for the jacket of this book.
David, the artist, could hardly contain his excitement. But what,
to me, was thrilling beyond belief was to be able to see every
feature of this particularly compact battlefield, astoundingly little

changed in the intervening 190 years. The farming villages of 1805 were all there, grown but little; roads were all but unchanged; no woods had grown up to obscure the contours. All at once the amazing genius at work in choosing this site for battle against the superior foe, who was moving in for the kill, become plain – as did every component of Napoleon's plan.

On no battlefield that I have ever visited was the course of it laid out before my eyes with such extraordinary clarity. One could not fail to see in most minute detail how it had all evolved, and developed.

Later on in our trip we visited the site of the Battle of Wagram in 1809, Napoleon's last victory. Here, in complete contrast to Austerlitz, it was hard to see why Archduke Charles chose to fight on this totally featureless plain; equally hard to follow the progress of the battle over terrain which had now become extensively absorbed into the suburbs of Vienna. Even the course of the Danube had been radically changed over the years, so that the Island of Lobau, critical to Napoleon's success in two separate phases of the campaign, was no longer an island. A good deal of exploring, studying of maps and deployment of imagination had to be done before one could figure it all out.

Apart from the excitement and immeasurable benefit I derived from these first visits to the fields of Austerlitz and Wagram, what new insights have I been able to muster in the following pages? In addition to re-examining the story of six further Napoleonic campaigns, and fifteen battles, I have brought in more about Napoleon's civil innovations; more about his tangled love life, which ended in his divorce and remarriage, bringing him neither happiness nor the dynastic stability he so craved. Britain's Continental Blockade assumes an increasingly dominant role in the story from 1807 onwards, thus I have introduced more about the Royal Navy, and more about the fascinating Talleyrand – both of them decisively at war with Napoleon in their different ways. I have tried to illuminate corners of that vast canvas which seemed to me to have been neglected. One, for instance, is the amazingly silly War of 1812 between Britain and the United States (why, I have often wondered, is it usually taught in US schools as 'American History', rather than in the context of the Napoleonic Wars? As I endeavour to show, had it gone otherwise, it could so easily have led Napoleon to victory at Waterloo). Then there is the intelligence war conducted so ruthlessly by Napoleon's unpleasant henchmen Fouché and Savary, and with no less zeal by the British, with undertones which were to be echoed by SOE in the Second World War. Finally, there are the adoring Marie Walewska's brave but deceived Poles, the most enduring of all Napoleon's allies – poor romantics that they were – about whose contribution to his side too much has hitherto been overlooked.

A historian's viewpoint changes – and so it should – in tune with events closer to his eye-level. Since 1979 we have had wars in the Falklands, in the Persian Gulf and in Yugoslavia; we have seen the end (only temporarily, perhaps) of the Cold War with the collapse of Stalinism–Leninism – the challenge of which, incidentally, led to the creation of a coalition – NATO – which lasted twice as long as all the seven which confronted Napoleon, and probably rather more effectively. In the 1990s run-up to the fiftieth anniversaries of D-Day and VE-Day, I found myself thinking and writing much about the Second World War, and about leadership, both political and military, in general. All wars have their echoes and reflections in other wars, which tempt the historian to make parallels, valid or tenuous as these may be. Thus, at various intervals in the pages that follow, I have made parallels with Hitler's record (a curious coincidence, for instance, is that both launched their invasion into Russia, which was to destroy them, on almost the same day of June). Of course, the parallels can go too far; remarkable warlord that he was, Hitler was ever the guttersnipe who in his twelve years bequeathed nothing to Germany but ruins, and nothing to Europe but a pyramid of skulls (tragically for Europe, with his blinkered knowledge of the world limited to the trenches of the First

World War, Austria and Germany, Hitler was incapable of learning from the mistakes of Napoleon, otherwise he would never have ventured to attack Poland in 1939). Napoleon, on the other hand, brutal as his conquests were, would never have contemplated an act of genocide, while he left a legacy of permanent contributions to French life and culture that are still with us today.

Yet there is a general moral to be drawn common to both warlords – and indeed to all from Alexander the Great on down: it is the old repeated maxim of conquest leading only to further conquest; dictators and nations can win striking victories, but still lose wars – and the peace. Then follows the exhaustion, failure or death of the dynamic leader, and everything collapses. Wellington understood. 'A conqueror, like a cannon-ball,' he observed, 'must go on; if he rebounds, his career is over'. Napoleon and Hitler never perceived this; Talleyrand did; Hitler had no Talleyrand.

THIS BOOK OWES a special declaration of gratitude to Nicky Byam-Shaw, my Publisher-in-Chief over most of my past thirty-eight years with Macmillan, and an old friend always in the background – sometimes steadfastly in the foreground.

I am indebted to William Armstrong for the propulsion he provided for the writing of this book, and for editorial advice at various stages. Without Peter James, whose patience, sense of humour and supportive encouragement in those laborious final editorial stages was vital for a fourth time, I doubt if I should pick up the (metaphorical) pen again.

Once more, too, I was hugely aided in all manner of research and assistance by Anne Whatmore.

For the third book in a row, as well as in fifty-odd megabytes expended on other tasks, in common with many other authors these days, I feel I owe thanks of a different kind to the invisible geniuses at Apple Mac. Some writers regard the word-processor as the greatest invention since the wheel; whether it be the friend or enemy of style remains an open question – all I know is that its organizational powers now enable me to start the day with a smile on my face.

David Mynett, the painter and himself a Napoleonic 'buff' of distinction, was a superb travelling companion, deploying a skilled artist's eye and some critical appraisals on our enjoyable visit to the battlefields of Austerlitz, Wagram and Aspern–Essling.

Among museums and libraries, not for the first time I am appreciative of the friendliness accorded by the Musée de l'Armée, located so close to Napoleon's tomb in the Invalides; and I am perennially grateful to the excellence of the London Library and its long-suffering staff.

Only those sources actually consulted or referred to have been listed in the Select Bibliography. Certain primary material (for example, Napoleon's correspondence) has been used throughout, and among the secondary accounts similarly exploited is that of Adolphe Thiers. For details of warfare techniques, both of Napoleon and of his enemies, I found G. E. Rothenberg's concise book valuable. Among many sources used in the wider background of both Revolutionary and Napoleonic France, George Rudé's *Revolutionary Europe 1783–1815*, J. C. Herold's *The Age of Napoleon* and Simon Schama's more recent and brilliant contribution *Citizens: A Chronicle of the French Revolution* seemed particularly useful.

I am beholden as ever to the works of David Chandler. *The Campaigns of Napoleon* remain an inseparable companion for any work of this kind, as does his *Dictionary of the Napoleonic Wars* – a masterpiece of conciseness when one requires an instant reference to events or personalities. Not so easy to lug around the battlefields, but equally indispensable, is the first-class West Point *Atlas of the Napoleonic Wars*. Among recent works that have earned my admiration is Evangeline Bruce's delightful study, *Napoleon and Josephine*. Two days after publication Evangeline, a dear friend, lost her sight. The light was never to return during the remaining year of her life, but she left behind a book of an exceptional visual quality, rendering (for me at any rate) Josephine an infinitely more appealing person than heretofore.

About to go to press, I read with benefit Rory Muir's recently published and thoughtful *Britain and the Defeat of Napoleon, 1807–1815*. His conclusions on the foolish War of 1812 (though somewhat different to my own) I found most worthwhile and I am grateful to his drawing my attention to the book of Harry L. Coles, *The War of 1812* (Chicago, 1965) – though alas too late for my researches. In this context I remain always indebted to that marvellous American historian, the late Samuel Eliot Morison.

Arthur Bryant has recently fallen under a revisionist cloud for his wrong-mindedness over Hitler; but it seems to me he more than atoned for this with his superb *Years of Endurance* series, which so inspired British readers by their unspoken parallels during those other years of endurance, 1942–5. On re-reading, for me he remains as good as ever.

Turville, May 1996

How far from Austerlitz?

Napoleon 1805–1815

ONE

The Rise of the Adventurer

1795—1801

... it were better not to have lived at all than to leave no
trace of one's existence behind.

Napoleon

THROUGHOUT THE DAY of 24 June 1807, the hammers of
the *Grande Armée* had clattered frantically to complete a large raft
on the River Niemen in faraway East Prussia. The little town of
Tilsit – which lies not far from Rastenburg, where Hitler was to
locate his 'Wolf's Lair' headquarters, and where he was narrowly
to escape assassination in July 1944 – had been ransacked for the
richest materials it could provide, to furnish an elegant pavilion
of striped canvas aboard the raft. At opposing ends the pavilion
was surmounted by the Imperial eagles of Russia and France.
Napoleon was determined that no pomp should be missing at this
meeting of the two most powerful rulers on earth, which had
been proposed earlier that day by Tsar Alexander 1, his armies
recently humbled on the battlefield of Friedland. For Napoleon,
the Corsican adventurer receiving on terms almost of condescen-
sion rather than equality the Emperor of All the Russias, this first
encounter was to represent the pinnacle of glory in a career of
already meteoric achievement.

Completed, the raft was anchored exactly midway between
the shores of the river, on which were encamped the rival forces
that only ten days previously had been at each other's throats.
Simultaneously, with superb military timing, at one o'clock on
25 June, boats carrying the two potentates set off from either

bank. With Napoleon came his brother-in-law, the dashing cavalry-
man Murat; Marshals Bessières and Berthier, the ever-faithful
Chief-of-Staff, newly dignified Prince of Neuchâtel; generals
Caulaincourt, Grand Equerry, future Foreign Minister and chronicler, and Duroc, Grand Marshal of the Empire. Tsar Alexander
was accompanied by, among others, the Grand Duke Constantine
with his unpleasing countenance, and General Bennigsen, whose
army it was that had just received such a drubbing at Friedland.
Perhaps because he disposed of the more efficient oarsmen,
Napoleon arrived first at the raft — thus acquiring for himself the
air of host on this freshly declared neutral territory. Nevertheless,
the first act of the rival emperors on boarding was to embrace
each other warmly. The Niemen at that point was no wider than
the Seine, consequently the gesture was clearly visible in both
camps and wildly applauded. It seemed as if lasting peace was
already a reality.

The two emperors then withdrew into the privacy of the
pavilion. 'Why are we at war?' they asked each other (so Adolphe
Thiers tells us) with Alexander following up: 'I hate the English
as much as you do!' To which Napoleon exclaimed, 'In that case
peace is made!' Alexander condemned the false promises with
which the absent perfidious ones had lured Russia into a disastrous
war on their behalf, then abandoning her to fight it single-
handed.[1] That first 'summit talk' lasted an hour and a half; after
it, Napoleon confided in a letter to his Empress Josephine his
delight with the former adversary: 'He is a truly handsome, good
and youthful emperor; he has a better mind than is commonly
supposed. . . .'

For a fortnight the intimate talks, the courtesies and the fêting
continued. Napoleon praised Bennigsen and the Grand Duke
Constantine, whom he had first encountered at the head of the
élite Russian Imperial Guard at Austerlitz; Alexander praised the
martial prowess of Murat and Berthier. Alexander was invited to
inspect the French Imperial Guard; Napoleon was shown Alexander's fierce Cossack and Kalmuck warriors. They went for long

rides together along the banks of the Niemen, while Napoleon unfolded the various new projects his restless mind was already conceiving. Day by day a cordiality, almost an affection, seemed to grow between the two men. On one occasion (according to Baron Méneval)[2] when Napoleon had pressed the Tsar to remain in his camp for dinner, he offered his guest the use of his own gold toilet-case with which to change. How much further could fraternity be taken! But, behind all this, much hard bargaining was going on. While Napoleon spared no effort in his endeavours to charm the apparently impressionable young Tsar, not quite the same degree of camaraderie between equals was reserved for the latter's unhappy ally, Frederick William, King of Prussia. His armies having been vanquished and his dominions overrun the previous year, in the utmost humiliation that Napoleon had inflicted upon any of his foes, the heir to Frederick the Great was made to wait, like a poor relation, in the rain on the Russian bank, to be admitted to the councils of his fellow rulers only after their cordiality *à deux* had already been established. 'Sad, dignified and stiff' (according to Thiers) Frederick William was easily bullied by Napoleon. It was left to his attractive queen, Louise, to turn on the charm. 'She is full of *coquetterie* toward me,' Napoleon wrote to Josephine, but was able to assure her (in this case with conviction): 'do not be jealous, I am an oilcloth off which all that sort of thing runs. It would cost me too dear to play the *galant*.'

On 7 July, Napoleon signed a formal peace treaty with Alexander at Tilsit. Pointedly, a similar settlement with broken Prussia was not signed and ratified until several days later. In the public treaty between Napoleon and Alexander, much play was made of their newly discovered fraternal feelings for each other and their hopes for active co-operation in the future. More to the point, under the secret articles attached, the Tsar was to abandon any romantic crusading notions about liberating Europe from the revolutionary French; instead, at the expense of Napoleon's ally, Turkey, he was encouraged to pursue expansion along the traditional Russian route – towards the south-east. As a penalty to the Swedes for their rashness in joining the Coalition Wars against Napoleon, Swedish Finland was to be ceded to Russia. But it was, of course, against the still-unvanquished and physically almost untouchable distant arch-enemy, England, that Napoleon's ire was chiefly directed. She was to be excluded totally from Europe, with Russia joining the Continental System if by November Britain had not agreed to Napoleon's terms.

If the terms granted Russia were flatteringly and calculatedly benevolent, those for Prussia were correspondingly harsh. Despite the *coquetteries* of Queen Louise, Prussia was to be shorn of half her territories. Those west of the Elbe would be transmuted into a new Kingdom of Westphalia for the benefit of Napoleon's brother Jérome. To the east, Prussia's Polish provinces were to be handed over to create a new Grand Duchy of Warsaw (in itself a source of some disappointment to Napoleon's recently acquired mistress, the patriotic Marie Walewska, who, in giving herself, had hoped for nothing less than restored nationhood for her proud but oppressed people). Crushing war indemnities were imposed upon King Frederick William, plus a permanent French military occupation; and, to ensure that Prussia would henceforth never aspire to be more than a second-rate German power, the remainder of the German states had been organized into a puppet Confederation of the Rhine.

On 9 July, Napoleon took leave of his new friend (who was tactfully wearing the *Légion d'Honneur* for the occasion), bestowing on him one last warm embrace, and watching until Alexander disappeared out of sight on his bank of the Niemen. Earlier Napoleon had written to his Minister of the Interior, Fouché, instructing him: 'See to it that no more abuse of Russia takes place, directly or indirectly. Everything points to our policy being brought into line with that of this Power on a permanent basis.'

News of Tilsit reached London only in the third week in July, during a summer of heat so stifling that haymakers were fainting in the fields of Buckinghamshire. No intimation of the secret clauses had been received from her former allies, but it was abundantly clear that, at Tilsit, the two emperors had effectively divided the continent between them into two spheres of influence in which England was to be permitted no part. From Gibraltar to the Vistula and beyond, Napoleon now ruled either directly or through princes who were his creations (over the previous two years he had given out more crowns than the Holy Roman Emperors had in a thousand), or his dependants. Before Austerlitz Napoleon had been an object of fear, after Tilsit he held Europe spellbound with terror. He was its undisputed master. 'One of the culminating points of modern history,' a starry-eyed supporter declared of Tilsit; '. . . the waters of the Niemen reflected the image of Napoleon at the height of his glory.'[3] The next time he ventured on to the Niemen, just five years later, he would be *en route* for his first great defeat, and the beginning of his eclipse.

HOW, IN SO SHORT A SPACE OF TIME, had Napoleon managed to acquire these trappings of mastery which Tilsit now seemed to vest in him? One needs, rapidly, to turn back the clock some twenty years. At Tilsit he was still only thirty-seven, and – because of his youth at the conclusion of his most famous run of victories – one tends to forget that he was born under the reign of Louis xv and started his military career under Louis xvi. If he was a child of the *ancien régime*, he was also very much a product of that event dubbed by Thomas Carlyle 'the Death-Birth of a World', and was steeped in the French Revolutionary heritage, without which he would surely never have got as far as Tilsit. His father, Carlo Buonaparte, was an impecunious lawyer, originally of minor Italian nobility, who had set up a not notably successful law practice in Ajaccio, Corsica. (The island was taken over by France in 1768, the year before Napoleon's birth.) After producing eight children that survived – five died in infancy – Carlo died of cancer in 1785 when Napoleon was only fifteen. His wife Letizia, later always known as *Madame Mère*, who had married at fourteen, was a strong-minded woman who would outlive her famous son by fourteen years. Her favourite, cautionary utterance was 'Just so long as it lasts.' Young Napoleon had a rough passage through the school to which he was sent at Brienne in Champagne, where he was distinguished chiefly for his fierce Corsican nationalism and a certain aptitude for mathematics: 'reserved and hardworking . . . silent, capricious, proud, extremely egotistical . . . much self-esteem . . . extremely ambitious,' his reports read. He was then commissioned a second lieutenant in the French Army at the age of sixteen, making his first real mark on military affairs some eight years later, at the Siege of Toulon. The key naval base was then held by an English fleet under the command of Admiral Hood; Napoleon, as a twenty-four-year-old artillery captain, was brought in to advise the not very distinguished commander of the French Revolutionary forces besieging it. With his genius for the swift *coup d'oeil* which was later to stand him in such good stead, he gave the brilliant appreciation that, if the Le Caire promontory overlooking Toulon harbour could be seized, guns sited there would make the harbour untenable for Hood's ships. The strategy succeeded, and the British were driven out; wounded in the thigh,* Napoleon became a hero in the ranks of the incompetent Revolutionary Army (though still unknown outside it), was promoted to the dizzy rank of *général de brigade* when he was still only twenty-four, and was made artillery commander to the Army of Italy.

After a brief, fallow period of considerable frustration his next opportunity came when, by chance, he happened to be in Paris on sick leave during the autumn of 1795. A revolt was pending against the Convention and Napoleon was called in by his friend and protector, Paul Barras, to forestall it. He positioned a few

---

* One of the remarkable things about Napoleon's career was how, after this wound, he was – like Wellington – hardly to be touched in any of his battles, in which he exposed himself without concern. This was to give rise to a legend of immortality that lasted him to the end.

guns (brought up at the gallop by a young cavalry captain called Murat) on the key streets leading to the Tuileries Palace. Three years previously he had witnessed the mob storm the same palace, and the weakness of the King on that occasion had made a lasting impression on him. 'If Louis xvi had shown himself on horseback, he would have won the day,' Napoleon wrote to his brother Joseph. He was determined not to repeat the same error and showed no hesitation in giving the order to fire. Discharged at point-blank range, the historic 'whiff-of-grapeshot' of the *Treizième Vendémiaire* left 400 dead and put the mob convincingly to flight. For the first time since 1789 the Paris 'street', which had called the tune throughout the Revolution, had found a new master whom it would not lightly shrug off. Barras, grateful but also nervous at having Napoleon too near the centre of power, now appointed him – at the age of twenty-seven – Commander-in-Chief of the French Army of Italy.

Ever since 1792, France had been at war with the First Coalition of her enemies, who were bent upon reversing the revolutionary tide that seemed to threaten all Europe, and restoring the *status quo ante* in France. As Thomas Carlyle saw it, the guillotining of Louis xvi had 'divided all friends; and abroad it has united all enemies . . .'; on the other hand, in the view of Friedrich Engels and others, had it not been for the stimulating effect of foreign intervention, the Revolution might quietly have choked on its own vomit. It was a question of the chicken or the egg. The fortunes of war had swung back and forth; lack of adequate preparation and incompetence among the new leaders of the revolutionary French forces had been matched by differences of interest and lethargy among the Allies; the stiff forms of eighteenth-century warfare, unaltered since the days of Frederick the Great, had encountered a new revolutionary fervour, though it was lamentably supported with guns and equipment. Marching into France, the Duke of Brunswick and his Prussians were halted and turned about, surprisingly, by the cannonade at Valmy in September 1792, first harbinger of a new form of warfare.

In 1793 the French forces, resurgent under the organizational genius of Lazare Carnot (whom even Napoleon was to rate 'the organizer of victory'), and fired by their first victories to carry the Revolution to all the 'oppressed nations' of Europe, swept into Belgium and threatened Holland. During the bitter winter of 1794–5, one of France's few naval victories was achieved when French cavalry captured the Dutch fleet by riding across the frozen Texel. By June 1794, Jourdan had chased the last Coalition soldier across the French frontier. The British bungled a landing at Quiberon Bay, while – defeated, and invaded in her turn – Prussia abandoned the First Coalition the following year. But, over-extended, under-equipped and unhelped by the dithering and corrupt rule of the Directory, France's new 'Army of the Sambre-and-Meuse' now experienced a series of defeats across the Rhine at the hands of the Austrians.

It was at this point that, called in by Barras, Napoleon was sent to Italy to wrest the initiative from the Austrians. He found the army unpaid, hungry, poorly equipped and on the verge of mutiny. Stendhal cites the example of three officers who owned but one pair of shoes, one pair of breeches and three shirts between them; elsewhere in *The Charterhouse of Parma*, he relates how, at Napoleon's legendary action on the 'Bridge at Lodi', another French officer had the soles of his shoes 'made out of fragments of soldiers' caps also picked up on the field of battle'.[4] As this ragged army set forth, Napoleon issued one of his most famous orders of the day:

> Soldiers, you are naked and ill-fed; though the government owe you much, it can give you nothing . . . but . . . I will lead you into the most fertile plains in the world. Rich provinces, great cities will be in your power; you will find there honour, glory and riches. . . .'[5]

It was an open invitation to looting. But, by his extraordinary capacity to inspire, Napoleon totally transformed the forces under him within a matter of days. One of his officers, Colonel

Marmont, later a marshal, said years after the Empire had foundered, 'we marched surrounded by a kind of radiance whose warmth I can still feel as I did fifty years ago'.[6] Over the next eighteen months the young General caused his troops – with minimal resources – to win a series of remarkable victories. These ended with the Battle of Rivoli, as impressive a battle as any the world had yet seen. In Italy, aided and almost abetted by an inept Austrian command, driven on by violent Corsican jealousy at the infidelities of Josephine while he was away at the front, Napoleon took risk after extravagant risk, but his string of successes there laid the foundation for the legend of his invincibility. To Colonel Marmont he remarked, 'Fortune . . . is a woman, and the more she does for me, the more I will demand from her. . . . In our day no one has conceived anything great; it is for me to give an example. . . .'[7] By October 1797, he had defeated seven armies, captured 160,000 prisoners and over 2,000 cannon, and chased the Austrians to within a hundred miles of Vienna. Here, for the first but not the last time, he forced the beaten Austrians to sign a peace with France, thus marking a definitive end to the wars of the First Coalition.

Napoleon now became the idol of France, his star irresistibly in the ascendant as he returned in triumph to Paris. 'From that moment,' he wrote after the first Italian campaign, 'I foresaw what I might be. Already I felt the earth flee from beneath me, as if I were being carried into the sky.'

At the Treaty of Campoformio (17 October 1797), Napoleon dictated his first peace to the defeated Austrians. He was in a hurry, to get back to Paris and the unfaithful Josephine, and it was not a good peace. At one point, he flew into a rage and shouted brutally at the Habsburg generals, 'Your Empire is nothing but an old maidservant, accustomed to being raped by everyone!'[8] He then dashed to the ground an enormous porcelain tea-service, a treasured gift from Empress Catherine of Russia, declaring, 'This is what will happen to your monarchy!' To

NAPOLEON,
as Commander-in-Chief,
1795

Vienna, the Austrian delegation reported that he had 'behaved like a madman'. It was an insult that would never be forgotten. Nevertheless, France was now ceded Belgium and the left bank of the Rhine. These were frontiers for which Louis xiv had fought so hard; but the prospect of Belgium (where Antwerp was often described as a 'dagger pointed at the heart of England') in menacing hands was guaranteed to keep Britain at war with Napoleon. It was, after all, what would bring her to fight the Kaiser and her former German allies a century later. In return for Venice and its territories, Austria recognized France's establishment of an Italian satellite state, the Cisalpine Republic – from which seed, eventually, was to germinate the modern united nation of Italy. Of her foes of the First Coalition, only the British remained at war with France, but with no weapon to strike at her across the Channel; so England contented herself by extending her Empire at the expense of both enemy and allies. After Campoformio, however, in exchange for a durable peace, she too declared herself ready to accept France's 'natural frontiers' and even to hand back colonies captured during the past hostilities. At last, Revolutionary France was offered the security for which she had fought so passionately for the previous five years; it looked like a good time to make peace with England.

Nothing, however, succeeds like success, and it now went to the weak head of the Directory. Back in 1790, the Constituent Assembly had declared the noble ideal: 'The French nation renounces the undertaking of any war with a view to making conquests, and it will never use its forces against the liberty of any people.' But, not unlike the heirs to Lenin in the twentieth century, the Directory, inflated by Napoleon's achievements, now let itself be enticed into graduating from a basically defensive war, with an aim of saving the Revolution and securing France's frontiers, to one of expansion and enrichment. A story familiar to the twentieth century, it is instructive that France's wars of aggrandizement began, not under the Consulate or the Empire, but under the Revolutionary movement. Returning to France in 1797, Napoleon was acclaimed in the Luxembourg Palace with full honours by the Directory, its members clad in scarlet togas emulative of Ancient Rome. Every beautiful *Parisienne* crowded into the courtyard, but, 'in spite of the luxury, the elegance of the women's clothes and the sumptuous costumes of the Directors, every eye was fixed on the spare, sallow, sickly-looking man in a simple coat, who appeared to fill all the space around him'.[9] A few days later, Talleyrand, Napoleon's future Foreign Minister, threw a magnificent ball for him, egregious in its unrevolutionary extravagance.

The following year, the new hero was put in command – briefly – of the Army of England, charged with carrying the war across the Channel. In 1797, General Hoche with 14,000 troops and sixteen ships of the line had made an abortive descent on Ireland, which had been disrupted by storms. After an inspection in January 1798 of the 120,000 troops mustered between Étaples and Walcheren in Holland for an invasion attempt, Napoleon abandoned the idea as 'too chancy to risk *la Belle France* on the throw of a dice'. Instead, he placed in the mind of the Directory the idea of striking at British sea-power by a campaign in Egypt, and in the Eastern Mediterranean – the key to England's empire and trade in the Orient.

With England's Pitt still under the misapprehension that he was heading for Ireland, Napoleon sailed for Egypt and for what was to prove, militarily, his most disastrous campaign to date. Josephine rushed down by coach, to see him off. (She had also hurried out to be with him in Milan, during the Italian Campaign. One cannot but be struck by the astonishing distances Napoleon, and Josephine – and not just his armies – covered, at phenomenal speed and under conditions of considerable discomfort.) As an unhappy augury, the flagship of the fleet ran aground as it was leaving the *rade*. Ensuing operations followed the familiar course, with Napoleon winning round after round on land (for example, the Battle of the Pyramids) and with Nelson sweeping the seas (Aboukir Bay and the Nile). The fighting moved up into Palestine and the Levant, and in his massacre of prisoners at Jaffa Napoleon revealed himself at his most ruthless and cruel.* His own forces were decimated by plague (to which Napoleon himself seemed miraculously immune), with the Revolutionary General Kléber growling that he was 'the kind of general who needed a monthly income of ten thousand men'. Meanwhile, encouraged by British naval successes, before the end of 1798 a Second Coalition comprising of England, Naples, Austria, Russia and Turkey had come into being, and had begun to threaten the French position in both northern Italy and the Netherlands. Abandoning his battered army in the Middle East (as he was to do in Russia

---

* An explanation for these out-of-character atrocities has sometimes been found in Napoleon's rage at continuing to be *cocu* by Josephine. It was in Egypt, apparently, that Major Andoche Junot blunderingly revealed to him her affair with the alluring Lieutenant Hippolyte Charles – on which account, possibly, Junot never became a marshal.

thirteen years later) and dodging Nelson's patrols, Napoleon hastened back to France, landing secretly at Fréjus on 9 October 1799. In Paris, he found the Directory tottering. On 9 November – *18 Brumaire* in the Revolutionary Calendar – he attempted a *coup d'état* which would end the rule of the Directory. The Deputies abandoned their red togas with indecent haste; but it was touch and go for Napoleon – the resourceful policeman, Fouché, took no chances and closed the gates of Paris, preparing to arrest the General in case the coup failed. France was in a terrible state, her economy was tottering and she was at war with most of Europe – and even with the United States. But Napoleon's coup was successful and he at once established himself as First Consul, with a tenure of ten years and dictatorial powers greater than those of Louis xiv at the height of his glory. Both within France and beyond, this was heralded as signifying the end of the Revolution. In Russia, the mad Tsar Paul – already at odds with his Austrian ally over Italy – withdrew from the Coalition; in France, even the critical Madame de Staël (an amazingly tiresome woman, not only to Napoleon through most of his career, but also to almost everyone else in her life) was delighted, though her father, the banker Necker, cautioned, 'Your nerves are overwrought. . . . Unfortunately, everything rests on the life of one man.'

But the war still continued. Consolidated in power politically, Napoleon set off once more to chastise the Austrians. By an astonishing feat of transporting an army of 50,000 secretly over the 8,000-foot Great St Bernard Pass, still covered in snow in the May of 1800, Napoleon struck the unwary Austrians from the rear. June brought him his stunning victory at Marengo, north of Genoa. It was a copybook classic of manoeuvre, though, as was characteristic of Napoleon, the panegyrical bulletin he issued afterwards (aimed in part at further terrifying a demoralized foe) made it sound rather more of a calculated, according-to-plan result than was actually the case, and disallowed the element of opportunism that had played an integral part in the victory, as it so often did with his other triumphs. The *coup de grâce* to Austrian arms was administered by Moreau's victory at Hohenlinden in Bavaria on 3 December. It was a small consolation that, the following summer, General Abercromby's British expeditionary force was to defeat Napoleon's abandoned Army of the Orient and expel the last Frenchman from Egypt; for the Second Coalition – as ineffectual as most of its successors – had now collapsed in ruins.

The resulting Peace of Lunéville in 1801 with the Austrians, which forced them out of most of northern Italy, was followed by the Peace of Amiens with England in March 1801. Under its provisions a smarting England agreed to part with most of her recent colonial acquisitions, including Malta, while Napoleon was left – for the time being – in unchallenged military supremacy, and a grateful France confirmed him Consul for life. On the other hand, Nelson at Copenhagen (2 April 1801) had once again demonstrated to Napoleon the impotence of his attempts to gain control of the seas. Neither side was particularly happy with the peace terms: England deeply concerned by Napoleon's hegemony over Europe and resentful at her territorial deprivations; France soon finding England in default for not withdrawing her forces from Malta. Nevertheless, for the first time in a decade, a glimmer of lasting peace flickered over the battered European nations, and, once again, it looked like as good a time as any for bringing the sequence of wars to a definitive end. But peace was to prove illusory. As Napoleon had written prophetically to his lieutenant and potential rival, Moreau, during the more ecstatic moments of 1800: 'Greatness has its beauties, but only in retrospect and in the imagination.'

TWO

An Uneasy Peace

1801–1805

> He always applied all his means, all his faculties, all his
> attention to the action or discussion of the moment. Into
> everything he put passion. Hence the enormous advantage
> he had over his adversaries, for few people are entirely
> absorbed by one thought or one action at one moment.
>
> Caulaincourt

AFTER AMIENS, what the English uncharitably dubbed 'the
peace which passeth all understanding' heralded for both France
and Napoleon a halcyon period. But it was brief. During the
thirteen months it lasted, English tourists, the curious and the
spendthrift, poured across the Channel in their tens of thousands.
French goldsmiths, jewellers and makers of fancy-goods worked
night and day to provide wares to satisfy their greedy visitors. In
September 1802, many were drawn to the great industrial
exhibition mounted to celebrate the revolutionary 'Year X' at
which Richard Lenoir, the cotton-spinner, alone took 400,000
francs worth of orders. The gallants found their fancies much
stimulated by the manifest seductiveness of the ladies of Parisian
society, in their high-waisted, see-through gowns inherited from
the Directory. Those foreigners privileged to be invited to the
First Consul's birthday celebrations were agreeably surprised by
the gracious *bonhomie* with which the great man greeted them.
With the utmost regard for the sensibilities of his English visitors,
he displayed, on either side of his chimneypiece, busts of Fox and
Nelson. The court around him exuded a certain brilliance – 'a
newly-born government', he told his secretary, 'must dazzle and
astonish' – but, in contrast to the glitter of the generals and

Mameluke orderlies that accompanied him on military parades, Napoleon's own uniform was striking by its simplicity, reminding the visitors more of an English sea captain in undress. Could this really be the monster who, so recently, had terrorized all Europe? At home he was undoubtedly at a peak of popularity that year, and success seemed to imbue him with a new aura of security. At first sight, the English visitors had to admit themselves favourably impressed by appearances of life under the new régime.

What might possibly have escaped their gaze was the depth and intensity with which the ideals of the Great Revolution still impinged upon French life and thoughts, and on which was now grafted a growing personal loyalty to Napoleon. It was, after all, little more than a decade since the principles of *Liberté, Égalité, Fraternité* had first swept the country. In our era, historians and psychologists still puzzle over how Hitler was ever able to carry away a sensible race like the Germans, to follow him with fanatical devotion to a very bitter end. To that extent, it is understandable that the extraordinary mystique of the French Revolution is also sometimes hard to grasp. It was not just France; hand in hand with the Romantic movement, it liberated an inestimable wave of idealism throughout Europe. Byron, Heine, Goethe, Hegel and Beethoven were all seduced by it. And, at the beginning of the new century, the young Napoleon seemed like the embodiment of all its ideals. At about this time, Beethoven, for instance, was at work on his *Eroica*, intending to give it the name of 'Bonaparte', while *Fidelio* still stands for that sense of individual liberty which 1789 was supposed to represent. Certainly, as of 1801, the mystical ascendancy which the First Consul had already come to assume among thirty-three million Frenchmen was in no way to be underestimated. The legacy of revolutionary zeal would in part explain how, after he had lost whole armies in the three successive years of a disaster of 1812, 1813 and 1814, each time France would be ready to provide him with new ones.

It was during this fleeting period of peace that Napoleon, acting with the same speed and remarkable concentration of energy which characterized all his military operations, established the majority of the civil reforms that were to provide France with a new constitution, set her finances in order, and comprise – *inter alia* – the *Code Napoléon*: his most durable achievements. He reduced the number of tax collectors from 200,000 to fewer than 6,000; the yields doubled. He was helped by the clean sweep already effected by the Revolution, which had abolished all those institutions it regarded as outmoded. But, if Napoleon had never fought a battle, these achievements would surely still leave him one of the world's great constructive rulers.

Paris, with its 547,000 inhabitants to London's 850,000, at the turn of the century seemed to its British visitors a dilapidated place, full of foul-smelling mud and still with open sewers. Cattle were driven through the main thoroughfares on their way to market. In no way did Napoleon succeed more triumphantly than in the ambition he had declared in 1798 to 'make Paris not only the loveliest city that is, or that ever had been, but the loveliest that ever could be'. Sparked by the catastrophic floods of the previous winter, which had partly inundated the Champs Élysées, Napoleon began by reorganizing the quays of the Seine; he decreed, in 1802, the construction of the Quai d'Orsay, which he eventually extended all the way to the École Militaire. Grandiose plans for canals and reservoirs were laid down, providing Paris with her modern water supply; streets were renumbered on a basis that survives to the present day. Christened the Musée Napoléon, the Louvre was completed in 1803 to house the Italian art treasures shamelessly looted in his recent campaigns. Inevitably there would come the grandiose architecture dedicated to military conquests; the charming Arc du Carrousel and the Vendôme Column (both to commemorate the Austerlitz triumph of 1805), and the Arc de Triomphe itself (not to be completed until the reign of Louis-Philippe). There were also works of purely economic significance, like the Bourse (the foundation stone of which was laid in 1808, although the idea was conceived by Napoleon much earlier), and the vast Halle des Vins – designed to make Paris the foremost trading centre for wine in northern Europe.

The list of works initiated is an imposing one, especially considering the short amount of time Napoleon was able to spend on the home front: the Rue de Rivoli, Rue de Castiglione, Rue Napoléon (renamed Rue de la Paix), the Conseil d'État and the Cour des Comptes, four new bridges, the Madeleine transmogrified into a Temple of Victory with, facing it across the Concorde, the portico of the Palais Bourbon remodelled in Roman style to match. Everywhere new fountains and parks were constructed, and – not least – churches which had been vandalized during the Revolution were to be restored over the next twelve years at a cost of some £4 million.

In this last endeavour, Napoleon was not influenced entirely by architectural values. The withering away of the Revolution had been accompanied in the last years of the old century by a marked religious revival, hand in hand with the new Romantic movement, as exemplified by Chateaubriand's work, *Le Génie du Christianisme*, published in 1802. Returning to France in 1800 after seven years' self-exile, Chateaubriand had been deeply shocked by the ravages still left by the Revolution, particularly in its excesses of atheism: 'the ruinous castles, the belfries empty of bells, the graveyards with never a cross and the headless statues of saints'.

Immediately sensitive to the prevailing mood, however, Napoleon, with one stroke of consummate skill, had healed the wounds that still divided France by his *Concordat* with Pope Pius VII. Ratified in 1802, the *Concordat* re-established the Roman Catholic Church as 'the religion of the greater majority of Frenchmen'; but at the same time it clearly demarcated its spiritual and temporal powers. The settlement was to last over a century, until the Church was disestablished in France. Meanwhile it removed the main grievances that had kept civil war smouldering in the Vendée, and helped gain for Napoleon the sympathies of Catholics in France as well as in the subject, or about-to-be-subject, nations. Although rejected by Louis XVIII's government in exile, the *Concordat* was supported by most of the returning émigrés, including Chateaubriand, who found a Paris where 'the émigré was returning and talking peaceably with the murderers of his nearest and dearest . . .'.

Largely a tactical device, however, the *Concordat* did not imply any religious fervour in Napoleon himself. Under his régime, notes one writer, 'Congregations were treated to extracts taken from the Bulletins of the *Grande Armée*, and informed that the paths of conscription, as much as of holiness, led to Heaven.'[1] Though the churches were to be repaired, there was no suggestion of returning the actual properties sequestrated by the Revolution.

Before 1782, education had been left largely in the hands of village priests and religious orders like the Jesuits. In 1795 a new secular system had been introduced by the Revolution on to which stem Napoleon now grafted, in 1802, one of the most famous and enduring of all his reforms – the *lycées*, or state secondary schools. Like so many of his reforms, the system was designed, at least in part, to serve his own aims by providing a steady flow of military and administrative cadres essential to the Napoleonic machine. At the same time he transformed the high-grade *École Polytechnique*, founded by the Convention in 1794, into a military college for gunners and engineers. He also set his seal on the *École Normale Supérieure*, likewise initiated by the Convention and still today the breeding ground of a particular genre of French intellectual leadership. Typical of the fervent intervention in cultural matters that went *pari passu* with military campaigning was the 'living encyclopaedia' of scientists, oriental-ists and zoologists – including Monge the great mathematician and Champollion the Egyptologist – whom Napoleon had taken to Egypt with him. He had lost the war in Egypt, but discovered the Rosetta Stone.

Though the Directory had done much to improve France's political structure, between 1799 and 1804 the Constitution was extensively remodelled by Napoleon, of course greatly to the increment of his own personal power. As it did in his military technique, rationalization also lay at the heart of all Napoleon's civil reforms. In February 1800, the various departments were placed under the charge of Prefects; the following year the metric system was introduced, and in 1802 a new national police force was raised. France was to become more tightly centralized than ever it had been under the *Roi Soleil*. Prior to Napoleon, France had been bedevilled by the existence of 360 separate local *codes*; he now set about the immense task of unifying them into one set. By 1804 the *Code Civil* (later, and better, known as the *Code Napoléon*) was voted through the legislature. Though comprising over 2,000 articles, it took only four years to complete and is still largely operative. Typical both of his energy and of his personal interest in the work of administrative reform, Napoleon managed, almost incredibly, to attend no less than 57 of the 109 meetings devoted to the *Code Civil*. Regulating virtually every function of life, the *Code* insisted *inter alia* on the equal division of property among sons, thereby in fact doing more than the Revolution had done to fragment the big estates. Much emphasis was laid on the authority of the male, removing many of the contractual rights women had enjoyed under the *ancien régime*; this reflected his own, very Corsican disbelief in feminine equality.

Indispensable to Napoleon in all these endeavours at civil reform was the person of Jean Jacques Régis de Cambacérès, aged forty-five when he became Second Consul in 1799. Cambacérès was a known homosexual and pretentious gourmet, but also an outstanding jurist, administrator and manipulator in the corridors of power. With a capacity for work rivalling even Napoleon's, as President of the Senate, the Council of Ministers, the *Conseil d'État*, the *Conseil du Sceau des Titres* and the Privy Council, there was scarcely any aspect of Napoleon's 'Peace

Machine' that lay outside his ken. Incapable of decision himself, over the five years that Napoleon was absent from Paris during his fourteen and a half in power, Cambacérès faithfully drafted him a daily report. Unlike Fouché and Talleyrand, he was to remain totally loyal to his master, being created a Prince of the Empire and Duke of Parma for his pains. Napoleon's Minister of Police, the thoroughly odious, unscrupulous but eminently efficient Fouché, had, like Talleyrand, started life in the Church. Typically, although he had ruthlessly suppressed a revolt against Robespierre in Lyons, when *Thermidor* arrived he acted with equal zeal against him and the Jacobins. During his sixty-one years, he would work – always, like a mole, underground – in turn for the Revolution, the Directory, the Consulate, the Empire and, finally, the Bourbon Restoration. Portraits show him to have been personally as unpleasant as his morals; 'only the red rims of his half-closed eyelids relieved the identical colour of skin, hair and eyes'.[2] After the fall of Toulon in 1793, Fouché gloated to a colleague in Paris, 'Tonight we will execute 1,213 insurgents. *Adieu* – tears of joy flow from my eyes.'[3] But he was said to be a kind father and devoted husband; he was certainly one of the most accomplished politicians of all time.

Inevitably, one thinks in the same breath of Talleyrand, the greatest and the wiliest diplomat of them all. He and Fouché were forever coupled by Chateaubriand's devastating remark, as the two entered the room, *bras dessus, bras dessous*, at the time of the Restoration: 'A vision of Vice supported by Crime.'[4] To one Scottish duke, Talleyrand was 'the most disgusting individual I ever saw. His complexion is that of a corpse considerably advanced in corruption.' So suave was his duplicity that when death finally overtook him his king reacted to the news with the admiring epitaph, 'But there is no judging from appearances with Talleyrand!' Like Fouché, Talleyrand was a true Vicar of Bray, serving them all in sequence – including, once he had defected from Napoleon after Tilsit, his enemy, the Tsar of Russia. The self-defrocked Bishop of Autun, married, and –

probably on account of his devastating wit – fairly irresistible to
women despite his club-foot, Charles Maurice de Talleyrand-
Périgord had highly developed venal and acquisitive tastes. The
orator Mirabeau, never a man to mince words, remarked of him,
'The Abbé de Périgord would sell his soul for money; and he
would be right, for he would be exchanging dung for gold.'[5] He
was already forty-three when appointed Minister of Foreign
Affairs in 1797, on return from his exile in America, where he
had escaped the Terror. For the next ten years he would serve
Napoleon well; then, after Tilsit, serve against him with equal
zeal and amorality. In the well-chosen words of his biographer,
Duff Cooper, the difference between Talleyrand and Napoleon's
police chief was that for the former 'the word politics meant the
settlement of dynastic or international problems discussed in a
ball-room or across a dinner-table; for Fouché the same word
meant street-corner assassination, planned by masked conspirators in dark cellars.'[6]

The shaky French economic and financial system also received
the full benefit of the two Consuls' attention, accompanied by
often draconian measures. The Banque de France was established
in 1800, and granted total control over the national debt and the
issue of paper money. Industrial prosperity was stimulated by
ubiquitous government intervention, and various innovations of
social welfare encouraged – though along largely paternalistic
lines. However, trade unions were ruthlessly stamped on as
'Jacobin' institutions, or as diseases exported by the insidious
British. Unemployment was kept at a low level, but labour was
hard and the hours long. In summer, builders worked from
6 a.m. to 7 p.m.; the life expectancy of bakers was under fifty,
and up to 1813 children under ten were still employed in the
mines. From 1803 onwards every working man had to carry a
registration book stamped by his employer, without which he
was treated as a vagabond, and when it came to litigation it was
the employer's word that was always accepted. In rural France,
the life of the average peasant – though improved by the

revolutionary land settlement – was not much affected by either the Consulate or the Empire. The great roads built by Napoleon radiated out towards frontiers with distinct military purposes, but did little to bring the countryside into contact with the modern world.

In general, however, both peasant and urban working classes seem to have been better fed than they were either before 1789 or after 1815 – partly because of strict government controls placed on corn exports and price levels – and they came to regard the Napoleonic era as one of relative prosperity. Napoleon claimed to have gained the allegiance of the working classes by 'bread and circuses', and certainly the appeal to native jingoism of great victories such as Marengo went far to mitigate discontent for any loss of civil or political liberties. But, as with most dictators, it also meant that he had to keep on going, producing one triumph after another abroad. At the other end of the social scale, there were also great (and often scandalous) opportunities for self-enrichment; Talleyrand, the negotiator of the Peace of Lunéville, made a fortune by buying up Austrian bonds issued in Belgium, through knowing that one of the stipulations of the Treaty was that these bonds were to be honoured. Meanwhile, by 1804 the bourgeoisie owned approximately twice as much land in parts of northern France as it had done in 1789.

With perhaps just a passing similarity to the Soviet Union at the peak of its imperial power in the late 1970s, one class that was less than impressed by the compensation of 'bread and circuses' for an authoritarian régime was the intelligentsia. Not agreeing with Goethe's ecstatic view that Napoleon epitomized 'all that was reasonable, legitimate and European in the revolutionary movement . . .', a disenchanted Madame de Staël found that her France had become 'a garrison where military discipline and boredom rule'.

Culturally, the decorative arts probably thrived most under Napoleon: the Lyons silk industry was revitalized to satisfy the copious demands of the Bonaparte family, and by 1807 Jacob

Desmalter, Napoleon's favourite furniture-maker, was employing no less than 350 craftsmen. Everywhere the influence of the soldier left its impact on the austere built-to-last neo-classicism of Empire style ('Simplify. This is for the Emperor,' Napoleon scrawled across the sketch for a candelabrum submitted by his architect, Perrier); the pharaonic motifs and fiery poppy shades brought back from the Egyptian campaign; the Winged Victories symbolizing military triumph; and the mythology and artefacts of Rome borrowed later to lend flavour to the new imperial mystique. At Malmaison, the love-nest Napoleon set up with Josephine, the council chamber was fitted up with striped canvas to resemble a campaign bivouac, within ten days of Marengo. On moving into the Tuileries Palace as First Consul, Napoleon promptly ordered the erasure of red republican caps, symbols of liberty, that were painted on the walls: 'I don't like to see such rubbish.' These were replaced by busts of Alexander and Frederick the Great, along with Brutus and Demosthenes. Exemplifying the Roman 'high-seriousness' of the Empire was the painter David, who had abandoned the eighteenth-century frivolity of his uncle, Boucher ('It is pure, it is great, it is beautiful as antiquity,' he once said of Napoleon's head), and the great tragedian, Talma.

But the theatre fared less well under the heavy hand of Napoleon. By 1806, Fouché's Ministry of Police had acquired the right to censor all plays, and by the following year the list of theatres receiving government support had been reduced to eight. Already by 1803, Napoleon had ordered all new books to be submitted to the censor; when he came to power there had been over seventy newspapers in Paris, within a year these had been reduced to thirteen, all under strict censorship. Among other things, no caricatures of the ruler or his policies were permitted; which accounted for the serious dearth in the cartoonist's art of the times. (When the British Opposition leader, the much caricatured Charles James Fox, visited Napoleon in the autumn of peace of 1802, and rashly remarked that no one in England minded being abused in the press, his host shouted 'It is another thing here!' and strode away. He nevertheless showed an almost morbid fascination with the savage British cartoons of himself. Neither the Revolution nor the Empire was to produce any great music, leaving it to Beethoven to rhapsodize the feats of Napoleon. Apart from Chateaubriand and Madame de Staël, notable novelists were few. Since Napoleon had no faith in freedom, he gave little support to arts and letters, which always tend to wither in a climate of despotism. Perhaps more than from direct political persecution, artists suffered 'from the restrictive, stifling atmosphere produced by fear, flattery and censorship. There was something distinctly "second-hand" about much of the art of the period. . . .'[7] It was in this stifling atmosphere that Madame de Staël, her salon having become a focus of the opposition, was forced into exile in Switzerland by 1803. It was also this atmosphere and its essential lack of liberties which, once their gaze had penetrated the shiny surface of Napoleonic France, gradually disenchanted the liberal visitors from England, making them think themselves perhaps better off after all in their own backwardly libertarian society.

By means of his civil initiative, Napoleon had contrived to gain successively the loyalties of most elements of French life: the Catholics, the bureaucracy, the peasantry and the bourgeoisie. With the old aristocracy his policy of reconciliation had been less successful, and it had continued to keep a mistrustful distance. So Napoleon decided to create an élite of his own, faithful to himself as the fountain-head of rewards, and in May 1802 he created the institution of the *Légion d'Honneur*.

By the end of the following year, Napoleon's authoritarian rule seemed to be totally established, with virtually all wires in the nation leading back to his one pair of hands. But one lynchpin in the whole structure was missing: the continuity of succession. Already in December 1800, the fact that the First Consul might be less than immortal had been suggested when, on his way to the opera, he had narrowly escaped the explosion of a powerful

mine which killed several bystanders. The Jacobins were implicated (although Fouché held the Royalists responsible), and
severe penalties were meted out. On being made Consul for life
in August 1802, Napoleon was granted powers to nominate a
successor, but his ambitions lay further. At the beginning of
1804, two further plots were uncovered – one led by a Vendée
Royalist called Georges Cadoudal, the other by two generals,
Pichegru and Moreau. Cadoudal (in whose conspiracy the
Addington government had rashly connived but which had been
adroitly turned by that master-spy, Fouché) was executed, as
were a dozen others in one of the few mass guillotinings of the
Napoleonic era; Pichegru was found strangled in prison, while
Moreau as the popular hero of Hohenlinden was permitted to
disappear into exile, thereby removing one of the few potential
rivals to Napoleon. (Moreau eventually returned to Europe to
fight for the Russians against Napoleon, and was mortally
wounded at the Battle of Dresden.) The Cadoudal plot provided
Napoleon with just the excuse he needed to give himself an
imperial crown and ensure the hereditary succession of the
Bonaparte dynasty; but it was also to lead to his most deplorable
blunder, the murder of the Duke d'Enghien. 'I came to make a
king,' declared Cadoudal as he died; 'and I have made an
emperor . . . !'[8]

Acting with a grandeur that was indicative of the vast power
that he had already acquired in Europe, Napoleon summoned the
Pope to Paris to officiate, on 2 December 1804, at Notre Dame
while he himself placed the Imperial Crown on his own head –
and Josephine's. The whole façade of the cathedral had been clad
with a mock Gothic exterior for the occasion, provoking the
comment from a wit that 'so much work has been done that God
Himself would lose his bearings!' On the Place de la Concorde,
a vast star was hung, in questionable taste, at the exact place
where Louis XVI's head had rolled. To one *Parisienne*, Napoleon
in all his coronation finery looked like the King of Diamonds.
Ominously, for the superstitious, it was the coldest day of the

year. As he ascended the steps to the immense throne, Napoleon is said to have murmured to his brother, 'Joseph, if only our father could see us now!'

There were moments of dissonance that day; between the altar and the throne, a slight altercation broke out between Josephine and her jealous sisters-in-law carrying her train, with the result that she was momentarily arrested in her procession. Chagrined by receiving only two tickets for the coronation, David the court painter sought revenge by painting himself into the ponderous formal tableau; while in Vienna, when Beethoven learnt that Napoleon had proclaimed himself emperor, he scratched out his name from the *Eroica* in a rage. Napoleon, he is said to have exclaimed, was 'nothing more than an ordinary mortal'; he would 'trample on all human rights . . . [and] become a tyrant'. Madame de Staël was indignant: 'for a man who has risen above every throne, to come down willingly and take his place among the kings . . . !' she exclaimed.[9] In a state of *post coitum triste*, the new Emperor gloomed to his secretary, Decrès, the day following the great ceremony: 'I have come too late; men are too enlightened; there is nothing great left to do. . . .' This was not, however, a view widely shared by the denizens of the new Empire, bemused by the 'bread and circuses' feat *par excellence* of free feasting and fireworks which had accompanied the dazzling occasion. It merely seemed as if Napoleon had ascended to yet another pinnacle of glory, and of these there still promised to be no end.

At this moment when he had vested himself in the pomp and circumstance of power comparable only to that of the Roman Caesars, of Charlemagne and of the Holy Roman Emperors, the man like his fortune stood at his zenith both physically and intellectually. Now still only thirty-five, *le Petit Caporal* or *le Tondu*, as the army called him affectionately, was beginning to show just a few signs of thickening; his cheeks were fuller, the waistband of his breeches tighter, his complexion sallower. Already he had been *cocu* by Josephine (and vice versa). He suffered from the alarming inferiority complex of the small man, and, as a lover, he was always reputed to suffer physically from a *faiblesse dans le deduit d'amour*. Some of his less intimate officers thought possibly his gaze was a trifle duller, and they would reflect apprehensively among themselves that it was now over four years since he had won that last great military victory, at Marengo; could it be that 'perhaps the crown has squashed his brains'? But they would soon be proved wrong.

Millions of words have been written about Napoleon's complex personality, re-examining its mysteries and paradoxes (and sometimes, even, manufacturing new ones). He hunted, not because he enjoyed it or was even particularly good on a horse, but because he deemed it part of the regal apanage. He espoused pageantry, insofar as it was a function of the courtly life designed to bedazzle the impressionable, but in fact was happier himself amid the almost martial simplicity which Josephine had created for him at Malmaison. He was also no gourmet. He derided ambition in others, remarking disdainfully of his own creation, the *Légion d'Honneur*, 'it is by such baubles that men are governed', yet was boundless in his own ambition. He was bred on the egalitarian ideals of the Revolution, but was to found a new aristocracy and a new despotism of his own.* He condemned sexual love as 'harmful to society and to the individual happiness of men', yet was incapable himself of avoiding both its entanglements and torments of jealousy. He leant towards mathematics and sciences of the reason, while mistrusting anything to do with human passions, yet he could never quite escape from being a child of the Romantic movement himself.† He was (wrote George Rudé) 'a man of action and rapid decision, yet a poet and

---

* As once remarked revealingly to Benjamin Constant: '*Je ne hais point la liberté. Je l'ai écarté, lorsqu'elle obstruait ma route; mais je la comprends, j'ai été nourri dans ses pensées.*'

† A measure of his suppressed romanticism is revealed in his own little-read novel, *Clisson et Eugénie*, written in purple prose during the fallow summer of 1795, and in which the hero, an aspiring young soldier, seeks a hero's death in battle on discovering that his wife, Eugénie, has fallen in love with his friend.

dreamer of world conquest; a supreme political realist, yet a vulgar adventurer who gambled for high stakes . . .'. About certain facets of Napoleon's character there has been little argument. One was the extraordinary impact he had on people. 'The terror he inspires is inconceivable,' wrote Madame de Staël. 'One has the impression of an impetuous wind blowing about one's ears when one is near that man.'

As for his relationships with his soldiers, perhaps the single most remarkable feature was the total dedication he was able to exact; the *grognards* would march to Moscow and back for him – and then, once again, pick up their muskets during the Hundred Days. Another incontrovertible asset of Napoleon's was his almost superhuman reserve of energy. It was his energy which enabled him to be, so his admirer Goethe thought, 'in a permanent state of enlightenment, which is why his fate was more brilliant than the world has ever seen or is likely to see after him . . .'. He could concentrate eighteen hours a day without his mind clouding. 'I work the whole time,' he once explained to Count Roederer. 'It is not a *génie* that reveals to me suddenly what I have to say or do in a circumstance which may surprise others, it's my reflection, it's meditation.'

By the beginning of 1805, that capacity for work was certainly undiminished. So too was the retentiveness of that remarkable, questing, restless mind and his genius for total concentration. As Caulaincourt, his trusted aide, explained, 'He always applied all his means, all his faculties, all his attention to the action or discussion of the moment. Into everything he put passion. Hence the enormous advantage he had over his adversaries, for few people are entirely absorbed by one thought or one action at one moment.'

'An infinite capacity for taking pains', 'an intuitive sense', 'an indomitable will to power', 'a firmness of aim'; these are some of the many qualities attributed to Napoleon. Perhaps above all he was a man of reflexive action, as opposed to meditation. A remark made in his youth revealed clearly his extrovert inclinations: 'when a man asks himself "Why do I exist?" – then, in my opinion, he is the most wretched of all. His machine breaks down, his heart loses the energy that is proper to men.' Even if it did not lead to happiness, he thought action was better than introspection, which inevitably showed the way to wretchedness. Insofar as he (a Voltairean sceptic) had any, this also applied to his religious beliefs. Such beliefs were perfectly acceptable for others (and particularly women), but where he was concerned 'I am glad I have no religion,' he confided to his intimate, Bertrand: 'It is a great consolation I have no imaginary fears. I do not fear the future.'

His mistrust of intellectualism perhaps lay at the root of his aversion for Madame de Staël and her fellow ideologues. 'They talk, talk, talk,' he complained to his brother, Lucien. Occasionally it also led him into faulty conclusions, as when he rejected a blueprint by the American genius, Robert Fulton, for the invention of a submarine: 'All these inventors, all these project mongers are either schemers or visionaries. Don't mention him again.'

'Men are moved by two levers only: fear and self-interest,' he once declared. To some extent he approved of Robespierre's Terror, regarding it – like the actions of a late-twentieth-century terrorist – as 'one of the inevitable phases' of revolution, a process that 'can be neither made nor stopped'. In no way ashamed of his own relentless looting of treasures in Italy, he regarded the acquisition of the booty of war by his subordinates as just one of the elements comprising the lever of 'self-interest'.

If it was his addiction to action that placed him on a treadmill leading, ineluctably, from one conquest to another, in terms of both strategy and tactics he did, however, also possess the rare capacity to bide his time, waiting for the *moment juste*. It was, he admitted, a characteristic to which the 'Gallic temperament' was ill-suited: 'yet it is solely in virtue of this that I have succeeded in everything that I have done'.

In all his personal relations, self-interest stood foremost. 'I have always been the victim of my attachment to him,' declared Jean Lannes, and there was no one more devoted among all Napoleon's marshals; 'He only loves you by fits and starts, that is, when he has need of you.' This same rather unattractive quality manifested itself in Napoleon's associations with women which played so important a part in his life. His philosophy was very much that of the eternal Mediterranean male; the function of women should be confined to bed, family and Church. The aim of education must be 'not that girls should think, but that they should believe'. He complained: 'We Westerners have spoilt everything by treating women too well. We are quite wrong to make them almost our equals. The Eastern peoples have been much more sensible.' As with his essential lack of interest in *la bonne table*, he endeavoured to keep his amorous affairs on a matter-of-fact basis.

He was, however, by no means immune himself to passion in all its facets; there was the famous occasion when he collapsed senseless from excess in bed with Mademoiselle George, the celebrated actress (who, prefatory to their liaison, had provoked an explosion of applause in the theatre by reciting, just as Napoleon entered his box, the line *'Si j'ai séduit Cinna, j'en seduirai bien d'autres!'*). He could also be relentless when rebuffed, as he was with the virtuous Madame Récamier, who preserved her virginity – it was alleged – even with her boring banker husband. Nor, much as he may have affected to despise women, could he ever entirely restrain his passions from spilling over into his professional life, notably, of course, where Josephine was concerned.

This complex relationship between Napoleon and Josephine is superbly portrayed in the outstanding, highly sensitive biography of the pair published in 1995 by Evangeline Bruce – from which Josephine emerges as a gentle, highly feminine and utterly delightful but doomed personality. Bruce calls theirs 'an unlikely union'; and, indeed, it is always something of a mystery how Napoleon and the Creole Vicomtesse de Beauharnais, conveniently widowed at the age of thirty-one by Robespierre, ever became destined for each other. There was no cogent reason for Barras, master of the Directory, to hand over a perfectly good mistress to a relatively insignificant young general* (although he appears to have retained certain rights for a few years afterwards); or for Josephine to marry an impecunious young officer. Napoleon deluded himself that she was wealthy enough to pay his debts and to provide him with heirs, on both of which counts he was disappointed.† (She also lied to him about her age.) Wildly extravagant, Josephine in fact increased his indebtedness, purchasing Malmaison for the astronomic sum of 325,000F, which she had no means of paying, while Napoleon was away in Egypt. The match began inauspiciously, with the future Emperor being bitten on the leg by Josephine's pug while making love to her on their wedding night, and little time elapsed before she was flagrantly unfaithful to him. Although he once declaimed haughtily, on the subject of separate bedrooms, 'Crimes only divide the husband from the wife . . . only *one* for me and Madame Bonaparte', *male* fidelity was not rated quite so highly in the Corsican scale of things. In Egypt, Napoleon in his separation was solaced by a lady called *la Bellilote* who concealed a well-rounded pair of buttocks in tight officer's breeches, and there were a series of ladies like Mademoiselle George (whom an enraged Josephine once flushed *in flagrante* from the Imperial bedchamber).

But for most of his life it was Josephine, the highly sexed

---

* On one occasion, Napoleon, much given to ordering the private lives of his siblings, expressed displeasure when brother Lucien announced his intention of marrying his mistress. Lucien, piqued, retorted that it was surely better to marry one's own mistress than someone else's. He was never forgiven.

† Although Josephine had two children, Eugène and Hortense, by de Beauharnais, and both Marie Walewska and Marie-Louise proved Napoleon's potency, one might well speculate on the causes of Josephine's later barrenness on examining the villainous douching devices, resembling brass garden syringes, that are laid out for the edification of tourists at Malmaison — not to mention her numerous, presumably crude, abortions.

Creole with the bad teeth from chewing too much West Indian sugar-cane, who held some special magic for Napoleon. 'Sweet and matchless Josephine. . . . How strangely you work upon my heart!' he wrote in one of his many, deeply moving letters to her, letters that all too often brought no reply. Abandoned for months on end, creating the garden at Malmaison, growing her beautiful roses there and commissioning Redouté to paint them was not enough to keep the hot-blooded young woman occupied. Napoleon knew this and while campaigning in distant lands she was constantly in his mind, driving him on and plaguing him with doubts:

> I have not spent a day without loving you; I have not spent a night without embracing you; I have not so much as drunk a single cup of tea without cursing the pride and ambition which force me to remain separated from the moving spirit of my life. In the midst of my duties, whether I am at the head of my army or inspecting the camps, my beloved Josephine stands alone in my heart, occupies my mind, fills my thoughts. . . .

Then there would come the inevitable note on professional matters: 'ps The war this year has changed beyond recognition. I have had meat, bread and fodder distributed. . . . My soldiers are showing inexpressible confidence in me; you alone are a source of chagrin to me; you alone are the joy and torment of my life. . . .' A year later he was writing from Verona: 'I love you no longer; on the contrary, I detest you. You are a wretch, truly perverse. . . . You never write to me at all, you do not love your husband. . . . What business is so vital that it robs you of the time to write to your faithful lover?' And a few days afterwards: 'I have defeated the enemy . . . I am dead with exhaustion. I beg you leave with all speed for Verona; I need you. . . .'

He had few illusions. 'She wanted everything,' he once complained. Late in life he admitted to Bertrand in what seems like more than passing honesty: 'I really did love her . . . but I had no respect for her. . . . She had the prettiest little ———— imaginable.' Whatever it may have been, it was for many years to wield a most powerful influence over the most powerful man in Europe, in peace as in war.

Those two rare years of peace that opened the century would be cherished by Napoleon and Josephine as the happiest of their lives. The same could probably be said for many millions of Europeans.

THREE

Partners in Coalition

1804

Thou art free,
My country! and 'tis joy enough and pride
For one hour's perfect bliss, to tread the grass
Of England once again. . . .

Wordsworth, 'Sonnets Dedicated to Liberty', 1802

ALAS FOR NAPOLEON'S imperial grand design — and alas for Europe — in the words of Winston Churchill 'the tourist season was short'.[1] The peace which followed the Treaties of Lunéville and Amiens was to turn out to be something like the Ribbentrop–Molotov Non-Aggression Pact of 1939 — a brief unnatural truce which both sides sought to vitiate, while laying the blame on the other. What has been called the 'experimental peace'[2] (the terms of which were in fact more preferential to France than to England) was based on premises that were altogether too insubstantial.

It was not just the fact of the undiminished alarm which Napoleon's dynamism continued to arouse among his neighbours, but what he had inherited. The Great Revolution had so fundamentally shaken the whole European system that it was being excessively optimistic to presume that equilibrium could be restored by the exchange of an island here and a province there. If, in France, Napoleon was most intrinsically both product of it and heir to it, then beyond her frontiers there was also barely a nation whose institutions had not been profoundly affected by the Revolution and its consequences. In Poland, Tadeusz Kosciuszko, sparked by what he had experienced in America (where, as a skilled engineer, he had put his country on the map by helping to fortify the key bastion of Saratoga) and what he had observed in France, launched an abortive insurrection against the Russian oppressor in 1794. In Prussia, where intellectuals like Kant and Hegel, Goethe and Schiller, were sharply divided by the Revolution, Silesian peasants in 1792 had declined to pay their tithes to their Junker landlords; in Piedmont, Italian peasants had rioted for land reform. In England radical agitation had spread through the Corresponding Society, although perhaps a more influential phenomenon was the religious revival (especially within the Nonconformist churches) provoked by outrage at the excesses of French atheism. And in Austria, where the reigning Habsburg had been forced to watch impotently while his sister had been first humiliated, then guillotined, there were also those dynastic considerations not lightly to be papered over. Moreover, in the words of Pitt at the time, 'the dreadful sentence which they had executed on their unfortunate monarch applies to every sovereign now existing'.

Not unlike other periods that precede great upheavals (such as Europe on the eve of 1914), the years leading up to the French Revolution had been a time of growing commercial prosperity for almost the whole continent, including Russia. Yet, by the time of his coronation and in comparison with the powerful, modern apparatus, both civil and military, which he was forging in France, Napoleon could with some justice regard his European rivals as looking conspicuously archaic, indeed almost fragile. They also seemed paralysed by endless division, both internally and among themselves. We will speak of purely military matters later, but in Austria Maria Theresa's successor, Joseph II, had made earnest endeavours towards civil reform before his death in 1790. He abolished torture and serfdom, and dissolved 700 monasteries to help finance education and poor relief. But too often his reforms represented more a private Utopia rather than what his subjects specifically wanted at any given time. Like Louis Napoleon, a century later, he might well have been dubbed 'the well-intentioned', and he too had a knack of going about things the wrong way. He offended the Bohemians by imposing German officials on them, and most of his reforms were wrecked by the Church and nobility whom he had alienated. He longed to prove himself a great military leader and expand his already unwieldy Empire, but a series of silly wars, in the best Austrian tradition, only left his country at odds with her neighbours; and outraged Bavaria was particularly to prove a thorn in Austria's side throughout the Napoleonic campaigns. His wanton share in the partition of Poland resulted in Austria's permanent enmeshment with both Prussia and Russia. He died six months before the storming of the Bastille, leaving an embittered epitaph: 'Here lies Joseph II, who failed everything he undertook.'

His more level-headed successor, Leopold II, managed to shore up the tottering throne and showed every promise of succeeding where his brother had failed. Yet even his endeavours as peacemaker in the Netherlands only had the effect of upsetting both England and Holland, with further disastrous consequences for Austrian policy in the early wars against Revolutionary France. Then, after a bare two years' reign, Leopold was dead of dysentery. His successor, Francis I, aged thirty-six when he succeeded to the throne in 1804, immediately found himself plunged into war with France.

It was under the benevolent influence of Maria Theresa and her two sons that Vienna had become the musical centre of gravity of Europe, drawing to it Gluck, Mozart, Haydn and eventually Beethoven. But, as Arthur Bryant observes, Austria's highly civilized denizens also continued – in the gentlemanly eighteenth-century manner – to view war rather 'as a professional activity to be performed, like music, according to clearly recognized rules and conventions . . .'. For military success has never been Austria's highest distinction. And there was also the eternal disadvantage of the hotch-potch of *Mitteleuropa* nationalities which, in varying degrees of resentfulness, comprised the Empire, and which were to cause its final break-up a century later. As for Francis' allies in the various coalitions, the only interest shared with Austria was the negative factor of opposition to Revolutionary and Napoleonic France. Fortunate for Francis was his own endowment with the Habsburg talent for survival, developed to the highest degree.

The social institutions of her north German neighbour, Prussia, were yet more archaic than those of Austria. If anything, since the death of Frederick the Great, serfdom had received further impulsion as peasants were bullied by landlords to increase grain output to exploit boom export markets. In East Prussia they were sometimes committed to five or six days' work a week for their Junker; it was not therefore surprising that, as previously noted, they had reacted in sympathy with the principles of the French Revolution. In terms of military efficiency, Prussia since Frederick had also declined in inverse ratio to the age of its commanders. Having received a drubbing in the Revolutionary Wars, she was reluctant to risk her neck against Napoleon's France and would prove to be little more than a posthumous entrant in the next round.

As in contemporary Prussia, in the late-eighteenth-century Russia of Catherine the Great and her son, mad Paul I, serfdom had actually increased its hold. Like the Austrians, Catherine abolished torture and she also talked about agrarian reform, but most of her radical ideas were cured by the immense alarm which the Pugachev Rebellion provoked. Thus, in effect, serfdom spread to embrace a still wider class of Russians, and to the Ukraine as well; while bonds between the landowners and the ruler became even closer. Autocracy took another turn under the dark, brief reign of Paul, who closed down most of Russia's printing presses not banned by his mother, and – in a manner familiar to modern times – outlawed all Western books. He gave away as personal 'presents' some 600,000 serfs, while at the same time introducing a decree (which was entirely unenforceable) limiting serfdom to only three days a week. Stepping to the throne over the strangled body of his father in 1801 (for whose murder many held him responsible in some degree), young

Alexander I initiated the steady move towards emancipation of the serfs, although the number receiving their freedom was the merest drop in the ocean, and it is recorded that, by the time of Napoleon's invasion of Russia, some 58 per cent of all Russians were still not free men. To escape from the deprivations of serfdom Russians flocked to join the army, where Catherine had benevolently reduced the terms of service from life to a leisurely twenty-five years. 'God, how sad our Russia is!' sighed Pushkin on reading *Dead Souls*, Gogol's powerful indictment of serfdom. But no Russian serf blamed the Tsar for his troubles. The Tsar was purely ill-advised, and when called to do so they would fight for him to the last breath in their bodies.

Alexander was prompt to introduce numerous other timely reforms – in education, in censorship, in recasting governmental administration (thereby incorporating some lessons learnt from Napoleon), and in reordering Russia's finances, while at the same time he was also to reverse Paul's inconsistent foreign policy, which had ended by coming down on the side of Napoleon. Much of Catherine's boundless energy had been channelled into south-easterly conquests, at the expense of the Ottoman Turks and greatly to the alarm of England. Such alarms were by no means diminished by a crazy scheme concerted between Paul and Napoleon to invade India with a force of Don Cossacks, and Nelson was actually on his way to take punitive action in the Baltic when Paul was assassinated.

Brought up in a frugal and virtuous atmosphere which owed something to the principles of Jean-Jacques Rousseau, Alexander was still a virgin when married (at sixteen). He was only twenty-four when he succeeded to the throne, but it was soon apparent that the new Tsar came out of a totally different mould from either his father or grandmother. Napoleon remarked of him patronizingly that, 'to be very able, he lacks only decision', yet he was to prove a most tenacious adversary. The fact remained, however, that Alexander's Russia was no more a natural ally of England – or, for that matter, of Napoleon's other enemies –

than Catherine's Russia had been. Therein lay a constant advantage to France, with her strategically central position and internal lines of communication placed astride Europe – an advantage that Kaiser Wilhelm and Hitler were to enjoy a century later.

Although, in the years 1805–7, on dry land the killing of Frenchmen and the dying was to be accomplished by Austrians, Russians and Prussians,* behind the whole scheme of things hovered the shadow of England, enigmatic, aloof, but immensely powerful – and inestimably rich. She had made a remarkable recovery from the crippling costs, and the humiliation, of the American War of Independence, which had ended with a pious hope of 'a Christian universal, and perpetual peace'. It was only a decade later, however, that the French Revolutionary Wars exploded. The twenty years and more of conflict that were to ensue would cause the shelving of much urgently needed social reform; yet Wordsworth was not being totally smug when, on returning from France in the summer of 1802, he could write:

> Here, on our native soil, we breathe once more.
> . . . Oft have I looked round
> With joy in Kent's green vales; but never found
> Myself so satisfied in heart before.
> Europe is yet in bonds; but let that pass
> Thought for another moment. Thou art free,
> My country! and 'tis joy enough and pride
> For one hour's perfect bliss, to tread the grass
> Of England once again. . . .

More than anything else, it was this sense of personal freedom that distinguished England from her continental allies. Prussians and Russians would later fight with maximum ferocity when their sovereignty had been trampled underfoot, or the war carried

---

* The British Army never put more than 40,000 men into action at any one time; the whole Peninsular War cost less than 40,000 British dead (Napoleon suffered almost that number of casualties in one battle, Leipzig).

deep into their own homeland; but the dogged determination of the English stemmed from being the only European people who could in any way term themselves 'free men'. They alone had a monarchy subject to parliamentary democracy — even though George III exercised more influence over policy than any of his successors (and though the onset of porphyria inflicted him with bouts of madness which placed its burden on government too). English society, if one may trust that great contemporary chronicler Jane Austen, was obsessed with wealth and rank; yet its privileges were becoming as open to wealth as to birth, in this nation of shopkeepers where the merchant was now as 'respectable' as the aristocrat. Though England remained largely an agricultural economy, industrially she still headed the world by a long lead. But her true prosperity lay in her mercantile marine — incomparably the world's greatest — which in turn depended upon the protective supremacy of the Royal Navy. Between 1793 and Waterloo, English coffers were able to pay out £52 million in subsidies to the Allies alone. At the prevailing value of the pound (approximately twenty-five times its rate today), it was indicative of the amazing extent of British prosperity.

With English merchants, profiteers, landlords and farmers getting inflated prices for their produce during the war, it was France who was to suffer more from the boycott of the 'Continental System'. But this was a prosperity that was, however, far from universal in England. Reforms that were as badly needed, here as elsewhere, were adjourned (for instance, virtually the only major reform passed was Wilberforce's prohibition of slavery in 1807). 'While desires increase,' George III wrote gloomily to the younger Pitt in 1787, 'the means of satisfying the people have been much diminished.' It could have been said of many other pre-revolutionary times in history. In 1795, a year of terrible weather which ruined crops, killed lambs by the intense cold and sent the price of food soaring, mass demonstrations in London had shouted, 'No war, no Pitt, no King!' The King's coach was stoned by hungry subjects, and Pitt began to have serious fears of the Revolution crossing the Channel. In Ireland conditions were grimmer than usual, not helped by the ingenuity of Government forces who, at this time, invented a device called 'pitch-capping' whereby the forefathers of the IRA had their heads smeared with pitch and gunpowder and set alight. In 1798 there was a brief rebellion, dangerously fanned by France.

Throughout the Napoleonic Wars conditions were harsh for the poor, and poverty spread. Because of the blockade, wheat trebled in price between 1792 and 1812. In the country, bread and cheese became the staple diet of the labourer, washed down with tea or beer; meat – let alone John Bull's traditional joint of beef – was seldom seen. In a nation that listed 200 capital offences on its statute books, the laws were savagely tilted against the hunger-driven poacher. Things were worse in the grubby, overcrowded cities to which the underpaid and underemployed countrymen had flocked, unable to bring with them the compensatory joys of rural life. Badly built slums innocent of sanitation sprawled, uncontrolled by any kind of planning. Factory and mine workers existed forgotten, without social welfare, distractions or hope – except that provided from Nonconformist pulpits. Their children were required to labour cruel hours; women, forced out of decayed 'cottage industries', made city nights hideous with 'the harlot's cry from street to street'; and it was the age of the Luddite smasher of machinery.

Yet it could in no way be said that, overall, England was unhappy, or the mood of the country unhealthy. Over the past quarter of a century, the crude world of Hogarth had been replaced by Gainsborough, mirroring fashionable taste. As David Cecil tells us, Jane Austen's England was now one of 'good sense, good manners and cultivated intelligence, rational piety and spirited sense of fun'.[3] By comparison with other nations, and even (or perhaps especially) by today's standards, there were many aspects of English life at the turn of the century that seem to have been wistfully good. The country cried for reform, but not for revolution; it had a strong sense of fair play and was law-abiding, though still without a police force. If a man was knifed in the street, passers-by did not hurry on, and Southey reckoned that contemporary Britons would put out an insurrection as they would a fire. From top to bottom, England had never been more dedicated (until, perhaps, the 1960s) to the pursuit of pleasures, some healthier than others. Fornication was regarded as an essential proof of virility; as an indication of the scale of the industry the splendidly outrageous diarist Harriette Wilson (who later smuggled her memoirs out of Paris via the diplomatic bag) and both her sisters were all 'kept ladies'. The example was set by the frivolity of the Prince of Wales, married secretly to Mrs Fitzherbert in 1785, and his world. Not for the last time in British history, the domestic antics of the family Wales provided succulent material for Grub Street. It was also at the height of the Napoleonic Wars that dandyism, coupled with the name of 'Beau' Brummel, reached a peak of extravagance. With its nightly balls and masquerades, London society was seen by Wordsworth (rather censoriously) as 'glittering like a brook in the open sunshine':

> The wealthiest man among us is the best:
> . . . Rapine, avarice, expense,
> This idolatry; and these we adore:
> Plain living and high thinking are no more.

With the improvement of the fowling-piece, the *Sportsman's Directory* could declare in 1792, 'The rage for shooting was never at a higher pitch than at present . . . the art of shooting flying [i.e. birds on the wing] is arrived at tolerable perfection. . . .' Duelling flourished, and, in further pursuit of the stimulus of danger, the upper classes had become hunting mad; in 1790 steeple-chasing was introduced, and in 1801 the Duke of Richmond laid out a racecourse at Goodwood.

Pleasure, however, was by no means the prerogative only of 'the wealthiest man'. On horse or on foot, people would travel almost any distance to attend a prize-fight and reports of such sporting events would often eclipse news from the battle-front. Because of popular pressure a bill to end bull-baiting failed in 1802, and the hardly less cruel sport of cock-fighting continued to thrive under the patronage of 'Prinnie'. For all the hardships, there was also much wholesome joy to be found in humbler rustic life, as the childhood memories of Wordsworth and Cobbett record. 'The beauty of field and wood and hedge, the immemorial customs of rural life,' writes G. M. Trevelyan, '. . . the village green and its games, the harvest-home, the tithe feast, the May Day rites, the field sports – had supplied a humane background and an age-long tradition to temper poverty.'[4] Rural England and its picturesque market towns would never again be so unspoilt, and this was also the great age of Constable, Turner and Morland. Poetry, too, was on a high plateau – reflecting, perhaps, as Wordsworth noted, a:

> central peace subsisting at the heart
> Of endless agitation. . . .

It has often been remarked that the novels of Jane Austen barely mention the wars raging beyond the Channel – perplexing, perhaps, when one considers that she had two brothers in the navy; Frank was an admiral, and a prolific letter-writer, who had the bad luck just to miss the Battle of Trafalgar.* American visitors were also usually struck by the absence of any signs of war. There were no fortifications, and few soldiers to be seen on the streets (the explanation was simple, of course – England had few soldiers). Even 'those far-off ships' of which the great American naval historian Admiral Mahan wrote and which alone stood between England and French conquest were, for most of

---

* After the battle, he met the unfortunate Admiral Villeneuve, who, he observed, was 'so much of a Frenchman as to bear his misfortunes with cheerfulness'. Six months later, however, Villeneuve committed suicide. Cecil's comment was: 'perhaps the Austens were too English to understand foreigners' (*A Portrait of Jane Austen*, p. 101).

the time, as unseen to English eyes as they were to Napoleon's. The fact is that, because of the many distractions at home, Englishmen found little time to think about the war. High among such distractions was, of course, the perennial spectacle – as diverting as a good prize-fight – of the politicians Pitt, Sheridan, Fox and Addington mauling each other, mostly on domestic matters. If the war came home to Englishmen it was generally through the heavy taxes levied to finance it (there was no end to Pitt's inventiveness, past and present; taxes on windows, on horses, and even on ladies' hats); or via the vituperation of the cartoonists. Headed by Gillray, Rowlandson and many others, the Napoleonic Wars fuelled one of the greatest periods of English political caricature. Immensely skilful, and boundlessly imaginative, the cartoons were often of a viciousness hardly exceeded in Goebbels' Germany, and usually of an unrestrained coarseness. The royal family, and even the King, were by no means sacrosanct, while Napoleon generally appears as a contemptible little figure, a Tom Thumb, or a Lilliputian Gulliver being chastised (or sometimes copiously excreted upon) by a robust, Brobdingnagian John Bull. With comparable inaccuracy, Gillray portrays Josephine as a mountainous, blowsy tart. The cartoonists undoubtedly succeeded in whipping up patriotic emotions against Napoleon, but they also did a grave disservice by causing the British public vastly to underrate him. At the same time, by depicting – with almost equal savagery – the British political scene as one of total anarchy, they contributed materially to leading Napoleon to commit the same errors about England.

Anarchic, frivolous, venal, greedy, slothful, disloyal, disorganized, untrustworthy and unwarlike; this was how Napoleon saw *Perfide Albion*. It was perhaps not all that different from Britain at the end of the next century. Napoleon was later to attribute the staunchness of the British infantry line purely to the benefits of flogging. He was quite incapable of comprehending the basic ruggedness that lay behind the unattractive and unimpressive façade, or, more important, the deep attachment to freedom that united, and would continue to unite, Englishmen of all walks of life whenever they felt menaced by his system. When invasion loomed, Wordsworth echoed the jingoism of his compatriots with his 'We must be free or die . . .' and

> We are all with you now from shore to shore:
> Ye men of Kent, 'tis victory or death!

It was a fundamental misappraisal that was to lead Napoleon into the same kind of faulty speculation and disaster which later befell the Kaiser and Hitler. On his journey round the West Country during the 1802 peace, Nelson, in his quiet, understated way, judged the mood better: '. . . I have not the slightest doubt, from the result of my observations during this tour, that the native, the inbred spirit of Britons, whilst it continues as firmly united as at present, is fully adequate.'

SOMETHING REMAINS TO BE SAID, briefly, about the new-born giant across the Atlantic – the United States of America – although she was to play no active role in the campaigns of 1805–7, but also just for that reason. Already American naval presence on the high seas could make itself felt (as Britain was to discover in 1812), and possible US involvement in the war was a factor not lightly to be dismissed. Politically the 'American example', reinforced by the involvement of Lafayette and Tom Paine, had had a powerful influence on the origins of the French Revolution. When, in 1793, Revolutionary France decreed a 'war of all peoples against all kings', the recent rebels were swept with almost hysterical enthusiasm. It waned somewhat on the news that she had guillotined the good friend of the 'embattled farmers', Louis XVI. Though Jefferson still regarded France's as 'the most sacred cause that ever man was engaged in', he and Washington opted for a benevolent neutrality. Then France sent as an envoy Citizen Genet, well described by Samuel Eliot Morison as the 'quaintest of many curious diplomats sent by European governments to the United States'.[5] Genet's instructions were to exploit the US as a privateering base, which was bad enough, but he went further by proceeding to inaugurate Jacobin Clubs wherever he set foot on his travels. It was as if in the 1950s a Soviet ambassador had toured the country implanting Communist cells; and America reacted comparably. Recalled in disgrace, Citizen Genet saved his head by marrying an American heiress and settling down in New York.

Together with a certain disenchantment with France, America's infant commerce now realized its need for British capital. Then, in September 1797, came Washington's famous Farewell Address, establishing the cornerstone of US foreign policy for many years to come:

> Europe has a set of primary interests which to us have none, or a very remote relation. Hence she must be engaged in frequent controversies, the causes of which are essentially foreign to our concerns. . . . Our detached and distant situation invites us to pursue a different course. . . . 'Tis our true policy to steer clear of permanent alliances, with any portion of the foreign world. . . .

There now ensued an uncertain period with the US Navy defensively involved in a quasi-war against French privateers (in which uss *Constellation* acquitted herself with distinction), followed by comparable clashes with Britain at sea, and a Teddy Roosevelt-style sideshow (perhaps not in accord with the strictest interpretation of the Farewell Address) against the pirates of Tripoli. Meanwhile, Napoleon had come to power and grandiosely declared his intent to make his country paramount in the New World as well, once he had finished in Europe. In 1800, by secret treaty with Spain, France took over the vast (and largely virgin territory) of 'Louisiana' as a substitute for those lost *'quelques arpentes de neige'* (as Voltaire had scathingly termed them) in Canada. At the same time a French expeditionary force was despatched to seize Toussaint l'Ouverture's negro republic of freed slaves in Hispaniola (Haiti). Castro's installation of Soviet rockets in Cuba was hardly more disturbing to American tranquillity. 'The day that France takes possession of New Orleans,' President Jefferson wrote to his minister in Paris in April 1802, 'we must marry ourselves to the British fleet and nation.' The following year he sent James Monroe as envoy extraordinary to treat with Napoleon.

Although it was to turn out to be the best bargain in American history, Monroe's opening bid was excessively modest, with a fall-back offer of $7.5 million just for New Orleans. But, if this failed, his instructions were to break off and seek 'a closer connection with Great Britain'. His negotiating partner was the astute Talleyrand, who, as a royalist exile, had spent two years in America.* At the Philadelphia bookshop of Saint Mery (who, as a sideline to books, had introduced contraceptives to the grateful Americans), Talleyrand mixed with a curious group of expatriate aristocrats, who had fought for liberty in America while opposing it in their own country. He allegedly shocked Philadelphians by consorting publicly with a coloured lady. Nevertheless, during his time in the US he had ingested the clear lesson that the country was still, at heart, more English than not, and that its 'utility' to England would 'increase in proportion as the English Government gives up its present haughtiness of demeanour in all its relations with America'.[6] Therefore, on the eve of renewed war with England, France would have to lean over backwards to prevent America falling into the English camp.

Meanwhile, his forces decimated by yellow fever in Hispaniola and his restless eyes already focusing elsewhere, Napoleon had lost interest in the New World. On 11 April 1803 (by which time Anglo-French relations were once more on the brink of

---

* On the eve of his departure from England, he had asked an American general, who chanced to be staying in the same inn, for letters of introduction. The General replied sadly: 'I am perhaps the only American who cannot give you letters for his own country.' His name was Benedict Arnold.

rupture), Talleyrand staggered the American negotiators by offering to sell the entire 'Louisiana' Territory, as big in area as the whole of the existing United States. Three weeks later the Louisiana Purchase was signed, at a price of $15 million, or only twice what Monroe had been briefed to offer for New Orleans alone – and this regardless of Napoleon's promise to Spain never to sell to a third power.

'You will fight England again,' Napoleon remarked hopefully as he shook hands on the deal with the Americans. But at least the US would remain strictly neutral in the now imminent War of the Third Coalition; and on 7 November, as Napoleon was closing in on Vienna, Jefferson's army explorers, Lewis and Clark, were to reach the Pacific, thereby blazing the trail for America's 'Manifest Destiny' to possess the whole continent from burning sea to burning sea while the rest of the world, distracted, grappled in the heart of Europe.

Thus to Napoleon all the omens seemed to favour his getting what he wanted – hegemony over Europe – and possibly by peaceful means. The United States had opted for neutrality, and his former enemies in Europe seemed reluctant to face war again. With thirty-three million* to England's fifteen, Prussia's six and Austria's twenty million, France had the largest population from which to draw fresh soldiers – except for Mother Russia's thirty-nine million – and the efficiency of her existing forces showed that she could beat any combination that might attack her. The potential coalition powers had, as previously noted, no common interest to bind them together, except opposition to France, and England and Russia looked as if they might easily come to blows over conflicting interests in the Near East and the island of Malta; while, internally, England herself seemed anarchic, led by a weak and aimless government under 'Doctor'

---

* Over the century following Napoleon, France's population grew remarkably slowly, to reach only 39.6 million by 1914; partly, in itself, a delayed consequence of the losses suffered during the Napoleonic Wars.

Addington, and with no land forces worth mentioning. (Addington, the natural pacifist, had actually halved the army, disbanded the militia 'Volunteers' and discharged 40,000 sailors in order to abolish Pitt's income tax.) The only four remaining factors of menace to Napoleon were the Royal Navy, the manpower resources of the Russian Army, the plottings of the Bourbons and 'Pitt's gold', the British funds capable of mounting a fresh coalition. However – especially with Pitt ailing and safely out of power – these factors showed no serious sign of combining against him, and by the beginning of 1803 Napoleon's voice had taken on a more strident note. He annexed Piedmont (although his guarantee of the integrity of the Italian states had been a *quid pro quo* for England's surrender of Malta), and sent Marshal Ney to invade Switzerland, which enraged even 'Doctor' Addington.

On her side, England by 1803 was becoming increasingly alarmed by France's naval activity, which included the construction of large numbers of flat-bottomed invasion barges. Her fears were not without reason; Napoleon intended to use the years of peace to construct twenty-five ships-of-the-line annually which, within six or seven years, would make him (at least theoretically) unbeatable at sea. Addington infuriated Napoleon by refusing to withdraw from the key naval bastion of Malta. What Fox called 'reciprocal Billingsgate' mounted in the press of both countries, and with it national feeling. In March, Napoleon had lost his temper at a public *levée*, shaking his cane at the English ambassador, Lord Whitworth, to the point where Whitworth expected to be struck, and exclaiming, 'Now you mean to force me to fight for fifteen more years!'

After another month of terse negotiations, Whitworth received what amounted to an ultimatum to pass on to Napoleon: England would recognize the Italian annexations, in exchange for Napoleon's evacuating Holland and Switzerland and accepting a ten-year English tenure of Malta. Enraged that anybody should present *him* with an ultimatum, at the same time taking it no more seriously than Hitler was to take Chamberlain's 1939 guarantee to the Poles, Napoleon rejected the British terms. It was the first big mistake of his career. Instead of the years of peace he had hoped for, in which he could have made his power virtually unassailable, on 18 May 1803 France found herself again at war with England. The following day the blockading ships of Admiral Cornwallis were once more in position outside Brest.

Then, nearly a year later, Napoleon followed up this error with an even greater one. Shaken by the Cadoudal conspiracy against him, he decided upon an act of sheer terror that would deter his royalist foes once and for all. The thirty-two-year-old Duke d'Enghien was (says Duff Cooper), 'not only the least blameworthy but the most admirable of the Bourbon princes. . . . Young, handsome and chivalrous he resembled more a hero of romance than a prince of the nineteenth century.'[7] While prepared to fight for his family rights with the *Armée des Émigrés*, he alone had steadfastly refused to have any dealings with the conspirators against Napoleon, and lived quietly – following the pursuit of love – in the independent German state of Baden. On the night of 14 March 1804, he was kidnapped by a French cavalry detachment sent by Napoleon, and spirited off to the sinister Château de Vincennes. A week later, after a perfunctory court martial which produced no evidence against him, he was executed by firing squad, with his inseparable dog, and buried in a grave which had been dug well in advance. All Europe was outraged by the killing; in Russia, Tsar Alexander, the body of whose own murdered father was barely cold, felt personally affronted, ordered court mourning and despatched a protest to France. It was Napoleon's blackest deed, but it was also, in the immortal phrase of Talleyrand, whose own hands were far from clean, 'worse than a crime, it was a blunder'. Chateaubriand resigned as Napoleon's envoy in Switzerland, declaring later that the murder of d'Enghien changed the course of his life, 'as it did Napoleon's'. Indeed, for Napoleon it was to become the Ghost of Banquo, haunting him for the rest of his life; but, more immediately, it was to provide one of the principal causes of the renewal of coalitionary war against him.

Only a few weeks before the murder, George III had caught a chill and had gone off his head again, having to be restrained from addressing Parliament with the words 'My Lords and Peacocks!' This made inevitable the departure of his feeble and unpopular favourite Addington, and the return of Pitt. On 19 May 1804, the reins of power were taken up again by the bellicose Pitt, bent – as always – on confrontation with Napoleon. It was the same day that, in Paris, a *Senatus Consultum* declared Napoleon Emperor of the French.

FOUR

The Army of England

1804–1805

They want us to jump the ditch, and we *will* jump it!

Napoleon

'PITT IS TO ADDINGTON, As London is to Paddington', wrote George Canning at a time when Paddington was an undistinguished outer suburb.[1] To every English schoolboy Pitt the Younger has long come to embody the spirit of warlike resistance to Napoleon; probably his more successful contribution lay in times of peace rather than of war. As a successful war leader, he had certainly not proved himself to be in the same league as his father, great Chatham; on the other hand it was a very different France he had to face. During the first Revolutionary Wars he had erred by frittering away his forces on minor expeditions – for instance, to the West Indies, where disease (such as Napoleon was to encounter in Hispaniola) had been victor* – instead of concentrating all on Europe. Like his father, however, Pitt was totally uncompromising in his determination to break the power of France. 'He possessed perseverance and courage and never flinched from criticism,' remarks Winston Churchill, and indeed it was with Churchillian oratory that Pitt could turn upon his opponents. Fox, he once declared:

---

* Nearly half the total death-roll during the twenty-two years of war (about 100,000 for Britain) was suffered in Pitt's West Indies campaign.

defies me to state, in one sentence, what is the object of the war. I know not whether I can do it in one sentence, but in one word I can tell him that it is 'security'; security against a danger, the greatest that ever threatened the world. It is security against a danger which never existed in any past period of society. . . .[2]

Later, he recalled for the Commons:

what we have to contend for. It is for our property, it is for our liberty, it is for our independence, nay, for our existence as a nation; it is for our character, it is for our very name as Englishmen, it is for everything dear and valuable to man on this side of the grave.[3]

A cold and lonely personality who never married, proud and unlovable, if there was one thing Pitt hated almost as much as France it was fecklessness. He disciplined himself with an icy self-control (he had once had a painful tumour removed from his cheek without flinching). His constant need to raise taxes in order to prosecute the wars was not destined to endear him to the good-living merchants of England, and it was Pitt's added misfortune to have lived at that time of peak viciousness in political satire, where his extenuated, angular figure proved a godsend to the cartoonists. It was only towards the end of his days, and afterwards, that he achieved anything resembling universal popularity.

With the war going badly again, in 1800 Pitt had found himself more unloved than ever before and the following year he resigned over the issue of emancipation for the Irish Catholics, after seventeen years in office. His successor, Addington ('that mass of conciliation and clemency' as his enemies called him), had promptly opened peace negotiations with Napoleon. Out of power, but appointed Warden of the Cinque Ports, an archaic honour later also bestowed on that other custodian of an embattled Britain, Winston Churchill, Pitt passed his time riding, sailing and partridge-shooting, planting fruit-trees and growing wheat at Walmer Castle, his official residence, or gazing out over the Kentish cliffs, in deepest concern, at Napoleonic France. As 'Addington's peace' looked less and less appealing, so Pitt's allure was rekindled. At a party to celebrate his birthday on 28 May 1802 (from which Pitt was absent), a thousand guests rose to toast Pitt's health and sing the doggerel composed by George Canning:

> And O! if again the rude whirlwind should rise,
> The dawning of peace should fresh darkness deform,
> The regrets of the good and the fears of the wise
> Shall turn to the pilot that weathered the storm.

Returning to the Commons on the outbreak of war the following May, Pitt made one of the greatest orations ever heard there: 'and all for war, and for war without end', noted Creevey the diarist.

Having started his prime ministerial career at the absurdly early age of twenty-four, Pitt was still not quite forty-four when recalled to power in 1804. Yet already he was a very sick man; often in pain, he had difficulty sleeping at night. Never physically robust, at the time of his resignation Pitt had been warned by his doctor that, unless he took a proper holiday and a 'cure', he would not survive the next parliamentary session. His chronic gout was not improved by excessive port-drinking, and in 1802 friends were deeply shocked by his bloated face and shaking hands. But, whatever the state of his health, nothing would in any way deflect him from pursuing the war against Napoleon with the utmost resolve.

The heroic view of Pitt is, of course, not entirely shared on the continent:

> *Their* ploughshare was the sword in hireling hands,
> *Their* fields manured by gore of other lands . . .

so noted even England's Byron of his nation's farmers, enriched by the war. To continental eyes, indeed, Pitt more often appears as the paymaster, 'buying' others to fight England's battles for her, at *their* expense in blood, while she aggrandized herself with fresh colonies. If Pitt had been less dedicated to the destruction of Napoleon, could not a compromise settlement have been achieved, thereby saving Europe – and France – untold misery? Yet it is doubtful whether, by 1804, with Napoleon firmly set on his imperial path of unlimited ambition, confrontation could long have been avoided. One thing was certain; as long as Pitt and Napoleon faced each other, no negotiated peace would be possible.

On returning to office, Pitt set himself two immediate objectives: to woo the Tsar, still outraged by the murder of the Duke d'Enghien, and to restore the effectiveness of the Royal Navy. The threat of Napoleon's naval construction programme, and the more immediate one of the growing flotilla of invasion barges, was very real in British eyes. When war with France had broken out in 1793, the navy had been in a bad state; four years later, not without cause, the mutinies at Spithead and the Nore broke out. Nevertheless, by the following year Nelson was able to wipe out the French fleet off Egypt. It was a reverse from which perhaps Napoleon's navy – already shaken by the havoc wreaked by the Revolution's purges of the officer corps – never properly recovered professionally. As Napoleon himself wrote of that abortive campaign: 'If it had not been for the English I should have been emperor of the East, but wherever there is water to float a ship, we are sure to find [them] in our way.'

The problem, for England, was to provide enough of those ships, and keep them there. Much of Pitt's restless energy was dedicated to reform and ship-building. Conditions gradually improved, and yet they were still appalling and it was, by modern standards, inconceivable that any human being should have tolerated them. There was the brutality: the press-gangs on shore, and the floggings on board ship – a dozen lashes, the normal penalty for petty theft (double that for drunkenness), sufficed to rip the skin off a man's back. At sea the crews experienced months in disgustingly cramped quarters, rats eating the bandsmen's bagpipes, weevils in the hard-tack ('we were fed with putrid beef, rusty pork and bread swarming with maggots', recorded a contemporary report),[4] the boredom of prolonged blockade duty – and scurvy.* Then, when the few minutes of battle at last came there were the horrible scenes of carnage, the dreadful wounds caused by cannon-ball and jagged splinters of oak inadequately tended in the surgeons' hopelessly ill-equipped cockpit, the badly wounded dumped overboard together with the dead. Nevertheless, the one quality the British sailors never lacked was enthusiasm, and the stimulus did not lie just in the greedy lure of prize money. 'The contrast between their grievances and their indiscipline on the one hand and their splendid spirit in action and on the blockade service may seem unaccountable . . .', writes G. M. Trevelyan, continuing (perhaps a trifle eulogistically):

> The explanation lay in this: the men before the mast knew that, for all the ill treatment they received, the nation regarded them as its bulwark and glory; that at the sight of one of Nelson's men with his tarry pigtail, the landsman's eye kindled with affection and pride. The country that used them so ill looked to them confidently to protect her, and they knew it.[5]

At the time of the renewed outbreak of war in 1803, however, the Royal Navy was also a highly professional force. It was (in contrast to the army) in the hands of the educated sons of gentlemen of modest means, like Nelson. Relations between officers and men were, particularly under Nelson, generally excellent. At the top Pitt had appointed, as First Lord, Admiral Sir John Jervis, who had taken his new title of St Vincent from

---

* Strange as it may seem, since Pepys' day, a century and a half earlier, the known cure for scurvy, citrus fruits, had been lost. Admiral Lord St Vincent had rediscovered it. Consuming oranges by the thousand, Nelson's Mediterranean Fleet had by 1804 the best sick record of any.

the battle which had saved England in 1797. A close second only to Nelson, it was 'Jarvie' to whom Britain owed most for her survival, then victory, at sea. Already aged sixty-nine in 1803, he had joined the navy the week of his fourteenth birthday, and by the time he was twenty-four he had witnessed Wolfe's assault at Quebec, in command of the *Porcupine*. He was a square, oak-like, small figure, but with twinkling eyes, a man of irresistibly forceful personality, and with a dread reputation as a most stern disciplinarian. It was reputed that he had once administered a dozen lashes to a captain of the maintop who had failed to uncover during 'God Save the King'.

During the alarming mutinies in Spithead and the Nore of 1797, which could have devastated the fleet had they spread, St Vincent (then Commander-in-Chief, Mediterranean) had had to act with extreme measures. On the *Marlborough*, a 'very bad ship', he ordered a mutineer to be hanged from the yard-arm by his own shipmates; a launch with a 'smashing carronade' was sent alongside to blow the ship out of the water in case the order was refused.[6] In another ship under his command, two homo-sexuals were hanged for their 'unnatural crime'. Four mutineers were ordered to be hanged immediately, but, as it was a Sunday, St Vincent's second-in-command, Vice-Admiral Thompson, pro-posed a delay. He was promptly sacked. The word went round: 'If old Jarvie hears ye, he will have you dingle-dangle from the yard arm at eight o'clock tomorrow morning.' Yet, though severe, 'Jarvie' was not a cruel man, and was respected both for his rigid sense of justice and for his hatred of unfairness. Like Montgomery in a later world war – and though quite out of phase with his own times – he was much harder on the officers than on the men; and he was correspondingly loved for it.

Having suffered a crushing blow during the 'Terror', when the guillotine had almost wiped out its officer corps, the French Navy had never really recovered. The quality of the French ships was often superior to that of the ageing British vessels, worn out by years of service (Nelson's *Victory*, for instance, had been laid down in the 1760s), but discipline on board ship was poor. Perhaps more than to any other factor, the ability of British ships to stay at sea, and endure longer than the French — which would eventually decide the war — could be ascribed to that fierce, almost inhuman, discipline maintained by St Vincent. Under him, too, far-reaching reforms of pay and conditions were also carried out. When commanding the Mediterranean Fleet, he found more than one of his exhausted men-of-war to be worn out by non-stop operations: 'altogether in such a crazy and infirm state, as to be totally incapable of a passage back to England'.[7] After the period of the 'Phoney Peace' in 1802, Addington had imposed certain ill-chosen economies, and the navy's ships were in a terrible state when St Vincent took over as First Sea Lord; but somehow he was able to transform its 'hulks of dubious wood and canvas into a fighting fleet' — and just in time to meet Napoleon's greatest threat to England. An unflappable figure, it was 'Jarvie' who, during the 1803 invasion scare, had declared challengingly, 'I don't say the French can't come. I say they can't come by sea.'

Body and soul, he stood for the all-out, offensive blockade of Napoleon's ports. He was replaced, briefly, by Lord Melville, who was in turn to be succeeded in April by Lord Barham. Very much Pitt's appointee, Barham (previously Admiral Sir Charles Middleton) had resurrected the navy after the war with America. Although aged seventy-eight, he was still full of vigour, and knew more about reactivating ships than anybody in the business. In the short time that was to elapse before the ultimate showdown at Trafalgar, Barham was to prove the greatest naval adminis-trator since Pepys.

Just below came a galaxy of brilliant sea commanders: 'Billy-go-tight' Cornwallis, the sixty-year-old Commander-in-Chief of the Channel Fleet; Collingwood, who had served so long at sea it was said his children scarcely knew him; Cotton, Calder, Cochrane and Pellew — and, above, the genius of the frail but fearless Nelson. It was they who maintained the superb standards boasted by the navy of that day. Ships-of-the-line, though minute by twentieth-century measurements, then represented the pinnacle of the high-tech and constructional skill of their age; Nelson's *Victory*, for example, had been six years in building (it was already forty years old at the time of Trafalgar); it had required the felling of 2,500 oaks, had 27 miles of rigging and 4 acres of sail, displaced 3,500 tons, carried 104 guns and had cost £63,176 (about £3 million in today's money). After decades of hard training, the British handling of these exquisite, yet primitive, pieces of equipment was unsurpassable, and so was the tactical seamanship of the commanders. When it came to the crucial factor of gunnery, nobody could concert a broadside with such deadly efficacy; it was something that Napoleon's navy, for all its enthusiasm, could never emulate.

Yet, on the outbreak of war in 1803, England could count no more than fifty-five capital ships against France's forty-two, though because Addington's declaration had taken Napoleon by surprise only thirteen of these latter were ready for immediate service. Nevertheless, the margin was still uncomfortably slim by the critical spring of 1805 when – with Spain and Holland aligned against her as well – Barham had only eighty-three battleships in commission, and many of those badly in need of repair. But the spirit made up for much; putting to sea in May 1803, Nelson wrote to Emma Hamilton, 'I have no fears,' and the following year (to his friend, Alexander Davison):

> . . . I am expecting the French to put to sea – every day, hour and moment; and you may rely that, if it is within the power of man to get at them, it shall be done; and I am sure that all my brethren look forward to that day as the finish of our laborious cruise.

Of 1803–5 it could be said with truth that *only* the Royal Navy of St Vincent, Barham and Nelson stood between Napoleon and world domination. Fortunately for Britain, although sailors like the courageous, doomed Villeneuve would do their best, the

French Navy, however, was never a high priority with Napoleon, any more than the German Navy was with Adolf Hitler, which was the fundamental reason why both would ultimately be defeated. Certainly, had the Royal Navy proved unable to prevent Napoleon landing a substantial force in England, her prospects would have been dim, for the British Army came out of a very different mould from the navy. It was, according to one contemporary description:

> lax in its discipline, entirely without system, and very weak in numbers. Each colonel of a regiment managed it according to his own notions, or neglected it altogether; professional pride was rare; professional knowledge even more so. Never was a kingdom less prepared for a stern and arduous conflict.

In marked contrast to the French Army, with its revolutionary principles, officers (including the future Duke of Wellington) had to buy their way in, and upwards; advancement by merit alone was rare. The system produced some brave and capable officers, but in essence they remained amateurs, regarding war more as a sport than as a profession. As for the rank and file, even Wellington once declared (admittedly in a fit of anger) that they 'all enlisted for drink!' Corporal punishment, even more brutal than in the senior service, endeavoured to maintain discipline.

Administration at the top in the army was chaotic; throughout the war, with Parliament fearful of the odium conscription might bring, voluntary enlistment was the only means of obtaining troops. Under Addington's peace economies, the army had actually been reduced to under 150,000 — scarcely enough to garrison Ireland and the Empire, and less than Napoleon would later be able to throw into just one of his big battles. To make up the deficit, a body of militiamen, or Volunteers, had been formed; a horde of untrained, unarmed, undisciplined but eager amateurs, they could only have further confused the Regular Army's task had an invasion ever materialized. There was a long way to go before General Bell could boast of the Peninsular

Army as being 'the bravest, the best, the finest disciplined and well-seasoned army in the world' or that a French officer could admiringly rate the British soldier as having 'no superior in the world; fortunately there are only a few of him'.

On the marriage of his favourite sister Pauline in 1803, Napoleon had instructed her, 'the only nation you must never receive are the English'. Throughout his remarkable career, whether fighting by land amid alpine snows, in the sands of Egypt or on the endless plains of eastern Europe, Napoleon had never been able to forget that it was England who was his principal, uncompromising adversary. It was England who had mounted, and financed, the successive coalitions against France; yet, weak though her army might be in relation to his own apparently irresistible land forces, she remained protected by the wide moat of the English Channel and that ubiquitous Royal Navy. Napoleon had tried to strike at the arch-enemy by disrupting her communications with India, but Nelson had thwarted this design at Aboukir Bay in 1799. He had tried to strangle her by barring her trade with the north European ports, but Nelson had brought the League of Armed Neutrality to ruin at Copenhagen in 1801. There remained only a direct invasion of the British Isles.

As far back as 1797 the possibilities for such an invasion had looked enticing when a French raiding party landed in Ireland, pinning down for nearly three weeks the entire British garrison. That same year Napoleon, in his brief command of the 'Army of England', had begun the building of a flotilla of flat-bottomed vessels, and from the collapse of the peace in 1803 onwards he concentrated his thoughts on invasion. 'They want us to jump the ditch,' he declared in a fury, 'and we *will* jump it!' With characteristic vigour and resourcefulness, he set thousands of navvies to work dredging out the invasion ports and digging new basins to accommodate his flotilla of 2,000 craft. Shipyards all along France's Channel coast and the Low Countries reverberated with hammering and sawing. Napoleon himself specified the prototype of 'A flat-bottomed boat able to transport 100 men across the Channel. There would be a mortar in the bows and stern . . .' – not unlike the landing-craft which took off for D-Day in 1944. He busied himself with such details as the numbers of cooking pots and pioneer spades to be carried in each barge, and even drew up an elementary rowing drill for the unfortunate troops who were to propel their own *péniches*. On the command 'Row!', 'the men holding the butt of the oars stretch forward together; they lean on the butt so that the blade does not plunge into the water until they have fully extended their arms . . .'. As it evolved, the invasion fleet comprised three kinds of vessel: large sail-driven *prames* over a hundred feet long, and each carrying 150 men; well-armed *chaloupes cannonières*, transporting guns, ammunition and horses; and – the most numerous – sixty-foot *péniches*, each containing fifty-five infantrymen. Ingenious 'terror' propaganda rumours were also circulated suggesting that Napoleon might also be planning to land troops by balloon, or even by a Channel tunnel or a bridge. He himself planned to disembark 120,000 picked troops, plus 6,000 horse and supporting artillery; he was prepared to accept 20,000 casualties drowned on the way. 'One loses that number in battle every day,' he reckoned, 'and what battle ever promised such results as a landing in England?' No doubt as a result of misreading the scurrility of the British cartoonists, he also expected to 'have found partisans enough in England to effect a disunion sufficient to paralyse the rest of the nation'. He planned to reach London within five days.

Throughout the glorious Indian summer, continuing through the October of 1803, the east wind blew in the invaders' favour, but still the fleet did not leave its harbours. Napoleon moved his headquarters to a château at Pont-de-Briques near Boulogne, and at the end of November he instructed Cambacérès to 'have a song written to the tune of the *Chant du Départ* for the descent on England. . . .' But in fact things had fallen badly out of joint; there were hopeless delays in the shipyards and money was running short; harbours were still so inadequate that it could take several days to get all the barges out to sea; and meanwhile the English frigates prowled everywhere, arrogantly close in-shore, like hungry sharks lurking to snap up an unwary vessel. Worst of all, the flat-bottomed barges, built without keels so as to ease beaching and unloading on the Kentish coast, proved hopelessly unseaworthy in anything but mill-pond waters rarely encountered in the notoriously capricious Channel. Sly jokes began to make the rounds in Paris about 'Don Quixote of *La Manche*'; in December winter gales closed down the invasion season, and almost immediately Napoleon's thoughts were distracted by the Cadoudal conspiracy.

Having examined one of the invasion barges that had been picked up, drifting helplessly in the Channel, a British admiral dismissed the prospects of such 'contemptible and ridiculous craft' achieving anything. Nevertheless, totally ill-prepared as England was to meet any invasion on land, the threat was received in deadly earnest (not altogether unmixed with the farcical). English babes went to bed terrified by such cautionary lullabies as:

> Baby, baby naughty baby,
> Hush you squalling thing, I say;
> Hush your squalling, or it may be
> Bonaparte may pass this way.

> Baby, baby, he's a giant,
> Tall and black as Rouen steeple;
> And he dines and sups, rely on 't,
> Every day on naughty people.

Church doors had Henry v's stirring words from the Siege of Harfleur pinned to them; the caricaturists took on a new note of belittling savagery, while blood-curdling posters depicted the horrors of invasion – mass rape of women and slaughter of infants – not to be improved on even in 1914. Songsters so bad they might have been hard-pressed to find employment with the BBC in a later age, had a heyday:

The French are coming, so they declare,
Of their floats and balloons all the papers advise us,
They're to swim through the ocean and ride on the air,
In some foggy evening to land and surprise us! . . .

We'll announce to the world his detestable Fame;
How the traitor RENOUNCED HIS REDEEMER and then
How he murdered his Prisoner and poison'd his Men!

Spy-mania was rife, with innocent holidaymakers being arrested for raising a telescope to their eye as a ship passed by, and there were more ugly rumours about a rising in Dublin.

Jingoism was orchestrated by no one more than Pitt, who cheerfully toasted 'a speedy meeting with our enemies on our *own* shores'. Then still out of power, he found himself so preoccupied in training his battalions of Kentish Volunteers that, even by December 1803 when the danger had (at least temporarily) passed, it was 'impossible for me to think of going to town until the week after'. To Winston Churchill, writing a century and a half later and with a detectable note of envy:

> Few things in England's history are more remarkable than this picture of an ex-Prime Minister, riding his horse at the head of a motley company of yokels, drilling on the fields of the South Coast, while a bare twenty miles away across the Channel the Grand Army of Napoleon waited only for a fair wind and a clear passage.[8]

Meanwhile, in London even the pacific Addington took to appearing in the House in uniform; further north, Dorothy Wordsworth watched the Grasmere Volunteers marching back and forth, while in Scotland Walter Scott polished up his swordsmanship by slashing at turnips stuck on poles, and at Selkirk a forebear of a future prime minister amused his Volunteers by singing an old Border song: 'Up with the souters [shoemakers] of Selkirk and down with the Earl of Hume!' Lord Auckland was even convinced that, if the invasion came, 'you would see all the ladies

The KING of BROBDINGNAG and GULLIVER. *(Plate 2.) Scene."Gulliver manœuvring with his little Boat in the Cistern." Vide Swift Gulliver*

'*I often used to Row for my own diversion, as well as that of the Queen & her Ladies, who thought themselves well entertained with my skill & agility. Sometimes I would put up my Sail and then my art by steering starboard & larboard; However, my attempts produced nothing else besides a loud laughter, which all the respect due to his Majesty from those about him could not make them contain... This made me reflect, how vain an attempt it is for a man to endeavour to do himself honour among those, who are out of all degree of equality or comparison with him.*' *See Voyage to Brobdingnag*

GILLRAY, 'The King of Brobdingnag . . .' 1804
King George III and court await invasion, 1804

letting their nails grow that they might scratch at the invader' for 'You never saw so military a country,' he observed; 'nothing but fighting is talked of.'[9]

In its spirit of defiant determination, the mood of England then seems to have resembled that of the summer of 1940. Martello towers were built at key points along the coast – James Joyce later lodged in extreme discomfort in the one protecting Dublin – and floating batteries anchored off the more vulnerable beaches. At first the Government talked seriously of countering the invaders with a desperate 'scorched earth' policy in southern England; but more sensible was the proposal by Major-General John Moore (later of Corunna fame) to harass them with guerrilla tactics.

In the event, winter passed, followed by an unusually calm and lovely spring and summer, and still no invasion came. The fervour abated in England. Neglected, Boulogne harbour began to silt up with sand again, and, because of the Royal Navy's successful blockade, the training of Napoleon's crews suffered, as did the equipment of their vessels. Yet still he persisted with the project, to the extent of striking a superbly over-confident victory medal, with the inscription '*Descente en Angleterre, frappé à Londres en 1804*'.

On 20 July 1804, against the advice of his admirals, Napoleon insisted on holding a review of the invasion flotillas, in the teeth of an onshore gale. Over 2,000 men were drowned as a result. On 16 August 1804, amid magnificent panoply with 1,300 drummers on parade, he revisited the Army of Boulogne to bestow on its leaders the coveted *Légion d'Honneur* created by him two years earlier. By the time of his coronation as emperor that December, he had assembled 177,000 men and more than 2,000 invasion craft on the Channel. As a fighting force it was incomparable, and morale was still magnificent:

> From England we'll bring back treasure
> That won't have cost us a sou . . .

they sang with lusty expectancy in the taverns of Boulogne. After repeated exercises, Napoleon had proved that 25,000 men could now be embarked in ten minutes, but he had also at last come to the realization that he could not invade by means of his flat-bottomed barges alone. Everything depended on his weaker navy being able to achieve local supremacy for a limited period, to cover the invasion force.

'Let us be master of the Channel for six hours and we are masters of the world,' he wrote to Admiral Latouche-Tréville in July 1804. That Admiral, France's best, died however of a sudden heart attack. He was replaced by the more timid Villeneuve, and – once again – the invasion was called off for 1804. But the intent remained, with Napoleon vowing to his new Empress, 'I will take you to London, madam. I intend the wife of the modern Caesar to be crowned in Westminster.'

Meanwhile, British heavy-handedness had come to his aid that winter by bringing Spain into the war on his side. This meant that the campaigning season of 1805 would open with France granted useful naval bases at Cadiz and Ferrol (on the north-west tip of Spain), and her naval strength reinforced by the addition of thirty-two Spanish ships-of-the-line.

Although war had reopened between France and England in May 1803, there had continued to be virtually no fighting through that year and 1804, a kind of 'Phoney War', while France threatened invasion and both camps armed and trained for the next round. However, in the realm of diplomacy Pitt had not been idle. Despite the dislike and distrust most red-blooded Englishmen felt for Russia and the Russians – which was mutual, and which Nelson exemplified when, at Copenhagen in 1801, he had told the battered Danes he only wished they had been Russians – Pitt had skilfully been fanning Tsar Alexander's indignation at the murder of d'Enghien. Equally he had been exploiting the Austrians' still smarting sense of humiliation, compounded with their anger at Napoleon's fresh annexations in northern Italy. On 11 April 1805, a secret 'provisional' treaty signed in St Petersburg laid the foundation of the Third Coalition, consisting of England, Austria, Sweden and Naples, with a big question-mark hovering over hitherto neutral Prussia. Through the dangerous early summer months, however, all continued to hang on a thread. Russia had still to be persuaded of the altruism of England's continued occupation of Malta, which she coveted herself as a warm-water port, while at home Pitt was very much at bay. In the Commons he had sat helplessly with tears streaming down his face as MPs voted to impeach his friend, Melville, now Treasurer of the Navy, for speculative improprieties. There was bad news from the West Indies about raiding successes by the French Navy, while the shortage of British ships was giving rise to serious fears that the continental blockade could not long be sustained.

It was the British blockade, however, that drove Napoleon into the ultimate act of provocation. In June he annexed the Ligurian

Republic, with the excuse that he had to have its ships and seamen to help defeat England. This was in flagrant violation of his treaty with Austria, and it threw Tsar Alexander into an implacable rage. Napoleon, he declared, 'is a scourge of the world; he wants a war and he shall have it'. Russia now committed herself to a new war against France. Combined with Austria, and with contingents from a host of lesser German states as well as Sweden, this Third Coalition would – so Pitt hoped – be able to field more than half a million troops by Christmas. On top of this, there also seemed a fair hope that Prussia might finally make up her mind to join the Allies. Apart from the war at sea, England's role in all this was to finance her continental allies to the tune of £1,250,000 per 100,000 soldiers per year, an astronomic sum in those days. Altogether, at least on paper, France would now be confronted by the most powerful land force yet mounted against her.

The war aims of the Third Coalition were to 'return peace to Europe', forcing France to withdraw from her conquests and accept, in essence, the territorial *status quo ante* of 1791. To achieve these aims, the basic Allied strategy for 1805 was as follows: in the south, the Austria Archduke Charles (who had proved himself the most competent Austrian leader during the 1797 campaign) would attack in northern Italy with the intention of pinning down a substantial portion of Napoleon's forces on the wrong side of the Alps; to the north, an imposing body of some 200,000 Russian troops, under Kutuzov and Buxhöwden, would join up with the main strength of the Austrian Army, led by Archdukes Ferdinand and John, to thrust through the territory of Napoleon's Bavarian ally. The Russo-Austrian force would then strike across the Upper Rhine, into France's vulnerable eastern flank. At the same time expeditionary forces comprised of 50,000 English, Swedes and Neapolitans would open other diversionary fronts along the European periphery. On paper, at least, it looked like a perfectly sound strategy. Secret as the Allied designs were, however, they were not to escape Napoleon for long as the summer of 1805 wore on.

FIVE

Preparing for a New Campaign

1805

Rely on my activity; I will surprise the world by the
grandeur and rapidity of my strokes!

Napoleon to Cambacérès, August 1805

ON 3 AUGUST 1805, Napoleon had arrived at Boulogne.
Three days later he summoned his élite shock formation, the
Imperial Guard. His deep hatred for the English then far
transcended anything he felt for his other enemies. Day by day
his stocky, impatient figure paced the coastal heights gazing in
frustration at those famous white cliffs just visible in the distant
haze, waiting impatiently for Admiral Villeneuve and the Combined Fleet to appear in the Channel. Today, as that narrow strip
of water presents a rather less imposing obstacle, those white
cliffs an altogether less alluring goal, it is hard to avoid the
parallel between Napoleon and that other warlord of 135
summers later. Both had risen meteorically from lowly station to
head a nation not their own, and to command, in a short space
of time, the world's most invincible land force; both were
restlessly daemonic men of small stature and both were at the
zenith of their power as a commander; it was almost the same
time of year; the grand design was approximately similar; and
each would end, in frustration, by turning his great war machine
eastwards instead. For Hitler too, with Europe then at his feet,
the omens for the grand project (which had occupied Napoleon's
fantasies intermittently over the previous seven years) had never
seemed more propitious.

Experience had taught Napoleon that, even with the added strength of the Spaniards, there was still no prospect of his matching the Royal Navy, ship for ship. Therefore he would aim, as he had intended the previous year, to obtain local superiority in the Channel, just long enough for him to load and discharge on to British soil his overwhelming land force. To achieve this, in his third and final Grand Design issued on 22 March 1805, Napoleon ordered his scattered fleet to take to sea and make for the West Indies. By threatening British possessions there, and recalling how mistakenly Pitt had reacted to the threat in the previous decade, Napoleon reckoned he would draw Nelson and the main weight of the British battle fleets after him. Villeneuve and Ganteaume would then elude the British in the Caribbean, and double back with all speed (about $5\frac{1}{2}$ knots) and force, to appear in the Channel in July with the Combined Fleet of nearly sixty battleships.

It was with considerable misgiving that Villeneuve, driven by fear on the one hand of his master, on the other hand of interception by Nelson's blockaders, left Toulon for the Straits of Gibraltar. Already that January his fleet, with its inexperienced sailors and unbattleworthy tackle, had nearly met disaster when making a sortie in a storm. Nelson and the Mediterranean Fleet narrowly missed Villeneuve off Majorca; and then the French had disappeared, according to plan, into the Atlantic. Napoleon's expectations also appeared to be fulfilled by Nelson following his quarry, westwards. Although he made the trip from Gibraltar to Barbados in the record time of little over three weeks, misled by faulty intelligence Nelson proved equally unable to overhaul the French in the West Indies. Obeying his orders, Villeneuve headed back eastwards for the Channel, but, pursuing him, Nelson was still able to make the return Atlantic crossing in a fortnight less than Villeneuve. What was even more fateful for Napoleon's Grand Design, however, was that Barham and his admirals had not been taken in by the French fleet's 'deception play'. The Duc de Decrès, Napoleon's able Minister of the Marine, had warned him that — whatever the crisis — the Royal Navy would *never* be enticed to disperse its effectives so as to leave the Western Approaches unguarded. It was a tradition that was to run through to the 1940s, and Decrès was to be proved right, Napoleon wrong. As if by radio communication, in an era when the fastest and farthest-reaching signal was the flag and the swift sloop, but in fact as a consequence of years of superlative training, the British admirals seemed to know instinctively what to do without waiting for orders from above. When Nelson left for the West Indies, reinforcements were mustered in readiness to bolster the Channel Fleet — just in case.

The danger, for Britain, remained extreme. The enemy had all but succeeded in concentrating a superior force at the decisive point. Nelson, still off Cadiz, beating northwards on the day that Napoleon had arrived at Boulogne (3 August), wrote gloomily in his diary, 'I feel every moment of this foul wind. . . . I am dreadfully uneasy.' In England the invasion alarms were sounding again; the Volunteers were on alert; Walter Scott galloped a hundred miles in a day to attend the muster of Dalkeith, while Sir John Moore's men practised combating invaders breast-high in the sea. On 18 August, the *Victory* brought Nelson back to England on his final homecoming. After hunting Villeneuve for 14,000 miles with total lack of success, he had hardly expected a friendly reception; as it was, he was quite overcome by the affection and admiration he encountered everywhere. When he re-embarked less than a month later many were in tears, recorded Southey, and 'knelt down before him and blessed him as he passed'. Returning to his weary ships, *en route* for Trafalgar, Nelson remarked simply to Hardy, 'I had their huzzas before. I have their hearts now.'

By this time, however, the immediate threat to England had passed, though it was by no means apparent at the time. A brig carrying Nelson's despatches, the *Curieux*, had sighted Villeneuve heading for the Bay of Biscay and reached London with this vital information on 9 July. Naval reinforcements were rushed to bottle up the Channel off Cape Finisterre. On 22 July Rear-

Admiral Sir Robert Calder with fifteen battleships joined battle there with Villeneuve's twenty. An elderly officer apparently concerned at his inferiority in numbers, Calder did not press the attack and — after an inconclusive action — Villeneuve was allowed to escape. Although Calder had only acted with a circumspection which would not have shamed Admiral Jellicoe at Jutland a century later, all England cried out for his blood and he returned to a court-martial and disgrace. Nevertheless, the Battle of Finisterre was enough to have a decisive influence upon Villeneuve's subsequent moves. In sharp contrast to Nelson's forces, after the summer's arduous sailing Villeneuve's ships were in poor shape, his crews reduced by scurvy and dysentery and those of his Spanish allies verging on mutiny. 'Our condition', he reported to Decrès, 'is frightful.' He personally had also never held much faith in Napoleon's invasion scheme. Thus, after the brush with Calder, instead of continuing northwards, Villeneuve retired nervously into Ferrol. On 13 August he sailed southwards again, for the greater safety of Cadiz, where he was promptly sealed in again by Nelson's returning fleet, ultimately to be driven out to his doom off Trafalgar two months later.

Meanwhile, unaware of what had happened to Villeneuve, Napoleon was pursuing his plans to their climax at Boulogne. One hundred thousand men were drawn up on parade in a single line along the shore, an awe-inspiring spectacle. But time was not standing still. Napoleon — well informed by spies — was aware of the ponderously mounting threat of the land forces of Austria and Russia, combined under Pitt's Third Coalition. Yet he still considered that he had time to invade England, then return to deal Austria a crippling blow. Back and forth across the cliffs he strode, waiting impotently for the change of wind (which would never, in any event, bring Villeneuve). Reproachfully he wrote, on 13 August, to his Empress, absent at a spa:

It is not often one hears from you. You forget your friends, which is wrong. I did not know that the waters of Plombières had the same effect as those of Lethe. It seems to me that it was drinking these same Plombières waters that once made you say, 'Ah, Bonaparte, if ever I die, who will there be to love you?' That was a very long time ago, wasn't it? Everything passes, beauty, wit, sentiment, even the sun, all but one thing that is endless; the good I wish you, your happiness. I cannot be more loving even if you laugh at me for my pains. Goodbye, dear friend. I had the English cruisers attacked yesterday; everything passed off well. . . .

Summer would not last for ever. The letter to Josephine coincided with fresh orders to Villeneuve to hasten with all forces to the Channel, Napoleon being unaware that it was also the same day that Villeneuve was setting his sails in the opposite direction, for Cadiz. Uncertainty about Villeneuve's movements threw Napoleon into a terrible rage. Grossly calling the unhappy admiral a 'Jean-Foûtre', he accused him of little short of cowardice and treason, charges which drove Villeneuve to despair and, later, to suicide. The three days, 18–20 August, marked the period of Napoleon's highest expectations for the Channel crossing, although he was constantly receiving fresh warnings from Foreign Minister Talleyrand of Austria's warlike preparations to his rear. On 22 August, still ignorant of Villeneuve's true movements (of which the latter had not dared inform him), Napoleon wrote again to him at Brest, commanding; 'Sail, do not lose a moment, and with my squadrons reunited enter the Channel. England is ours. We are ready and embarked. Appear for twenty-four hours, and all will be ended. . . .'

It was perhaps significant of Napoleon's own waning confidence that the six hours' mastery of the Channel he had required of Admiral Latouche-Tréville the previous year had grown to twenty-four by August 1805. On 23 August a letter to Talleyrand reveals his restless thoughts already beginning to move elsewhere. If Villeneuve were suddenly (and magically) to appear, then there would still be time to launch the invasion; otherwise 'I shall raise my camp and march on Vienna.' An abject letter from Decrès assured him that Villeneuve had sailed to Cadiz, and urged him to regard this as a decree of Fate and cut his losses. 'It is a misery for me', he lamented, 'to know the trade of the sea, for this knowledge wins no confidence nor produces any effect on Your Majesty's plans.' For several days longer, Napoleon remained in a state of indecision, intolerable to his nature. Then, abruptly, he set to preparing orders for the new operations. On 26 August he instructed his chief staff officer, Marshal Berthier, to move the Army of Boulogne against Austria. On 5 September, amid early-autumn sunshine after a long, cold summer a captured schooner revealed to England the joyous news that the enemy had marched out of Boulogne, 'because of a new war with Russia'. England was saved.

Napoleon's decision to march east in 1805, and abandon (forever, as it was to turn out) his dream of leading a victorious army through the streets of London, looks to have been extraordinarily precipitate. But historians continue to argue over whether he did *seriously* intend to invade England in 1805. Among other indications, however, the arrival of both the Imperial Guard and the cavalry suggest that it was more than a bluff. Equally, shortage of horses, and the far-from-complete marching array of the French Army when ordered to about-turn, indicate that there was little premeditation about his change of plan. Could an invasion have succeeded? Given the overall superiority of the Royal Navy in seamanship, if not in ships, it would have been a highly risky operation. But *if* Villeneuve had arrived in the Channel according to the Grand Design, and *if* the Third Coalition had not begun to menace France's back door, the risk might have seemed an acceptable one to the arch-gambler that Napoleon was. On the other hand, Arthur Bryant may not have been wrong in his estimation that 'Only the prudence or timidity of his admiral had saved his fleet from a fate as awful as that of the Spanish Armada.' As it was, his abandonment of the much vaunted invasion project constituted perhaps the most serious strategic reverse in Napoleon's career up to that time; therefore, all the more did he who lived on success need a stunning victory elsewhere. Had the invasion aborted, however, as Thiers remarks, it would:

> at least have exposed him to a sort of ridicule, and would have exhibited him to the eyes of Europe as in a real state of impotence in opposition to England. The continental coalition, furnishing him with a field of battle which he needed . . . drew him most seasonably from an indecisive and unpleasant situation.[1]

Thus there was little doubt that, to some extent, Napoleon was himself relieved by what his despondent Minister of the Marine termed a 'decree of Fate'; certainly the new course of action imposed on him came as the most welcome kind of relief after all the months of frustrated inactivity facing out across the Channel. A brave new world of military possibilities in his own element (which, indubitably, the sea was not) opened itself to Napoleon – now, at last, the supreme warlord of France. 'For the first time,' says Thiers, '. . . he was free, free as Caesar and Alexander had been. . . . All Europe was open to his combinations.'

As it was to evolve, Napoleon's new plan of operations indeed seemed hardly less audacious than the one he had just abandoned. For six unbroken hours he dictated it to Daru, Lieutenant-General of the Army. The fact that he should have utilized so eminent a dignitary as a mere scribe denoted the extreme secrecy with which Napoleon prepared his campaign; for secrecy was absolutely essential to its success. Thus only Daru and Berthier – Napoleon's Minister of War and chief staff officer – were kept privy to the master-plan.

On the other hand, the total lack of secrecy of the Allies presented Napoleon's excellent intelligence service with as clear a picture of their intentions as if Napoleon himself 'had been present at the military conferences of M. de Winzingerode, the Austrian Chief-of-Staff, at Vienna'.[2] A great mass of 300,000 men (with more to follow) was mobilizing against him. Heading from south to north there was first of all Archduke Charles facing across the River Adige in northern Italy with some 100,000 troops. Next was Archduke Ferdinand, with roughly another hundred thousand, heading westward for Bavaria and already on the River Inn. Dividing the two archdukes, however, was the great mountain massif of the Tyrol, with its few viable and easily blocked passes, held by a small linking force under Archduke John. Then, far away to the east were three ponderously moving Russian armies totalling another 100,000. Under Kutuzov and Buxhöwden, two were already on the borders of Austrian Galicia and clearly intending to join up with Archduke Ferdinand. Finally, further north, there was Bennigsen's army sitting on the eastern frontier of Prussia so as to exert pressure on its wavering king, Frederick William III, and with the (rather distant) ambition of awaiting Swedish and English reinforcements to move through Pomerania on Hanover and Holland.

Thus there would be three main Allied efforts developing across the continent of Europe: south, centre and north. All this was evident to Napoleon. It was equally evident that the gravest threat to France would come in the centre, once Ferdinand was joined by the Russians. His extraordinary intuition, aided by a comprehension of the rigid traditionalism of the Austrian military mind and its passion for fortresses, led Napoleon to calculate that Ferdinand would aim to establish himself in the Bavarian stronghold of Ulm on the Upper Danube Valley (a favourite standby of past Austrian tacticians). There he would wait for the Russians, then thrust into the French flank at Strasbourg with crushingly superior forces. With what was to prove uncanny accuracy, Napoleon predicted the positions the Austrians and Russians would reach several weeks ahead, and the routes they would take.

Above all, however, his genius for the *coup d'oeil* immediately revealed to him the essential flaw in the Allied strategy. The enemy forces were widely dispersed over Europe. Because of the obstacle of the Tyrolean Alps, the Austrian archdukes would have extreme difficulty in supporting each other. But what most attracted his gaze was the immense distance that separated Ferdinand, pressing on aggressively westwards towards Ulm, and the slow-moving Russians coming up behind him at a snail's pace. They must inevitably be several weeks' march apart. (Kutuzov had in fact already started ten days later than reckoned; it appears, unbelievably, that one of the problems of the Allied timetable was the unallowed-for fact that the Russians were still using the Julian Calendar, which was twelve days behind that of their Western confederates!)

Here lay the key to Napoleon's hopes. He could reckon that at Boulogne he was closer to Ulm than was Kutuzov. If he could but move quickly enough he could isolate Ferdinand from his allies, and smash him before the Russians arrived, then hasten eastwards toward Vienna, to deal with Kutuzov. The campaign would be decided by two battles of annihilation in the Danube Valley. Everything would depend on speed – and this was a predominantly Napoleonic quality.

In a series of staccato orders, letters and decrees, the Emperor poured forth his campaign plan to the overworked Daru. Napoleon once claimed, 'I never had a plan of operations.' It was quite untrue. He was, recalls Baron Jomini (the Swiss military historian, the Liddell Hart of the era):

> in reality his own Chief of the Staff; holding in his hand a pair of compasses . . . bent, nay, often lying over his map, on which the positions of his army corps and the supposed positions of the enemy were marked by pins of different colours, he arranged his own movements with a certainty of which we can scarcely form a just idea. . . .

Aided by an elaborate card-index system, every detail, down to regimental level, came out of this one voluminous mind. Once when Napoleon came across a unit that had got lost during the approach march to the Rhine, he was able to inform its astonished officer, without consulting any orders, of the whereabouts of its division, and where it would be on the next three nights, throwing in for good measure a résumé of its commander's military record.

The essential component of Napoleon's strategy was that the Austrians at Ulm must not be attacked frontally; otherwise they might simply fall back on their Russian allies advancing from the east. 'My only fear', he confided later to Talleyrand, 'is that we shall scare them too much. . . .' The Austrians would expect him to approach, conventionally, from the west via the Black Forest; so, instead, he would swing his armies southwards through Germany to throw an unbreakable barrier across the Danube downstream from Ulm, then roll up the enemy from the rear. Marlborough had followed roughly the same route, to Blenheim, a century earlier with 40,000 men; but to transport an army five times as big with all their cannon and impedimenta from Boulogne (500 miles as the crow flies) in an epoch when the fastest speed was that of his slowest grenadier's feet, and still take the enemy by surprise, presupposed no mean feat.

Thus, for speed and secrecy (and in conformity with his axiom of 'separate to live, gather to fight'), Napoleon split his forces into seven 'streams'. From the north Bernadotte, already stationed in Hanover, would push almost due south, through Würzburg. Next to him, Marmont's corps from Holland was to cross the Rhine by Mainz, and then wheel south; on his right came Davout, then Soult, rated as 'the most skilful at moving large masses of troops' of any European commander, and with the largest force (41,000), Ney and Lannes, later famous names of the Empire — all performing a similar manoeuvre at intervals lower down the Rhine. Finally, Augereau, hurrying all the way from Brittany, would constitute the army reserve. Ahead of them all was to hasten the world's most formidable cavalry force, 22,000 strong, under the impetuous and dashing Murat, with the task of providing a screen to hide Napoleon's true design. Once across the Rhine, Murat would move ostentatiously through the Black Forest. He departed immediately to reconnoitre the way himself, under the *nom de guerre* of 'Colonel Beaumont'. On 25 August, General Bertrand was despatched to Bavaria to make notes of all he saw, particularly the Danube crossings in the area around Donauwörth; and then to study the terrain all the way to Vienna. 'Everywhere his language is to be pacific,' ordered Napoleon; 'he will speak of the invasion of England as imminent. . . .'[3]

In fact, only a minimal covering force consisting of the third battalions of a few regiments was to be left on the Channel in the role of guard against any English diversionary raids. As part of the grand deception plan, Napoleon himself would remain at Boulogne to the very last; rigorous censorship was applied, with post offices occupied and newspapers muzzled. To all but the handful conversant with the plan, Napoleon declared that he was sending only a defensive contingent of 30,000 men to the Rhine: and Talleyrand was instructed to spin out negotiations with the Russians and Austrians as long as possible.

Finally, down in Italy with only 50,000 men, Napoleon's most reliable tactician, Masséna, was instructed to pin down Archduke Charles' vastly superior army by adopting a defensively aggressive stance.

Already on 27 August the great machine, nearly 200,000 men strong – or roughly half of all the effectives of the Empire – began its immense march. By any standard the plan was one of the most brilliantly conceived, and speedily executed, of all time. There was little time left in the campaigning season. However, of the many risks it entailed there hovered one above all others: Prussia. As with the two great encirclement strategies by which Germany nearly defeated France in 1914, and did succeed in 1940, Napoleon's plan depended on an infringement of neutrality. The *Blitzkrieg*-speed marches of Bernadotte and Marmont could not be made without traversing the Prussian state of Ansbach. Napoleon told Talleyrand to soften Prussia's indignation by offering her Hanover as a sop. Talleyrand was thrown into despair; as he once sighed, 'the most difficult person with whom Napoleon's Foreign Minister had to negotiate was Napoleon himself'. Opposed to the new war in the first place, he had admitted to the Prussian Minister in Paris that if he were able to prevent it 'he would consider such an action the most glorious event in his tenure of office'; now, by marching through Ansbach, it seemed inevitable that the nation of Frederick the Great must sooner or later range itself with the rest of Napoleon's enemies.

To Napoleon it was a calculated risk; if he violated Prussian territory to inflict a terrible blow upon the Allies it would probably serve to frighten the hesitant Prussians on to his side. In fact Prussia was outraged; the following year she would declare war on Napoleon, but too late; and it would only lead her to defeat at Jena. Had Prussia fought at once, Napoleon might have been defeated in 1805; as it was, though only Hardy's 'Spirit of the Years' could then have seen the prospects of Blücher and Waterloo shimmering in the distance, Napoleon's act of arrogance was to contribute to his ultimate downfall.

The Army of England now became designated the *Grande Armée*, heading for eastern Europe and the unknown instead of Kent and London. After all the months of intensive training put in while waiting at Boulogne, it was, in the Emperor's own view, 'the finest army that has ever existed'. Indeed, his confidence that it could execute so phenomenally taxing a manoeuvre seemed indicative of its quality.

SIX

La Grande Armée

He [Napoleon] kept on winning his battles, not because he
was a genius (I am convinced he was very far from that), but
on the contrary because he was more stupid than his
enemies, could not be carried away by logical deductions
and only bothered about seeing that his soldiers were well-
fed, embittered and as numerous as possible.

Tolstoy, *War and Peace*

IF ONE WERE TO CONSIDER the immense advances in
military technique witnessed in the twentieth century, the purely
technical aspects of warfare in Napoleon's day seem not to have
progressed dramatically when compared with the previous century. In all armies, the basic infantry weapon was still the
flintlock, smooth-bored musket with its detachable socket bayonet, the latter used more to frighten than to kill.* Capable of
an accurate range of little more than 170 yards (although in the
heat of battle the average infantry man often missed at 50 yards)
and a maximum rate of fire of two rounds per minute, rapidly
fouled and unserviceable in wet weather, the infantry musket
was virtually the same as in the day of Marlborough or Frederick
the Great. The cannon, too, showed an evolution that was largely
relative. A 12-pounder, the standard 'heavy' field-piece, had a
maximum range of a little over 1,000 yards, or only 700 with

---

* Studying wounds suffered in a number of hand-to-hand combats, Napoleon's
Surgeon-General, Larrey, could count only five actually caused by bayonets
compared with 119 bullet wounds; a conclusion that could be paralleled with
remarkable accuracy in the two world wars, where the majority of bayoneted
men were generally on the point of surrender anyway!

canister;* muzzle-loading, a good gun crew could get off no more than one round a minute, and had to re-lay after each shot because of the lack of any recoil mechanism. The cavalry still charged with *arme blanche* (literally 'cold steel') – swords or sabres according to whether they were heavy or light cavalry, both weapons which had developed perhaps least of all over many centuries. It was only well after Waterloo that, with the flowering of the industrial revolution, warfare was to be truly revolutionized by such delights as the rapid-firing rifle, followed by the machine-gun and steel breech-loading artillery capable of hurling a high-explosive shell five, ten or fifteen miles.

As a result, by 1805 anyway, the battlefield had changed but little in terms of geographical scale and character. Although the clouds of smoke obscured most of it from the average participant (one thinks of the British commander ordered to advance at Waterloo who asked Wellington, 'In which direction, my Lord?'), the short range of weapons compressed it into an area where one individual could usually exercise effective overall control. (At Austerlitz, during much of the battle, Napoleon would actually have most of his units in sight.) Because of problems of supply and logistics, battles – even Waterloo – were largely one-day affairs, unlike the protracted slogging matches of the First World War or even the American Civil War. It is also to be noted that the successes of the Revolutionary and Napoleonic armies were due in part at least to innovations brought in, or at least proposed, during the *ancien régime*. Therefore it is elsewhere that one needs to look for what distinguished the Napoleonic battle.

To begin with, the coming of the French Revolution had completely modified the style and objectives of warfare; the same

---

* Charged with small balls, this was principally used against massed infantry at short range. In 1784, the British had invented the shrapnel (named after its inventor), a shell that exploded above the heads of the infantry, but it was still not widely in use.

was to happen in the twentieth century, in the aftermath of the Soviet Revolution of 1917. Before 1792, a battle had been a passionless, elegant and gentlemanly affair (*Messieurs les gardes françaises, tirez!*), fought between professionals for a limited advantage, usually dynastic rather than ideological or even territorial. In the eighteenth century, it was considered proper to declare war, and plunder was restrained so that even Adam Smith, who deplored its wastefulness, could reckon that it 'is so far from being a disadvantage in a well-cultivated country that many get rich by it . . .'.

Commanders took along with them their hairdressers, and sometimes even their wives; weighed down by their vast administrative tails, armies moved slowly and deliberately, and at the onset of mud and frost they disappeared, like squirrels, to re-emerge in the spring. The height of strategy, suggested Major-General Henry Lloyd in his *History of the Late War in Germany* (published in 1781) about Frederick the Great's campaigns, was to: 'Initiate military operations with mathematical precision and to keep on waging war without ever being under the necessity to strike a blow.' Such Barry Lyndon kind of battles were rarely fought 'to the last man'. It was a world that began to vanish with the cannonade of Valmy on 20 September 1792 (shots that were, indeed, 'heard around the world'), when a French 'people's army' defeated the Duke of Brunswick's regulars. Goethe, accompanying the Prussians, declared prophetically: 'From this place and day commenced a new epoch in the world's history.'

After Valmy came the revolutionary *levée en masse*, which – almost overnight – was to furnish 450,000 men for the French armies; conscripts who, in the words of a French historian, Louis Madelin, 'driven in their thousands to the frontiers, trembled as they reached them, and then made all of Europe tremble'. The day had arrived of the mass, and ever-expanding, conscript army, which, imbued with fanaticism, would turn the battlefield into a place of mounting carnage and horror. Whereas in the Augustan eighteenth century, Saxe and Turenne had never maintained an army of more than 50,000, and the highest number even Frederick the Great had mustered at any one battle had been 77,000 (at Hohenfriedberg), at *seven* of his battles Napoleon would command over 100,000 men, reaching 175,000 on the bloody field of Leipzig (1813), in which was also suffered the previously unheard-of total casualties to both sides of 120,000. Finally, it was left to Napoleon to introduce, or reintroduce, the 'total war' that toppled dynasties and shattered existing balances of power.

Under the old European purchase system, an officer could well reach the rank of colonel at the age of twenty, having spent more time at Court than with his regiment. But in France, with the Revolution, birth ceased to be a prerogative for advancement; many of the old, aristocratic officers were purged and commissions were made open to all. At first the purges seriously impaired the effectiveness of the army (the navy, as has already been noted, possibly never recovered), but later this democratization provided Napoleon with an immense advantage. By 1802, when he created the *École Spéciale Militaire*, the new French officer corps was already becoming an imposingly élite body. In 1804 he reinstituted the title of marshal, abolished by the Revolution, and it could be said with truth that every French soldier carried a marshal's baton in his knapsack. A ranker and lawyer's son called Bernadotte would become King of Sweden, while Masséna, one of Napoleon's finest marshals, was the orphaned son of a grocer, and went to sea as a cabin-boy at the age of thirteen. Only two out of the twenty-six marshals had noble antecedents, and, by 1805, half of the whole officer corps had risen from the ranks. They were also young, because the Emperor reckoned no commander had any enterprise left in him after his forty-fifth year; of the corps commanders at Austerlitz, Bernadotte at forty-two was the oldest, Davout was only thirty-five. He was exacting in what he demanded of his senior officers, who were expected to share the privations of the simple soldier, sleep in the open, and lead from the front (later, as the victorious generals and marshals grew grander, this keenness for the rough life tended to wane). If Napoleon's generals had a fault it was that they lacked initiative on the wider tactical level; for — such was his ascendancy — they always looked to him for guidance on every issue. It was a shortcoming that was to lead to serious problems in the 1805 campaign.

Organizationally, the French Army had been totally transformed since 1792. First, Napoleon had institutionalized the compact division (introduced by the Revolutionary armies), composed of 6,000 to 9,000 men and never more than five or six infantry regiments strong, which, with its rapid mobility, had proved the key to his early victories. Next, in the Camp of Boulogne, he had invented the army corps, self-contained, fast-moving and hard-hitting formations, each consisting of two or three divisions, with its own artillery and cavalry, and commanded by one of the stars in the Imperial firmament. In order to confuse enemy intelligence Napoleon would frequently vary their battle strengths. Each corps was, in effect, a miniature army capable of engaging or pinning down a vastly superior force for several hours, until its neighbouring corps could hasten up in support or prise the enemy apart from a flank. The corps would advance to battle behind a reconnaissance screen of light cavalry, their infantry columns preceded by a dense swarm of 'skirmishers' ('as sharp-sighted as ferrets and as active as squirrels'). These light infantry sharp-shooters picked holes in the enemy lines, while the main punch formed up behind them. During the months at Boulogne, infantry, cavalry and artillery arms within each corps had trained more closely together than ever before, with the result that the First *Grande Armée* of 1805 was probably the best trained force Napoleon ever commanded.

To a large extent, the striking power of Napoleon's new army corps was provided by their self-sufficiency, and therefore speed, on the approach march, as will be seen shortly. It was a cardinal principle that baggage had to be reduced to the barest minimum. This, in effect, meant living off the land, or in Napoleon's own parlance 'making war support war'. Already, twenty years before the Revolution, the French military philosopher, the Comte de Guibert, had urged this procedure and the Revolutionary armies had taken to it with gusto. By breaking away from the depot system of supply of the eighteenth century, they had profited immensely from mobility; but, if carried too far, the policy of 'living off the land' could eventually prove to be a wasting asset, in more than just the literal sense. Of General Jourdan's revolutionary army invading Germany in 1796, Marshal Soult said it 'could exist only by plunder, and this both raised the country against us and destroyed the discipline of the troops'.

Here was a predicament that would plague Napoleon in the course of time. The supply trains bringing up ammunition and stores were still, strangely enough, in the hands of civilian contractors; in 1805 they would *just* prove adequate, but two years later the system was to break down seriously in the Polish campaign. Always verging on the ramshackle, always within an inch or two of collapse, Napoleon's logistics system was both a strength and a grave weakness. At Austerlitz, Davout's corps would save the day by covering 100 miles in forty-eight hours, and arrive fit to fight. But it was also these demands on the local populace that would, eventually, prove a factor in unleashing the 'War of Peoples' – which would bring Napoleon to defeat in 1813.

Under Napoleon (but more especially under his dashing brother-in-law, Murat, the giant with the black corkscrew curls falling over the collar of his doublet, flashing blue eyes and fierce moustache, twelfth child of a Cahors innkeeper), the French cavalry was transformed from a laughing-stock into a very potent instrument. It fell into two main types, light and heavy, each with clearly differentiated functions. The light squadrons belonged to the divisional and army corps cavalry, and were employed for deep reconnaissance and protective screening in front of an advance, a role that was to assume particular importance in the advance to Ulm during the first part of the

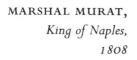

MARSHAL MURAT,
King of Naples,
1808

1805 campaign. Their role as intelligence-gatherers was prime, but they were also used for pursuit following a victorious engagement – notably at Jena in 1806. Unlike the daring generals of the American Civil War, however, Napoleon never used these cavalry squadrons for large-scale raids any distance away from the main body of the army. They were comprised, in 1805, of twenty-four regiments of *chasseurs à cheval* and ten of Hussars; in later years, having noted painfully the expertise of the Russian Cossacks with their 16-foot lances, Napoleon was to introduce new Units of Lancers, originally Polish levies. The Hussars, a reckless and hard-swearing lot clad in heavily braided dolmans (tight-fitting jackets of Hungarian origin and the showiest uniforms in the army) and wearing long pigtails, seemed particularly to embody much of the panache associated with the French cavalry as a whole, which had changed but little from pre-Revolutionary times. General Marbot describes a typical *maréchal de logis* (sergeant-major) who had trained him:

> Shako over the ear, sabre trailing, face disfigured and divided
> into two by an immense scar; upturned moustaches half-a-foot
> long, stiffened with wax . . . two great plaited tresses of hair
> hanging from the temples . . . and with this what an air! – the
> air of a swaggering ruffian. . . .

Another cavalry general, Lasalle, allegedly claimed that any
Hussar 'not dead at thirty' must have been a malingerer. (He
himself was killed, aged thirty-four, at Wagram.)

THE HEAVY CAVALRY consisted of two regiments of
Carabiniers, twelve of Cuirassiers heavily armoured with bullet-
proof breast- and back-plates and thirty of Dragoons. (The
Dragoons were the standard cavalry of the line; less heavily
armoured than the Cuirassiers they would either charge with the
heavy cavalry or support the light cavalry.) The heavy cavalry
was held in massed formations ready to launch powerful charges
against weak points in the enemy line at the critical moment – a
fundamental feature of the Napoleonic battle. In contrast to the
curved, slashing sabre of the light cavalry, the principal weapon
of the heavy regiments was a straight thrusting sword; at varying
times both categories also carried short muskets or carbines, and
pistols. Until they were able, after 1806, to remount their
regiments with captured steeds, the French heavy cavalry was
notably less well mounted than its continental enemies, particularly the Russians, who had perhaps the best horses of any army.
The French rode lumbering Norman and Flemish animals,
probably not unlike a percheron, that were great weight-carriers
but very slow; far removed from the traditional image of the
charge at the full gallop, they would sometimes be unable to
break out of trot. But this deficiency was, in Wellington's view,
more than made up for by the fact that the French heavy cavalry
'excelled in battle drill and tactical handling, and the larger the
formation the more this superiority told'.

Napoleon's philosophy of boldness was not unlike Guderian's handling of his tanks in 1940; the cavalry was never to be used 'with any miserly desire to keep it intact. . . . I do not wish the horses to be spared if they can catch men . . .'. For the opposing infantry, a charge by the French Cuirassiers was always a terrifying experience.

Although its basic weapons and their capabilities remained much the same, the artillery arm – which was, after all, Napoleon's own speciality – was constantly being expanded and streamlined. 'Today the artillery indeed decrees the destiny of armies and of people,' he once declared. In numbers, however, his artillery was relatively small, hardly bigger than that mustered by Frederick the Great. Among his earliest triumphs he had won the battle of Rivoli in 1796 with less than twenty cannon; but they had been well placed. These numbers were to rise to a maximum of 700 guns at Leipzig, but here – as on several others occasions – he was to be considerably outnumbered by the Allied artillery. (At Eylau in 1807, for instance, the Russians – historically renowned for their mass use of cannon – actually had a superiority of more than two-to-one; while, of Soult's forty-eight guns, all but six were Austrian booty.) In 1805, the First *Grande Armée* counted a ratio of roughly two pieces to every 1,000 men, arriving at Austerlitz with 139 cannon to the 278 of the Allies.

However, it was how Napoleon deployed his guns that was decisive. As in many other things, he had benefited from innovations that had preceded him. Already before the Revolution, a Frenchman, Comte Jean de Gribeauval, had greatly enhanced the mobility of cannons by substantially reducing their weight. This had been achieved by casting barrels thinner and shorter, and making the carriage lighter; with the result that, for instance, a Gribeauval 8-pounder weighed just half as much as its predecessor. This meant, in effect, that the guns could now keep pace with the infantry on an approach march and, drawn by horses instead of oxen, would not even lag too far behind the cavalry. Tested with success during the American War of Independence, the Gribeauval guns also attained a remarkable degree of standardization. Napoleon further reduced his standard pieces to four: the 6-pounder, the 8-pounder, the 12-pounder (he affectionately called them his *belles filles*), which still weighed two tons and required twelve horses to move it, and a $5\frac{1}{2}$-inch howitzer, designed for indirect fire over crests, with explosive shell. Typical of Napoleon's rationalization, this last weapon — replacing a 6-inch one — meant that each ammunition wagon could carry seventy-five rounds instead of the fifty previously. The standardization of calibres resulted, initially, in Napoleon having fewer guns to draw upon; on the other hand their reduced weight enabled him to gallop his pieces from one end of the battlefield to the other, thereby diminishing the drawback of their short range and affording himself a rapid concentration of firepower to batter the enemy to shreds at the critical point. 'It is the artillery of my Guard', declared Napoleon, 'which generally decides my battles, for, as I have it always at hand, I can bring it to bear wherever it becomes necessary.' Here, in its tactical handling, lay the true superiority of Napoleon's artillery.

Eye witnesses at Napoleonic battlefields speak of the constant, sinister and mysterious humming noise of the cannon-balls flying overhead. The artillery played an immense part in sustaining the morale of the French infantry, but to advance towards enemy guns firing directly at you at short range was perhaps the worst of all battle experiences; a hit from one round shot could disembowel or smash to a pulp three men at a time. At Waterloo, one British company square suffered twenty-five killed and wounded from the same shot. The effects of exploding shell, such as mortally wounded Tolstoy's Prince Andrei at Borodino, were immeasurably less lethal than those of a century later; on the other hand, the impact of cannon firing grape-shot at point-blank range into charging cavalry was appalling. In return, the gunners were often overrun and sabred by the cavalry; but, as the latter seldom had time to stop and spike the pieces, they would often be brought into action again by courageous and resourceful gunners.

Napoleon's infantrymen looked more like an army in rout after a long march, straggling, dishevelled and apparently indisciplined; perhaps not unlike the hard-hitting but scruffy Israeli soldier of the 1960s and 1970s, and appearances were equally deceptive. Carrying no baggage trains, they were often dangerously short of ammunition, ill-paid, ill-shod and ill-fed; and yet they constituted the finest fighting force in Europe. 'The first quality of a soldier', declared Napoleon, 'is fortitude in enduring fatigue and hardship.' He also considered that 'tents are not healthy, it is better for the soldier to sleep out'. The French infantryman marched weighed down by a 58-pound pack (the Guard, burdened with its extra 'ceremonials', was privileged to carry 65 pounds),* which contained sixty rounds of musket ammunition, rations for a week, a spare pair of pants, two shirts and two extra pairs of boots; but, mass-produced and glued rather than sewn together, the boots often fell apart on the march and so the infantrymen were happiest when they could relieve their better-equipped enemy (or sometimes allies) of their footwear. Also with Napoleon's troops, courageous and robust *vivandières* sometimes travelled. They, in addition to other services rendered, did their best to repair tattered uniforms.

On paper the basic ration of one pound of 'munition' bread, four ounces of meat, two ounces of dried vegetables and one ounce of brandy meant that the infantryman was better fed than many a French civilian, but because of the afore-noted vagaries of the supply system theory quite often did not become practice; the bread ration more frequently took the form of a hard biscuit, tied by string around the soldier's neck. To compensate for all these hardships there was no corporal punishment, as there was in the British Army; instead men were goaded on by a coveted

---

* In the Peninsular War, British riflemen staggered under 80 lb of equipment, which sometimes led to needless deaths from exhaustion on the march.

system of awards and decorations. Nevertheless, like the fighting men of the other nations, they would inevitably arrive on the battlefield wet and cold, hungry and fatigued.

The standard infantry weapon was still, with small improvements, the Model 1777 musket, with all its limitations and unreliability. (According to one expert, at reasonable ranges hits were seldom registered at a better rate than one in every 3,000 to 4,000 shots fired.) Yet John Keegan suggests that, because of its greater concentration and control, an infantry regiment of the Napoleonic era was 'arguably more dangerous to approach than a late-nineteenth-century – Boer War – one'.[1] With terrifying impact, in the space of every minute a well-trained battalion could fire 2,000 heavy leaden musket balls, each capable of shattering a limb at a hundred yards' range. To obtain this maximum advantage of firepower, all depended on formations and their tactical deployment. At this, of course, Napoleon was unbeatable. Breaking away from the eighteenth-century tradition of advancing to the attack in a beautifully 'dressed' line, Napoleon had come to prefer the principle of the 'battalion column'. This was much more adaptable to an approach through broken country (such as Napoleon was to encounter at Austerlitz); with an exposed front of perhaps no more than fifty yards, it presented the minimum target to the enemy, and, with skilful control, could very swiftly be spread out into line order for 'fire action'. Later Napoleon experimented successfully with various forms of *ordre mixte* in which battalions would advance part in column, part in line, according to the circumstances, preceded by those clouds of infuriating and damaging 'skirmishers', a role greatly suited to the born individualism of the French soldier.

To his confidant on St Helena, General Gourgaud, Napoleon declared that, as far as his strategy was concerned, the whole art of war was 'just like all beautiful things, simple; the simplest manoeuvres are the best'. (This simplicity inevitably brought with it a degree of predictability, so that after 1807 Napoleon's opponents were less liable to be taken by surprise.) The naval historian Admiral Mahan once observed that 'not by rambling operations . . . are wars decided, but by force massed and handled in skilful combinations'. Combined with the Emperor's superb – indeed unique – comprehension of the interactions of time and space, this very much conformed with Napoleon's basic philosophy. As a key to his strategy, he had declared in 1797, 'There are in Europe many good generals, but they see too many things at once; as for me I see only one thing, namely the enemy's main body. And I try to crush it, confident that secondary matters will then settle themselves. . . .'

Again, two years later (to General Moreau), he had stressed the imperativeness of moving so as always to achieve local superiority, even against a force that was in total superior to his own, then 'beat it [the broken remnants] in detail'. In consequence 'the victory which was the result was always, as you see, the triumph of the larger numbers over the lesser'. At no battle would this policy work to better effect than at Austerlitz, and it was cardinal among his five principles for conducting a campaign. Others included moving his main force so that it was always placed on the enemy's flank or rear,* and enabling it to act against enemy lines of communication, while guaranteeing its own. Between 1796 and 1815, Napoleon would employ his famous *manoeuvre sur les derrières* (or what Liddell Hart called the 'indirect approach') no less than thirty times; again, never with greater effect than at Austerlitz. Once on the battlefield, the image of Napoleon as the daring gambler without limits has also been over-stressed; at various times he would show extreme prudence, especially when it came to keeping in hand powerful tactical reserves for an opportunity, or against the contingency of a reverse.

Although there was no aspect of staff planning over which

---

* 'They sent a young madman,' an Austrian officer complained characteristically during the Italian campaign, 'who attacks right, left and from the rear. It's an intolerable way of making war.'

Napoleon would not exert a personal influence (and, with a passion for detail, he was very much a hands-on commander), behind him he had a far more impressive and weighty back-up machinery than is often assumed. Already by 1805 Imperial *Grand-Quartier-Général* numbered more than 400 officers and 5,000 men; by 1812 the officer complement had escalated to 3,500. Headquarters was divided between two separate organizations: Napoleon's *Maison*, or Military Household – which David Chandler rightly describes as 'the true nerve centre of the French war effort'[2] – and the General Staff proper. The most important personage in the staff bureaucracy was Louis-Alexandre Berthier, 'small, stout, ever laughing, very full of business' and known to the soldiers as 'the Emperor's wife'. Although rated (by David Chandler) as having 'rarely served as more than a glorified chief clerk', because of the way Napoleon took so much on his own shoulders, Berthier was rather more important than this by reason of the nexus and the factor of continuity which he represented. Already aged fifty-two in 1805, as the son of a high-ranking officer and a pre-Revolutionary officer himself he was one of the few to provide a continuum with the Staff Corps of the *ancien régime*; promoted general in the Revolutionary armies in 1795, he became Napoleon's Chief-of-Staff the following year and was to hold the post until he switched to the monarchy at the end of the 1814 campaign. At the same time, by being Vice-Constable, Minister of War and Master of Hounds, he also held a key position in the *Maison*. Although Napoleon's proclivity for secrecy was such that he would occasionally keep even Berthier in the dark, he regarded him as indispensable.

Important figures later in the *Maison* were Duroc, the Grand Marshal, and Caulaincourt, Master of the Horse, as well as a cluster of lesser generals entrusted with the most vital missions as aides-de-camp. At the heart of the *Maison* was the Imperial Cabinet, from which emanated in genesis all Napoleon's plans. It consisted of only a handful of personnel among whom the geographer Bacler d'Albe was the most essential cog. A 'little

MARSHAL BERTHIER,
'The Emperor's Wife'

dark man, handsome, pleasant, well educated, talented and a good draughtsman', the poor fellow would be summoned by Napoleon at any hour of the day or night. As soon as the site for Imperial Headquarters in the field had been decided, d'Albe would set up Napoleon's 'operations room', the centre-piece of which would be a vast map table of the theatre of war, so large that the Emperor and his topographer would often be forced to lie on it full length together. 'I have seen them more than once,' wrote Baron de Fain, the Cabinet archivist, '. . . interrupting each other by a sudden exclamation, right in the midst of their work, when their heads had come into collision.'[3] It was symptomatic of the immense importance which Napoleon always attracted to topography, which was to pay dividends particularly at Austerlitz.

After such a session on the map table, Napoleon would then begin dictating orders like a machine-gun, walking slowly about the room. 'As inspiration came to him,' says his private secretary, Baron de Méneval:

> his voice assumed a more animated tone, and was accompanied
> by a sort of habit, which consisted in a movement of the right
> arm, which he twisted, at the same time pulling the cuff of the

sleeve of his coat with his hand . . . expressions came without effort. . . .

Because of the speed of his dictation, this would be scribbled down by the secretaries in rough draft and finally worked up on large sheets of 'elephant paper', sometimes a metre in length.

On the march, Napoleon's entourage would be further compressed to a 'Little Headquarters', or tactical headquarters, which might move several days ahead of the main body. Napoleon himself would travel in a light *calèche* when distances were small, but more often in a heavy *barouche*, drawn by six powerful horses. On the box would be Roustam, Napoleon's Mameluke *valet de chambre* (acquired during the Egyptian campaign); inside, Berthier would be sitting up attentively while:

> with his head covered by a checkered handkerchief, the Emperor could sleep in his carriage as though in his bed. In the interior of the carriage were a number of drawers with locks and keys containing news from Paris, reports, and books. . . . A large lantern hung at the back of the carriage and lit up the interior, whilst four other lanterns illuminated the road. . . .

Though he was an indifferent horseman (Odeleben says scathingly, 'Napoleon rode like a butcher. . . . Whilst galloping, his body rolled backwards and forwards and sideways')[4] and was thrown more than once; but when roads were poor he would take to horseback, once covering eighty-six miles in five and a half hours.

At the hub of the whole Napoleonic war machine stood – and would continue to stand, right up to the last dreadful minutes at Waterloo – the Imperial Guard. Consisting of all arms, it was about 7,000 strong in 1805, but in 1814 it would escalate to 100,000, virtually an army in its own right. Élite of the élite, and envy of other nations, the Guardsman had to be over 1.78 metres tall (5ft 6in) – a fair height in those days of undernourishment – had to have fought in three campaigns or have been wounded twice, and had to read and write. He was not allowed to frequent places of ill-repute, and if he should escort a proper lady under no circumstances was she to be seen on his arm. To the Horse Grenadiers (sometimes nicknamed 'big heels', because of their vast boots, or simply 'gods' because of their haughtiness) it was forbidden that 'any woman under forty come in to make soup for them'. Old in experience rather than age, they averaged between twenty-five and thirty. Respectfully addressed as 'Monsieur' by their officers (the ordinary soldier of the line even used to joke that donkeys used by the Guard were promoted to 'mules'), the Guard enjoyed many special privileges such as higher pay and better rations and quarters. (Before Eylau, for instance, after the Russians had pillaged everything, only the Guard had its own ration wagons; the rest of the army came close to starving.) Above all, theirs was the privilege of guarding the Emperor; and, in turn, of being thrown into battle at the decisive moment as a constantly dependable reserve. The spectacle of these giant-like figures, exaggerated by their two-foot-high shakos, coming out of the fog of battle at its critical moment inspired terror in all but the bravest enemy infantryman. The *grognards* – as Napoleon himself had nicknamed the 'Old Guard' – grumbled and groused, but always went on, and on. As was to be said of it, immortally, at Waterloo, the Guard 'died, but never surrendered'. On the other side of the coin, some military historians hold the Imperial Guard to have played an injurious role, to the extent that its élitism drained the rest of the line. Nevertheless, its morale was unbeatable, and set the tone for the whole army.

Speed and mobility counted for everything with Napoleon. To this end, good intelligence was essential. In the field, the light cavalry were his eyes and ears, supplemented by audacious espionage forays carried out by generals like Savary, who, in the Austerlitz campaign, ranged far ahead of the army in disguise. Even commanders like Bertrand and Murat were not above disguising themselves as peasants to carry out spying missions.

One of Napoleon's most celebrated double-agents, an Alsatian called Carl Schulmeister, was infiltrated into General Mack's staff – thereby providing Napoleon with information that was to help lure the Austrian to his doom at Ulm.* A card-index system, hardly less elaborate than that relating to his own armies, was kept on enemy forces down to battalion level.

At higher levels, ever since Henri IV in the sixteenth century had given France her first letter-opening service in the form of a *Cabinet Noir*, successive regimes have put varying degrees of effort into intelligence collection; but Napoleon, first under Fouché, elevated espionage into an extensive and efficiently run state enterprise. After police failure to detect the Cadoudal plot in 1804, its activities soared – to excess. The most important office in Fouché's Ministry of Police was the *Sureté*, which was run from 1800 to 1814 by Pierre-Marie Desmarest. He came to rank as the 'third most powerful man in France',[5] described by Fouché as 'my trusted ferret'. Much of the *Cabinet Noir* work was carried out under the authority of the Postmaster General, Lavalette, a diminutive figure only five feet tall. Often 200 letters, or diplomatic despatches a day would be opened. Every letter written by that busybody Madame de Staël and her lover, Benjamin Constant, evidently winged its way swiftly to Napoleon's own desk – even when he was a thousand miles from Paris, in remote East Prussia during the Friedland campaign. He said he read them 'for recreation', but obviously he persuaded himself that Madame de Staël was in touch with some conspiracy preparing to seize power.[6] In the end, his Corsican obsession with espionage, intrigue and conspiracy may have led him into a hopeless wastage of effort – just like the KGB in its prime. Nevertheless, as of 1805, he could say with confidence, 'A leader has the right to be beaten, but never the right to be surprised.'[7]

Widespread and active as they were, Napoleon's spy networks

---

* When the Austrians invaded Alsace in 1814, they were said to have taken care to destroy Schulmeister's estate.

under Fouché, Desmarest and Savary were as nothing compared with the twentieth-century terror apparatuses of Hitler and Stalin. Moreover, he could with reason assert the need for extreme vigilance. Operations carried out by British agents on the continent were themselves conspicuously ruthless. From 1792 onwards had been born the precursors of modern British intelligence agencies, of the Secret Intelligence Service and the Special Operations Executive of the Second World War; in fact, when SOE began life in 1940 its clear instructions were 'to do to Europe what Pitt did to France before 1807'.[8] In alarm at the possibility of revolutionary agents infiltrated among the influx of genuine French refugees, the 'Alien Office' had been created January 1793, to check on surveillance of suspects coming into England. Its job initially was, quite simply, to scotch the possibility of revolution. Just as in France, letters at first were opened under the aegis of the Post Office. Then, in 1793, all such counter-espionage activities became concentrated in the person of a metropolitan magistrate, William Wickham. Two years later he chalked up his first success when a Colonel Edward Despard, and four others, were convicted of high treason and publicly executed. In a manner disquietingly similar to the widely deplored techniques of the French Terror, the heads of the condemned were cut off and held up to the crowd, with the words 'This is the head of a traitor.' When *démarches* were received in London, purportedly from high-ranking members of the Convention, inviting Britain to overthrow that body and restore the monarchy in Paris, Wickham was promptly transferred to Switzerland by Lord Grenville, Pitt's Foreign Secretary.

As chargé d'affaires in Bern, Wickham busied himself in pumping funds into northern France to rig elections there, setting up a cell of double-agents inside the French intelligence networks, fomenting 'resistance' uprisings in the Vendée and Brittany, and plotting with renegades like Pichegru and Moreau* to over-

---

* See p. 26 above.

throw, or assassinate, Napoleon. At one stage he was even reported to be working on Bernadotte, the marshal who would later become conspicuous for his disloyalty to Napoleon. Meanwhile in Vienna Madame de Stael was contacted by one of the top British agents in the German-speaking world. It has been suggested that Wickham's Alien Office also had a hand in the assassination of Tsar Paul of Russia in 1801.* Funds available to Wickham (generally via a special account in the eminently respectable royal bank, Coutts and Co.) would have seemed vast beyond belief to any twentieth-century British Secret Service; by 1800, the almost incredible sum of £3,682,520 had been passed to Wickham. One of his great successes was to penetrate French endeavours to spark rebellion in Ireland; all but two of the leaders of the 'United Irishmen' (precursors of Sinn Fein) were arrested, and executed in utmost secrecy.

Exposed to the Swiss by Fouché's agents, Wickham was forced to move from Switzerland to Frankfurt in 1797, where he set up a 'Swabian Agency'. From here he supported the efforts of Cadoudal, which culminated in the abortive assassination attempt of 1804;† and he was involved, more disreputably, in the killing of two French emissaries on their way to Rastadt to ratify the Treaty of Campoformio — which was to lead to Austria abandoning the war against Napoleon. Wickham failed in his main objective of achieving counter-revolution in France, and was later to suffer impeachment by Parliament for his lack of success. Yet his operations reveal that Britain's hands in the secret war were little cleaner than those of Fouché.

There was one quality the *Grande Armée* of 1805 had to excess: it was morale, or sheer fighting spirit. 'If you discover how',

---

* Mad Tsar Paul had thrown in his lot with Napoleon; his death put into reverse all Napoleon's hopes of blockading Britain, or even driving her out of the Mediterranean, through the League of Neutrals. Three months after his death, and the accession of his son, Alexander I, Russia resumed friendly relations with Britain.

† See p. 26 above.

wrote one of Britain's most revered commanders, Field-Marshal Wavell, many years later '. . . he inspired a ragged, mutinous, half-starved army and made it fight as it did . . . then you will have learned something.' Like so much else, the explanation had its roots in Revolutionary times. After the initial setbacks against the First Coalition, special 'political commissars' (not unlike those introduced by the Soviet Army) called 'Deputies-on-Mission' were despatched to the armies to instil a new spirit. Although the purges and punishments they carried out were – as might have been expected – often bloody and unjust, they did succeed in their mission. The early urgency that the Republic was fighting for its life, on its own territory; the new egalitarianism, as far as advancement was concerned; the awareness that, unlike the impressed serfs of the other continental nations, the French soldier alone felt he had a personal cause worth fighting for, plus that extra indefinable something to be found in almost all 'revolutionary armies' of the twentieth century, provided the rest of the mix. Napoleon simply carried on all that was best of the Revolutionary zeal; 'We suffered, but were proud of our sufferings,' wrote a Grenadier, 'because our officers, with their packs on their backs, shared our meagre rations.' But Napoleon, of course, grafted his own special – indeed unique – morale-boosting magic on to the Revolutionary stock.

First of all, even though he was a Corsican, he understood the mentality of the French soldier uncannily well. The soldier, said Napoleon, 'is not a machine to be put into motion, but a reasonable being that must be directed. . . . [He] loves to argue, because he is intelligent. . . .' Like Montgomery with his Eighth Army before Alamein, he believed in making the simplest soldier party to his plan and understand what was to be demanded of him. As has already been noted, the degradation of corporal punishment had been abolished and replaced by a system of glory, awards and riches. On the other hand, no flogging-through-the-ranks could be more searing than a flaying from the Emperor's tongue when in one of his terrifying rages. Describing his outburst against a regiment that had lost an 'Eagle' at Austerlitz, the Comte de Saint-Chamans was to admit, 'my flesh crawled. I broke into a cold sweat, and at times my eyes were coursing with tears. I do not doubt that the regiment would have performed miracles if it had been led into action at the very next instant.'[9]

Equally no one was more aware of the positive force of his personality than Napoleon himself. 'The 32nd Brigade would have died for me,' he once observed. 'Because after Lonato, I wrote: "The 32nd was there, I was calm." The power of words on men is astonishing.' Napoleon also used this 'power of words' often quite unscrupulously when framing his famous Bulletins in the aftermath of a battle. Mediocre victories would be transformed into epic triumphs; while, particularly after assuming the Imperial Crown, Napoleon himself did his best to foster superhuman legends, *inter alia* in popular engravings, all designed to suggest he was endowed with powers beyond the natural. This mixture of half-truths and downright lies employed in his Bulletins was probably designed as much to exhilarate his own forces as to demoralize the enemy (a leaf from his book which Montgomery was usefully to borrow). Throughout his career Napoleon was conscious of having constantly to keep up a certain moral momentum to hold the enthusiasm of the French Army. 'I had to act with éclat', he said after his first triumph in the 1796 Italian Campaign, 'to win the trust and affection of the common soldier.' 'A man does not have himself killed for a few halfpence a day, or for a petty distinction,' Napoleon recognized; 'you must speak to the soul in order to electrify the man . . .' – and this was a skill at which he was unrivalled.

The troops of the *Grande Armée* with habitual cheeriness spoke of 'setting off for the marriage feast' as a campaign approached, and, as the Emperor personally took leave of his departing cohorts at Boulogne, their display of ardour after the long months of boredom and frustration waiting on the Channel was overwhelming. It was rivalled only by the glumness of those left behind to protect the coast (to whom Berthier promised an invasion next spring, once the Emperor had 'punished the continent for its aggression'). Those Frenchmen of 1805 had already defeated most of the soldiers of Europe, and consequently despised them. The long, perilous march into the heart of the continent held little horror or fear for them. Says Thiers:

> They set off singing and shouting 'Vive l'Empereur!', begging for as speedy a meeting as possible with the enemy. It is true that, in those hearts, boiling over with courage, there was less pure patriotism than in the soldiers of '92; there was more ambition, but a noble ambition, that of glory. . . . The volunteers of '92 were eager to defend their country against an unjust invasion; the veteran soldiers of 1805, to render it the first power in the world.[10]

It was a valid distinction. And, though that mesmeric spell of Napoleon, under which his *grognards* would march to hell and back for him, would endure through 1812 and beyond, now it was at its all-time peak of potency. These soldiers of 1805 would never be surpassed.

SEVEN

Ulm and on to Vienna

2 September—28 November 1805

The Emperor has discovered a new way of waging war; he makes use of our legs instead of our bayonets. . . .

Anonymous French soldier, 1805

HAVING DISPATCHED HIS TROOPS, Napoleon set out for Malmaison on 2 September 1805. In Paris there were some distractingly aggravating domestic problems to be dealt with; a disappointing harvest had made bread prices soar and finances were in a mess. The budget showed an immense deficit, and, as it was against all Napoleon's principles either to borrow or to print paper money, a heavy increase in taxation was his only recourse. Rumours that he was reaching down into the bottom of the national coffers in order to pay for the new war were spreading financial panic. This, plus a call-up of 80,000 to provide him with a contingency reserve, did not enhance his popularity in the capital. On 23 September when he explained to the Senate the causes of the new war, laying the blame squarely on the Allies, the Senators evinced little more than token enthusiasm. During his return to the Tuileries, he was vexed by the unwonted lack of warmth shown by the populace. Disagreeably aware that civilian morale was not of the same high order as that of the *Grande Armée*, Napoleon left Paris for Strasbourg knowing how imperative it was for him to win a swift and decisive victory, if for no other reason than that the country might otherwise face bankruptcy.

At Strasbourg, the gloom was intensified by Talleyrand, the venal ex-Bishop of Autun turned Minister of Foreign Affairs, who for both national and personal reasons disapproved of the new war. With his club-foot and love of comfort, he dreaded the pain that resulted from the long marches trailing behind his master. The rest of his entourage was also suffering from presentiments that, like Turenne or Charles XII, the irreplaceable leader might possibly be struck down by a stray ball. The Empress herself, so Thiers alleged with just a touch of cynicism, 'was the more strongly attached to him the more fear she felt about the duration of her union with him'. Having got over his latest transient infatuation with twenty-year-old, musical Madame Duchatel that spring, Napoleon displayed a renewal of his passion for Josephine and there was an emotional (and public) farewell scene. Napoleon wept and vomited, and according to Talleyrand suffered something like a convulsion – news which was warmly received in London as signifying that the arch-enemy had been laid low with an epileptic fit. 'It really is painful to leave two people one most loves,' grieved the Emperor, embracing them both and then setting forth, on 1 October, on one of his rare campaigns without a woman.

Once on the other side of the Rhine, things immediately looked brighter. Only a short time behind the schedule laid down by Napoleon, on 26 August the *Grande Armée* was concentrated perfectly in conformity with his plans and was marching superbly. It was probably one of the first times in warfare that roads were to be used so extensively for transportation of an army on a large scale. The infantry strode forth in two parallel files at the side of the dusty roads, leaving the centre free for the cavalry and heavy wagons, each division spread out over three miles in precise march discipline. With straws between their teeth so as to keep their mouths closed, the troops would begin their march at between 4 a.m. and 6 a.m. and bivouac before midday. Every hour there was a five-minute halt when the music – clarinets, flute and horn – played, and when the men showed signs of sleepiness on the march the drums began to beat. Anything to keep them on the move.

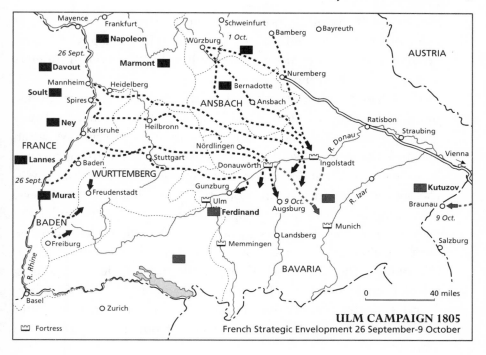

ULM CAMPAIGN 1805
French Strategic Envelopment 26 September–9 October

Among the Guard, even though they carried heavier packs than the Line, discipline was of course superb; at Ettlingen they rendered honours in immaculate full dress when the Emperor was received by the Grand Duke of Baden. Desertions were minimal; out of Marmont's 20,000-strong II Corps, only nine men were missing when it reached Würzburg. 'The Emperor has discovered a new way of waging war,' grumbled the infantry, 'he makes use of our legs instead of our bayonets. . . .' As previously noted, the speed of Napoleon's forces on the march was legendary. Advancing into the German states, the *Grande Armée*, travelling light, was preceded by the quartermasters, who arranged billeting and requisitioning. Fortunately, at any rate in the early stages, food was readily available in rich Württemberg and Bavaria. 'It was the height of the potato season,' Corporal Jean-Pierre Blaise wrote to his parents from Germany. 'How many times did we blight the hopes of a villager! We plundered him of the fruits of a whole year's work. However we were, as you might say, forced to do so. . . .' The unhappy German peasants tried to bury their food supplies, but the French foragers soon ferreted them out.

Then bad weather struck and in the sodden bivouacs morale slumped. François-Joseph Joskin wrote, 'Oh mother, what a great misfortune has befallen me to become a conscript! What an unhappy life it is to be a soldier!' Food supplies were uncertain, boots were holed and the horses were beginning to break down. Davout was asking permission to shoot hungry marauders. Something of that Boulogne euphoria began to dissolve under the icy rain. But Napoleon was in no way dejected; to Josephine he wrote exuberantly on 2 October, 'Our grand manoeuvres are in full swing. The armies of Württemberg and Baden are joining mine. I am in good health, and I love you. . . .' By 7 October, Murat's cavalry had crossed the Danube downstream from Ulm. The *Grande Armée*'s front concentrated from 125 down to 50 miles.

In contrast to his own performance, Napoleon noted (on 2 October) how 'the enemy is marching and counter-marching and appears to be embarrassed'. Though nominally under Archduke Ferdinand, the Austrian expeditionary force on the Danube was in effect commanded by his quartermaster-general, General Karl Mack. Aged forty-three at this time, Mack had been born in Bavaria of a lower-middle-class Protestant family and had worked his way up through the ranks. In 1799 he had been defeated by Napoleon in Italy and captured, escaping the following year. He had not handled that campaign with particular distinction, and Nelson — with whom he had collaborated in Naples — went so far as to declare him 'a rascal, a scoundrel and a coward!' This was unduly harsh, and Mack seems to have been a courageous soldier at least as competent as most of the leaders thrown up either previously or subsequently by a nation whose greatest talent never lay in the art of warfare. As *Generalquartiermeister*, Mack had done his best to modernize the Austrian Army, but his efforts had been resisted as too 'revolutionary' by Vienna's hidebound military establishment.

Basically, the Austrian Army of 1805 remained that of Maria Theresa and Joseph II. Its bible was still the *Generals-Reglement* of 1769, which stressed drill and rigidly linear tactics and a cautious strategy based on secure communications, coupled with a traditional Austrian proclivity for fortified bases. The Commissariat was regarded as too socially inferior to be administered by officers-and-gentlemen; hence it was rotten with corruption, and barely functioned. Between 1801 and 1804 the national military budget had been cut by more than half. Most of the Austrian infantry still carried the 1754 musket, and had very little practice with it. Artillery was sprinkled about in penny-packets among the infantry, much as the French were to use their tanks in 1940. Baggage trains were huge, partly due to the requirements of officers' personal kit.

Greatly impressed by the mobility of Napoleon's army, Mack had undertaken a series of reforms in the spring of 1805; but it had been too late, and Mack himself seems to have been somewhat carried away by optimism at what he had already achieved. More realistically, the best Austrian commander, Archduke Charles, had unsuccessfully resisted involvement in a new war on the ground that the army was simply not ready for it. He was overruled by the 'hawks'; thus, when war came, the Austrian Army was caught in the middle of change and reform, its organization still antiquated and its movements ponderous. The High Command was in the hands of the slow-witted and argumentative Aulic Council. Its deliberations with the Russian leaders were sadly shown up by Napoleon's axiom that, 'nothing is so important in war as an undivided command. For this reason, when war is carried on against a single power, there should be only one army, acting upon one base, and conducted by one chief.' Moreover, within the Ulm camp, there was already a fundamental clash of personalities between the aristocratic, overbearing Catholic Archduke Ferdinand (given titular command not least to keep it out of the hands of the mistrusted Russian ally) and the despised Lutheran ex-ranker, Mack, who was to bear the shame and responsibility of the coming disaster.

Under the impulse of Ferdinand and the Aulic Council, Mack had committed the fatal error of crossing the River Inn into Bavaria on 8 September, without waiting for the Russians, who were still east of Vienna. This was exactly what Napoleon had foreseen (aided no doubt by the presence at Mack's headquarters of the double-agent Schulmeister). Equally Mack and Ferdinand had perfectly swallowed Napoleon's deception plan, expecting the main French offensive to be delivered in northern Italy, as in 1796 and again in 1800; they were also distracted by such carefully planted rumours as that the British had landed in Boulogne and that a coup had been launched in France against Napoleon. Refusing to believe that he would risk breaching Prussian neutrality by marching through Ansbach, they had their eyes riveted to their west, on the Black Forest where Murat's cavalry had been ostentatiously swarming about. A series of contradictory intelligence reports were reaching Mack. As a result he continued to sit paralysed at Ulm, ordering up reinforcements from the Tyrol – only to increase Napoleon's eventual bag of prisoners. When Marshal Soult's corps crossed the Danube at Donauwörth on 8 October, the officers of a reconnaissance force despatched by Mack were taken by surprise in the middle of their dinner. The surprise was universal. As Thiers remarks:

> Never was astonishment equal to that which filled all Europe on the unexpected arrival of this army. It was supposed to be on the shores of the ocean, and, in twenty days, that is to say the time required for the report of its march to begin to spread, it appeared on the Rhine, and inundated South Germany.

Although, with the arrival of the *Grande Armée* on the Danube, the curtain was now rent asunder, Mack could still not be sure of precisely what Napoleon was planning to do. He seems to have nursed a wishful belief that, since Napoleon had crossed the Danube and then swung westward again, he might be heading back to Paris to cope with the domestic crises that Mack too had heard about. Consequently he went on wavering, adopting scheme after scheme and then abandoning them. In turn his irresolution made it the more difficult for Napoleon to form an appreciation of how his enemy would react once the jaws of the trap closed behind Ulm. There were basically three options open to Mack. He could stay in Ulm and sit it out until the Russians arrived, a contingency for which he had neither the strength nor the provisions. He could try to break out of the trap and retreat on Vienna along the north bank of the Danube; but this route lay across the main line of march of Napoleon's forces and he would be sacrificing his own communications with the Tyrol. Or he could withdraw southwards up the River Iller, to withdraw on Vienna through the Tyrol, linking up on the way with Archdukes John and Charles.

This last seemed to Napoleon the most logical contingency, and upon this judgement he went on to commit his first major error of the campaign, which, had the Austrians been less ineffectual, might easily have led to catastrophe. To prevent Mack breaking out southwards, he despatched the main weight of his army — Lannes, Soult, Davout, Marmont and the Guard — across the Danube, concentrating on Augsburg. Bernadotte was sent eastwards, as a covering force against the Russians, leaving only Murat, with Ney under his command, to control the Danube River itself on both sides.

With their vaunting pride, rivalry and ambition, one of the chief faults of Napoleon's marshals was that they seldom took well to being subordinated to one another. Murat, the thirty-eight-year-old innkeeper's son, who became commander-in-chief of the newly formed Guard in 1799 and Napoleon's brother-in-law the following year, was the most over-weaningly ambitious of them all. Tall, vain, handsome and a brilliant horseman with a passion for fine horses and extravagant uniforms, Murat was renowned in the army for his rash courage (even though he was bullied by his wife Caroline). General Savary remarked acidly that 'it would be better if he was endowed with rather less courage and rather more common sense', and his mixture of impetuousness and self-interest was to lead Napoleon to the brink of disaster on more than one occasion during the Austerlitz campaign. He was the most resented of Napoleon's marshals, and Ney, the thirty-six-year-old cooper's son, immediately chafed at being placed under his command. Red-headed Ney was also courageous to a fault; of only moderate intelligence he could show initiative, but often at the wrong time, and his front-line style of leadership tended to lead him to ignore units not immediately within his sight.

Relations between the two marshals were thus immediately strained. On 11 October, when (in interpretation of Napoleon's instructions) Murat ordered Ney to move his whole corps across to the south bank of the Danube, there was a violent row in front of many witnesses which nearly ended in a duel between the two commanders. Finally only General Dupont's division of 6,000 men was left on the north bank of the Danube, muddled by conflicting orders that resulted from the marshals' altercation. Murat – and certainly Napoleon – was unaware of just how weak the French forces now were that side of the river.

Meanwhile, Mack had captured orders revealing Ney's dispositions and realized that an escape route north was open. Suddenly the unfortunate General Dupont found himself confronted by 60,000 Austrians 'in an imposing attitude', some twenty miles north-east of Ulm. Typically of the spirit of the *Grande Armée*, however, Dupont hurled forward two regiments in a savage bayonet attack. The Austrian front line recoiled, leaving behind 1,500 prisoners. For the next five hours there was violent fighting in and around the village of Haslach, between Dupont and 25,000 Austrians. Dupont's division was cut to pieces, and possibly only saved from being overrun by the fact that Mack himself had been wounded in the battle. But Dupont held; if he had not, the Austrians — says Thiers — 'would have fled into Bohemia, and one of Napoleon's most splendid combinations would have been completely frustrated . . .'. Certainly there would have been no Austerlitz.

Opinions differ over who was to blame for this near-disaster; Thiers says it was Murat, Ségur blames Napoleon. Wherever the fault lay, Napoleon on hearing of Dupont's plight immediately took over the reins himself, ordering Ney to push vigorously across the Danube upstream from Dupont. On 14 October, Ney, enraged by this decimation of one of his divisions and Murat's overbearing manner, seized Murat's arm and shook him violently in front of the Emperor, exclaiming angrily, 'Come, prince, come along with me and make your plans in face of the enemy.' He then galloped off, in full uniform and decorations, to supervise the relief operation 'amid a shower of balls and grape, having the water up to his horse's belly.'

Dupont's valour, however, had provoked fatal dissension in the Austrian camp. On 12 October, Archduke Ferdinand wrote bitterly to his kinsman, the Emperor, 'General Mack has already projected and put into execution today three absolutely different plans.' Although the French error had opened an escape route out of the Ulm trap, Ferdinand had thrown it away by pressing the attack on Dupont so half-heartedly; yet he now urged Mack to agree to his escaping from Ulm in that same direction with at least a part of the army. Mack protested that, left with only 30,000 men until the Russians should arrive, this would abandon him completely to the mercy of Bonaparte, while Ferdinand's force would just be chopped up piecemeal by the French cavalry. But, with true Habsburg arrogance, the Archduke challenged him: 'Confine me in the fortress if you wish to prevent me. Does your power extend to that!'

Ulm, and the Austrian army there, was doomed. On 12 October Napoleon wrote triumphantly to Josephine, 'The enemy are beaten and don't know what they are about. It all looks like the most successful, the shortest and the most brilliant campaign ever fought. . . .' The following day he issued a proclamation to the army, declaring, 'Soldiers! It is only one month since we were encamped on the Ocean, facing England. . . . Soldiers! Tomorrow will be a hundred times more famous than the day of Marengo; I have placed the enemy in the same position.'

By the night of 15 October, Ney had retrieved the situation on the left bank of the Danube by winning a brilliant victory at Elchingen (which was later to earn him the title of Duke of Elchingen), and had established himself on the Michaelsberg heights overlooking the city from the north-west. That day the Emperor, while gazing down on Ulm, came under heavy fire himself when a concealed Austrian battery poured grape-shot into the Imperial group, and Lannes had to seize the reins of his horse to lead him hastily out of danger. (At another time, on the River Lech, the Emperor had also narrowly escaped death or serious injury when his horse, stumbling, had fallen on top of him. The episode had been kept a strict secret from the rest of the army.)

The citadel of Ulm was now held in a vice on three sides, with Soult moving up on the fourth from the south-west. Napoleon called on Mack to surrender; Mack refused. He was like 'a tethered goat in an Indian village awaiting the visit of a tiger'.[1] On 16 October, Napoleon ordered Ulm to be bombarded with a few warning shells. Conditions in the city, largely as a result of the Austrians' chaotic Commissariat, were already appalling: 'Many thousands of men made their quarters on the open streets, where they cooked and slept. . . . The whole city was a latrine, permeated with a pestilential stench. . . .' Meanwhile, as threatened, Ferdinand had pulled out with 20,000 men, abandoning Mack altogether. Equally, just as Mack had predicted, the Horse Guards pursued them, putting the unhappy fugitives to the sword at every turn; the Bavarian peasants plundered them as well, cutting the traces of the artillery to steal the horses. Finally, only 2,000 men struggled into Prague.

Blindfolded, Napoleon's aide, the Comte de Ségur, was led

into Mack's citadel to renew cease-fire negotiations. Until that moment the unfortunate Mack had still no idea that he was encircled by 100,000 enemy troops, plus another 60,000 between him and the Russians. With his own army now divided in half, his position was clearly hopeless but still he refused to surrender. Finally, on 19 October he gave in and on the following day Napoleon, mounted on a white horse, watched as the army that was to have taken Strasbourg and Paris passed into captivity. The incessant rain of the previous weeks had suddenly turned to glorious sunshine. A conversation took place between Mack and Napoleon, whom a captured Austrian officer described in his moment of glory as dressed 'in the uniform of a common soldier, with a grey coat singed* on the elbows and tails, a slouch hat without any badge of distinction on his head, his arms crossed behind his back, and warming himself at a camp-fire'. To Mack, a 'powdered old man in a splendid uniform of blue and white', Napoleon remarked, 'I don't know why we are fighting each other. . . . I did not wish it; I did not intend to fight any but the English, when your master came along and provoked me,' adding (prophetically, as far as his own was concerned), 'All empires come to an end.'

Napoleon was never to win an easier success. Mack disappeared into ignominy. While Archduke Ferdinand was to become the darling of Vienna for his flight from Ulm, the plebeian Mack was made scapegoat for the defeat; he was court-martialled, broken from service, and thrown into a dungeon for several years.

On 21 October, Napoleon issued his victorious proclamation:

Soldiers of the *Grande Armée*:
  In a fortnight we have made a campaign; we have accomplished what we intended. We have driven the troops of the house of Austria out of Bavaria. . . . The Army, which, with equal

---

* A hole had apparently been burned in it by a spark from a bonfire.

ostentation and imprudence, came and placed itself on our frontiers, is annihilated. . . .

Of the hundred thousand men who composed that army, sixty thousand are prisoners; they shall go and replace our conscripts in the labours of our fields. . . . Soldiers, this success is owing to your unbounded confidence in your Emperor, to your patience in enduring fatigues and privations of every kind. . . . But we shall not stop there; you are impatient to commence a second campaign. That Russian army, which the gold of England has brought from the extremities of the earth, shall share the same fate. . . .

It was a classic victory, and was won with an extraordinary economy in casualties on the French side; however, Austrian losses (including those inflicted in the ensuing sweeping-up operations) are reckoned to have totalled almost 60,000 men. Including those lamed by the long march, Napoleon lost no more than 2,000 men *hors de combat*, most of them from the single, battered division of General Dupont.

News of Ulm, when it reached England, was greeted with a mixture of shock and outrage. Lord Auckland declared that a captain of the London Volunteers would have done better than Mack. Lady Bessborough wrote, 'I am so terrified, so shocked with the news I scarcely know what to wish. This man moves like a torrent . . .', while Lord Grenville was incredulous: 'An army of 100,000 men, reckoned the best troops in Europe, totally destroyed in three weeks. . . . Yet even this, I am afraid, is only the beginning of our misfortunes. . . .'[2]

Events would prove this to be no exaggeration. Yet there was one shadow in Napoleon's triumph, the shadow that would always haunt and eventually destroy him. That same glorious day of 21 October was also the day that Admiral Villeneuve with his ill-trained, sick and mutinous fleet, driven out of Cadiz by his Emperor's repeated taunts of cowardice, had been smashed by Nelson's ships off Cape Trafalgar. Abandoning the old, formal line of battle, parallel to the enemy fleet, Nelson had adopted

TRAFALGAR, *'Crossing the T'*, 1805

revolutionary new tactics* of breaking through Villeneuve's
line, thereby cutting the enemy force in two. Ironically, he was
triumphing at sea with something very close to the tactics with
which, on land, Napoleon was about to shatter the Austro-
Russian armies at Austerlitz. In the oft-quoted words of Admiral
Mahan: 'Those distant, storm-beaten ships, upon which the
Grand Army never looked, stood between it and the dominion
of the world.'† Though British glory at Trafalgar was hardly of
any immediate consolation to the humiliated Austrians, whatever
successes might now fall to Napoleon on land, ultimate victory
would henceforth always elude him.

---

* In fact similar tactics had been tried and proven a generation earlier by
Admiral Rodney in his famous victory over the French at the Battle of the Saints
off St Lucia in the Caribbean.
† In one sense this was an obvious, if not faintly absurd, remark; how *could* the
Grande Armée have set eyes on the Royal Navy's ships, any more than the
Kaiser's or Hitler's land-locked armies were to do a century later?

It was not until some time later that Napoleon learned of the disaster at Trafalgar; he expressed himself 'mortified', ordered the minimum to be made of it in the French press, otherwise showed only moderate distress, and refused to be distracted from the pursuit of the decisive contest ahead. After Ulm he wrote to his Empress:

> I have been rather overdone, my good Josephine. Eight days spent in the soaking rain and with cold feet have told on me a little; but . . . I have accomplished my object; I have destroyed the Austrian army by simple marching. . . . I am on the point of marching against the Russians; they are ruined. . . .

Napoleon rested four or five days longer at Ulm before moving on eastwards down the Danube Valley – first stop Munich. Accorded a warm welcome there by his 'liberated' Bavarian allies, he was in an ebullient and generous mood, presenting his Guard with one thousand pairs of new boots. At Munich, however, he was caught up by his hobbling and fatigued Foreign Minister, bringing with him a variety of headaches. In France, the financial crisis was worsening; several bankers had been declared bankrupt, including M. Récamier, husband of the famous Empire beauty. An outraged Prussia was taking the French violation of Ansbach's neutrality worse than anticipated. In revenge, Russian troops were being allowed passage through Silesia, and on his way to Vienna young Tsar Alexander had paused in Berlin to captivate the Queen and cajole her vacillating husband into signing the Potsdam Treaty, whereby Prussia would intervene on the Allied side as soon as her mobilization could be completed, early in December. Thus, as Napoleon advanced further 'into the very entrails of Europe', there was the ever-increasing danger that the jaws of a gigantic trap – sprung by Prussia in the north and Archduke Charles moving up from Italy in the south – would close on his rear.

Seeing all this, Talleyrand beseeched Napoleon to try now to seduce the battered Austrians out of the coalition by means of 'soft' peace terms. Austria – urged Talleyrand, as always, taking the longer view – must be transmuted into the ally of France, as an eastern bulwark against Russia. With the scent of military victory in his nostrils, however, Napoleon was little inclined to heed Talleyrand. On 28 October he left Munich to begin the march to Vienna, 250 miles distant. Either way the risks were the greatest he had ever taken. If, instead of advancing, he adopted a defensive posture, within little more than a month he would have to face the combined weight of 120,000 Austrians, 100,000 Russians and 150,000 Prussians. On balance, comments Thiers, his decision to press on 'was the wisest, though apparently the rashest'. Napoleon's strategy now was, on the one hand, to continue to keep the Austrian armies of Archdukes John and Charles (in the Tyrol and northern Italy respectively) out of the Danubian theatre of war; on the other, to catch and destroy Kutuzov somewhere *south* of the Danube, before Russian re-inforcements could reach him. The one fear that dominated all Napoleon's thinking from this time onwards was that the Russians might escape northwards, back across the great river barrier.

On the day of his departure from Munich, the southern jaw of the potential Allied trap was in fact badly bruised when the dependable Masséna, with his 50,000 men, forcefully attacked Archduke Charles's 80,000 troops outside Verona. The Second Battle of Caldiero (as it came to be known) was a model of aggressive defence. It inflicted 11,000 casualties on the Austrians, and pinned them down so that they would be unable to join in developments north of the Tyrol. Napoleon could now march eastwards along the narrow, vulnerable route between the Alps and the Danube, fairly confident that his southern flank would be safe. However, he did take the precaution of establishing supply dumps at various intervals which could serve either for the advance or for a withdrawal if it were to be forced upon him. He also organized a flotilla of mobile pontoon barges to link the forces moving along both sides of the Danube.

Conditions on the new march were far from excellent. On All Saints' Day, a foot of snow covered the ground; at times the revictualling broke down, and the army was scourged with hunger. Corporal Jean-Pierre Blaise wrote, 'It was again one of the most wretched nights that we had spent; we could hardly remain lying down, such was the steepness of the slope. . . .' The corps commanders were constantly receiving such bossy reminders from Berthier as: '. . . I repeat that in a war of invasion and of rapid movements which the Emperor is waging there can be no depots, and the generals in command have themselves to see to it that they procure the necessary supplies from the countries which they traverse.'

Then, on 5 November, Murat and Lannes caught up with the Russians at Amstetten, just south of the Danube and 100 miles west of Vienna. It was the *Grande Armée*'s first encounter with this new, redoubtable enemy. Kutuzov — who had only recently heard of the disaster at Ulm, since Archduke Ferdinand had persisted in sending him nothing but optimistic news — fought a brief battle to save his baggage train, then disengaged.

Since 25 August, when, under the Allied grand strategy, the one-eyed old Russian veteran had set off westwards from Galicia, Kutuzov's columns had had a wearisome time. Under orders from the Tsar, a sixth column had been sent back to watch the frontier with Turkey; then the order had been countermanded, the column wearily trying to catch up with the main body. Pressed by Emperor Francis, Kutuzov had been urged, in September, to speed his march so as to join up with Mack, though grumbling to Czartoryski, Alexander's Foreign Minister, 'our soldiers have already endured much fatigue, and they are suffering badly', and again, on 1 October: 'They have had to march barefoot, and their feet have suffered so badly on the sharp stones of the highways that the men are incapable of service. . . .'[3]

By 26 October he had been reinforced by some 27,000 fatigued Russians and 18,000 Austrian survivors from Ulm and elsewhere. Relations between the two Allies were already strained, with the Austrian commander, Lieutenant-General Max Merveldt, complaining to Vienna that Kutuzov 'seems unacquainted with the art of war. . . . He leaves time and distance completely out of account, and is most unwilling to risk his troops.' In fact, Kutuzov had already made up his own, highly independent mind to conduct one of those long, stubborn retreats for which he was to earn his place in history.

Whereas the Austrians' obvious priority was now the defence of their capital, Vienna, Kutuzov's was the preservation of his unbattleworthy army. In the event, a compromise was forced on him. He was to concentrate on holding the permanent bridge over the Danube at Krems, some forty miles upstream from Vienna. This would enable him both to cover the approaches to Vienna and to keep open an escape route northwards. Then, as a result of conflicting orders received from the Aulic Council (but what at the time looked remarkably like cowardice), on 1 November Merveldt had withdrawn his main force southeastwards, leaving Kutuzov unsupported at Amstetten to fend off Murat's cavalry. Three days later Merveldt was fallen upon by the combined forces of Davout and Marmont and destroyed on the snow-covered field of Mariazell. It was a further episode hardly calculated to improve Austro-Russian relations. Kutuzov proceeded with a savage scorched-earth withdrawal, burning everything behind him – something the French had never yet encountered, but would learn more about in 1812. Arriving at Krems, Kutuzov discovered that the Austrians had not fortified the bridgehead. He now took the major strategic decision to pull his army out, northwards across the Danube.

Misjudging his new adversary, Napoleon calculated (and hoped) that Kutuzov might stand and fight a decisive battle at St Pölten, some thirty miles further east from Amstetten. At this moment the Emperor and his staff were still at Linz, further behind the vanguard and more out of touch with developments than was his wont, which was perhaps a contributory factor in the second* major error of the campaign that the French were about to commit. On 7 November Murat intercepted messages revealing Kutuzov's intention to retreat across the Danube at Krems. From this it seemed clear that the Russians were planning to abandon the capital of their allies, and fall back north-eastwards into Moravia whence they had only recently arrived. If they succeeded it meant that they would escape Napoleon's trap, and his grand strategy of a swift battle of annihilation would collapse. However, the dazzling prospect of the open, defenceless city of Vienna lying just ahead was too much for the vainglorious Murat to resist. After Marengo, the victorious French had come close to Vienna in 1800, but otherwise no western army had ever occupied it. Here indeed was a prize worthy of Murat's boundless ambition; perhaps he had already thought of himself as Duke, or even King, of Vienna? Momentarily he was like a headstrong stallion that has ripped the bridle out of the grasp of its handler and bolted.

Kutuzov, his forces increased to 40,000 by the arrival of the jaded sixth column, soon perceived that — with Murat and Lannes galloping for Vienna — the French had only one *ad hoc* army corps, Mortier's, advancing in extended order along the north bank of the Danube. The supporting troops were well behind him, as was the Danube flotilla which provided the only means of transferring troops from one side to the other of the now wide and largely bridgeless river. Kutuzov swiftly turned about and, on 11 November, despatched nearly 15,000 men to strike Mortier's 6,000 from the front, flank and rear in a narrow defile at Dürrenstein — where Richard Coeur de Lion, returning from the Third Crusade, had been captured and incarcerated on Christmas Day, 1192. The situation was almost a repeat of Dupont's reverse before Ulm, except that, this time, the odds were not so great. The Russians, however, pressed their attack

---

* His first had been to leave the north bank of the Danube so weakly held by Dupont's division on 11 October.

with much more vigour, although allegedly impeded by the weight of their heavy overcoats. The rugged but rather slow-witted General Mortier (the subject of a contemporary pun, 'the big mortar [*mortier*] has a short range'), fighting sword in hand at the head of his Grenadiers, was nearly captured. It was Dupont, again, who came to the rescue and the Russians were driven back; but with heavy French losses – 4,000 on each side.

Russian historians claim that, at Dürrenstein, Napoleon had been dealt 'a serious blow in the eyes of all Europe' for the first time in his military career. Indeed, it was a close-run thing, and if Mortier's corps had been wiped out it would have gone far to dilute the results of Napoleon's triumph at Ulm. In all probability the set-back would not have happened had Napoleon been more closely in touch with the advance troops. Thiers goes so far as to criticize it as a 'negligence scarcely ever to be met with in operations directed by Napoleon', and largely exculpates Murat. As it was, with his usual alacrity the Emperor restored the imbalance, taking it out on his brother-in-law Murat, with one of his most searing reprimands:

I cannot approve your method of advance; you proceed like a scatterbrain [*étourdi*], and you pay no heed to the orders I send you. Instead of covering Vienna, the Russians have recrossed the Danube at Krems. This extraordinary circumstance should have made you realize that you ought not to move without fresh instructions. . . . Without knowing what plans the enemy might have had, or being aware what my intentions were in this new state of affairs, you go and set my army at Vienna. . . . You have made me lose two days, and have considered nothing but the petty triumph of entering Vienna. There is no glory except where there is danger. There is none in entering a defenceless capital.

Napoleon should perhaps have remembered this in 1812.

Kutuzov had escaped Napoleon's first trap, and a chastened Murat now redeemed himself by a Machiavellian ruse the following day. Arriving at the great bridge leading over the Danube to Vienna, he realized at once that the bridge was mined; in fact, an Austrian gunner was standing by with a lighted fuse as the French approached. But the Austrian troops guarding it were commanded by a general brought out of cold storage after a dozen years' retirement – Prince Auersperg. Disingenuously shouting 'Armistice, armistice!', Murat and Lannes talked their way across the vital bridge, and at the other end they managed persuasively to assure the defenders that an armistice had been signed: 'How is it that you have heard nothing about it? Peace is being negotiated! Lead us to your general.'

While the bemused Auersperg was pondering what to do, a detachment of French Grenadiers doubled across the bridge, and the key to the Austrian capital was in Napoleon's hands. Emperor Francis declared himself 'all the more hurt since this stupid and unpardonable blunder has destroyed the whole trust of my allies at a single stroke'. In fact, by uncovering the flank of the retreating Kutuzov, considerably more than just trust was now at risk. Among the francophone Russian officers, a bitter jest (according to Tolstoy in *War and Peace*) went the rounds: '*c'est comme à Ulm . . . c'est du Mack. Nous sommes Mackés!*'

Napoleon was delighted by this rather underhand coup, and promptly forgave Murat his earlier transgression. On 14 November, seventy-three days after leaving the English Channel, the Emperor rode with calm dignity and a much beplumed train into the Austrian capital. Hating the savage Russians whom they reckoned to have left them in the lurch, those Viennese who had not abandoned the city greeted him more like some conquering Austrian general (though they could hardly have seen many).

Vienna was then a small, feudal city, neatly enclosed within its ancient walls, but it was the grandest capital Napoleon had yet taken, and the centre of a great empire. Mozart's *The Magic Flute* was currently being performed at the Opera; a week later, the first night of Beethoven's just-completed *Fidelio* would flop in front of an audience full of French uniforms (Beethoven himself, disillusioned with Napoleon whom he had once venerated, refused to watch his procession through Vienna). In the Vienna arsenals Napoleon discovered 2,000 cannon, 100,000 muskets and a vast store of ammunition negligently left behind by the Austrians. They would prove useful against the Austrians and their allies at Austerlitz, and the city itself provided the French with an invaluable supply and hospital base.

Meanwhile, in the south, Archduke Charles had withdrawn from Italy. With Masséna close on his tail,* he was obliged to keep up a running fight while trying to come to the aid of Vienna. Napoleon now sent Marmont southwards to Leoben in Styria to block him off. As a result, Archduke Charles's army and Archduke John's force from the Tyrol were harried eastwards across what is now Yugoslav Slovenia and into Hungary. Neither would be able to play any role in the coming operations. Here Napoleon's original strategy had been perfectly executed.

Kutuzov now hastened his pace north-eastwards. Behind him came the *Grande Armée* in pursuit, looting as it went. An old Austrian cavalry officer described one French unit as clad:

> in sheepskin or the fur of some wild animal; others are rigged out in the most strange manner and carry long sides of bacon, ham, pieces of meat hanging from their belts. They are veritable walking larders. Others march with their bodies hung all over with loaves of bread and bottles of wine. . . .

The Austrians, however, suffered even more from their own allies – in the best tradition of Russian armies down through the ages – acting as if they were in enemy territory. On the withdrawal from Krems, they 'plundered, ravaged, even murdered, behaving like downright barbarians, so that the French were almost regarded as deliverers . . .'. They so stripped the

---

* Napoleon's orders to Masséna (on 22 November) were: 'pursue the enemy with your sword in his ribs so that he may not be able to attack us, as we are now in the presence of the whole Russian army'.

surrounding area of both food and horses as to make a prolonged stand there improbable, and disease began to run through the cold, hungry army. They treated the Austrian troops with arrogance and contempt, sneering at them and blaming them (not without reason) for the disasters of the campaign to date. Relations between the two armies were noticeably deteriorating.

Commanding the advance guard, which he had spurred on at a killing pace, on 15 November a red-eyed Murat beat the Russians to Hollabrünn, a small centre where he was able to revictual his forces. However, remembering the disaster that had nearly overtaken Mortier, and conscious of the presence of the bulk of Kutuzov's army somewhere close by, he felt distinctly nervous. So it was with ill-disguised relief that he was suddenly informed of the arrival, under a flag of truce, of Russian emissaries, asking for a temporary armistice in advance of peace negotiations. Lannes was suspicious, but Murat acceded, falling into a trap which suitably paid him out for his own deceit on the Vienna bridge. According to Weyrother, the Austrian Chief-of-Staff, 'if the Russians, with their peculiarly Byzantine cunning, had not contrived to repay the deceitful French in their own coin . . .' it seemed as if Kutuzov must have been destroyed. As it was, the twenty-four hours during which Murat stood still were sufficient for the Russian to extricate his tired forces, and put a healthy distance between them and Murat. When (simultaneously with the arrival of fresh details about the disaster at Trafalgar) Napoleon heard of Murat's latest error of judgement, he flew into a terrible rage and unleashed yet another venomous shaft against his headstrong brother-in-law:

It is impossible for me to find words with which to express my displeasure to you. . . . You are causing me to lose the fruits of a campaign. Break the armistice at once and march on the enemy. . . . The Austrians let themselves be taken in over the passage of the Vienna bridges; you have let yourself be taken in by an aide-de-camp of the Tsar!

Kutuzov had escaped a second trap, causing Napoleon to lose more time that he could ill afford. As he wrote to his brother Joseph on 15 November, 'The fate of the world may depend on a day.'

Stung by this latest rebuke, Murat thrust ahead once again, fighting a brisk engagement at Schöngrabern – immortalized in *War and Peace* – against Prince Bagration's rearguard, which cost it 3,000 men. The following night was passed by one French colonel in a grisly enough bivouac prepared by his Carabiniers: 'they dragged together a number of Russian corpses, face to the ground, and spread a layer of hay on top.' Kutuzov, nevertheless, congratulated the Georgian Prince: 'I shall not ask after your losses. You are alive, and that is enough for me.'

On 19 November Murat occupied the Moravian capital of Brünn (Brno), happy to find it full of badly needed provisions. Some of the French officers were also happy to discover in the city 'extremely pretty women, got up in the most tasteful and tempting way'. Less fortunate troops, frozen with the damp cold, dismantled entire houses and their furnishings to fuel camp fires, to the dismay of the wretched peasants who had greeted them as liberators from the Russians. On that same day, Kutuzov came to rest in Olmütz, some forty miles away to the north-east. Here he linked up with the second Russian army under Buxhöwden, at last arrived from Galicia, 'completely fresh and in splendid order', in contrast to Kutuzov's force which (as described by one of its officers), 'had been ruined by perpetual hardship, and broken down by the lack of supplies and the foul weather of late autumn . . . their footwear had almost ceased to exist. Even our commanders were arrayed in ill-assorted, almost comic attire.' Five days later the splendid Russian Imperial Guard, 10,000 strong, arrived all the way from St Petersburg: 'a magnificent force, composed of enormous men, who appeared by no means exhausted by such a long march'.

The two great opposing forces now stood and contemplated each other, for the first time in the campaign; equally for the first time it seemed as if the strategic advantage might lie with the Allies. It was also plain that a full-scale confrontation on the battlefield could not now be long postponed. For Napoleon, irrevocably committed in the very heart of Europe, the critical moment had arrived. The alternatives open to him were either to win a decisive victory, and quickly, or to face annihilation. With Prussia's entry into the war seeming to come closer every day, the whole of Europe had become, potentially, a deadly trap for the *Grande Armée*. Certainly, this is how it must have looked, unmistakably, to any neutral observer. There was absolutely no time to spare; disturbing news was also reaching the Emperor from Paris that the Treasury was running out of funds with which to pay the army. There was a serious threat of bankruptcy, on a scale not encountered before. The future held four daunting prospects for Napoleon. If Kutuzov withdrew out of reach again, denying him the decisive battle he sought, Napoleon would be lost. He would also be lost if he were to fight a drawn game, leaving the enemy forces undestroyed. Thirdly, if he were forced to attack a superior enemy force on ground of its own choosing, Napoleon would be at a grave tactical disadvantage. He was thus left with a fourth and risky option: to entice the Allies to attack him where and when he wanted. And this is what he intended to do.

Everything depended on the Russians taking Napoleon's bait. He would have to persuade them that they now outnumbered him by two to one, and that – become suddenly aware of his extended position – he was frightened. For the next ten days he busied himself with reconnaissance and espionage, bluff and counter-bluff, and – a skill in which he had few rivals – play-acting. Thirty-one-year-old General Savary, an adept at intelligence work, was despatched to the Tsar's camp at Olmütz, to spy out the land and gauge the Russian mood, but also to drop meaningful hints that a worried Napoleon would now be quite grateful for a negotiated peace. While the army sat unprovocatively motionless, liaison officers sped out to summon up the corps of Davout and Bernadotte and all other available forces for the coming confrontation. Ceaselessly Napoleon himself roamed over the countryside between Brünn and Olmütz, poring over maps with Bacler d'Albe, and consulting accounts of battles that had been fought in the Moravian hills by Frederick the Great. He also had with him some useful notes which that twenty-six-year-old Swiss military genius, Colonel Jomini, currently accompanying Ney on the campaign, had written only the previous year in his *Traité des Grandes Opérations Militaires*: 'Between Olmütz and Brünn there are several little rivers tucked away among the mountains which provide very favourable camps. On the whole, Moravia can be defended against a superior army. . . .' According to one of Napoleon's officers, Brigadier Thiébault, however, the name Moravia had sinister connotations for the French. It 'signified for them *mort à vie*. . . . In ten years of campaigning many of our officers had risked their lives in one battle after another, without ever thinking that they ought to draw up their wills. But they made them now. . . .'

Suddenly Napoleon stuck his pin in the map midway between Brünn and the small village of Austerlitz, some thirteen miles to the east. Notwithstanding all his minute study and deep reflection of the past days, it seemed almost as if a divine intuition was guiding his hand at this moment.

EIGHT

'Le Beau Soleil d'Austerlitz'

28 November–2 December 1805

When I read the story of the Battle of Austerlitz I saw every
incident. The roar of the cannon, the cries of the fighting
men rang in my ears and made my inmost self quiver.

Balzac, *Louis Lambert*

AS NOVEMBER DREW TO ITS END, inside Olmütz Castle
the highest councils on the Allied side found themselves, once
again, in a state of discord, as they had been during the critical
moments before Ulm. There were the hawks convinced that
now, at last, they had the archfiend, Bonaparte, beautifully
cornered – and the doves who were urging caution. Chief among
the hawks was Count Dolgorukov, aide-de-camp to the Tsar and
exerting a potent influence on the twenty-eight-year-old autocrat;
arrogant in the extreme, he was a kind of Russian counterpart to
the headstrong Murat. On 28 November Napoleon, hinting at
negotiations, had requested a personal interview with the Tsar,
and Dolgorukov had been sent to the French camp as spokesman.
Haughtily he offered the enemy Emperor 'peace at once if you
give up all Italy immediately. . . . But, if France goes on with
the war, it will be Belgium, Savoy, Piedmont. . . .' With
difficulty Napoleon had controlled his temper, keeping up the
role that his strategy dictated, but afterwards he had exploded,
slashing at the ground with his riding crop and slating Dolgorukov
as 'a youthful trumpeter of England': 'These people must be mad
to expect me to evacuate Italy when they find it impossible to
get me out of Vienna!'

Dolgorukov, however, had conveyed exactly the desired

impression back to his master; Napoleon he described as 'a little figure, extremely dirty and ill-dressed', and his army on the brink of doom. In particular, he delivered one nugget of intelligence. The previous day Soult, on Napoleon's orders, had abandoned both Austerlitz and the dominant Pratzen Heights behind it. This, declared Dolgorukov triumphantly, must provide evidence of Napoleon wanting to avoid battle. The young Tsar, who (according to the émigré General, the Comte de Langeron) above all 'wished to experience and win a battle', and the firebrands of his entourage had been persuaded.

Among the doves stood the 'honest and grave' Prince Adam Czartoryski, Alexander's Polish Minister of Foreign Affairs. He felt strongly that the Tsar, sickly and subject to occasional fits bordering on epilepsy, should not have been with the army in the first place. 'He had never served; he could not know how to command . . . surrounded by young, giddy, ignorant, presumptuous men. . . .' Czartoryski recommended that the Allies should withdraw further north-eastwards into Silesia until Prussia entered the game. Equally cautious was Emperor Francis of Austria, at thirty-seven years old already prematurely old, with a complexion blotchy from good living and in his Habsburg eyes 'the look of the crowned conserver of the existing order'. Still shaken by Mack's downfall at Ulm, he also knew (many times over) what it was like to be mangled by Napoleon. Another dove was the sardonic Langeron, probably one of the smartest intellects in the Allied camp.

Most noteworthy of the doves, however, was Tolstoy's hero of *War and Peace*, General Mikhail Golenishchev Kutuzov. Already sixty, but with his greatest fame still seven years ahead of him, Kutuzov had fought in Poland and under the great Suvorov during the Turkish Wars. His character revealed a mass of typically Slav contradictions: he was in turn lazy and ambitious, ill-read and obtuse, but he had an earthy shrewdness, and combined extremes of refinement and coarse grossness. A tremendous drinker, he habitually travelled with three wenches in his baggage train, and on the eve of an important battle he would often summon all three. In his various defensive actions along the Danube, he had deserved far more credit than historians have given him. But, as a result of these earlier experiences, he had also derived the poorest opinion of Austrian generalship, which at Olmütz he made little attempt to hide. (The Russian dislike of their Austrian allies, lumped together with other Teutons as 'Germans',* come through in every line of *War and Peace*, often seeming to eclipse their hatred of the French. Typical of the Russian view is Prince Bolkonsky's contemptuous dismissal: 'Ever since the world began, everybody has beaten the Germans. But they never beat anybody. Only one another. He [Napoleon] made his reputation fighting them.')

In the Allied councils, Kutuzov urged a fighting withdrawal into the Carpathians, 'for the further we entice Napoleon, the weaker he will become'. It was very much the strategy that would present itself to him in 1812. In 1805, however, it was clear from the start that he did not enjoy the hawkish Tsar's confidence, who on one occasion told him curtly, 'That is none of your business', when the Commander-in-Chief had enquired about his operational intentions.

In their turn, the Austrians were full of mistrust for their blustering, semi-barbarian Russian ally who constantly reminded them that they had come to save the poor incompetent Habsburg Army. By 1 December – or 19 November in the Julian calendar of the Russians – relations were more strained than ever. Over the previous ten days twice that number of plans had been put forward; 'everybody had an opinion . . . and everybody expressed it'. But eventually the hawk party had triumphed, headed by the Tsar, whose lust for glory had been further seasoned by the arrival of a courier from St Petersburg who

---

* The Russian word for a German, *Nemyets*, originally signified any alien who spoke 'incomprehensibly and unclearly', the Germans being the first group of aliens to come to the Slav countries.

declared, 'All Russia is quivering with joy, Sire, at the thought of their beloved leader taking into his own hands the fate of the army. . . .'

So an offensive battle was decided upon for the following day, but not till after midnight (because of the still-raging arguments and counter-arguments) did the joint Allied staffs meet to receive their orders. Kutuzov, in disgust, had by now more or less washed his hands of the coming battle; as the baggage train with his ladies had got bogged down somewhere, he comforted himself by getting drunk instead ('hardly a good beginning to a battle', wrote that renowned puritan, Field-Marshal Montgomery of Alamein). During much of this crucial meeting he was half-, or completely, asleep – and many of the other participants were semi-comatose. Of all the generals present, says Langeron, only little Dokhturov even bothered to study the map.

The briefing was conducted by General Weyrother, the Austrian Chief-of-Staff, described as 'a veteran of the Viennese offices', who had become a hawk in opposition to his own Emperor. He was (or should have been) intimately acquainted with the terrain, as he had recently conducted manoeuvres over it, and it was his battle plan that had finally been accepted for the next day. In a boringly pedantic, Teutonic fashion Weyrother droned on, unfolding on the table (wrote Langeron):

> an immense and most accurate map of the environs of Brünn and Austerlitz, and read the dispositions to us in a loud tone and with a self-satisfied air which indicated a thorough persuasion of his own merit and of our incapacity. He was really like a college teacher reading a lesson to young students.

Weyrother's strategy was to fix Napoleon opposite the commanding Pratzen Heights (which Soult had abandoned with such apparent folly), and give the impression that he faced the main threat of a frontal attack there, by superior Allied weight of men. In fact, however, 55,000 men out of the total force of approximately 89,000 (under command of Buxhöwden) would be slipping southwards to smash into the French right flank between Telnitz and Sokolnitz. Once across the Goldbach brook and through the French defence, Buxhöwden's powerful spear-head would fan out to sever French lines of communication with Vienna, roll up the *Grande Armée* from the rear, and encircle it. This grandiose flanking manoeuvre was indeed a leaf borrowed from Napoleon's own book. While it was under way, the rest of the Russian line would be held defensively on the right by Bagration (13,700 men), and the Pratzen Heights in the centre by little more than the 10,000 élite troops of the Russian Imperial Guard, the sole reserve, under command of Grand Duke Constantine.

At this point only Langeron (on his own evidence, which may have been wisdom after the event) asked the key question: 'If the enemy forestalls us, and attacks us near Pratzen, what would we do?' Weyrother parried this by stressing Napoleon's weakness – 'If he has 40,000 men, that's putting it too high' – and therefore his inability to launch a dangerous attack himself. In addition to this crucial flaw in his 'Dispositions', Weyrother also erred in presuming that the Allied army could act in conformity and with speed, and – indeed – that the Russian commanders would be able to understand the orders given them. Apart from this, says a modern Sandhurst historian, Christopher Duffy, Weyrother's 'Dispositions' 'would gain high marks as an operational order in a military academy today . . . .'.[1]

Finally, after three hours' silence, Kutuzov emerged from his coma to break up the meeting with: 'There is nothing more important than to sleep well. Gentlemen, let us take some rest.' The die was cast.

From the vast Allied camp, six miles long, rose a mounting hum of activity. One Russian major expressed admiration for the apparent precision with which the Austrian staff moved such masses of troops – but it was not a view that would outlast the battle. The preparations, says Tolstoy in *War and Peace*, were like:

the first movement of the centre wheel of a great tower-clock. One wheel moved slowly, another set in motion, then a third, and wheels began to revolve faster and faster, levers and dogwheels to work, chimes to play, figures to pop out and the hands to advance in measured time, as a result of that activity.

How may one evaluate this new enemy Napoleon now faced? Under Tsar Paul I, and his brutal favourite, Alexei Arakcheev, the Russian Army was reckoned to have been 'set back by half a century'. Alexander had attempted reforms from his accession in 1801 onwards, but Arakcheev remained on for many a year; now Inspector General of the Artillery, he had been known to scalp his men by wrenching out their hair, and – on the long march from Russia – had personally sliced off several heads for 'insolence'. In sharp contrast to the French, the Russian soldiery was still driven on by fear and the lash of the knout; army service, as we have seen, had been reduced from life to twenty-five years, but during this time the soldier–serf hardly ever had leave,* so that a common social phenomenon in Russia was the 'soldier's wife' who became a part-time whore, raising children her husband knew nothing of. About the only way the soldier could escape was by such self-inflicted injuries as knocking out his front teeth, which were essential to tearing open the nineteenth-century musket cartridge.

The standard of the senior officers was perhaps typified, if not by Kutuzov, certainly more by his fellow army commander Buxhöwden, an Estonian German with the good sense to have married Catherine's illegitimate daughter, but described (by the Moravian parish priest on whom he was quartered) as being 'of very little education', and who 'carried about with him a train of hunting dogs, as well as other creatures which I shall not specify out of fear of offending the ears of decent people. The whole

---

* This harshness of service was not much modified even under the Soviet system; in the Second World War, Red Army soldiers often fought until killed or disabled, without ever returning home.

took up eleven coaches and as many carts . . .'. Probably the best of the Russian leaders was forty-year-old Prince Peter Bagration, normally taciturn and rather shy, but whose Georgian blood sometimes led to violent eruptions; he was fiery, utterly fearless, but also totally reliable, and an inspiring leader of men. Better than the average, too, were such column commanders as Lieutenant-Generals Dokhturov, Miloradovich and the French émigré Langeron. But, lower down, according to that critical British observer Major-General Wilson, the inadequacies 'of regimental officers is more felt in this army than in any other in Europe',[2] and, in the eyes of another British officer, they 'spent their time drinking, gambling or sleeping'.

As already noted, the Russian heavy cavalry were the best mounted of any army and were supported by swarms of irregular Cossacks; incredibly dextrous with their 14- to 18-foot lances, they were also highly indisciplined, equally happy when raping and plundering friendly peasants as when attacking the enemy. The artillery was numerically imposing: 'No other army moves with so many guns and with no other army is there a better state of equipment, or more gallantly served', Wilson was to write of the Russians in the 1806–7 campaigns, but in 1805 the standard Russian 'unicorn' was badly out-ranged by the French field-pieces, and the Commissariat so hopeless that batteries were constantly running out of ammunition; witness Tolstoy's superb account of the plight of the courageous little Captain Tushin. Clad in grey–green, the Russian infantryman was better camou-flaged than others, but he was miserably fed and equipped, with inferior muskets and a passion for bayonet-work, though as an Austrian ally uncharitably remarked, 'they are so clumsy that they never manage to catch anyone!'[3]

The greatest redeeming feature of Tsar Alexander's army, however, was the unquenchable courage and endurance – under every adversity – of the simple soldier, of all arms. As a French officer (Marbot) was to record of an episode in the 1807 campaign, 'our soldiers fired at the enemy at 25 paces but he

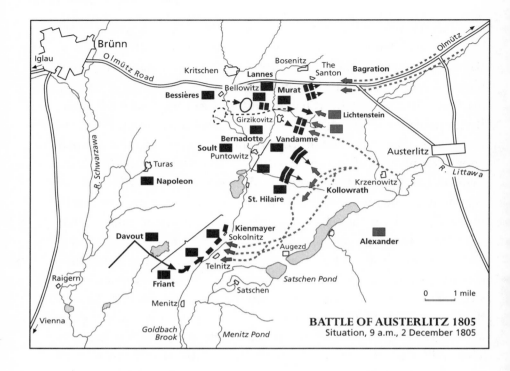

BATTLE OF AUSTERLITZ 1805
Situation, 9 a.m., 2 December 1805

continued to march without a sound'. On the eve of Austerlitz, the Russian forces were still exhausted and undernourished from their gruelling three months' march. Through the unwieldiness of their columns (each infantry regiment requiring some 50 wagons and 300 horses) much of their battle supplies had not yet arrived, which was one good reason why Kutuzov had wanted to avoid a major battle. Nevertheless, in their stolid way, morale was excellent. Says Tolstoy: 'nine-tenths of the men in the Russian army were at that moment in love . . . with their Tsar and the glory of Russian arms'.

The scene of Austerlitz remains today one of the most compact of all history's decisive battlefields, its salient features and their impact on the battle vividly evident. The terrain over which the gigantic clash was to take place was compressed into so small an area that the whole of it could have been seen by a high-flying eagle. From Brünn to Austerlitz was thirteen miles and the length of the front from north to south less than ten. There were few outstandingly striking features in the landscape. The Goldbach Brook and its tributary the Bosenitz, which divided the field, were marshy streams meandering roughly from north to south, hard to find on any map. Nothing overlooking the Goldbach could be termed more than a hillock, with the dominant Pratzen Heights standing at only 1,000 feet above sea level and rising less than 100 yards in a gentle slope out of the Goldbach valley. The north of the battlefield was bounded by the wooded hills of the so-called Moravian Mountains, in which it would be impossible to fight a battle of manoeuvre, thus providing an anchor to the line on both sides. Between them and the east–west Brünn to Olmütz highway there rose on the French side of the lines a mound some hundred feet high which the French nicknamed the Santon, whose curious shape reminded them of the pyramids they had seen in Egypt. It was to play a crucial part in Napoleon's plan of battle. South of the highway came the Pratzen Heights, now in Russian hands and commanding the whole battlefield; opposite across the valley, and less dominant, rose high ground between the hamlets of Bellowitz and Schlappanitz. Further southwards the hills dwindled, with the Goldbach weaving indeterminately between the villages of Kobelnitz, Sokolnitz – with its game park and pheasantry, enclosed in a low wall – and Telnitz; then it wended its way through boggy meadows containing a series of small shallow lakes or ponds that have since disappeared. Though the weather was thawing, making the ground muddy and slippery, the ponds were still frozen over.

These, in effect, were the essential features of the battlefield, Austerlitz itself being little more than a cluster of houses surrounding the charming small baroque Castle of the Counts of Kaunitz which had once entertained Empress Maria Theresa. Even today, nearly two centuries later, the geography remains remarkably unchanged. Only the scar of a new motorway now runs across its northern corner, severing the Santon from the

SCHLOSS AUSTERLITZ,
1995   *David Mynett*

Pratzen Heights. The lynchpin position of the Santon, still clearly defined like a miniature volcano, surprises one by its tiny size: it could have contained little more than a battery of guns. To the south, the shallow Menitz and Satschen ponds, which were to play so sinister and lethal a role in the final stages of the battle, have been filled in; there the military historian's imagination has to work. Otherwise, the villages are the same, only slightly expanded; the line of the tiny Goldbach is easily traceable by the line of poplars running along it; the gentle slopes of the Pratzen, now with a large monument atop it and covered with orchards, are clearly visible from all directions; the Schloss and its park walls at Sokolnitz are still there; and so is the small chapel on the southern slopes of the Pratzen from which Napoleon watched the last stages of his victory. But perhaps most striking of all is the panorama that unfolds below from the unsuspected eminence of Turan (now called Žuran). Marked only by a couple of trees, a tiny car park and a vandalized map table, it is at once obvious just what a brilliant choice it was for Napoleon's battle command post. From it everything is visible, as if laid out on a Sandhurst sand-table.

As early as 21 November, Napoleon (according to Ségur) had warned his officers, 'Gentlemen, examine this ground carefully;

it is going to be a battlefield; you will have a part to play upon it.' With his uncanny genius for the *coup d'oeil*, he had taken in all the features of the terrain, his gaze lingering particularly on the Pratzen Heights. As he explained two days before the battle:

> If I wanted to prevent the enemy from passing, it is there that I should post myself; but that would lead only to an ordinary battle and I want decisive success. If, on the other hand, I draw back my right towards Brünn and the Russians pass these heights, they are irretrievably ruined . . .

Over the next ten days Napoleon's plan was to evolve and be modified to meet shifts in the enemy dispositions, but its basic aim would be to invite the Allies to outflank him to the south. This, in turn, would involve the Allies in taking the risk of exposing their own flank on the Pratzen Heights as they swung southwards, a risk that Napoleon had endeavoured to make acceptable to them by his show of nervousness and his abandonment of the Heights.

The key was the Santon, which he intended to employ as a cornerstone in the battle and which, therefore, on no account should fall into enemy hands. Accordingly Lannes had been vigorously engaged in fortifying it, this activity promptly being interpreted by Weyrother and the hawks as proof that Napoleon was preparing to fight a defensive battle against a frontal attack at the north end of the line. Napoleon further aided them in the formulation of their battle plan by denuding his defences between Kobelnitz and Telnitz so as to leave an enticing hole there. Meanwhile, his main punch, a powerful concentration of 30,000 men consisting of Soult's Corps backed by Bernadotte and Bessières with the Guard, would be forming up behind the centre of the line – out of sight of enemy eyes and shielded by the familiar light cavalry screen posted across the Goldbach. Once the Allies had committed themselves to their flanking march, and had moved the bulk of their forces off the Pratzen Heights, Soult would smash through there, apparently the most unassailable point of the enemy line and hence where an attack would be least expected. If successful, he would then envelop from the rear the enemy columns, pressing them back against the Menitz and Satschen ponds. Having shattered this main body of the Allied army, Napoleon intended to swing northwards to trap Bagration's force, which Murat and Lannes would have been pinning down on the left of the line.

Like all Napoleon's major stratagems, it was superbly simple, but even more full of risk than normal. During the last days of November he had difficulty disguising his anxiety, which was, evidently, contagious. On that one evening he found three of his key marshals – Murat, Soult and Lannes – nervous and quarrelsome. Everything depended, still, on the Allies' willingness to conform to the plan he was imposing on them. Had Kutuzov been allowed to refuse battle, Napoleon would have found himself placed in the almost impossible predicament of having to withdraw sooner or later. As previously noted, however, the hawks had already done almost everything Napoleon required of them; admittedly, under the circumstances, it would have been difficult for them to reject the bait offered. Thus, while the Allies remained unaware of Napoleon's plan, Napoleon had the supreme advantage of knowing theirs and – remarks Field-Marshal Montgomery – 'knowing that it was bad, because he had forced it on them'.[4] Herein lay Napoleon's mastery as king among generals. Yet, even after Weyrother had taken Napoleon's bait, the French would still face the grave danger that their deliberately weakened right wing might indeed be pierced, bestowing success on the enemy plan. Here all depended on the arrival in time of Davout, whom Napoleon had kept off the stage (so as to reinforce his appearance of numerical weakness), and who was now hastening up from Vienna by rapid forced marches.

On the morning of 1 December, the French watched anxiously as the massive Allied formations manoeuvred across their front. The Russians 'stood in the open, and every here and there the green line of their infantry was interrupted by groups of stationary Cossacks and regiments of cavalry uniformed in white'. They were so close that one of Napoleon's own escort, a crack marksman, unsaddled with a single shot 'a Russian officer who had drawn our attention by the startling whiteness of his uniform'.

That afternoon, Napoleon carried out his final inspection of the *Grande Armée*. For the first time he was wearing, over the green, white and red uniform of a colonel of the Guard's *chasseurs à cheval*, the *redingote gris* which was to become a legend after Austerlitz. Ignoring the scruffy dress of his men, the piercing eye missed nothing when it came to inspecting weapons. He tasted and smelt the gunpowder with all the knowledgeability of the artillery expert, and nagged and rended defaulters: 'The tips of your flints must be rounded and set as the colonel ordered. . . . And you: what have you done with your scouring rod? . . . You've lost it? Admit it then, you fucker!' Few generals have ever used grosser language to the troops than Napoleon; the *grognards* feared it and loved it. Here the Emperor would pause to swap a coarse soldier's jest with a veteran whose face he recognized: there, to pinch the ear affectionately of another. It was a moment when that inexplicably magic touch sent morale soaring to the skies, as could no other great commander. 'Look how happy he is!' exclaimed Sergeant Coignet of the Guard, as Napoleon passed by. He managed to impart to his men a miraculous sense of immortality, and 'Even if one had to die, what did it matter? Death was beautiful in those days, so great, so splendid in its crimson cloak. It looked so much like hope . . . the very stuff of youth.'[5]

By nightfall on 1 December, Napoleon had made all his dispositions, placing most of the guns himself. The enemy continued to react as he wished, steadily shifting their forces southwards, and he revealed himself filled with confidence – almost too much. He had selected his battle headquarters up on the high ground near Bellowitz, where his sappers had constructed for him a sort of woodman's hut, and dictated his final orders to Berthier. In a proclamation to the *Grande Armée* he announced:

Soldiers:

The Russian army is presenting itself before you in order to avenge the Austrian army of Ulm. . . .

The positions we occupy are strong, and as they advance to turn my right, they will expose their flank to me.

Soldiers, I shall direct your battalions myself. I will hold myself far from the firing if, with your accustomed bravery, you carry disorder and confusion into the ranks of the enemy. But, if victory should for a moment be uncertain, you will see your Emperor expose himself to the first blows. . . .

As usual his speech ended with a reference to the distant arch-enemy:

we must defeat these hirelings of England, who are animated by so great a hatred for our nation.

This victory will end the campaign. . . .

NAPOLEON

As Jomini commented, 'Never in the history of the world has a leader of an army revealed his plan in this way to the whole of his forces.' It was taking a grave chance with security. Fortunately, however, the revealing proclamation* never fell into enemy hands – and, if it had, such was Weyrother's obsession with his own ploys it would probably have been ignored.

At dinner that night Napoleon was unusually relaxed and expansive. 'Entering the thatched cottage near by with us,' writes Ségur, 'he sat down gaily at table.' Silver candlesticks and goblets appeared from nowhere, and the fare was sumptuous, although the Emperor's favourite Chambertin suffered from

---

* There is, however, some doubt about its authenticity; it might have been fabricated or subsequently tampered with.

having been shaken up on the long marches. Jovially, Napoleon called on General Junot for the latest news from Paris. Junot reported that a porpoise had been seen in the Seine, but was promptly cut short: 'I expected you to tell me about the arts.' The conversation passed to the Opera, where Mozart's *Don Giovanni* had registered a great success, and thence to the theatre. Having castigated contemporary dramatists, the Emperor declaimed, 'Look at Corneille! What a creative force! He could have been a statesman!' From there the talk drifted back to war, with some of the wilder-eyed members of the Imperial entourage suggesting that the army should drive on to Constantinople. At this point, however, Napoleon's much wounded aide, General Mouton, interjected with a Cassandra-like note that broke up the party: 'My conscience obliges me to tell you that the army can do no more. If it were led still further, it would obey, but against its will. It is showing such fervour on the eve of battle only because it reckons on finishing tomorrow and returning home.'

This douche of cold water was not exactly what Napoleon wanted in such a moment of transitory euphoria. He broke off to visit the field hospital where, on the morrow, Surgeon-Major Baron Larrey (who, in contemporary portraits, looks like a curly-headed boy) would be operating up to his elbows in blood. Clausewitz was to reckon that, along with the shortcomings of Napoleon's food and supply system, neglect of medical requirements was among the most important factors in the ultimate destruction of the *Grande Armée*. Larrey, who by the end of his career would have been present at sixty battles, had striven to improve the prospects of the wounded by speeding treatment with 'flying hospitals', and had himself invented a rudimentary prototype of an evacuation ambulance. Yet between 1801 and 1804 the numbers of surgeons had actually been halved, and Napoleon was not exaggerating when he rashly declared, 'strictly speaking there is no medical corps'. Thus in 1805 the medical services, such as they were, were inadequate and demoralized, making Larrey's domain the least inspiring component of the *Grande Armée*.*

Although disease still carried off ten soldiers for every combat death, and the actual damage inflicted by the low-velocity musket ball was far less atrocious than that caused by HE shells in the First World War, or by the high-velocity conical bullet of today, the fate of the wounded in a Napoleonic battle was still a terrible one. Standing orders dictated that they were not to be removed from the line during the battle; yet within two hours from the start of it Larrey's field hospitals might already be full. For the wounded, piled on the straw-covered ground, amputation was the treatment most frequently administered by the ill-trained, brutal and sometimes drunken apothecaries. There was always a shortage of sedatives, so that most of the butchery would be performed with no more than a swig of brandy to deaden pain. Chances of recovery from surgery were roughly fifty-fifty. Without antibiotics, or even the 'wonder' sulfa drugs that revolutionized military surgery in the Second World War, the cleansing of wounds was largely left to the maggots (though, curiously enough, modern medicine is now apparently finding merits in this atavistic cure).

But if things were bad on the French side, they were infinitely worse across the lines; afraid of contagion, senior Austrian physicians would often avoid the field hospitals completely; and Russian standards were summed up by a remark made to the Tsar by the Cossack General-in-Chief Platow: 'God and your Majesty forbid; the fire of the enemy is not half as fatal as a drug.' The British observer, Wilson, was deeply shocked to hear a senior Russian officer declare (during the carnage at Friedland) that 'a cannon-ball was the best doctor for men without limbs'.

Shortly before midnight, an exhausted Davout rode up to

----

* But it would be quite wrong to deduce from the deficiencies of medical arrangements that Bonaparte was in fact taken by surprise by the enemy's advance, as have some historians.

Napoleon's headquarters. His men had covered 100 miles in two days. They were broken with fatigue, and still some distance away. Nevertheless Davout promised they would be in position by 8 a.m. the next morning; but only just. Napoleon was overjoyed, and went to his bivouac to sleep, contented that one of his major worries was overcome. It was after 11 p.m., and Napoleon's custom on the eve of battle was to bed down for a few hours, then rise before the dawn to issue final orders based on the latest possible information; but within an hour he was roused by an aide reporting heavy musketry fire in the direction of Telnitz. Napoleon set off promptly, and typically, on a personal reconnaissance. In the darkness, he narrowly escaped falling into the hands of a Cossack outpost (and then how the course of history would have been changed!), but what he saw persuaded him of two things. First, the main weight of the Allied army was being committed southwards, as he had hoped; secondly, it was moving a few miles further south than he had expected. The shift made the hole which Davout was to plug look that much more vulnerable. Swiftly Napoleon despatched fresh orders to Soult, slightly tilting the axis of his thrust towards the south, and detaching a force of 3,000 men to reinforce the defence of Telnitz, if necessary.

Meanwhile, on the Allied side an unhappy omen had taken place; during a last inspection the Tsar's horse had stumbled on a tussock and thrown its rider. The staff were also making heavy work on translating Weyrother's ponderous instructions into Russian, not even starting until 3 a.m., so that the battle would have begun before some of the commanding generals even received their orders.

On Napoleon's return from his reconnaissance, an extraordinary spontaneous demonstration took place. Suddenly an unknown Frenchman recalled that 2 December was the first anniversary of the Coronation. Cries of *'Vive l'Empereur!'* burst out through the camp, and excited soldiers began waving torches. Fire caught a pile of straw, and all at once the whole French camp turned into a mass of flame and wild enthusiasm. On the other side of the Goldbach, Allied sentinels gave the warning that the French were launching a night attack, and there was a brief moment of alarm. Napoleon himself was temporarily enraged by this breach of discipline. Yet the demonstration had also touched him and assured him, once and for all, of the unsurpassable morale of the *Grande Armée* on the eve of Austerlitz. As he finally returned to his bivouac towards 4 a.m. for what was left of the night, he was heard to admit, 'This is the finest evening of my life.'

As first light filtered through a heavy ground mist, 73,000 Frenchmen with 139 cannon faced 89,000 Allied troops (of which all but 15,700 were Russian) with 278 guns.* It was one of the heaviest concentrations seen in any battle of modern history to date. By 7 a.m. the higher hilltops were beginning to appear like islands floating in mid-air, with the mists shrinking down into the valleys in a milk-white sea. Above, there was a dark clear sky. Near Allied headquarters up at Krzenowitz, just west of Austerlitz itself, the two emperors were suddenly revealed to their troops riding side by side, the Austrian in a white uniform on a black charger, the Russian in a black uniform with white plumes in his hat and mounted on a bob-tailed chestnut. Kutuzov was there, looking worn and irritable and affecting a show of disengaged obsequiousness which little pleased his Tsar.

Shaking off the exhaustion and hunger with which the nine-teenth-century infantryman inevitably entered battle, thousands were on the move, formed up behind their different colours,

---

* Figures for the numbers involved at Austerlitz vary considerably from source to source. On both sides, a substantial number were infirm from the march, or *hors de combat* for one reason or another. One figure (Duffy) puts the actual French effectives at possibly no more than 60,000; while, according to the official French commentary after the battle, less than 50,000 fired a shot. Thus the numerical disparity between the two forces may have been even greater than it seemed on paper.

each 'with face newly washed and shaven and weapons cleaned and rubbed up to the final glitter'. Behind them, wrote Tolstoy:

> with measured hoof beats and the jingling of trappings, rode the cavalry, elegant in blue, red and green laced uniforms, mounted on black, roan or grey horses, bandsmen in front, their jackets covered with lace. Yonder, the artillery was crawling slowly into place between infantry and cavalry, the long line of polished shining cannon quivering on the gun-carriages.[6]

Further behind still bustled the busy staff officers in their grey cloaks, between the generals, their red necks squeezed into stiff collars, and the flamboyant pomaded officers of the Court of St Petersburg. Everywhere there was the clatter of hoofs and the rumble of gun-carriages, with an occasional sparkle as a bayonet caught the feeble sun on the heights. A testy exchange now took place between Kutuzov and Alexander, later immortalized by Tolstoy.[7] To Kutuzov's explanation of why the advance was not already under way, the Tsar retorted impatiently, 'But we are not on the Empress's Meadow, where we do not begin a parade until all the regiments are formed up!' to which came the crushing reply: 'Your Highness! If I have not begun, it is because we are not on parade, and not on the Empress's Meadow. However, if such be Your Highness's order . . .'.

With no show of enthusiasm, Kutuzov then gave the order to advance, and the vast bodies of men disappeared into the fog as they descended from the Pratzen Heights, heading southwards.

In command of the three Russian columns that constituted the massive and unwieldy flanking force was the unimpressive General Buxhöwden. Leading the advance guard, opposite Telnitz, was Kienmayer, a survivor of the Ulm débâcle, with 6,800 men – most of them Austrian. It was Kienmayer's premature fumblings, during the night, which had warned Napoleon that the enemy thrust was aiming further south than expected. Next came little General Dokhturov with 13,700 men and Langeron, full of scepticism for the Allied plan, with 11,700. Further north came the Pole, Prszebyszewski, with 7,800, and finally — the last to move off the Pratzen Heights — 23,000 men under the Austrian General Kollowrath and the florid-faced Russian Miloradovich.

In the valleys through which they were moving the fog was so dense it was impossible to see more than ten paces ahead. Bushes loomed up like gigantic trees, and level ground seemed like cliffs and slopes. Marching without any advance guard or proper liaison between units, some regiments of Kollowrath's column became horribly tangled together, and confusion reigned. To make matters considerably worse, Austrian Prince John of Lichtenstein (in command of the Allied cavalry) committed an appalling map-reading error. Instead of deploying opposite Murat at the north end of the line, his horses suddenly appeared three miles further south, cutting across the line of march of the three cumbersome great infantry columns. Commanders were enraged and the confidence of the troops shaken. Bitter reproaches passed between Austrian and Russian. Finally the situation was saved by Langeron grabbing Lichtenstein's bridle and turning him and his thousands of chafing cavalrymen sharply about. But, as it was, the disorder caused was to delay the unleashing of Buxhöwden's assault by one critical hour.

At about 7 a.m. the first blow in the battle was struck when Kienmayer's Austrians, eager to avenge Ulm and vindicate themselves in the eyes of their supercilious allies, hit the end of the French line at Telnitz. With Davout's III Corps still not yet in position, the whole of the danger area from Telnitz to Kobelnitz was held by General Legrand's thinly spread division of 6,000 men — upon which Buxhöwden's 55,000 troops were ponderously converging. Telnitz itself was covered by just the 3rd Regiment of the Line, plus a battalion of Corsicans who, most skilful marksmen, were cunningly concealed in broken ground and vineyards. As the mist cleared in patches, the Corsican *voltigeurs* picked off the Austrian Hussars with deadly accuracy.

What began with an attack by a few squadrons of cavalry now

escalated rapidly, with Kienmayer throwing in the Szekler Infantry Regiment, followed by the remainder of his foot battalions. The skirmishing surged back and forth, and within the first hour the Szeklers had lost two-thirds of their effectives. Then, at 8 a.m., an hour later than intended as a result of the disorder in the fog, Dokhturov's column appeared on the scene. The Russians pushed the 3rd of the Line out of Telnitz, and back across the Goldbach brook. Into the hole, Kienmayer threw his fourteen squadrons of cavalry. These were bravely resisted by small light cavalry units belonging to General Margaron, which Napoleon had detached from Soult's IV Corps in the final amendment to his orders. But they could not hold against such odds for long, and the line behind Telnitz buckled.

Meanwhile, further north at Sokolnitz (which lies to the west of the Goldbach) the situation was even graver. Here both Langeron and Prszebyszewski (known to the Tsar as 'the Pole with the unpronounceable name') with nearly 20,000 men were attacking together in overwhelming force. But, once again, because of Lichtenstein's blunder they were an hour late, and a further delay was caused when the vast Russian columns jammed the crossings of the Goldbach. But for these delays, it seems probable that the bolt holding the whole of Napoleon's vulnerable right wing might have been prised open. Somehow his last-minute change of orders was late in getting to Davout at Reigern Abbey, so that III Corps's vanguard under General Friant was already heading northwards for Kobelnitz. A galloping liaison officer from Soult overtook Friant, however, and turned him at the double towards the endangered Telnitz–Sokolnitz sector. The Allied delays enabled the 1st Brigade, led by Friant himself, to reach it just in time.

In the fog and the excitement of the moment, one of those unnecessary tragedies of war now struck the French. The hard-pressed 26th Light of Legrand's division suddenly saw the 108th Regiment from Friant's vanguard loom up on the other side of the Goldbach and, thinking it was the enemy, fired into them.

The 108th feared that their flank was being turned, and reeled backwards. The Allies were swift to profit from this disarray, and bit deeper into the French right wing. Fighting like a hero, General Friant himself rushed from one threatened battalion to another; but Langeron brought up thirty cannon and swept a hole through the thin French line. The odds were too great and thus, by 9 a.m., Dokhturov had taken Telnitz, Langeron was in Sokolnitz, and 'the unpronounceable Pole' in Sokolnitz Castle. From these bridgeheads across the Goldbach, the three powerful columns were preparing to debouch into the plain behind the French defences. At this end of the line, the day was beginning to look full of menace for Napoleon.

On the French side, various French commanders noted the uncanny hush with which the battle began. Shortly after dawn (according to Ségur), Napoleon said to his aides, 'And now gentlemen, let's go and do great things!' Moving up to his battle command post on the high ground by Bellowitz, he had all his thoughts concentrated on the Pratzen Heights, wreathed in mist just three miles to the south-east. He had already ridden nervously about for two hours, seeking signs to confirm the movement of the Allied forces, and was now waiting impatiently, his eyes trying to pierce the pervading mist. The behaviour of that mist was a vital ingredient of the master plan: if it dissipated too soon, the great mass of Soult's assault force, marshalled down in the Bosenitz valley at his feet, would be exposed to the enemy's gaze; if it lingered too long, Napoleon would be unable to judge when Buxhöwden had moved off the Pratzen, and whether the *moment juste* for the attack had arrived. But, as with his other reckonings, the fog factor had not been left to chance; in his detailed reconnoitring of the field over the previous days, Napoleon had duly observed the regularity with which the nocturnal mists filled the low land and were then slowly burnt off by the watery winter sun in the early morning.

Suddenly, behind the enemy lines, there appeared the great, red orb of the sun. It was now about 8 a.m. A few minutes more, and through the last wisps of vapour rising off the Pratzen Heights, Napoleon and his entourage could clearly see the enemy forces pouring 'like a torrent', southwards off the Heights. *'Le beau soleil d'Austerlitz!'* Whoever made that exclamation has also been lost in the mists of history, but it was to come to epitomize the Empire's summit of glory.

Short, bow-legged and supposedly with one foot slightly clubbed, thirty-six-year-old Nicolas Jean de Dieu Soult was the man of the moment. The son of a notary from the Midi, he had been captured with a broken leg by the Austrians in 1800, and received his *bâton* in 1804. Aptly nicknamed 'Iron Hand' by his troops and quite imperturbable, Soult was to gain at Austerlitz Napoleon's acclaim as 'Europe's first tactician'. 'How long will it take you to move your divisions to the top of the Pratzen Heights?' Napoleon now asked him. 'Less than twenty minutes, Sire,' Soult replied; 'for my troops are hidden at the foot of the valley, hidden by fog and campfire smoke.' 'In that case, we will wait a further quarter of an hour.'

Through his spyglass trained on the Pratzen, Napoleon watched attentively as Kollowrath and Miloradovich moved their columns off the vital plateau, leaving it almost empty. Then he gave the decisive order. 'One sharp blow and the war's over!' he declared in the hearing of Brigadier Thiébault. Hoarse voices shouted the command back and forth along the line, 200 drums beat the *pas de charge*. The 17,000 men of Soult's two divisions surged forward in the famous Napoleonic *ordre mixte*; skirmishers, then infantry battalions in both line and column, and the sombre blue batteries of gunners following up close behind.

Up on top of the Pratzen, Tsar Alexander I had been watching the departure of Buxhöwden's imposing force, when the hand of his Foreign Minister, Czartoryski, touched him respectfully on the arm: 'Look, Sire, at the brisk and purposeful march of those Frenchmen scaling the plateau. . . .'

'I see nothing else, *mon cher*! . . . What would you put their strength at? Two battalions? Three? Four?'

'Several regiments at least, Sire, if not several divisions. It's an attack by an army corps.'

'But they come out of a clear sky! How is it that we have had no warning?'

'Your Majesty should say rather that they come from hell. This cursed mist hid their troops from us.'

From that instant, says Thiers, the Tsar 'lost all the confidence which he had felt till then, and conceived a sinister presentiment which never left him during the engagement'.

After passing rapidly through a possibly dangerous Scylla-and-Charybdis bottleneck between Puntowitz and Girzikovitz, Soult's two divisions fanned out into two separate streams. On the right, St Hilaire (who had issued his troops a triple ration – almost half a pint – of the *Grande Armée*'s gut-rot brandy) swept like a tornado, on through the village of Pratzen (with explicit orders not to halt there) and up to the commanding knoll of Pratzeberg. Such was the total surprise of the attack that there was still little firing, most of the battle-noise being contributed by the drummers, the shouting of the company commanders and the untuneful bellowing of ribald marching songs. On the left, Vandamme's division was held up briefly by determined enemy resistance in Girzikovitz. But Dominique José Vandamme – brutal, violent, high-handed and renowned for his insubordination and (later) his looting (Napoleon once remarked to him, 'If I had two of you, the only solution would be to have one hang the other') – was a fighting divisional commander, one of the *Grand Armée*'s best. Wounded already, he threw his men at the Russian infantry with the bayonet, routed them, then overran their supporting artillery. In his impetus he then actually rushed past his objective, the Stari Vinobrady knoll on the Pratzen, which was held by five Russian battalions and artillery. He swiftly wheeled round and, in the teeth of heavy plunging fire, swarmed up the knoll, dislodged the Russians and seized their guns.

Vandamme had marched for half-an-hour, and fought for half-an-hour; St Hilaire had been in action for little more than twenty minutes in all. Before 9.30 a.m., Soult was master of the Pratzen Heights, the routed Allies falling back hastily in the direction of Austerlitz.

All this was observed by Kutuzov, with a mixture of detached gloom and vindication. It was *his* soldiers that were being hammered, but it was not his plan that was causing the defeat, although he had lacked the strength of will to have it altered. As soon as he had seen Soult's infantry emerging out of the mist in front, the old veteran had realized what was going to happen; Soult, in order-of-battle, would smash into the unguarded Allied flank while it was in order-of-march. Nothing but total disaster could ensue. As he stood there in silence, an enemy musket ball creased his cheek. He dabbed at the blood with a silk scarf, waving away the personal physician sent him by the Tsar, with the words: 'Thank the Emperor and tell him that my wound is not serious, but that the fatal wound is here,' pointing to the advancing French.*

* Tolstoy drew most of his historical material for Austerlitz from Mikhailovsky-Danilevsky's official account and generally with considerable fidelity, but here adds an interesting novelist's twist. In this memorable scene, in *War and Peace*, the physician is replaced by the fictional Prince Andrei, and it is to the fleeing *Russian* soldiers, not the French, that Kutuzov points.

NINE

'Soldiers, I Am Pleased With You'
2 December 1805

There is a movement in engagements when the least
manoeuvre is decisive and gives a victory; it is the one drop
of water which makes the vessel run over. . . .

Napoleon

WITH THE SURPRISE and devastating impetus of Soult's
attack, the scanty Allied force left on the Pratzen had collapsed
at once. Kutuzov bellowed to Miloradovich to form front with
the rear of his column still in the area, but only a few battalions
could be turned about in time. He then called on Grand Duke
Constantine to prepare to throw in the Imperial Guard, held in
reserve back at Krzenowitz. These were piecemeal remedies, and
Kutuzov has been sharply criticized for his 'indolence' in not
pulling back the main weight of Buxhöwden's force, so as to
retake the Pratzen and prevent the Allied armies being cut in
two. In this case, an orderly retreat could perhaps have been
made upon Austerlitz, and total catastrophe averted. Instead,
however, Kutuzov was 'content to parry the evil of which he
was an eyewitness'. However, in Kutuzov's defence, although
Napoleon's nimble army corps might have been capable of so
rapid a manoeuvre on such a grand scale, this was simply not
within the ponderous fighting style of the Russian Army, and
would almost certainly have only led to a multiplication of the
chaos of the early-morning approach marches. Meanwhile, the
actual author of the disastrous Allied plan, Weyrother, seems to
have maintained a curiously low profile; later, at the height of
the battle, he was to have his horse shot from under him.

Napoleon was swift to exploit his initial success in the centre. He ordered Soult to consolidate his gains on the Pratzen in anticipation of the inevitable counter-attack, while Bernadotte's I Corps was pushed forward in support. At forty-two the oldest of the corps commanders at Austerlitz, Bernadotte's height had earned him the nickname *Sergeant Belle-Jambe* in the 'Old Army'. With a Pyrenean's capacity for intrigue, he is generally reckoned to have been better cast as a king of Sweden (1818–44) than as a general, and was one of Napoleon's least aggressive commanders. By way of widening the breach, Bernadotte captured Blasowitz to the left of Soult's breakthrough, but a determined attack by two battalions of the Russian Imperial Guard promptly drove him out of it again.

Up to this point, the northern sector of the front had been relatively static. Clearly visible from Napoleon's command post at Turan, it formed a gentle slope of frozen fields, the flattest part of the battlefield and the only area suitable for a cavalry charge on a grand scale. By about 10 a.m., while there was a brief respite in the centre, the whole of the north erupted into violent combat. Napoleon had designated it as the secondary battle area, ordering the two Gascons who loathed each other – Murat and Lannes, the thirty-six-year-old former dyer's apprentice – simply to prevent Bagration, distinguished by his tenacity in attack and defence alike, from intervening in the main battle. Both Bagration and his opponent at Austerlitz, Lannes, were to be mortally wounded in battle: Bagration at Borodino, Lannes his leg shattered by a cannon-ball at Essling in 1809.

Bagration had started the day in a rage; he was receiving no detailed orders from Kutuzov or Weyrother, and Lichtenstein's cavalry who were supposed to be supporting him had strayed to the wrong end of the battlefield. Drawn by the noise of battle, it was on his initiative that the Imperial Guard retook Blasowitz. This in turn provoked Lannes to move his two infantry divisions forward, with the object of pushing Bagration away towards the north and widening the hole through which Murat's cavalry could then deploy. On the right was wooden-legged General Caffarelli's division, preceded at a steady jog-trot by the light cavalry of General Kellermann (son of the hero of Valmy), with the heavy cavalry of Nansouty and d'Hautpoul – Cuirassiers splendid in their red and gold tunics and armoured breastplates – in reserve at the rear. Prince John of Lichtenstein had in the meantime arrived, having had to make a detour round the Russian Guard to reach Bagration's left flank, and he promptly threw into the battle the first available cavalry units – the fearsome Uhlans of the Tsar's Imperial Guard.

So as to avoid being flung back on top of the advancing infantry, Kellermann cunningly withdrew his light horse, through the intervals between Caffarelli's battalions. The pursuing Uhlans were then caught on either flank by a withering musketry fire from the infantry squares – a favourite tactic of Napoleon's, taking advantage of a typical Russian error. 'Our cavalry, like the rest of our forces,' says Lieutenant-Colonel A. P. Ermolov (who was commanding a battery of horse-artillery in Lichtenstein's column, where he admitted to having understood but little of the Allied plan all day), 'acted largely on its own account, without any attempt at mutual support. And thus from one wing to another, our forces came into action by detachments, and one after another they were put into disorder. . . .' In the space of three minutes, Caffarelli's squares brought down 400 men, including the commanding general, and many horses. Kellermann, re-forming on a flank, now sliced into the Uhlans before they could mount a second charge on the infantry. To help them out, Lichtenstein sent in several squadrons of heavy dragoons, and a terrible, confused and steadily escalating cavalry battle now began. Back and forth the magnificent horsemen seethed, hacking and jabbing with sabres, thrusting with swords, dismounting to fire their short carbines into the mêlée, and inflicting hideous wounds on each other.

When Lichtenstein's cavalry dispersed, leaving the ground carpeted with dead and wounded, Caffarelli's division was seen to be still advancing steadily. But in the interval Bagration had brought up forty cannon which cut great swathes in the French infantry – one volley alone sweeping away all the drummers of Caffarelli's leading regiment. Lannes then galloped up every gun at his disposal and personally placed them; hatless, his curly hair matted with powder and grime, he disregarded pleas from his men to take cover. He had only fifteen cannon in all, but, with the mobility in which the French artillery excelled, each piece fired one deadly round, then moved before the superior enemy guns could bear on it. A murderous fugue of cannon-ball and grape-shot now took over from the earlier cavalry contest. During this cannonade, General Valhubert had his thigh smashed, but when his men wanted to carry him off the field he ordered them, 'Remain at your post; I shall know how to die all alone; six men must not be taken away for the sake of one.'

At about 10.30 a.m., the opposing infantry moved forward again. On the northern extremity of the line, Bagration tried to turn Lannes's flank by a vigorous attack on the Santon. This being the cornerstone of Napoleon's position, he had ordered its defenders under the steadfast General Suchet to die rather than relinquish it. Bagration's men captured the hamlet of Bosenitz and advanced some 450 yards, but were then halted by a combination of French skirmishing tactics, light cavalry and the dug-in Santon battery. At the other end of the sector, Lannes's infantry supported by Murat's heavy cavalry pushed back into Blasowitz in a bayonet charge which cost the life of its gallant commander, Colonel Casteix. As Caffarelli pressed forward beyond Blasowitz, Lichtenstein decided to launch an all-out cavalry attack to stop the French advance. Some forty squadrons, nearly 6,000 men, thundered forwards. Three times Caffarelli's footsoldiers beat off their attack. Then Murat with his usual *élan*, though outnumbered at that moment by almost two to one, threw in d'Hautpoul's and Nansouty's Cuirassiers. In the heaviest cavalry engagement so far that day, the two sets of 'horsemen cased in iron' met with a clash that could be heard far across the field, above the din of battle. For an instant the two lines seemed to stand still, but after about five minutes of slaughter the Allied squadrons broke and turned about. One regiment of Cuirassiers, beyond its General's control, followed too far in pursuit and in turn was nearly engulfed by the Allied cavalry. Hordes of riderless horses milled anarchically back and forth across the battlefield.

By midday, Lannes and Murat had won a praiseworthy, though still limited, success on the northern sector. Four thousand casualties had been inflicted, and as many prisoners taken – together with a large amount of booty belonging to Bagration's force. Bagration had been virtually excluded from joining the crucial battle in the centre, thus fulfilling Napoleon's intentions. However, his main body was still intact and would continue effectively to bar the road to Olmütz, down which Napoleon intended to sweep in the final, annihilating phase of his plan. Typically, it was Murat who sent the first message claiming success to the Emperor: 'Tell him . . . that my troops, together with those of Marshal Lannes, have succeeded in throwing Prince Bagration back towards Olmütz.' At the same time however, Bagration, still fuming at the absence of orders, was reporting to the Tsar: '. . . I have succeeded in keeping intact the whole of my army corps and we are only retreating foot by foot.'

At the other end of the front, the heavily outnumbered French were still fighting a critical and desperate defensive battle. But, good as his word, Davout was arriving with the main weight of his superb III Corps, after an eighty-seven-mile forced march that was a staggering feat by any standard. For the soldiers it had been a nightmare, with officers having to kick to their feet men who had had only five hours' rest out of the forty *en route*. Corporal Blaise records:

We left the village where we were lodging at nine in the evening. We marched until two in the morning when we halted in a wood. Then we lit some fires and slept until five when we

MARSHAL DAVOUT,
Duke of Auerstädt

FROM THE PORTRAIT BY TITO MARZOCCHI, AFTER CLAUDE GAUTHEROT, IN THE MUSEUM OF VERSAILLES.   ENGRAVED BY H. A. MÜLLER.

returned to the road. All day we marched and again camped in the woods; at 6 o'clock that evening we had not even had time to prepare our eagerly awaited soup when we were informed that we should be leaving again at nine. . . . Then, leaving our position, we marched on until 5 a.m. when the regiment halted. . . . The colonel, whose interest in our welfare had never flagged from the opening of the campaign, now gave us an abundance of wine. This rallied our strength. . . .

Halting that night (1 December) at 7 p.m., Blaise's unit was allowed a good night's sleep. Up at dawn the next morning, there was another long approach march before the footsore soldiers were thrown into a counter-attack at Telnitz – without support of the artillery, which was still lagging behind. Approaching the line, Blaise heard:

a most terrible fusillade which took place between the Russians and the 3rd Regiment of the Line, whose large number of wounded we came across. At that moment, we were made to double our step, which did not prevent me from eating the leg of a goose that I had on the top of my knapsack, well knowing I would scarcely have time during the battle. I was right; before ordering the charge, Marshal Davout, who did not leave us although the balls were beginning to bother us, reminded us of the Battle of Marianzelle [Mariazell]. General Heudelet placed himself at our head; we marched into battle very well until we were stopped near a ditch of such width that we could not cross it. General Heudelet ordered the Colonel to have us cross over a bridge to our left. . . .

In the confusion of crossing the Goldbach, Blaise and his fellows came under a devastating flank-fire from Kienmayer's Austrians, costing them many casualties. And so the battle raged back and forth; Telnitz was recaptured, but lost again by 9 a.m. General Friant, at fifty, one of the oldest veterans in the *Grande Armée*, was to have four horses killed under him before the day was done. At Sokolnitz the fighting was even more intense, with Langeron furiously flinging in every man and musket he could lay his hands on, from the Viborg, Perm, Kursk and 8th Jaeger Regiments. The ravaged village was defended largely by one French regiment, General Legrand's 26th Light, and it changed hands repeatedly. At one moment of close combat two French sergeant-majors were observed using the sanctified regimental Eagles like cudgels to defend themselves. What most assisted the embattled French was the continued jamming of the Goldbach bridges by the mass of Allied troops, which prevented the arrival of the vast reinforcements available to the incompetent Buxhöwden. But still they were outnumbered by some 35,000 Allies to less than 8,000 infantry effectives and 2,800 cavalry, for most of the morning.

It was fortunate for Napoleon that Davout was on the spot.

Aged only thirty-five, but prematurely bald, Louis Nicolas Davout (later Duke of Auerstädt and Prince of Eckmühl) was one of the few Napoleonic marshals to come from a noble though impoverished family, and had entered his father's old regiment, which initially slowed down his advancement. He was notably lacking in charm, and intolerant with civilians. Duchess Augusta of Saxe-Coburg-Saalfeld complained in 1809:

> Marshal Davout's visit has been got over; it was a weary business trying to enliven him, for it is impossible to be more stolid and uncommunicative than was this thoroughly unpleasant man. His face betrays that he can be very harsh and brutal though not specially spiteful, or intellectual. . . .

Very short-sighted, he wore special combat glasses fastening at the back of his head; because of the fog, however, myopia was a small disadvantage at Austerlitz that morning. But his men (even if not loving him) called him 'the Just', and they were invariably the best trained and most disciplined in the army. With a coldly agile mind, Davout was probably the ablest of Napoleon's marshals and the only one for whom Napoleon felt a certain jealousy, as a possible rival. Renowned for its clock-work administration and attention to detail, Davout's III Corps was a model formation, probably the finest in the world at that time.

Back and forth along his battered line Davout ran, ordering and exhorting, and regaining a few yards here and there. But the odds looked like proving too much. With one nervous eye constantly on Davout's predicament, Napoleon shortly before 10 a.m. ordered General Oudinot's grenadiers from the reserve to move south and bolster up the line.

By that time, however, the news of Soult's success in the centre was beginning to have its impact on the attacking Allied left. Langeron recounts graphically:

> Count Kamensky sent to tell me that the French had actually occupied the Pratzen Heights in strength, that he had made a

right-about turn with his brigade, that he had reascended the ridge and that he had very strong forces in front of him.

It was difficult for me to understand what had happened and how the enemy came to be behind us. . . .

The situation was little improved by Buxhöwden himself, apparently dead-drunk. Langeron thus left Sokolnitz and went to join Kamensky, on whose right he saw:

a few battalions who were faltering and appeared to be in retreat. . . . they were part of Kollowrath's Austrians who were withdrawing and were being pursued by the French.

It was eleven o'clock. . . .

Up on the Pratzen the expected Allied ripostes had materialized, creating a series of crises for Soult's spearhead. Whereas Vandamme, sabre in hand, had borne the brunt during the initial assault, it was now the turn of St Hilaire to his right. The slow start of Buxhöwden's infantry, caused by Lichtenstein's monumental error in the first phase, had in fact resulted in there being somewhat more enemy infantry left on the south-east slopes of the Pratzen than Napoleon had expected. St Hilaire thus found himself counter-attacked on three sides by the troops that Kutuzov was able to rally: on his right, by Kamensky's Russian brigade (from the tail of Langeron's column); to the front by Kollowrath's Austrians; and to the left by the Russian Imperial Guard. The main weight of the Allied effort descended on General Thiébault's brigade, on the bottom end of the French breakthrough and separated from its neighbour by Pratzen village. Having been told to expect no more than a chain of outposts, for nearly an hour Thiébault found that his three regiments – the 14th, 36th and 10th Light – were subjected to perhaps the fiercest pressure of the whole day. The 10th Light was first overrun by Kamensky's Russians, after suffering heavy casualties. The 36th, exposed to a murderous musketry and grape-shot fire at not more than thirty paces' range, tottered when its commanding officer was shot down. A brave sergeant-major, Adjutant Labadie, seized the colours and advanced towards the enemy shouting, 'Soldiers, here is your line of battle!' The line steadied, but (says Thiers) the three regiments 'would soon have sunk under a mass of cross-fires, had the conflict been prolonged'.

As it was, the divisional commander, St Hilaire, was already consulting Thiébault on whether they should withdraw, when Colonel Pouzet of the battered 10th Light interrupted with a roar of 'General, let us advance with the bayonet, or we are undone!' 'You are right, forward!' agreed St Hilaire, and with a violent last effort Thiébault's infantry managed to push back the attackers. In the time gained by this spirited bayonet charge, Soult, who had been watching Thiébault's predicament with disquiet, was able to gallop forward six 12-pounder cannon, the whole of the corps reserve artillery available. Soult himself came up to lay the guns. Thiébault, nicknamed 'the Butcher', ordered the gunners 'to aim for the men's belts and for the centre of the platoons, so that not a shot should be wasted . . .'.

Once his bayonet attack had expended itself, the guns 'abruptly unmasked right down the line, began one of the most destructive volleys ever made . . .', said Thiébault, describing the effect of Napoleon's *belles filles*. 'You can imagine how pleased I was when every discharge from my cannon opened great square holes in the enemy lines, and when their four regiments dispersed in mobs of fugitives.' Yet, in some of 'these terrible encounters, whole battalions of Russians got themselves killed without a single man leaving the ranks'.

Langeron himself now arrived to launch a fresh bayonet counter-attack in person against his countrymen. In the meantime, however, Thiébault had received valuable reinforcements in two fresh regiments sent up by Soult. In the absence of any orders from the drunken Buxhöwden, Langeron then took the initiative to return to Sokolnitz in order to bring back a large contingent to the Pratzen Heights. This action would take the

PRATZEN VILLAGE, 1995
David Mynett

pressure off Davout, but would be too late to save the Allied centre.

Meanwhile, on Vandamme's front nothing of comparable seriousness had occurred. The florid Miloradovich had thrown nine battalions against Stari Vinobrady knoll, but these were flung back within half an hour. Two of his generals were wounded, one of them captured. Mounted on a fine English horse, Miloradovich rushed back and forth across the battlefield conspicuously but ineffectively, drawing from Czartoryski the acid aside, 'Have you noticed how he never goes out of the Tsar's sight?' A second half-hearted effort was then jointly mounted by Kollowrath's Austrians and Miloradovich's Russians. This too was dispersed before noon, with the virtual destruction of two Russian regiments. Miloradovich reported to Kutuzov: 'now the cumulative effect of the catastrophic situation, their own exhaustion, the lack of cartridges . . . and the enemy fire which came in from every side, all made them give way in disorder'.

By midday, it was beginning to get bitterly cold – a reminder that the short winter's day was already more than halfway through. For the most of the combatants, all but a few square yards of the battlefield was obscured by the suffocating clouds of greyish-white smoke from the cannon, compounded by the dank mist undissipated in the still air. In isolated corners desperate episodes took place, invisible to the rest of the world, the cries of men were drowned out by the terrible din of guns and musketry, thundering cavalry and the sinister whirr of cannon-balls flying overhead. Many participants, seeing only the confused fringe of the fighting, may well have wondered afterwards, like Stendhal's Fabrizio (in *The Charterhouse of Parma*) at Waterloo, 'Was what he had seen a real battle?' Certainly only a privileged few could possess any idea of how the overall picture was developing. Yet, though the lines remained more or less static, and there was some savage fighting still ahead for Napoleon, a turning point in the battle had in fact been reached. Bagration had been neutralized in the north; the Allied counter-attacks had been repulsed in the centre, leaving most of the Pratzen firmly in Soult's hands; and on the French right flank Davout had managed (just) to hold out against the worst of the enemy encirclement thrust.

So far the battle had developed closely along the lines Napoleon had dictated; or, as he said with little modesty, 'as if both armies were performing manoeuvres under my direction'. Perhaps the most dangerous single moment had been when Thiébault's brigade wavered momentarily. If the Allied counter-attack here had been better co-ordinated and more forceful, Napoleon's gamble might have been thwarted. One French writer, Claude Manceron, considers that the true turning point at Austerlitz, that decisive 'one drop of water', had been Colonel Pouzet's plea to General St Hilaire to attack *à la baionnette*, instead of withdrawing.

By 11.30 a.m. on 2 December, Napoleon had moved his headquarters forward on to the Pratzen. Soon afterwards he estimated the time had come to launch the decisive phase of the battle. Accordingly he ordered Soult's corps to begin a quarter turn to the right, bringing them to bear against the flank and rear of Buxhöwden's force. The gap created on the Pratzen was to be filled by Bernadotte's I Corps, withdrawn from its fight with Bagration and instructed to sweep the defenders remaining in the centre back towards Austerlitz. Simultaneously Davout was to go over to the offensive against Buxhöwden. There were, however, still no fresh orders for Lannes and Murat on the left.

In the centre, only one obstacle now stood between Napoleon and success; the superlative cavalry and footsoldiers of the Russian Imperial Guard, which had started the day 10,000 strong under Grand Duke Constantine. Younger brother of the Tsar, but lacking his grave good looks, Constantine is described as possessing 'a face all bumps, the hands of a gorilla, the gait of a peasant'. He was a Dostoevskian figure whose life apparently alternated between bouts of wild debauchery and religious atonement, and it was rumoured that he had strangled valets who displeased him. He revelled in the danger of battle, and the men he now led in one last desperate effort were hardly matched even by their French counterparts. All giants over six feet tall, magnificent in white and green uniforms, these were the men who guarded the Tsar (and occasionally deposed him) and they were brave to a fault.

It was on the division of the pugnacious Vandamme that Constantine's blow fell. At the time, Vandamme himself was sitting on an upturned cart, having his wounds dressed; his division had, so far, had a relatively easy time and had just dispersed Miloradovich's battalions. Over-eager, however, to get at the French after a morning of frustrating inaction, the Semenovsky and Preobrazhensky foot regiments started their bayonet charge at a distance of 300 paces, reaching the enemy line badly out of breath. Nevertheless, the tremendous Russian impetus overwhelmed the first ranks of Vandamme's 4th of the Line, and Constantine's foot guardsmen – their ranks cruelly thinned – withdrew in good order towards Krzenowitz. At this moment, Vandamme received Napoleon's order and began to perform his right turn. This momentarily left the 4th and 24th out on a limb, because Bernadotte – who was certainly never one of Napoleon's fastest moving commanders, being usually more concerned with the integrity of his own corps than the fate of the rest of the army – was still lagging behind. (Ségur, sent by Napoleon to activate Bernadotte, found him 'disturbed and anxious. He had told his troops to be calm, but he was setting a pretty bad example.')[1] The 4th had also apparently yielded to the temptation to pursue the retreating guardsmen, and suddenly Constantine, waiting with the impatiently snorting cavalry of the Guard, saw an opportunity that was not to be missed.

On the other side of the lines, Jean-Baptiste Bessières, commander of the French Imperial Guard and the last officer still wearing his hair powdered and in a queue in the old fashion, had also been chafing at the bit all day. Observing Vandamme's regiments in front of him with an expert eye, he remarked to his aide, 'Laville, we are going to have a cavalry engagement.' Asked later how he knew, the experienced Bessières replied, 'Because the retreating soldiers kept looking back. When infantry retires before infantry they never turn their heads.'*

His diagnosis proved correct. Six squadrons of heavy cavalry, led by Constantine himself, shouting 'For God, the Tsar and Russia', had charged into the open flank of Vandamme's isolated regiments. With ear-splitting Slav war-cries of 'Hurrah! Hurrah!', their sabres rising and falling, the Imperial Guard hit the 4th and 24th completely by surprise and with terrible force. At the same time, the retreating Russian footguards had turned about and attacked the shaken French regiments again

---

* In his thought-provoking book, *The Face of Battle*, John Keegan appends a note on Waterloo that may well throw additional light on this particular episode at Austerlitz; it was, he claims, always the men at the *rear* of formations who broke and ran before those at the front – for the simple reason that the latter could not, trapped as they were between the attacking enemy and the ranks behind them.

frontally. In the ensuing shambles, a colour-bearer of the 4th of the Line had been killed. Trying to save the eagle, a subaltern was killed in turn; an NCO had snatched it out of his dying grasp, but he too was struck down and the eagle was borne off triumphantly by the Russian Guard. With its commanding officer and ten other officers killed, and some 200 men sabred, the battalion broke. According to Ségur, it 'got up to flee at full speed', and then;

> almost passed ourselves and Napoleon himself — our attempts to arrest it being all in vain. The unfortunate fellows were quite distracted with fear and would listen to no one; in reply to our reproaches . . . they shouted mechanically, 'Vive l'Empereur!' while fleeing faster than ever.

At Napoleon's side, the ever-present Berthier — his vision perhaps distorted by earlier successes — misinterpreted the scene, and remarked to Napoleon: 'What a splendid crowd of prisoners they are bringing back for you!' The first reverse of this kind all day, it was fortunate for Napoleon that, coming so late in the battle, there were no longer any Allied reserves capable of exploiting it. Calmly he gave Bessières the order he had been awaiting all too long: 'Take the cavalry of my Guard forward to support those brave fellows.'

Bessières, however, always economical with the lives of his valuable élite, at first sent in only two squadrons of *chasseurs-à-cheval* under Colonel Morland, renowned for his moustaches and for being one of the army's best horsemen. The Imperial entourage were shocked to watch the green-clad *chasseurs* beaten back by the Russian Horse Guards. Bessières next sent in three more squadrons of the legendary *grosses-bottes* (*grenadiers-à-cheval*), their great red plumes tossing angrily as they trotted forward. They were supported by the horse artillery of the Guard, who 'dashed to the front at a gallop, unlimbered within 550 yards of the enemy, and proceeded to tear with extreme rapidity a hole in the opposing battle formation with case-shot'.[2] Meanwhile

Bernadotte's line infantry were also at last reaching the scene, but still the Russian Imperial Guard fought back like madmen. Having seen enough of this slaughter, Napoleon now decided to administer the *coup de grâce*. 'They are in disorder yonder; that must be set to rights,' he told one of his aides, the Alsatian Brigadier-General Rapp, despatching him with two fresh squadrons of *chasseurs* and one of ferocious scimitar-wielding Mamelukes.

Disregarding the concentrated volleys of grape-shot, Rapp and his squadrons broke through the first line of the Russian Imperial Guard. Then Rapp discovered his impetus had carried him too far – an ever-present hazard in a cavalry engagement. Wounded twice by minor sword thrusts, he was surrounded by the Russian Horse Guards headed by their Colonel, Prince Repnin. But, with 500 men lying dead on the field, the magnificent Russian Imperial Guard had shot its bolt and the tide abruptly turned. In Rapp's graphic report: 'The Russians fled the field and disbanded. The guns, baggage, and Prince Repnin were all in our hands. With my broken sabre and covered with blood, I went to give an account of the affair to the Emperor.' Riding with his Mamelukes, Napoleon's own Egyptian servant, Roustam, returned with a Russian standard and offered to bring back the Emperor Constantine's head as well, a suggestion for which he was harshly censured as 'a ghastly savage'. Looking at the flower of the Russian aristocracy, which lay scattered across the Pratzen in bloodstained green and white heaps, Napoleon remarked, 'Many fine ladies will weep tomorrow in St Petersburg!' Losses of the French Guard in the ferocious mêlée had been comparatively light; they included, however, the gallant Colonel Morland, brought back mortally wounded.* The Allied centre had ceased

---

* Morland's death had a rather gruesome sequel; his viscera were buried ceremoniously in Brünn after the battle, the rest of his body being shipped back to the Invalides, embalmed by Larrey in a barrel of rum. When this was opened, it was discovered that Morland's famous moustaches, continuing to grow, now reached down to his knees!

to exist. Finding himself abandoned by the infantry regiment, to which his battery of guns was attached, Lieutenant-Colonel Ermolov describes how he 'extricated one gun from the press of our own cavalry, but we were able to get off only a few rounds before the enemy captured the piece. My men were cut down in the process and I myself was taken prisoner.' Escaping back to his division that was 'milling about in disorder', he passed an all-but deserted Tsar, his features 'lined with deep sorrow, and his eyes . . . full of tears'.

Swiftly assessing the situation, Napoleon declared exultantly, 'It only remains to reap the reward of our plans. . . . Forward against the enemy left.'

It was shortly after 1.30 p.m. that Napoleon swung the weight of the *Grande Armée*, more than 25,000 men, southwards, off the Pratzen to trap and annihilate Buxhöwden. The battle began to move at lightning speed. Within an hour Vandamme, now holding the left corner of the enveloping net, was at Augezd; thereby blocking any escape route eastwards, except across the more or less impassable bogs of the River Littawa. Next to him came St Hilaire, a sling supporting an arm broken in three places, thrusting down the east bank of the Goldbach. His men, sorely fatigued but still full of battle now that victory was in sight, were backed up by the Grenadiers from Oudinot's division; a general whose favourite party game was shooting out candles, but who had been only briefly in action that day.* Beyond the Goldbach, Friant, whose stoical defence action throughout the morning had cost him over 300 dead and 1,700 wounded, was already recapturing Sokolnitz, where the 'corpses were heaped up on one another, and it was almost impossible to ride across the tangle of weapons and broken human bodies'.³ Pinching the enemy up against St Hilaire, all along his sector the dependable

---

* Already wounded in the campaign, Oudinot was to become Napoleon's most battered marshal, collecting thirty-four wounds in his service; nevertheless, he lived to the age of eighty.

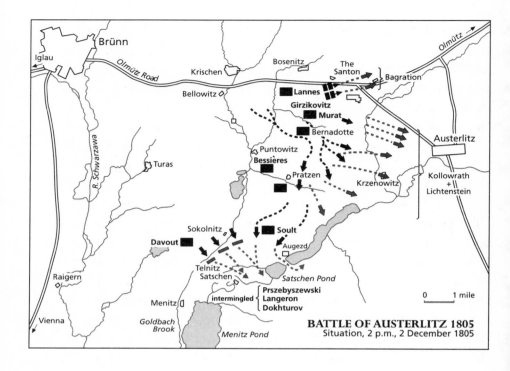

Davout had switched over to the offensive (though with some bitterness as it was clear that, while his corps had had the dirtiest work to do that day, Soult was going to carry off the laurels). His instructions were simply, 'Let not one escape.' Thus, remorselessly, the French net closed in on three sides, pushing Buxhöwden back up against the Satschen and Menitz ponds on the fourth. In the mounting ferocity of the battles little quarter was given. General Thiébault, whose brigade had suffered so heavily earlier on, records, 'Up to the last hour of the battle, we took no prisoners, it would not do to run any risk; one could stick at nothing, and thus not a single living enemy remained to our rear.'

On the Allied side, the confusion inside the net was unimaginable. A savage exchange took place between Langeron and Buxhöwden. When Langeron asked angrily why he had not yet ordered his three columns to retreat out of the trap, the Russian commander mumbled, 'Are you forgetting that I have taken Telnitz and that I still hold it?'

'Telnitz, but that's ancient history! . . . We now have the French at our backs, do you hear? At our backs! We are being taken in the rear!'

'*Mon cher ami*, you see nothing but enemies everywhere!'

'And you, *monsieur le comte*, are no longer in a state to see them anywhere!'

Before Buxhöwden could react to this deadly insult, a liaison officer from Kutuzov arrived bringing orders to withdraw. They had, apparently, been issued three hours earlier. As Langeron turned on his heel, he remarked to an Austrian officer, 'The rout has begun!'

From behind the pheasantry walls at Sokolnitz, Przebyszewski fought a desperate last stand, with the Russian gunners firing at such close range that they scorched the uniforms of the attacking French. Trapped, the gallant Przebyszewski later reported to the Tsar that, after eight hours in action:

> One of my subordinate commanders had been killed, another wounded, and the rest were reduced to confusion by the vicious salvoes of canister which came in from three sides. . . . we had no hope of support. With all this, we fought on against the enemy to the limit of our strength, according to the loyalty we owe Your Imperial Highness.

Two French officers, General Lochet and Colonel Franceschi of the Hussars, raced each other to take the sword of 'the Pole with the unpronounceable name'. At the bottom of the net and with his back to the ponds, Dokhturov courageously formed his remaining 5,000 men into three lines – cavalry in front, artillery in the second line and infantry behind – and then counter-attacked while Cossacks hastily reconnoitred an escape route between the ponds.

Dokhturov's stubborn last-ditch effort˙ sent Napoleon, who had moved up for the kill, into his first rage that day. He had just received word from the other end of the field that Murat and Lannes were, unaccountably, sitting still and doing nothing. A fine drizzle was falling and low clouds had brought nightfall closer. All of a sudden, victory seemed to be dwindling before his eyes. Peevishly he accused Soult's corps of being 'too slack': 'That's dreadfully slack! The Dragoons weren't thrown in wholeheartedly! It's inconceivable to press home a decisive charge so feebly.' Soult protested that the Russian artillery was 'still impressive'. Further enraged, Napoleon berated a returning Dragoon colonel, 'Tell the General who commands you, on my behalf, that he is nothing but a coward!' Then, changing his mind, Napoleon despatched another of his aides, General Gardanne, to lead the chastened Dragoons back into battle himself, with the instructions, 'Clear all those Russian pieces within twenty minutes. And break those people's last squares for me.'

Collapsing before the renewed French onslaught, Dokhturov's and Langeron's survivors became the victims of a tragic and dreadful finale. Although Kienmayer, the survivor of Ulm, had managed to lead his Austrians back between the ponds in reasonably good order after a courageous fighting withdrawal, the Russian reconnaissance squadrons were unable to find a negotiable route. Thus, in their despair, some of the fugitives tried to set off across the ice itself. When it seemed that it would hold up under the weight of even a gun carriage, cavalry, infantry and artillery piled up in their hundreds, trying to get across the ponds. Napoleon promptly ordered twenty-five cannon to fire red-hot balls into the panic-stricken mass. As a result of the thaw of the preceding days, the ice was already weaker than it looked. The combined effect of the cannon-balls and the Allied gun teams caused the ice to crack and break up in great slabs, cascading horses, guns and infantrymen into the chilly waters. And still the murderous red-hot iron kept falling among them in the semi-darkness.

When the guns ceased firing, 2,000 half-naked Russian prisoners were fished out of the ponds. In his bulletin after the battle, Napoleon claimed that 20,000 men had been drowned in this final catastrophe, but he seems to have been wildly exaggerating. Later, thirty-eight guns and the corpses of 130 horses were recovered from the shallow water, and probably human deaths amounted to at most 2,000.* Nevertheless, it was a frightful humiliation to be inflicted on so mighty and once proud an army. Most of the Russian cannon that were not lost in the ponds became stuck up to their axles in the boggy ground, and were left behind. Only a few groups of dispirited stragglers managed to escape through holes in Napoleon's net. Among them was the defeated and befuddled Russian commander, Buxhöwden; hatless, his uniform in disarray, he declared that he had been 'abandoned' and 'sacrificed'. 'I had previously seen some lost battles,' commented Langeron; 'but I had no conception of such a defeat.'

The only part of the whole Allied array which had remained relatively intact was Bagration's corps, on what seemed to have become the forgotten sector. Having effectively isolated Bagration from the main battle, shortly after midday, Murat, Lannes and Bernadotte had remained curiously inactive. At one point the Russians had come close to overrunning Suchet's division, many of them young recruits, in front of the Santon, but by 3 p.m. Bagration, who had received a slight wound in the thigh, had set in motion an orderly withdrawal down the Olmütz highway. He was, in fact, covering the getaway of the two defeated emperors and the forces remaining to them. Observing this, General Caffarelli, his uniform in shreds and begrimed with mud and powder stains, rode up to Lannes for further orders. But Lannes passed the buck: 'Go and see Murat. . . . You know very well I

---

* The grossly inflated figure of 20,000 drowned was probably another example of Napoleon's use of terror-propaganda in his bulletins. The figure of 2,000 comes from Thiers and others; some authorities put it as low, while the official Austrian history claims that 'just two men and a few horses' were found when the ponds were subsequently drained. An instructive exercise in the unreliability of computing war casualties.

am under his orders.' By the time he reached Murat's headquarters, Caffarelli was in a seething rage and demanded, 'Where
the bloody hell is Murat?' It appeared that Murat had ridden out
on reconnaissance, so Caffarelli was led to his Chief-of-Staff,
General Belliard, to whom he shouted, 'I have taken Krzenowitz,
where the enemy left me three cannon! Our skirmishers have
already crossed the stream and are spreading out to the rear of
the hills. . . . Think of it! I might have laid hands on the
emperors' carriages. . . .'

Trying to calm down the enraged divisional commander,
Belliard remarked that it was as well that Murat was absent,
otherwise Caffarelli would probably have ended the battle in
close arrest, then added bitterly, 'We have received one explicit
order, just one since noon, for the Emperor has lost interest in
us, it would seem. . . .' That order had been simply to preserve
communications along the routes between Brünn and Olmütz.
Yet, at the same time that Murat and Lannes were fretting for
want of orders, Napoleon had worked himself into a fury at their
passivity. Clearly it had been his original intention that, once
Soult had broken through in the centre and the enveloping
manoeuvre to the right was successfully under way, Murat was
to perform a similar sweep round the rear of Bagration. But by
4.30 p.m., when the firing had begun to die down in the north
and it was too dark to attempt such an ambitious cavalry action,
Murat had still not moved. In any event, Bagration had pulled
his hard-fighting corps back out of the trap, actually moving it
unimpeded across the front of the sluggish Bernadotte's I Corps,
which was battered but still in good order. His withdrawal was
to cheat Napoleon of the total victory he dreamed of.

What had gone wrong? There are various contributory expla-
nations, but a certain mystery remains. Lannes' infantry comprised a high proportion of inexperienced conscripts, which
slowed down his advance; Bernadotte's supporting corps had also
lagged, as already noted. Dispositions in the north had been
somewhat thrown off balance by Napoleon's last-minute tilting

of Soult's axis of attack southwards, and he had undoubtedly erred in not transmitting specific orders to Murat. But why? Had Napoleon allowed his attention to become so focused on Soult's and Davout's operations that he had, as Lannes and Murat felt, 'lost interest' in them? It seems out of character. Or had he, in fact, decided to keep Murat's cavalry in hand to the last minute, just in case any unexpected reverse (like the riposte of the Russian Imperial Guard) should upset the fine balance of success on the primary battlefield? Or did he simply assume that the dashing Murat, so apt to act on his own initiative anyway, knew what to do without further interference? This might well be the most plausible explanation. At the same time, to account for Murat's own reluctance to move, one must remember that already twice in the campaign (once before Ulm and once at Vienna) he had received the most savage upbraidings of his career – for using his own initiative, and blundering. So, quite possibly, in this last phase of his terrifying brother-in-law's greatest triumph, Murat was simply playing safe. On the other hand, some modern historians (Lombarès and Duffy)[4] hold that not nearly enough justice has been accorded to the *active* part played by Bagration's sturdy fight in spoiling the totality of Napoleon's victory, and here Tolstoy's fictionalized account is held in part culprit.

By 5 p.m. the guns were silent throughout the trampled, torn battlefield. Darkness and a flurry of snow blanketed the scenes of death and anguish. Napoleon had kept his promise of not exposing himself to danger that day, and had run about among his troops less than in any other battle he fought; he had not needed to, because – bar a few jarring setbacks – his battle plan, once set in motion, had proceeded so smoothly as to require little interference from on high. He had been able to stand there on his hilltop, coolly and detachedly pulling the strings. Throughout the battle, claimed a Prussian observer, Freiherr von Wolzogen, 'the stormy calm of his face hardly altered a second'.[5]

It was otherwise with the Russian Emperor. Shortly after the shock of Soult's men appearing on the Pratzen Heights, Alexander had become separated from Kutuzov, and his own entourage had gradually dissipated, until he was apparently left with no one but his English physician, James Wylie, two aides and two Cossacks. Totally out of touch with the course of the battle that he had so much desired, he had however not left the danger zone until the end, and at one point was covered with earth from a cannon-ball falling directly in front of him. During the final débâcle, he was found by an astonished Russian staff officer, Major Toll, dismounted and apparently feeling unwell. When Toll tried to comfort the crestfallen young Tsar, seated under an apple tree, he burst into tears (a scene which Tolstoy, in *War and Peace*, has young Nikholai Rostov witnessing). That night he spent as a refugee, collapsed on a pile of straw in a peasant's hut, several miles from the scene of defeat.

As so often, estimates of the casualties at Austerlitz differ. The French dead probably numbered at most 2,000, at lowest 1,300, with just under 7,000 wounded and 573 taken prisoner. But losses in individual units varied radically, according to their role that day. In St Hilaire's division, Thiébault's 36th of the Line had lost the grim total of 220 grenadiers out of 230; with Friant, Corporal Blaise's unit alone had lost four captains, two lieutenants and seventy men killed, while two toes smashed by a spent ball had retired Blaise himself from the fray, and excused him from more of the marching he so detested. On the other hand, the Foot Guard 'cried with rage' (in the words of the official Bulletin), because they had not been engaged at all that day, and had therefore suffered no casualties. By Thiers's reckoning, fewer than 45,000 troops could in fact be said to have fought that day, because of the inaction of the Foot Guard and Bernadotte's Corps. 'Thus 45,000 French had beaten 90,000 Austro-Russians.'

On the Allied side, losses seem to have numbered approximately 15,000 killed and wounded, of which 11,000 were Russians. Another 12,000 Allied troops were taken prisoner, making a total of 27,000, against fewer than 9,000 French.

Thousands more of the defeated were, however, to succumb in a typhus epidemic that followed the battle. Among the vast booty captured, there were also 180 guns and 45 flags.

As Napoleon roamed the battlefield that evening, praising his men and administering brandy and encouragement to the wounded — the fate of the abandoned Russians, with many having their wounds left untended for forty-eight hours, being particularly atrocious — he was stopped short by the ranting of a wounded Russian major, hardly more than a boy, who called out, 'Sire, have me shot. I am not worthy to live, I lost all my artillery!'

'Calm yourself, young man,' replied Napoleon. 'One may be beaten by my army without dishonour.'

The following day he despatched a triumphant order to the *Grande Armée*:

Soldiers, I am pleased with you. You have, on the day of Austerlitz, fulfilled all I expected of your intrepidity; you have decorated your eagles with an immortal glory. An army of 100,000 men, commanded by the Emperors of Russia and Austria, has, in less than four hours, been either cut up or dispersed. Those who escaped your steel have been drowned in the lakes. . . . Thus, in two months, this Third Coalition has been conquered and dissolved. Peace can no longer be far off.

. . . My people will greet you with joy, and it will be enough for you to say; '*J'étais à la bataille d'Austerlitz,*' for them to reply, '*Voilà un brave!*'

He closed his official Bulletin with bitter words, showing he had still not forgotten that other enemy he had faced so menacingly little more than three months previously: 'May the cowardly oligarchs of London suffer the penalty of so many evils!'

To Josephine he wrote in rather less grandiloquent terms:

. . . I have defeated the Russian and Austrian army commanded by the two Emperors. I am a little tired; I have been camping in the open for eight days and as many freezing nights. I shall rest tomorrow at the château of the Princes of Kaunitz where I count on sleeping for two or three hours. The Russian army is not only beaten, but destroyed. I embrace you. Napoleon.

The Empress appears, however, not to have been sufficiently impressed, for Napoleon was sending a somewhat acid follow-up two weeks later:

Mighty Empress, I have had not one single line from you since you left Strasbourg. You have passed through Baden, Stuttgart and Munich, without writing me one word. That is not very nice, not very loving. . . . Deign from the height of your splendours to take a little notice of your slave. . . .

It seemed an incongruous tone to be adopted by the mogul who had just won one of history's most remarkable victories.

From the other side, the fugitive Emperor Francis wrote to his wife what must have been the understatement of the age: 'A battle was fought today which did not turn out very well.' For his part, Kutuzov's report somehow managed to make Austerlitz sound almost like a Russian victory.

Inevitably the defeat had created a coolness between the two Allied emperors. Tsar Alexander pulled out with the remnants of his army to avoid an undignified pursuit, leaving Francis to cover his retreat, negotiate with the enemy and defray the expenses of defeat. Abandoning stragglers and wounded, he would be in Hungary in four days, back in Russia in ten. On 3 December, Prince John of Lichtenstein was sent to Napoleon to request an interview for his Emperor, which — without being hurried — Napoleon agreed to the following day. With all the courtesy of an almost bygone age and wearing his first clean shirt in eight days, Napoleon received Francis in a humble dwelling, apologizing wryly: 'Such are the palaces which your Majesty has obliged me to inhabit for these three months.'

'Your stay in them makes you so vigorous, that you have no

right to be angry with me for it,' replied the Austrian. An armistice was swiftly concluded, and General Savary hastened after Alexander to bring him the news.

The Tsar admitted to Savary, 'Your master has shown himself very great. I acknowledge all the power of his genius, and, as for myself, I shall retire, since my ally is satisfied.' Savary then gave a discourse on the battle, explaining the reasons for the French victory and adding, rather patronizingly (says Thiers), 'that with experience Alexander, in his turn, would become a warrior, but that so difficult an art was not to be learned in a day'. On his return to Napoleon, Savary observed the defeated Russian Army streaming homewards: 'No more than 26,000 men passed by . . . a great many were wounded, but they marched bravely in their ranks.' With them Alexander left Austrian soil, humiliated and his heart filled with the passion of revenge.

ONE OF THE LAST casualties of Austerlitz was Prime Minister William Pitt. His famous utterance, 'England has saved herself by her exertions and will, as I trust, save Europe by her example,' had done little to encourage his distant allies on the eve of battle. With his health deteriorating, he had spent the autumn months grossly over-working, over-drinking or else lying listlessly on a couch at Bath. When the first rumours of Austerlitz reached London at the end of December, 'Prinnie' had assured his guests that 'all was over with the French and that they had been sent to the Devil'. A few minutes later the full details of the disaster were coming through, and doubtless the despair they induced hastened Pitt's end. The following month, January 1806, he was making his remarkably accurate deathbed prophecy to his niece, Hester Stanhope, about rolling up the map of Europe: 'It will not be wanted these ten years.' 'In an age', runs the fitting epitaph to Pitt in the Guildhall, 'when the contagion of ideals threatened to dissolve the forms of civil society, he rallied the loyal, the sober-minded and the good around the venerable structure of the English monarchy.'

Austerlitz tempered the steel of the new *Grande Armée* into one of the finest weapons in military history. It was the victory of which Napoleon was proudest; justly so, for the results achieved, together with the risks they entailed, ensure its place as one of the greatest campaigns of all time. In twenty days the *Grande Armée* had marched from Boulogne to the Rhine; in two months, it had reached Vienna; within three it had shattered potentially the most powerful combination yet directed against France. The route was strewn with 'ifs': *if* the Russians had reached Mack before he was encircled at Ulm; *if* the Prussians had attacked Napoleon's long-extended flanks, in combination with the Austrian archdukes'; *if* Kutuzov had refused battle at Austerlitz, drawing Napoleon instead further into eastern Europe . . . Napoleon has been criticized for taking too many gambles in 1805, but he had several supreme advantages. Although even he confessed to being surprised by the true magnitude of his victory when, the following day, the Emperor of Austria in person came to sue for peace, so confident was Napoleon in his star (and his army) that he rejected the thought of being anything but *totally* successful. Moreover, far less had been left to chance than appeared to be the case. As Napoleon himself frequently repeated, 'Nothing is attained in war except by calculation.' With his extraordinary insight, he calculated exactly how the enemy would react to his every move; and, as has been seen, his calculations were in general correct, though this did not mean that the battle had been without its moments of extreme anxiety for him.

The Austerlitz campaign was *the* classic Napoleonic victory, with ingredients that would be repeated time and again. First of all, he had moved too fast for the Allies to join up, defeating first one army at Ulm and then the second at Austerlitz itself; secondly, on the Pratzen, he had split the enemy line, defeating each section in detail. It was a strategy which would work well until Leipzig, by which time the Allies had studied the form and would avoid the cornering of individual armies, until they could wear Napoleon down with superior numbers in a battle of sheer attrition. Austerlitz was also one of the last battles over which, tactically, he would be able to wield total personal control. Finally, doubtless as a direct result of all that intensive training at Boulogne, the *Grande Armée*'s numerical inferiority was counterbalanced by its supreme mobility. The key, wrote Savary, 'was that we moved about a good deal, and that individual divisions fought successive actions in different parts of the field. This is what multiplied our forces throughout the day, and this is what the art of war is all about. . . .'

Napoleon was much assisted by the blunders of the Allies. Above all, they suffered from the divergent strategy of a coalition: 'Nothing is so important in war as an undivided command,' declared Napoleon. In both world wars, and even during the brief Gulf campaign of 1990–1, under pressure the irresistible temptation is for separate components of a coalition to act in their own parochial interests. Just as the British fell back on Dunkirk in May 1940, so in 1805 the Austrians moved westwards to protect their territory, while the Russians looked back over their shoulder towards Mother Russia. Even in 'La Patrie en Danger' campaign of 1814, where the prospects were hopeless for Napoleon, the Austrians, when administered a bloody nose, immediately retreated on their lines of communication. It was, after all, only natural. At Waterloo, the following year, Wellington came close to defeat by concentrating his forces along the British natural axis of retreat to the Channel ports; fortunately, on the historic day of Waterloo itself, Blücher resisted the natural instinct and moved west and *away* from Prussia so as to assist Wellington. It was not what Napoleon had anticipated, and it was to win the day. Equally, at Austerlitz (and subsequently), diversionary operations by the British and Swedes (not to mention the Prussians) could not be co-ordinated in time to affect the main battle, and the joint Austro–Russian councils of war always ended by adopting the worst, compromise decisions. The Allied commanders consistently failed to explore what Napoleon's own intentions might have been, and at Austerlitz erred fatally in allowing themselves to be drawn into battle on Napoleon's terms. Once the battle was joined, they proved tactically incapable of bringing all their forces to bear, largely on account of the over-crowding and jamming of Buxhöwden's massive force in the early phases.

Napoleon, too, had made his mistakes. Had the Allies been less ineffectual, and more co-ordinated (the failing which was to dog them all the way to 1815), these could have resulted in a decisive defeat for Napoleon. Three of the gravest, as already noted, involved Murat: before Ulm, at Vienna, and – most seriously – in the pursuit of Bagration after Austerlitz. Some critics claim that the Eylau–Friedland campaigns of 1807 might have been avoided had Napoleon completely destroyed the Tsar's army at Austerlitz. But, with Russia's huge manpower reserves, the additional loss of Bagration's 10,000 men would have been a drop in the bucket. If anything, the fault lay – politically and psychologically – in Austerlitz being *too complete* a victory. As with Hitler in 1940, or, in more recent times, with the Israeli–Arab Six Day War of 1967, the defeated were *too* humiliated, the victor given *too* great a sense of superiority for the long-term future to consolidate the victory. If Austerlitz raised Napoleon to the pinnacle of his success, it also turned his head and filled it with the delusion that no force or combination of forces could now stop him conquering the world. On the Pratzen Heights were born the seeds of his ultimate destruction.

Summing up on the 'dazzling glory' of Austerlitz, Thiers was to write a generation later:

> A campaign of three months, instead of a war of several years, as it had first been feared, the Continent disarmed, the French Empire extended to limits which it ought never to have passed, a dazzling glory added to our arms, public and private credit

miraculously restored, new prospects of peace and prosperity opened to the nation. . . . For calm and reflective minds, if any such were left in presence of these events, there was but one subject for fear — the inconstancy of Fortune, and what is still more to be dreaded, the weakness of the human mind, which sometimes bears adversity without quailing and rarely prosperity without committing great faults.

TEN

'Uncheered by Fortune'

1806

Napoleon did not, after all, vanquish his enemies so much by
the battles of Ulm and Jena, however disastrous these were,
as by his incredible marches.

Count Yorck von Wartenburg

IMMEDIATELY AFTER AUSTERLITZ, Napoleon summoned Talleyrand to Brünn. He found it 'a horrible place —
there are four thousand wounded here at present. There are a
great many deaths every day. The smell yesterday was detestable. . . .' While Napoleon passed his time listening to Haydn
and Cherubini in Schloss Austerlitz, his devious but far-sighted
Foreign Minister constantly pressed him to conclude a magnanimous peace with prostrated Austria. Expanding on the arguments
he had produced after Ulm, Talleyrand pleaded with him to
strengthen, not weaken, the Habsburg monarchy because: 'Such
a power is necessarily weak, but she is an adequate bulwark
against the barbarians — and a necessary one. Today, crushed and
humiliated, she needs that her conqueror should extend a
generous hand to her. . . .' Talleyrand urged Napoleon to
compensate Austria for the last Italian territories he intended
taking away from her in the west, with the Russian provinces of
Wallachia and Moldavia in the east. This, he astutely calculated,
would make Austria an ally rather than an enemy, and alienate
her from Russia; at the same time Russia, driven out of Europe,
would inevitably come into conflict with Britain in the Orient.
His statecraft was not unlike Bismarck's after Sadowa in 1866.
But Napoleon, resembling more the triumphant Prussian generals

of that era, would hear none of this. The wars with the First Coalition had lasted five years, the Second Coalition, two years, and now he had shattered the Third within three months. The prodigious successes of the *Grande Armée* led him to believe that no possible combination of enemies could defeat him, militarily. Accordingly he instructed Talleyrand on 4 December 1805, 'Inform the Austrians that the battle has changed the face of affairs and that they must expect harder conditions. . . .'

Talleyrand went to work in despair, and with foreboding. Subsequent history was to vindicate him. The resulting peace terms were extremely harsh. In addition to the Italian provinces, Emperor Francis was to forfeit the Tyrol (to Bavaria) and other territories containing over two and a half million of his twenty-four million subjects, and producing one-sixth of his revenue. On top of this, he was to pay forty million francs in war indemnity (enough to help balance Napoleon's precarious budgets, though initially he had demanded 100 million). On 27 December, the Austrians signed the Treaty of Pressburg – but with bitterness and lasting resentment. It meant that, henceforth, they would no longer be the first German power; instead, Napoleon would now fill the vacuum thus caused by creating his own satellite 'Confederation of the Rhine', comprising Bavaria, Württemberg, Baden and the lesser German principalities.

In Frankfurt's Roman Hall, Goethe recalled how as a child he had once noted that the line of portraits of the Holy Roman Emperors left only one space, which was filled by Francis II in 1792. It seemed an omen; having created himself Emperor of Austria in 1804, so as not to be upstaged by Napoleon, in August 1806 the dispossessed Emperor finally doffed the thousand-year-old crown of the Holy Roman Empire (which, for a long time already, had been neither Roman nor particularly holy). Despite all this humiliation, Napoleon accused Talleyrand of being 'soft' on the Austrians. However, for Talleyrand, it marked the beginning of his all-out opposition to Napoleon which was to culminate in betrayal. He refused ever to visit the principality of

Benevento with which he was rewarded after Austerlitz, and when, in 1812, Napoleon planned to erect a monument to the Peace of Pressburg, Talleyrand refused to be associated with it. Beyond the ephemeral glories offered by the New Year of 1806, Talleyrand could see more bloodshed and disaster ahead. Like Versailles in 1919, Pressburg would drive a defeated enemy into drastically reforming their army. Similarly, the peace that followed Austerlitz was to prove only a pause between rounds.

When Napoleon returned, triumphant, to Paris on 26 January, the mood of the city was very different from that of the autumn. Fouché had been adroit in keeping from the public the full extent of the defeat at Trafalgar. But if Austerlitz had removed an Imperial crown from Francis's head, it had secured that on Napoleon's. Said the sober Cambacérès, 'The joy of the people resembled intoxication.' A popular cartoon of the time shows a street crier pointing to a sketch of a galloping Napoleon, holding out a letter in his hand, with the caption:

PEACE — THANKS TO . . . THE IMMORTAL NAPOLEON
It is I, *Messieurs les Français*, who offer you
the best New Year's presents.

Mementoes of almost twentieth-century bad taste, such as the famous Austerlitz table currently displayed at Malmaison, were run up to celebrate the famous victory. On a grander scale, the grateful Senate decreed the erection of a triumphal monument to Napoleon-the-Great; modelled on Trajan's Column, it would be set up in the Place Vendôme* with bronze reliefs depicting the glorious feats of 1805, and cast from melted-down enemy cannon seized at Austerlitz. Accompanying it was a triumphal arch, the Arc d'Austerlitz (now the Carrousel), but facing it on a hill two miles away up the Champs Élysées was projected a far more

---

* Only to be felled by Courbet and the anti-Imperialists of the Paris Commune of 1871: see Alistair Horne, *The Fall of Paris* and *The Terrible Year: The Paris Commune* (London, 1971).

grandiose structure that would commemorate all Napoleon's victories.

To his followers, Napoleon handed out the spoils of victory with largesse: out of the reparations milked from Austria, two million gold francs for his senior officers; an extra fifteen days' pay for each member of the Guard; liberal pensions for widows of the fallen. Battle orphans were formally adopted by Napoleon himself, and permitted to add 'Napoleon' to their christian names. On his family and intimates he also showered kingdoms and dukedoms as if creating so many corporals, causing Talleyrand to remark acidly, 'Since he had become an emperor, he no longer wished there to be any more republics.' In March 1806, Murat was proclaimed Grand Duke of Berg and Cleves (a territory with which Prussia had tried to buy Napoleon's friendship), and, three years later, he became King of Naples. Joseph Bonaparte was made King of Naples (later King of Spain); his sister, Pauline Borghese, became Duchess of Guastalla (which deeply disappointed her, when it turned out to be a mere village). Louis Bonaparte became King of Holland; Talleyrand, Prince of Benevento; Berthier, Prince of Neuchâtel; and Bernadotte (for no very clear reason), Prince of Ponte-Corvo.

With peace once more in his grasp, Napoleon's fertile mind now set anew to contemplating all manner of vast civil engineering projects – such as tunnels under the Alps. The Sorbonne (suppressed under the Revolution) was reopened, the Panthéon restored briefly to Catholicism, the desecrated cathedral of Saint-Denis restored. While David and the new court painters busied themselves with vast canvases of *la gloire d'Austerlitz*, one of the last – and greatest – of the old school died quietly: Jean Honoré Fragonard. Napoleon also set to work extensively reorganizing the Treasury, but it was here that he was forced to face, or rather to re-face, the less agreeable realities on the reverse side of the medallion of military triumph.

During the campaign, France's rickety finances had gone from bad to worse in the incompetent hands of brother Joseph, left behind as regent. Several banks had collapsed; the Minister of the Treasury himself was under suspicion of embezzlement, and the country faced bankruptcy. The British naval blockade was biting. With an ingenuity worthy of Hitler's *Ersatz* scientists, saltpetre for gunpowder was being produced synthetically, indigo dye had been made from a plant found near Strasbourg, substitutes for silk and cotton were being pursued, while efforts to obtain sugar from seaweed would lead (five years later) to the introduction of the sugar-beet as a major crop. Yet, for all this resourcefulness, the severance of France's foreign commerce was adding a further weighty burden on the already extreme debility of her economy. Unemployment was acute, and Napoleon sought to occupy the unemployed with such Rooseveltian projects as the excavation of the new Ourcq Canal, while prison sentences were freely meted out to workers who dared strike. The Emperor's presence was also badly needed in Paris to carry on with the work on the various half-completed *Codes*.

So, from the time of his victorious return in March 1806, Napoleon yearned once again for a period of peace in which to set his own house in order. But within a brief term of six months he would already be off to the wars again, the great industrial exhibition planned to celebrate Austerlitz – at the same time as it distracted minds from economic realities – somewhat eclipsed by the new campaign.

Following Austerlitz and the death of Pitt, none of Napoleon's adversaries looked more ready for peace than England. The collapse of Pitt's short-lived Third Coalition had left an expeditionary force of 25,000 of her scant army marooned on the freezing Elbe, at the mercy of the unpredictable Prussians, her Swedish allies having decamped back across the Baltic. Troops were alerted to deal with riots in London, and it seemed no exaggeration (nor unprophetic) when Captain Thomas Fremantle declared in May, 'If England gets out of the many difficulties that now press on her, she will be the greatest nation in the world.'

On the death of Pitt even his rival and antithesis in all things, Charles James Fox, groaned that it felt 'as if something was missing in the world'. Impetuous to the point (so it was said) of putting the shot into his gun before the powder when out shooting, he was regarded – not entirely without affection – by Sydney Smith as 'one of the most luminous eloquent blunderers with which any people was ever afflicted'. Dedicated equally to gambling and the championing of 'generous causes' (which included marrying his mistress in middle age), Fox had always stood for two great ideals – abolition of the slave trade, and peace with France. Now, as Foreign Secretary and the real power under Pitt's successor Grenville (in what was flatteringly dubbed the 'Ministry of All the Talents'), Fox hastened the pursuit of an accommodation. But Napoleon proved elusive, and greedy, while – stricken with dropsy – Fox was to follow Pitt to the grave less than nine months later. 'The giant race is extinct,' mourned a supporter, 'and we are left in the hands of little ones.'

For England, the next three years would be (in the words of Winston Churchill) 'uncheered by fortune',[1] with only two small rays of sunshine illuminating the glum year of 1806. The first, in the shape of the return home from India of a brilliant young general, Arthur Wellesley, was however to remain imperceptible for some time yet. The second was the success in July of a British amphibious operation at Maida, on the toe of Italy. With little more than 5,000 men, Major-General Sir John Stuart, acting on his own brief, routed the over-confident French defenders by his disciplined firepower.

'Such a thing has not been seen since the Revolution!' confessed one French officer. Admittedly on a very small scale, Maida dispelled the myth of the invincibility of the French line; more important it was one of the first fruits born of the seed of Trafalgar, while it proved as demonstratively as anything else could that at least England's seapower made her free of the terrors of invasion. Once Fox was gone, however, any serious prospect of peace with Napoleon was as remote as ever. In June,

Napoleon suddenly offered to return Hanover to George III; but, at a time when many Englishmen would have preferred to return both King George and his frivolous, obese heir to Hanover, it was a hollow gesture. The only impact it had was to incense Prussia. Ever since 1792, all the German states had suffered in growing anger from the rapacious depredations of passing French armies, living off the land like hordes of locusts, and from the arrogance of the occupation authorities. In August 1806, the French shot a nationalist journalist called Palm. This latest affront to the once proud Prussia of Frederick the Great caused that country to boil over, goading her finally into a suicidal war against France.

A month before Austerlitz, Frederick William III of Prussia and his vivacious Queen, Louise, had held a macabre tryst with Tsar Alexander. Inside the torchlit tomb of Frederick the Great, his successor – having wavered all year about supporting the Third Coalition – finally and solemnly pledged to join in the war against Napoleon. In effect, a kiss imprinted on the sarcophagus to seal the bargain dug the grave of the Prussian Army. Bearing what amounted to a declaration of war, Prussia's unenthusiastic envoy, Count Haugwitz, was despatched to Vienna but dallied so on the way that he was to reach Napoleon only after the Allies had already lost the day at Austerlitz. In some confusion, Haugwitz modified his missive to sound like an obsequious message of congratulations. Napoleon, always well informed about Prussian intentions, was not deceived. Treating Haugwitz – and, through him, his ruler – with contempt, the conqueror imposed the most degrading terms on Prussia. All of this the once proud soldier-nation was forced, in her isolation, to accept without having fired a single shot in her defence. Never had her reputation been so besmirched, and the humiliation rankled intolerably. As a result, a war party emerged in Berlin, headed by the spirited Queen and the nationalist Foreign Minister, Hardenberg. To them, compounded by all the slights that Prussia had suffered at Napoleon's hands beginning with the violation of

Ansbach's territory on the march to Ulm the previous year, the proposed transfer of Hanover to England came as the last straw. In August 1806 the weak Frederick William finally mobilized for war against France.

To have done so twelve months previously might have made sense, when there were powerful allies in the field, but now it was insensate folly. Says Thiers, 'Nothing short of the most fatal infatuation could account for the conduct of Prussia; but such is party-spirit, such are its incurable illusions. . . .' Such also, he might have added, are the consequences of a mortally wounded pride which Napoleon had grossly underestimated. The Prussian hawks based their miscalculation on precisely the same error that had brought Austria low at Ulm – that the plodding Russians would reach them before Napoleon. But, even more, they placed their faith mystically in the military inheritance of Frederick the Great. That, too, was utterly mistaken; for virtually nothing had changed (for the better) in the Prussian Army since the great victories at Rossbach and Leuthen half a century earlier. It is a popular illusion to think of the Prussians as always possessing a superlative military machine. Since the days of Frederick, her army had become a creaky affair, led by antique generals. The King's senior military adviser, Field-Marshal von Möllendorf, was a veteran of Leuthen and eighty-two years old, while the principal commander, the Duke of Brunswick, was seventy-one and had learnt little since his defeat at Valmy back in 1792. Even the most capable of the more junior generals, Blücher, was already sixty-four. Pugnacious to a fault – the Duke of Wellington later said of him that whenever there was a fight he was 'always ready and eager, if anything too eager' – Blücher was also a ponderous mover. He would suffer a nervous breakdown in 1811, when he declared to his friends that he was 'pregnant by an elephant' (a favourite Berliner expression, meaning in essence 'I'm losing my wool').

During the last years of Frederick the Great, the military art had already ossified, and by 1806, says General Fuller, 'Tactically

the Prussian Army was a museum specimen.'² In no way short
on courage, its men were educated to fight like automatons in
tight, rigidly disciplined linear formations, equipped with the
worst muskets in Europe, dating back to 1754. They moved even
more heavily encumbered than the Austrians, and when war
came in 1806 the army was just in the process of being
reorganized along divisional lines — the system abandoned by
Napoleon back in 1800. Commanders were totally inexperienced
in handling the new organization. Worst of all, at the top the
leadership was hopelessly divided.

In Paris, Napoleon hesitated a month before persuading himself
that the Prussians really meant business. On 10 September, he
was writing to Talleyrand: 'The idea that Prussia could take the
field against me by herself seems to me so ridiculous that it does
not merit discussion.' What particularly surprised him was that
the Prussian Army appeared to be concentrating *west* of the
mighty Elbe, with the formidable river barrier at their backs.
Were they planning to strike at the communications of the *Grande
Armée*, extended as it now was all the way from the Danube to
Holland? Or would they actually dare to repeat the operations of
1792, and thrust westwards across the Rhine? Nothing was clear.
Still hoping to avoid a new war, which he in no way wanted (for
all that he had provoked Prussia into it), Napoleon wrote to
Berthier at *Grande Armée* headquarters in Bavaria, 'If the news
continues to indicate that the Prussians have lost their heads, I
shall go straight to Würzburg or to Bamberg.'

On 18 September, Napoleon learnt that the Prussian Army
had shifted south-westwards into Saxony, bullying her reluctant
neighbour to join cause with her. This news meant that the
Prussians had indeed 'lost their heads', and war was unavoidable.
Napoleon now moved with his usual speed and decisiveness. On
the night of 24/25 September, accompanied by Talleyrand and
(this time) Josephine, he left Paris for Mayence, arriving there
on the 28th. (In the meantime a messenger had set out from
Berlin bearing an impossible ultimatum to Napoleon: withdraw

all French troops behind the Rhine.) Still without knowing exactly what the Prussian strategy was, Napoleon formulated his own. First of all he eschewed the notion of a straight thrust eastwards across the flat north German plain, over all those awkward rivers, like the route the victorious Anglo-Americans were to follow in 1945. Instead, without waiting to be attacked, he would seek out the main Prussian force, get between it and the approaching Russians, and destroy it in detail. In simplest terms, it would be a repeat of the Ulm manoeuvre.

Meanwhile, on the Prussian side mobilization had proceeded with sluggish inefficiency. Forces in East Prussia were not called in, perhaps partly out of traditional mistrust of the Russian ally. From an imposing potential of over 200,000 men little more than half reached the concentration area in Saxony. Towards the end of September endless inconclusive councils of war took place between the Prussian commanders, Hohenlohe and Brunswick, with the King shuttling between the two. By 7 October, a clear-sighted officer called Scharnhorst, Chief-of-Staff to Brunswick, was writing in despair, 'What we ought to do I know right well, what we *shall* do only the gods know.' What the Prussians *should* have done, says General Fuller, was to have retired behind the broad Elbe and 'to have disputed its passage until joined by the Russians'.³ Instead, Hohenlohe, with no general strategy agreed upon, decided on his own initiative to push part of his army south-westwards from Jena towards the River Saale. Brunswick and Rüchel remained stationary on the northern slopes of the Thuringian Forest. Thus, already, the Prussians were moving eccentrically, and dispersing their main forces over a sixty-mile front.

Napoleon, on the other hand, was concentrating his forces. On 30 September he revealed his plan in a long despatch to his brother Louis, who was commanding the forces in Holland. He would denude the entire area between the Rhine and Bavaria to bring all his might to bear on the extreme right. Only Louis's army of some 30,000 men would stand between the Prussians and a possible frontal attack across the Rhine. Louis for his part was to make aggressive noises to 'deceive' the Prussians into looking due westwards, while in fact Napoleon and an army twice as large as that which he had taken to Austerlitz was moving on to the Würzburg–Bamberg line, thence to strike obliquely north-eastwards into the heart of Saxony and Prussia. He would only count on Louis's forces, he told his brother, 'as a means of diversion to amuse the enemy up to 12 October, which is the date on which my plans will be unmasked . . .'. The remarkable accuracy of this projected date would indicate to what extent, once again, Napoleon was making the enemy dance to *his* tune. At the same time, he did not omit the element of caution: 'in case of a serious event, such as the loss of a great battle, while I make good my retreat to the Danube, you can defend Wesel and Mayence . . . and . . . hinder the enemy from crossing the Rhine and pillaging my estates . . .'.

By the beginning of October, Napoleon had made his mind up that the key to his plan lay in the Leipzig–Dresden area of Saxony. There he would seek his battle of destruction – manoeuvring 'in a *bataillon carré* of 200,000 men',* Napoleon told Soult (on 5 October) in one of his most instructive letters of the whole campaign. 'However, all that demands a little skill and some luck,' he admitted, while assuring Soult that 'With this immense superiority of force united in so narrow a space, you will feel that I am determined to leave nothing to chance, and can attack the enemy wherever he chooses to stand with nearly double his force. . . .' He stressed to Soult, as to his other corps commanders, how imperative it was to keep in *closest contact* with him, for the success of his plan. What Napoleon meant by his '*bataillon carré*' – a somewhat curious term for so vast a mass –

---

* The actual total forces Napoleon would be able to bring to bear would be 180,000, compared to 171,000 Prussians, thus reversing the numerical ratios of Austerlitz and giving himself an even greater advantage over a less impressive enemy. (On the other hand, the Prussians would be able to field well over twice as many cannon as the French.)

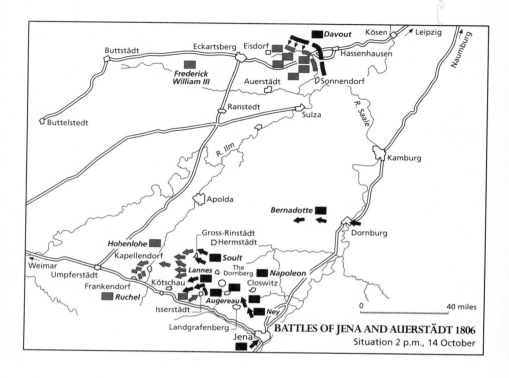

BATTLES OF JENA AND AUERSTÄDT 1806
Situation 2 p.m., 14 October

was a disposition that would enable him to fix the enemy with part of his army, while a second part was free to wheel against one of the enemy flanks or rear, and a third remained in reserve. Capable of operating against a force coming from any side, it was ideal for the opportunist 'encounter' battle likely to occur in the continuing uncertainty about Frederick William's thoroughly illogical intentions.

While the Prussian dithered, Napoleon's forces – greatly aided by Germany's excellent pavé roads – had mustered with great speed. For once the Guard had clattered part of the way in requisitioned post-chaises, covering 340 miles in just over a week. There were, of course, the usual signs of improvisation. At Strasbourg, the main replacement depot for the Austerlitz campaign, only 3,000 uniforms could be found for 15,000 new conscripts, while many troops marched eastwards without overcoats for an autumn and winter in the field. Reviewing

one of Augereau's regiments in Würzburg, Napoleon compli-
mented the soldiers on being 'the best marchers in the army; one
never sees anyone left behind, particularly when approaching the
enemy'. Then, observing the ducks and geese sticking out of his
soldiers' haversacks, he added, laughing, 'But to render you
complete justice I must tell you that you are also the worst
grumblers and the worst pilferers in the army!' Austerlitz having
cost 12,000 muskets, weapons were also in short supply, but
these would soon be made up from amply stocked Prussian
depots.

At dawn on 8 October, Napoleon began moving north-
eastwards, disappearing through the dense Thuringian Forest into
Saxony. A manoeuvre with similarities to Hitler's unanticipated
thrust through the Ardennes to Sedan in 1940, it enabled the
Grande Armée to pass unseen across the left flank of the Prussian
forces. By routing his army along three parallel defiles, two corps
to each, he saved himself several valuable days. The *Bataillon
Carré* was so disposed that it could rally on any one of its
component corps within forty-eight hours. As in 1805, it
marched preceded and masked by Murat's screen of light cavalry.
Bursting out of the forest, on 10 October, Lannes's V Corps
struck the advance guard of Hohenlohe's army at Saalfeld on the
River Saale. Commanded by the fiery nephew of the King, Prince
Louis Ferdinand, who had been a leader of the Prussian 'war
party', it consisted of only 8,300 men and so was outnumbered
two-to-one by Lannes's crack formation. Nevertheless, the Prince
pressed the attack in a fierce but uneven action which lasted four
hours. Leading a last desperate cavalry charge, Louis was hacked
down in hand-to-hand combat by Quarter-Master Sergeant
Guindet of the Hussars. At a total cost of less than 200 casualties,
Lannes wiped out nearly half the Prussian force, capturing thirty-
three guns and 1,800 prisoners.

This local defeat was to have greatly magnified consequences.
The effect on morale was disastrous, with Saxon troops at Jena
panicking hopelessly two days later and fighting with their

Prussian allies for supplies and firewood. When the news reached Prussian headquarters, all thoughts of further advance were promptly put into reverse. Brunswick gave the order to reconcentrate on Weimar, while both he and Hohenlohe prepared to fall back towards the Elbe – a course they ought to have adopted in the first place. Meanwhile, the engagement at Saalfeld had given a surprised Napoleon a first clue to the location of the enemy army, and an idea of what its line of retreat might now be. Accordingly he ordered Davout to hasten to Naumburg lower down the Saale, astride the main route to Leipzig, and to hold the bridgehead there. After one of his characteristically long-legged marches, Davout was in position with his 26,000-strong III Corps by the evening of 12 October, thereby sealing the Prussians from the rear in much the same way as the bulk of the *Grande Armée* had trapped Mack at Ulm. In view of what was to follow, it was indeed fortunate for Napoleon that he had selected his best marshal as the cork in the bottle. To the other leading corps commanders, his orders were: 'The game today is to attack everything we encounter, in order to beat the enemy in detail while he is uniting his forces.'

Realizing that the entire enemy force was on the far side of the River Saale, Napoleon now performed – with the flexibility and order for which the *Grande Armée* was famous – a 90-degree left wheel with his whole vast mass of men. This brought Lannes's V Corps on to the heights overlooking the small town of Jena on the River Saale. At 9 a.m. on 13 October, Napoleon received various pieces of intelligence which persuaded him that, in the first place, the Prussians were preparing to retire *due northwards* on Magdeburg, and secondly that Hohenlohe and the main weight of Frederick William's forces were massed within a few miles of Jena and Lannes's single corps. In all probability, Napoleon deduced, they would launch a spoiling attack on Lannes, so as to ensure their unimpeded withdrawal. 'At last the veil is torn aside,' he declared in a letter to Murat – but, in fact, he was about to commit one of his greatest miscalculations. At about 4 p.m. that afternoon he reached the Landgrafenberg Heights occupied by Lannes; looking down he could see some 30,000 of Hohenlohe's men encamped, and took them, erroneously, to comprise the whole Prussian Army, thereby confirming his earlier assessment. With utmost despatch, he now ordered up Soult, Ney and Augereau, plus the Guard, to reinforce Lannes at Jena — in other words, the bulk of the *Grande Armée*. Davout, already at Naumburg, was to cross the Saale and head south-west towards Apolda, so as to take the enemy in its left rear, cuttings its (supposed) line of retreat on Magdeburg. Bernadotte, on his way to back up Davout at Naumburg, was instructed to turn back to Dornburg, little more than seven miles downstream from Jena, in readiness to strike into the Prussian left flank. Napoleon himself resolved to attack the following dawn: 'There are moments in war when no consideration should override the advantage of anticipating the enemy and striking first.'

On the other side of the Saale, however, the situation was rather different. Morale was low. The Saxons, who had received almost no food for four days, were mutinous and threatening to leave the Prussians; even some of the Prussian battalions were down to half-strength as a result of straggling and desertion. In this sorry state, a council of war decided that Brunswick and the main army should withdraw immediately up the west bank of the Saale, taking the shortest route towards the Elbe — and Berlin; this meant adopting an axis closer to Leipzig than Magdeburg, which, in turn, would bring Brunswick into head-on collision with Davout. Meanwhile, Hohenlohe would act as a mere rearguard to cover the withdrawal, with Rüchel's 15,000 men hovering uselessly in the wings at Weimar. Thus, as the day of battle approached, Brunswick and 63,000 men were pushing down a single road towards Davout's corps of 26,000 men; while, at Jena, Hohenlohe and a force of 38,000 faced Napoleon with 55,000 troops already in hand and a further 40,000 that could reach him by noon on 4 October. It produced an intriguingly unbalanced picture.

At Jena, the night before the battle, there was confusion as Lannes's approach route was blocked when one of his cannon became wedged on a narrow trail; but Napoleon himself was on hand, calmly untangling the traffic snarl. As the attack went in at dawn, confusion was compounded by fog – thicker than at Austerlitz, and far less welcome. The first objective was for Lannes to seize, by straight frontal attack, the Dornburg plateau, so as to provide elbow room for the other three corps. With some disorder (Augereau getting his entire corps jammed into a ravine on the left flank), this succeeded by 11 a.m. Matters on the left were not helped by the impatient Ney, who, chafing at the bit for orders, plunged into battle in a foggy gap between Lannes and Augereau. This led him straight into the mouth of a powerful Prussian battery. Suffering terrible casualties, Ney overran the guns, but this impetus then carried him so far that he found himself cut off, and had to be rescued by the personal intervention of a displeased Emperor with the only available cavalry reserve.

More orderly was Soult's advance on the right, led by St Hilaire's men, who had acquitted themselves so superbly on the Pratzen the previous year. Towards midday, Hohenlohe led a concerted counter-attack on the centre of the line. His troops went in bravely with bands playing and colours flying, aligned as if on parade ground. When they reached the village of Vierzehn-heiligen, his 20,000 infantrymen were picked off for two hours by French marksmen firing from under cover of garden walls and broken masonry, with minimal losses to themselves.

By 2.30 p.m., Hohenlohe's army was reduced to fragments. But as he gave the order to retreat, Rüchel came marching on to the lost battlefield at last, with his 13,000 men from Weimar in a tight wedge formation. At first his attack shook the French, but after they had rallied Rüchel found himself exposed to fire from nearly the whole of Napoleon's four corps. Despite extraordinary bravery by some of the Prussian grenadiers, they broke, and retreat became a rout, with the French cavalry sabring and trampling the wretched fugitives in a six-mile pursuit. By 6 p.m., Murat was riding into the streets of Weimar contemptuously brandishing a whip instead of a sabre. It was how Austerlitz should have ended, but did not.

When the casualties were counted, French losses at Jena amounted to approximately 5,000; the Prussians lost 25,000 men, 200 cannon and 30 flags. Clausewitz was to write savagely of his nation's performance:

> When the Prussian generals . . . threw themselves into the open jaws of destruction in the oblique order of Frederick the Great, and managed to ruin Hohenlohe's army in a way that no other army has ever been ruined on the actual field of battle – all this was due not merely to a manner which had outlived its day, but to the most downright stupidity to which methodism has ever led.[4]

But, ultimately, sheer weight of numbers would have defeated Hohenlohe at Jena anyway. Far from being one of Napoleon's tidiest battles – it was certainly no Austerlitz – it was, rather, a collision of encounter and accident. Much of his initial plan had fallen apart, partly because events had occurred so rapidly as to prevent formulation of a careful plan, such as had won the day at Austerlitz. Comparing him to General Grant at Chattanooga fifty-seven years later, two American military historians, Esposito and Elting, also claim that 'he seems to have at times lost control of the battle. . . . Had the whole Prussian–Saxon army faced him, the struggle would have been desperate. . . .'[5]

Because of the intensity of the cannonade, sounds of a fierce battle some thirteen miles to the north had all but escaped Napoleon's attention. Thus, at the end of the day, he was surprised and aggravated to receive a staff captain sent by Davout who reported that the Marshal had won a great victory, defeating the main body of the Prussian Army near Auerstädt. Perhaps thinking of Davout's notorious short-sightedness, he snapped 'Your marshal must be seeing double!' but he was soon retracting his words.

In compliance with Napoleon's orders, Davout had begun moving his three divisions (one commanded by General Friant, the hero of the bitter defensive fight at Sokolnitz–Telnitz the previous year) towards Apolda at dawn. Reaching the heights of the key Kösen Pass, through which Frederick William intended to pass his entire army, Gudin's lead division ran into Blücher's cavalry in thick fog. Four times Blücher charged, but, with the speed at which Davout's superbly trained corps excelled, the infantry formed squares, repulsing all the Prussian attacks. By mid-morning, Friant's division arrived at the double and went into the attack directly in battalion column on the right flank. Blücher had his horse shot from under him and was sent reeling back towards Auerstädt. More serious was the threat to Davout's left flank, where at one point vastly superior forces under Schmettau and Wartensleben nearly enveloped Morand's division. Appearing personally to be at almost every critical point on the front at once, Davout brilliantly sited Friant's and Morand's guns (his maximum artillery potential was only 40, as against 230 for Blücher) so as to decimate Schmettau's infantry with interlocking fire. In the course of the battle, Schmettau was mortally wounded; the Duke of Brunswick, the army commander, was himself shot through both eyes, and died later; and the King's ancient adviser, Marshal von Möllendorf, was taken prisoner. With its command virtually wiped out, Frederick William's army at around midday lost its will to fight. Had the Prussians but known it, however, Davout by then had had to throw into the battle even his specialist (and preciously few) sappers, leaving himself with barely a battalion in reserve.

Nevertheless, realizing that the enemy were hesitating, Davout now thrust forward 'in a menacing crescent-shaped formation, horns pushed aggressively forward'.[6] For a while the Prussians fought back stoically, in murderous close-in fighting. Davout wrote in his *Journal*, 'We were within pistol range, and the cannonade tore gaps in their ranks which immediately closed up. Each move of the 61st Regiment was indicated on the ground by

Napoleon at Fontainebleau, brooding after defeat in 1814
by Paul Hippolyte Delaroche (1797–1856)

Josephine
by Vigor (after Appiani), 1797

Marie Walewska at Versailles
by Gérard, 1812

**Fouché, a deceptively benevolent
painting from Versailles**
by Houssaye, c.1813

Talleyrand, in old age
by Scheffer, 1828

'The <u>Arch</u> Duchess Maria Louisa Going to Take her Nap.'

Cartoon by Cruikshank, 1810

An acid double-entendre on Napoleon's stature. The bubbles read:
'My dear Nap. Your bed accommodations are very indifferent! Too short by a yard!
I wonder how Josephino put up with such things even as long as she did !!!'
and 'Indeed Maria I do not well understand you? the Empress Josephino who knew
<u>things</u> better than I hope you do, never grumbled – Le Diable! I see I never
will be able to get what I want after all !!!'

Triumph at Austerlitz, 1805
by Gérard (1770-1837)
Napoleon receives the defeated Russian Commanders.

Napoleon I receives Tsar Alexander I, Queen Louise and King Frederick William III of Prussia at Tilsit, 1807

by Gosse (1787–1873)

Wellington
by Derby
(after Lawrence and Evans), 1834

Pitt the Younger
by Hoppner (1758–1810)

Blücher
by Dawe (1781–1829)

Kutuzov
by Volkov, 1813

Wagram, 1809
Napoleon's passage of the Danube
by Swebach, 1810

Waterloo, 1815.
Marshal Ney, rallying his troops with a broken sword, a highly romanticized
French portrait from 1898
by Eugène Chaperon born forty-two years after the battle.

the brave men they left there.' Suddenly the defence broke, with demoralized units of Brunswick's army reeling back through Auerstädt on top of the fugitives streaming northwards away from Jena. Roads were blocked with abandoned wagons; hungry troops looted as they went. Having fought his most brilliant battle against far greater odds than even at Austerlitz, Davout had inflicted 13,000 casualties in six savage hours. But he had also suffered painful losses: 6,794 men and 258 officers — approximately one-quarter of his effectives. Many senior officers had fallen, and most of the rest had either been grazed by bullets or had at least one horse killed under them. One division (Gudin's, which had taken Blücher's first shock) had lost 41 per cent of its men — one of the heaviest losses on a victorious side ever to have been recorded.

Undoubtedly Davout's losses would have been a good deal less severe had he been supported by Bernadotte's 20,000-strong I Corps. But where was *Sergent Belle-Jambe* during the battle? He had reached Naumburg at 2 p.m. on 13 October, complaining that his troops were fatigued. Despite then receiving Napoleon's instruction of that morning, which ordered him back to Dornburg, he had dossed down for the night. At 3 a.m. Davout had received his final battle-order from Berthier, obviously drafted under extreme pressure, and adding a somewhat less than precise postscript for Bernadotte: 'If Bernadotte is with you, you can march together, but the Emperor hopes that he will be in the position assigned him, at Dornburg. . . .' Davout immediately passed this note to Bernadotte. But Bernadotte, apparently in a high sulk and professionally piqued at receiving orders via someone he considered his junior, refused Davout's repeated entreaties to move with him. Instead he insisted on carrying out to the letter the first order he had received. Behaving much as he had at Austerlitz, the Prince de Ponte-Corvo sauntered at an almost leisurely pace to Dornburg — *away* from Davout. Though all the time he could hear Davout's guns behind him, he turned a firmly deaf ear on them. He spent the rest of the day uselessly at Dornburg, making no attempt to join in the fight, either at Jena or at Auerstädt. At 4 p.m., when it was all over, Bernadotte headed towards Apolda, and had the nerve to claim that his arrival there had saved Davout.

Bernadotte's deplorable conduct could well have caused Davout's defeat at Auerstädt, and the mind boggles at what the outcome might have been had the roles of the two marshals been switched, with Bernadotte confronting Brunswick unsupported. Defenders of *Belle-Jambe* blame Napoleon for sending out inadequate orders – comparable to those which Murat and Lannes had (or had not) received when facing Bagration at Austerlitz. Indeed, one major failing of the whole Napoleonic command system was that few of his generals would act on their own initiative (save Davout, and Murat who often got it wrong); on the other hand if there was one axiom bred into all of them it was always to 'march towards the guns'.

In the aftermath of the battle, while Napoleon lavished praise on Davout for his victory – subsequently giving him the well-earned title of Duke of Auerstädt – his rage nearly cost Bernadotte his head. On St Helena Napoleon revealed he had actually signed a court-martial order, but tore it up, no doubt influenced by the fact that Bernadotte was married to his early love, Desirée Clary. The uncharitable, however, might well consider that a firing squad in 1806 would have saved Napoleon trouble seven years later, when *Belle-Jambe* was to betray him totally.

On 15 October there began one of the most famous pursuits in military history. On the previous night Murat had already gone on to capture the citadel of Erfurt, taking another 10,000 Prussians without a fight. Supported by Ney, he was now ordered to pursue what remained of Frederick William's forces, 'his sword point at their kidneys', while Soult and Bernadotte moved along parallel routes sweeping north-eastwards into the heart of Prussia. Napoleon, with Davout and the rest of the army, moved on Berlin. By 28 October, Murat was mopping up the last remnants of Hohenlohe's army twenty-five miles short of Stettin on the mouth of the River Oder, having covered 200 miles as the crow flies in the two weeks since Jena. Swinging westwards, he then joined up with Soult and Bernadotte in pursuit of Blücher, who, with characteristic pugnacity, fought back much of the way. By 5 November, Blücher was cornered in the neutral Hanseatic port of Lübeck, where he had hoped to find his Swedish allies; but most had already re-embarked. The next day the French stormed Lübeck, ruthlessly sacking it and committing grievous atrocities against its civilians. Although this was perhaps his principal contribution to the campaign, Bernadotte nevertheless managed to ingratiate himself with the Swedish prisoners there, thereby – ultimately – taking out an assurance policy for a comfortable old age. Having captured Blücher, Murat now reported laconically to the Emperor, 'Sire, the combat ends for lack of combatants!'

Meanwhile, on 24 October, Napoleon himself had reached Frederick the Great's capital at Potsdam, on the outskirts of Berlin. Respectfully, he went to pay homage at the tomb of the warlord he had most admired. Inside the tomb, according to Ségur, 'he remained nearly ten minutes, motionless and silent'. Nevertheless he could not quite resist the temptation to 'liberate' as trophies Frederick's sword, belt and Order of the Black Eagle, declaring, 'What a capital present for the Invalides . . . !' To Josephine he reported, 'I'm wonderfully well. . . . I found *Sans Soucis* very agreeable.'

For their distinction at Auerstädt, the honour of entering Berlin first was granted to Davout's III Corps, having completed another staggering march of 166 miles in fourteen days, as well as winning one of the Empire's toughest battles. On 27 October, Napoleon made his own triumphal entry, escorted by the Foot Guard (who had grumbled all the way from Jena, because they had not been permitted to fire a single shot there) up to the Brandenburger Tor, where he received the keys of the fallen city. Among his resplendent marshals, Napoleon seemed, 'with his penny cockade, the most poorly dressed man in the army', while one observer expressed surprise that such 'lively, impudent, mean-looking little fellows' could have thrashed the best troops of Prussia.

It was a glorious (perhaps *too* glorious) finale to one of the most remarkable campaigns in history; a true *Blitzkrieg* in which, over twenty-four days, the entire military potential of both Prussia and Saxony had been utterly destroyed. In addition to those killed at Jena and Auerstädt, 140,000 prisoners were taken, together with an immense booty totalling 4,000 cannon and 100,000 muskets in Berlin alone. For speed it would beat even Hitler's mechanized triumph in 1940 when he overthrew France in six weeks.[7] In England, Wordsworth wrote in total gloom:

> another deadly blow!
> Another mighty Empire overthrown!
> And we are left, or shall be left, alone. . . .

Yet it still did not bring peace for Napoleon; nor would Fortune send him any more such easy victories.

ELEVEN

The Raft on the Niemen

1807

So war was no longer that noble and universal impulse of
souls devoted to glory that he had figured it to be from
Napoleon's proclamations!

Fabrizio, *The Charterhouse of Parma*, by Stendhal

FOR ALL THE BRILLIANCE of Napoleon's victory over
Prussia, news of it was greeted with markedly less enthusiasm in
Paris than that of Austerlitz. 'So great was the public desire for
peace,' wrote the French historian, Louis Madelin, 'that it even
surpassed the gratification of pride. . . .'[1] A deputation was sent
by the Senate to Berlin, more to persuade Napoleon to make
peace than to offer congratulations. Her economic problems still
unresolved, France was wearying of war and wondering nervously – where next?

Although his army had been destroyed, his capital and most of
his country occupied, and he himself was a fugitive at Königsberg
in faraway East Prussia, Frederick William was still obstinately
refusing to accept peace terms. His resolve had been hardened
by the Tsar's promise to come to his aid (belatedly) with 140,000
men. Further disquieting reports reached Napoleon that the
conquered Austrians, too, were rearming at his rear. The danger
of Russian intervention (backed, as usual, by English gold) was a
very real one; so, to begin with, he found himself forced to
secure the line of the River Oder, then to take preventive action
across it. Next, the pursuit of the elusive Russians would lead
him to the Vistula; and finally across that river and on to the
Niemen, at the very gates of Holy Russia herself. Thus, instead

of peace, another eight months of the grimmest campaigning Napoleon had yet experienced lay ahead of him. Such are the laws that govern military conquest, and the penalties which so often requite the ancient sin of hubris.

First, on 21 November, to strike what he intended to be a mortal blow against that implacable English paymaster before yet another coalition could be mounted against him, Napoleon issued the famous 'Berlin Decrees' ordering the closure of all continental ports to British trade. All commerce was to be seized, even letters 'written in the English language'. To his brother, King Louis of Holland, he explained that he was 'going to reconquer the colonies by means of the land'. The beginning of the much vaunted 'Continental System', this signified a land blockade of sea-power – but as such it was to backfire. Immediately there proved to be numerous black-market loopholes, where vast profits were to be made and in which King Louis himself was one of the worst offenders. Meanwhile, says Winston Churchill, the British blockade wrapped Napoleon's Europe 'in a clammy shroud. No trade, no coffee, no sugar, no contact with the East or with the Americans!'[2] The greatest sufferers were the neutral mercantile nations, particularly the United States.

Pressed on by the logic of his own actions, Napoleon now moved into Prussian Poland to approach England's one remaining ally, Russia, and compel her too to accede to the Continental System. He also had a political motive. Down through the ages, history and geography have conspired together to give the Poles a worse deal that any other European people. None, observes an eminent student of Polish history, Norman Davies, 'has reaped fewer rewards for sweat and blood expended';[3] and this was to prove particularly true following Napoleon's lethal embrace. Though she had backed the wrong side in the Great Northern War of 1717 and been invaded by both Russia and Sweden, by the mid-eighteenth century Poland was the largest country in Central Europe – stretching from the Baltic to the Dnieper. But an exaggerated sense of personal liberty, amounting to anarchy and peculiarly Polish, reigned. For nearly a hundred years the Diet passed no laws. King Augustus III complained that he had encountered 'the greatest difficulties in preventing the selling of the Ministry of Finance to the highest bidder'.[4] The grandees, with their huge lands, raised their own private armies — while the peasants lived in dismal conditions. By the 1760s, Poland had become the joke of Western Europe; Frederick the Great remarked on how he had enjoyed dissecting Poland leaf by leaf, 'like an artichoke', and in 1795 the Third Partition between Prussia, Austria and Russia caused the name of Poland to vanish from the map. It was one of the peculiar tragedies of Poland that, both during the Napoleonic and First World Wars, Poles were to be found fighting with equal valour on either side — like, for instance, Prszebyszewski ('the Pole with the unpronounceable name') at Austerlitz, and Poniatowski who was to become Napoleon's first Polish marshal.

Yet, true to their irrepressibly romantic character, the Poles had responded more passionately to the clarion call of the French Revolution than any other European people. Ever since Louis XV had backed and given refuge to his father-in-law, Stanislaus Leszczynski, there had been a 'special relationship' with France, reinforced by the deep bond of Catholicism, and in 1795 General Henri Dombrowski had raised a Polish Legion which fought valiantly with Napoleon in the First Italian Campaign. Thus it seemed to the proud Poles that they had everything to gain from the man whose declared enemies of Prussia, Austria and Russia had been their traditional oppressors. But Napoleon's attitude towards Poland was entirely cynical. 'Poland?' he had remarked scornfully to one of Talleyrand's staff while in Berlin, 'so much the worse for them. They allowed themselves to be partitioned. They are no longer a nation, they have no public spirit. . . . I don't care what becomes of them in the end.' All he then saw was an opportunity to create a new ally in the east between his enemies by reconstituting Poland. More immediately he reckoned it could provide him with 50,000 superbly brave soldiers.

News was received that a powerful Russian army (the one which had materialized too late, again, to help Frederick William) was concentrating there. Following the disgrace of Kutuzov and Buxhöwden at Austerlitz, it was commanded by sixty-one-year-old Count Bennigsen, a Hanoverian who had preferred to choose the Tsar's service and was as yet unblooded in battle against Napoleon. He had been implicated in the murder of Tsar Paul I, and was described as 'a pale, withered personage of high stature and cold appearance, with a scar across his face'. Not lacking in courage, he was however a clumsy tactician. Bennigsen was also supported by some 15,000 Prussians under General Lestocq – all that was left of Frederick William's army, plus elements of Buxhöwden's army moving down from the Niemen. Contemptuously, Napoleon told his troops at Potsdam, 'The Russians boast of marching on us, but they will find only another Austerlitz. . . .' For the first time, however, he also found himself up against a new and far more dangerous enemy – 'General Winter'.

In sharp contrast to the excellent German highways along which the *Grande Armée* had rattled to the Danube and the Oder, the unmetalled Polish roads had been turned into bottomless morasses of mud by the October deluges. Then savage November frosts changed them into deep frozen ruts, followed by worse mud after an unseasonable thaw in December. Even with quadruple horse teams, cannons sometimes completely disappeared in the mud. The most the infantry could march was one and a quarter miles in an hour, and their sufferings were appalling; even for the favoured Guard. Wrote Sergeant Coignet of the Grenadiers:

> We sunk down up to our knees. We were obliged to take ropes, and tie our shoes around our ankles. . . . Sometimes we would have to take hold of one leg, and pull it out as you would a carrot, carrying it forward, and then go back for the other. . . . Discontent began to spring up among the old soldiers; some of them committed suicide. . . .[5]

Hospitals filled with the sick; according to Intendant-General Daru, out of every 196 hospital cases during the 1807 campaign, only 47 were wounded. Since the vast Polish plain west of the Vistula was one of the least fertile areas of Europe, it was no longer possible to 'live off the land', and food supplies became acutely short. Napoleon's ramshackle logistics all but broke down, forcing him to revert to the discarded depot system. All of this slowed down the army's movement. Morale plummeted, with General Rapp noting in December, 'Our soldiers were less satisfied; they showed a lively distaste to crossing the Vistula. Misery, the winter, the bad weather, had inspired them with an extreme aversion for this country.'[6] It was supposedly at this point that an ill-humoured Emperor gave his Guard the nickname of *grognards* (grumblers). 'General Winter' was also no respecter of persons; the coach carrying General Duroc overturned, breaking his collarbone, and even Napoleon was forced to ride on horseback into Warsaw, his carriages having been left bogged down on the road. 'God has created a fifth element – mud' was Napoleon's initial reaction to Poland. But the welcome accorded the French in Warsaw was ecstatic – with an irresistible warmth that Napoleon had encountered nowhere else. 'To understand what we felt at the sight of this first handful of warriors,' wrote Countess Potocka in her journal (even though Murat had made a gross pass at her), 'one must have lost everything, and hope for everything, like ourselves. They suddenly seemed to us like the guarantors of the independence we had been expecting from the hands of the great man, whom nothing could resist.'[7] Atop a triumphal arch, a vast inscription greeted Napoleon:

> Long live Napoleon, the Saviour of Poland
> He was sent to us straight from Heaven.

Alas for those poor, romantic Poles – they were to be deceived by Western appearances not for the last time in their tragic history.

True to form, the Russians had withdrawn across the Vistula, abandoning Warsaw without a fight. Murat occupied it on 28 November, with Napoleon arriving a few weeks later. Having crossed the broad Vistula, Napoleon now marched – or rather floundered – towards Pultusk on the River Narew, where he hoped to trap a reported Russian concentration. The attack began with Davout surprising Bennigsen in a brilliant night crossing of the River Wkra; this was difficult enough to achieve with all the technical innovations of the Second World War, but in 1807 – and in the appalling conditions that prevailed – it showed the sheer genius of Davout and his corps. Despite this first success, however, 26 December saw only two inconclusive battles at Pultusk and Golymin. If there was a victor, it was the mud which had prevented Napoleon from concentrating his forces. Little damaged, Bennigsen returned north-eastwards, towards the East Prussian capital of Königsberg. Thoroughly disconsolate, Napoleon returned to Warsaw to reorganize his logistics.

By way of compensation, there now occurred an interlude that was, for Napoleon, to be almost as important as a campaign, but rather more enduring. Its opening phases are graphically depicted in his own letters. On entering Poland, he had written to Josephine from Posen on 2 December:

> This is the anniversary of Austerlitz. I have been to a ball; it is raining; I am well. I love you and desire you. . . . All those Polish women are French. There is only one woman for me. Do you know her? I could draw her portrait; but I should have to make it too flattering if you were to recognize yourself; however, to tell the truth, my heart would only have agreeable things to say to you.
>
> These nights here are long, all alone. . . .

The cryptic references to 'all those Polish women' reveal how profoundly Napoleon's and Josephine's relationship had altered in the ten years since 1797, when, agonized with jealousy, he had written from Verona, 'You are a wretch. . . . You never write to me at all, you do not love your husband. . . . Who can this

wonderful new lover be who takes up your every moment . . . ?'
How the tables had turned! Now aged forty-four, six years older
than the husband for whom she was unable to produce an heir,
the Empress was sitting miserably in the boring provincial
German town of Mainz with no one to distract her, bombarding
Napoleon with jealous notes and begging to be allowed to join
him. But when he had written, from Prussia, 'Everything in this
world must come to an end,' though it was followed by all
manner of tender sentiments, she was filled with most sombre
premonitions. In Berlin, the Emperor had struck his entourage as
being 'very much alone'. He had had no mistress since the
Egyptian campaign. From Warsaw on 20 December, still complaining about the wet weather, he wrote, 'I hope, within five or
six days, to be able to send for you.' On New Year's Eve he was
writing from Pultusk, after the battles, 'I laughed heartily on
receiving your last letters. You create an image of the Polish
beauties that they do not deserve. . . .'

The next day he was eating his words. On his way back to
Warsaw he had met Countess Walewska and had been immediately stricken. With his customary despatch, Napoleon wrote to
her the following day: 'I saw only you, I admired only you, I
desire only you. A quick answer will calm the impatient ardour
of N.' The following day the enamoured male chauvinist was
writing again to Josephine in a cooler tone: 'Your pain touches
me; but one must submit to events. . . . I have a lot to deal with
here. I am inclined to think you should return to Paris, where
you are needed. I am keeping well. The weather is bad. . . .'

Blonde with an exquisitely white skin, intelligent but also soft
and yielding, Marie Walewska gazes disturbingly out of the
famous portrait by Lefèvre with passionate cornflower blue eyes.
In this young wife of an ancient nobleman, virtue vied with
patriotism. For nine days she held out, until Napoleon struck
her Polish Achilles heel, imploring, 'Oh come! come! All
your wishes shall be complied with. Your country will become
more dear to me if you take compassion on my poor heart. N.'

(Talleyrand, strongly in favour of an independent Poland and always susceptible to feminine beauty, was instantly struck by Walewska and his unerring political instinct possibly saw in her an instrument of policy, as he went out of his way to further the relationship.) Napoleon, meanwhile, was repeatedly telling Josephine (not without truth) that the roads were impassable, that he could not have her exposed 'to so much fatigue and danger', that she should return to Paris for the winter; and finally he was urging her to 'be gay and show some character'. On 1 February, he wrote berating her for her tears and adding, outrageously, 'the trouble is that you have no religion!' It was not long before details of Napoleon's new love were reaching Josephine. In February she recognized defeat, and crept back miserably to Paris. On 21 February the heartless husband wrote expressing his pleasure that she had been seen at the Opéra. Recovering, Josephine began to exact a woman's revenge, provoking angry letters from Poland with instructions to stop gossiping.

The beautiful, and now adoring, Countess moved into Napoleon's headquarters for the remainder of the campaign. But was he honourable in his intentions towards the cause for which Walewska had originally given herself? Constantly badgering him to make it a sovereign state, Talleyrand was probably a truer friend to Poland, while Napoleon seems to have had no genuine thought beyond creating a rump duchy or principality dependent upon himself, leaving half the Poles still under foreign domination.

In the middle of his Polish winter idyll, Napoleon was suddenly roused by the disturbing news that Bennigsen had launched a surprise attack on his extended left flank, driving back Ney and Bernadotte towards the west. It was the third week of January. By the end of the month Napoleon had regained his balance, and realized that the Russians, in thrusting westwards, had exposed their southern flank to him. He saw an opportunity to perform one of his favourite manoeuvres – to get in behind the enemy to

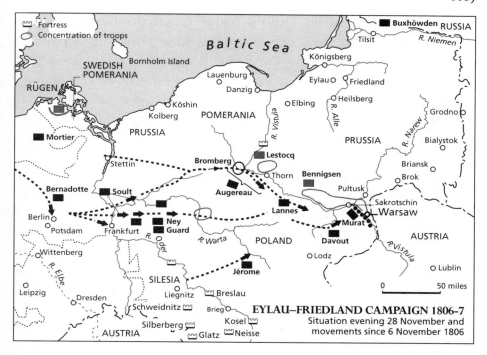

EYLAU–FRIEDLAND CAMPAIGN 1806-7
Situation evening 28 November and
movements since 6 November 1806

the east and cut him off from his base at Königsberg. But Fortune continued to play him false, at least on the battlefield. An inexperienced, newly commissioned staff officer sent with detailed orders to Bernadotte got lost and fell into the hands of Cossacks. On 1 February Bennigsen knew the full plan of Napoleon's envelopment manoeuvre. Exploiting the traditional Russian expertise for winter movement, he slipped out of the trap, withdrawing northwards on Königsberg. Napoleon stumbled after him, once again failing to allow for the state of the roads, now made worse by several feet of snow. On 7 February, Bennigsen turned and stood, like a cornered bear, at the small town of Eylau, only twenty miles south of Königsberg.

On the afternoon of 7 February, Murat and Soult in the van of the army fought a bloody but inconclusive action around the Eylau cemetery. Each side had lost about 4,000 men when Bennigsen pulled back to the ridge east of the town. It was clear to Napoleon that he faced a major action the next day. That night the *Grande Armée* experienced its most miserable night since marching out of Boulogne, huddled together in 30 degrees of frost. The Russians had pillaged all the food in the area; according to Baron Marbot, a young captain on Augereau's staff, one of his regiments had received no rations for eight days and now had to make do with potatoes and water.[8] Unlike the other countries, where the *Grande Armée* had lived ruthlessly off the land, here the foragers could find nothing. The cavalry ripped the thatch off the roofs of peasant hovels to feed their horses; 12,000 tents had to be cut up to provide hospital sheets – while ever since Jena the army itself had been seriously in need of a complete refit. Even the Emperor himself is described as begging a log and a potato from each squad of his Grenadiers, then squatting by the fire with them. The next morning the half-starved French attacked, into blinding snowstorms blowing from the east. Such was the chaos of his communications that, out of some 300,000 effectives in Prussia and Poland, Napoleon could immediately count on only about 45,000 men to face 67,000 Russians, with both totals rising to roughly 75,000 in the course of the day. But, as so often was the case, the Russians had more than twice the number of guns. Many of the famous names of Austerlitz were once again to the fore: Murat, Soult with St Hilaire and Legrand; on the other side, Dokhturov and Kamensky with Bagration in the wings. Notably absent was Lannes, who was seriously ill, while Augereau – on whom the main weight of the day was to fall – was so sick he could hardly ride. Neither Ney nor Bernadotte was to take part in the battle,* omissions for which, this time, Napoleon seems to have been to blame. Napoleon's deployment also bore a passing resemblance to Austerlitz: a thrust through the Russian centre (by Augereau's VII Corps), leading to a double envelopment, with Davout moving up from the south to strike

---

* Ney's arrival late in the afternoon did, however, influence Bennigsen's decision to withdraw from the disputed battlefield.

BATTLE OF EYLAU, *1807*

the Russian left flank. But nothing was to happen according to plan.

Early in the battle, the redoubtable Soult on Napoleon's left flank was severely mauled. A far worse fate befell the men of the sick but gallant Augereau. The son of a fruit vendor who at fifty was Napoleon's oldest combat marshal, Augereau permitted his corps to stray fatally to the left in the blizzard, presenting its flank to a powerful concentration of seventy-two Russian cannon. With the snow blowing from behind them, Bennigsen's gunners could see the advancing French, but not vice versa, and they raked them with a merciless hail of shot at almost point-blank range. Worse still, their straying brought Augereau's men under the fire of their own artillery, which was maintaining a blind bombardment into the obscurity. By 10.30 a.m. VII Corps had virtually ceased to exist (the first time that such a disaster had ever overtaken Napoleon); Marbot, who was later severely wounded, claims that the corps now numbered no more than two or three thousand. The French position was extremely precarious, and at one point Napoleon – up in Eylau's church tower – came perilously close to being engulfed himself by the advancing Russians. At 11.30 a.m., he called on Murat and his cavalry reserve to fill the vacuum in the shattered French centre. Now re-equipped with superb horses taken from the Prussians, Murat found his moment of true glory, sweeping forward into the massed Russians in one of the greatest cavalry charges in history. Behind followed the Horse Grenadiers of the Guard, the élite 'big heels', their colonel, Lepic, shouting 'Heads up, by God!' when they ducked the bursting shells: 'Those are bullets – not turds!'

After Eylau, Murat's action established the French heavy cavalry as 'the dread of Europe and the pride of France'; more immediately it had saved the day for Napoleon. In the respite provided, Davout's newly arrived corps bit into Bennigsen's left flank, bending his whole line back 'like a hairpin'.[9] By mid-afternoon it looked as if the Russians might break; then, in the nick of time, Lestocq arrived with his 7,000 Prussians and in turn took Davout on his exposed (right) flank. According to one of his officers, Pasquier, even Davout was about to sound the retreat as dusk fell, when, 'Putting his ear to the ground he recognized the distinct sounds of cavalry and guns on the move, and as the noise was receding . . . he no longer doubted that the enemy was in full retreat.' There was no question of any pursuit. Like Jellicoe at Jutland, Napoleon was left in possession of the field but he had suffered (again for the first time) far higher losses than the enemy. Before the battle he was boasting to Cambacérès, 'I am going to throw it [the Russian Army] the other side of Niemen'; afterwards, his letters reveal an unusual humility. To Talleyrand, he was revealing that the day had been 'pretty risky'; to Josephine, 'I have lost a lot of people'; while he made a rare admission that his 'soul was oppressed to see so many victims'.

But Napoleon's own figure of 1,000 killed and 4,000 wounded was cast ridiculously low; David Chandler puts the overall total possibly as high as 25,000, compared to 15,000 for the Russians (and Prussians). No fewer than twenty-three French generals were also among the casualties. The suffering of the wounded exposed on the frozen battlefield was unimaginable; it was not much better once they had been removed to the barns in the neighbourhood that had been converted into temporary hospitals, because the thatch from the roofs had been removed to feed the cavalry horses. Of those lucky enough to have been evacuated, many died on the long jolting journey back to base hospitals in Prussia. But, as always, the suffering was that much worse on the Russian side, where medical provisions were virtually non-existent.

When Napoleon visited his troops the following day, more surly cries of '*Vive la paix!*' and '*Du pain et de la paix!*' greeted him than the usual shouts of '*Vive l'Empereur!*', while Ney made one lapidary remark on surveying the battlefield: '*Quel massacre! Et sans résultat!*' If Eylau had any results, they were all unfavourable to Napoleon. It was the first time since Egypt, eight years previously, that he had experienced such a reverse on land. The 'Dynasts' at last seemed to be ganging up on him. After Eylau, something of the terrifying mystique of the *Grande Armée* had evaporated; for the first time also, it had been fought to a standstill, and was proved to be invincible no longer. The effect this would have on Napoleon's enemies in the long run was to be considerable. Unfortunately for France, five years later Napoleon would have forgotten the lessons of this bitter winter battle.

He now withdrew to reorganize his forces for a spring campaign, made inevitable by the drawn results of Eylau, and found solace whenever he could in the arms of his fair Pole. Reaching down deep into the barrel, Napoleon called up part of the class of 1808, eighteen months ahead of schedule, thereby raising a new army 100,000 strong, plus two new Polish divisions. But already it was not the same in quality as the First *Grande Armée* that had set off so zestfully from Boulogne eighteen months previously. On the other side, encouraged by Eylau, which Allied propaganda had converted into something resembling a major victory, a new 'Coalition' all but got off the ground. Under the Convention of Bartenstein on 26 April, Russia and Prussia bound themselves to drive Napoleon out of Germany, with Britain undertaking to subsidize Prussia with yet another million pounds. But a month later the fortified port of Danzig surrendered, after an old-fashioned siege lasting three months; this released another 20,000 French troops to join in the pursuit of Bennigsen.

By the beginning of June, Napoleon was on the move again, squeezing the Russians once more towards Königsberg. The roads had dried out to a dusty hardness. A rashly conceived attack by Bennigsen was broken, leaving the Russian commander off balance. Napoleon now slid northwards along the west bank of the tortuous River Alle, dangerously threatening Bennigsen's links with Königsberg. On 13 June, Murat and Soult were sent directly against the city from the south, thereby forcing a disagreeable choice on Bennigsen. He would either have to withdraw to the east, abandoning Königsberg and with it the rest of East Prussia and Poland, or else remain on the west bank of the Alle to fight and defend the city. Napoleon guessed correctly that Bennigsen would adopt the latter course; but where? At dawn the next day, Lannes came up against Bennigsen's main army holding the small town of Friedland, its back to the Alle. With only 26,000 men facing at least 45,000 Russians, Lannes realized at once that it was his duty to pin Bennigsen down until Napoleon and the rest of the army could arrive. This he achieved for some nine hard hours, by shifting his effectives skilfully from one end of the front to the other. On seeing the situation, Napoleon at once realized that he had Bennigsen at an impossible disadvantage; crushed into a small space on the wrong side of an unfordable river, and connected to the rear by only three hastily prepared pontoon bridges, Bennigsen's front was also bisected laterally by the Mühlen Fluss (or mill stream), with Bagration to the south of it and Gorchakov to the north.

Napoleon's staff urged caution: wait another day until Murat and Davout could bring the army up to overwhelming strength. But Napoleon was adamant: 'We can't hope to surprise the enemy making the same mistake twice.' By 4 p.m. he had 80,000 French opposing 60,000 Russians. Baron Marbot, sent by Lannes to report developments, found the Emperor 'radiating joy'. Smiling, he asked Marbot if he knew what anniversary it was.

'That of Marengo.'

'Yes, yes . . . and I am going to beat the Russians just as I beat the Austrians!'

Ney – who had missed Austerlitz (he had been clearing the Tyrol) and had played only a minor role at both Jena and Eylau – was selected to lead the attack, against Bagration on the Russian left flank. It was evidently just in time as Bennigsen, realizing his plight, was giving orders to withdraw across the Alle, where once again his army would have escaped destruction. Initially Bagration's cannon, massed across the river, inflicted heavy losses on Ney's infantry. Then Napoleon threw in I Corps, which he had been holding in reserve, now commanded by Victor. A new star among Napoleon's commanders, Victor (his real name was Claude-Victor Perrin) had started life as a bandsman in Louis xvi's army, and had served as Chief-of-Staff to Lannes in 1806. In marked contrast to his predecessor Bernadotte (who had retired with a head wound from a spent musket-ball) he was a combat officer full of thrust. Deploying his cannon in much the same way as Rommel was to use his anti-tank guns in the Western Desert, Victor wheeled thirty of them forward in a series of bounds, first to 600 yards from the Russians, then 300, then 150. At each bound the guns poured a devastating salvo into Bagration's densely massed men. Finally the guns halted at 60 yards, almost point-blank range, reducing whole companies to a shambles with canister-shot. Inside of twenty-five minutes, 4,000

Russian infantrymen had been bowled over, while cavalry trying to silence the deadly guns suffered a similar fate. At the same time the combined efforts of the French artillery set on fire Bennigsen's pontoon bridges. Trapped in Friedland, the Russians formed one vast and largely unprotected target. As his final effort, Bennigsen sent in the Russian Imperial Guard. Ney's infantry fell with bayonets on these 'northern giants . . . the last and redoubtable hope of the great enemy army'. It was, wrote a participant, 'a victory of pygmies over giants . . .'.[10]

Discovering a ford north of Friedland, Bennigsen managed to evacuate the ruins of his army across the Alle under cover of darkness, but leaving behind 11,000 dead and 7,000 wounded – a third of his effectives. Eighty guns but few prisoners were taken, and over the next days the local inhabitants – revenging themselves for months of brutal mistreatment and pillaging – mercilessly hunted down Russian stragglers. Bennigsen was a broken man. For a total French loss of fewer than 10,000, Napoleon had at last won the decisive victory that had eluded him over the previous six months' campaigning. To Josephine he reported, 'My children have worthily celebrated the anniversary of Marengo. The battle of Friedland will be just as famous and as glorious for my people. . . . It is a worthy sister of Marengo, Austerlitz and Jena. . . . Goodbye, dear friend, I am just getting into the saddle,' he added, ambiguously.

Next to Austerlitz, Friedland was probably Napoleon's most distinguished victory; but it had been a hard-fought one, and his manoeuvring beforehand had certainly not been as impressive as that which had preceded Ulm or Jena.

On 19 June, Murat's cavalry reached the River Niemen near Tilsit, over 1,000 miles from Paris. There they were met by the Tsar's envoys, sent to request an armistice. Internal pressures inside a hungry and disoriented Russia had become too great for him to continue the war. In the less than two years since he had paced the cliffs at Boulogne in deepest frustration, Napoleon had won Ulm, Austerlitz, Jena and Friedland. They added up to 'the longest, the most daring expedition, not through defence-less Persia or India, like the army of Alexander, but through Europe, swarming with soldiers as well disciplined as brave . . . unparalleled in the history of the ages . . .', wrote Thiers.[11] No unqualified admirer of the victor, he added, however, 'Everyone will ask himself how it was possible to display so much prudence in war, so little in politics.' Yet none of this was immediately apparent when, the following week, Napoleon, at the peak of his power, received the Tsar aboard his raft on the Niemen. At that sublime moment of glory, 'he dominated all Europe', says Winston Churchill: 'The Emperor of Austria was a cowed and obsequious satellite. The King of Prussia and his handsome queen were beggars, and almost captives in his train. Napoleon's brothers reigned as Kings at The Hague, at Naples, and in Westphalia. . . .'[12]

The treaties with both the Tsar and Frederick William were signed by 9 July, and that same evening Napoleon set off on the long journey back to Paris, bringing with him – so it seemed – prosperity and peace in his time. He was eager to resume the business that had been rudely interrupted by the Prussians the previous summer. To his Minister of the Interior he wrote menacingly, '*Monsieur le Ministre*, peace has been made with the foreigners; now I am going to make war on your offices. . . .'[13]

TWELVE

Talleyrand Defects

1807–1808

I served [Bonaparte] with devotion so long as I could believe that he himself was completely devoted to France. But when I saw the beginning of those revolutionary enterprises which ruined him I left the ministry, for which he never forgave me. . . .

Talleyrand

ON 27 JULY 1807, cannon thundering out from the Invalides announced that the Emperor had returned to Paris, victorious yet again, from the Eastern Front. He had been away at war for ten months, almost all of that year. Heralds clad in medieval costume and illuminated by smoking torchlight proclaimed the Treaty of Tilsit. Military bands and spectators jammed the broad avenues, as the Imperial Guard made its triumphal entry. There were endless parades, balls and fêtes – perhaps the most brilliant of them celebrating the Emperor's birthday on 15 August. That day, in Notre Dame, Napoleon declared, with hubristic grandeur, that everything 'comes from God. He has granted me great victories. I come in the premier capital of my Empire to render thanks to Providence for its gifts, and to recommend myself to your prayers and those of the clergy.'[1]

Hubris, the device that destroyed the Greek heroes of ancient mythology – was it now to be the undoing of Napoleon? Emulating Louis XIV after the Peace of Nijmegen in 1678, Napoleon bestowed upon himself the title *le Grand*. He now gazed down on an empire which stretched from the Pyrenees to the Niemen, ruled over either by puppet sovereigns or by members of his clan promoted to unimaginable heights. In addition to the elevations of his brothers Louis and Joseph and of Murat, Jérome became King of Westphalia; Lucien, Prince of Canino; and his stepson, Eugène de Beauharnais,* Viceroy of Italy. Ordering this Empire was a multinational army 800,000 strong, a number unprecedented in European history. The emperors of Austria and Russia, defeated once again, were Napoleon's humble allies — reluctant ones, it is true, their friendship secured by the most artificial of bonds. Only England remained defiantly unbeaten among his adversaries; but, shut out of almost every port of Europe, it might be predicted that atrophying trade would now rapidly bring her to her knees — and to her senses. Thus, for every reason, Napoleon Bonaparte seemed to stand securely on a pinnacle of success. Yet, except possibly for the ever optimistic Poles, France had no real friends in Europe.

The Imperial Court out at Fontainebleau was seen at its most brilliant. 'No language can convey a clear idea of the magnificence, the magical luxury, which now surrounded the Emperor,' gushed the extravagance-loving Laure Junot, wife of one of his generals, that autumn:

> the diamonds, jewels, and flowers, that gave splendour to his fêtes; the loves and joys that spread enchantment around, and the intrigues which the actors in them fancied quite impenetrable, whereas they were perhaps even more discernible than at the Tuileries.

When the Emperor went hunting,

> Nothing could be more exhilarating than the sight of seven or eight open carriages whirling rapidly through the rides of that magnificent forest, filled with ladies in their elegant dress, their waving plumes blending harmoniously with the autumnal foliage;

---

* Josephine's son by Alexandre, who had been guillotined during the Terror.

the Emperor and his numerous suite darting like the flight of arrows past them in pursuit of a stag. . . .[2]

Already there were shadows, however. The cheering of the crowds and their rejoicing at the Emperor's latest military triumphs was rather less unambiguous, and more clouded with anxiety than it had been the previous year, after Austerlitz. The Parisians knew what close-fought and bloody battles Eylau and Friedland had been. Following Eylau, the stock exchange had dipped sharply, causing Fouché to note the universal fear that 'each time, the destinies of France appeared to depend on a single bullet'. That terrible winter in Poland, when whole gun carriages of the *Grande Armée* had been swallowed up in the mud, had been grim in Paris too. The British Continental Blockade, biting ever harder since Nelson's formidable success at Trafalgar, meant that almost no rum, coffee, chocolate or sugar were coming in from the French West Indies. Like ordinary Parisians, even Court dignitaries were obliged to suspend a piece of sugar on a string from the ceiling, each member of the family allowed to dip it in their cup only briefly. And Napoleon had found a new foe in the shape of Pope Pius VII, now openly denouncing his demands for the closure of Italian ports to British trade, and threatening him with excommunication if he persisted with his policies.

Above all, in the character of the man on whom all depended, there had been since Tilsit a worrying transformation. After Austerlitz, Madame de Rémusat had observed of Napoleon that 'his despotism increased daily', and with it his passion for power. From his headquarters in East Prussia a thousand miles away, he had managed amazingly during the past year to run his Empire of 70 million people, involving himself in almost every facet of life. No less than 300 letters had been sent off in the spring of 1807. On 4 April, to his brother Louis in Holland:

> You govern your nation like a docile, timorous monk. . . . A king issues orders and does not beg. You had better apply those

paternalistic, effeminate traits you display in governing your country to your domestic life. . . .

On 20 April:

I am writing to the Minister of Police [Fouché] on the subject of that foolish woman, Madame de Staël. . . . She is to remain in Geneva. . . .

On 6 May (like some late-twentieth-century Eurocrat):

I want the whole of Europe to have one currency: it will make trading much easier. . . .

On 16 May, to his brother Jérome, who was suffering from piles:

The best way to make them disappear is to apply leeches.

Now that Napoleon was once more back in Paris, Tilsit had presented him with every scrap of power he could possibly need, and he seemed quite overwhelmed by it. Talleyrand found that he was 'intoxicated by himself'; even his voice sounded different. Orders were despatched to remove the last of the houses perched on the Seine bridges because they spoiled the view down the river; a new bridge was to be built, the Pont d'Iéna, named after the victory of the previous year. But the Emperor began to lose interest in the great institutions founded under the Consulate. To Fouché he declared that one newspaper – the official *Moniteur* – was sufficient, there was no need for others. The complaint fell on fertile ground. Censorship spread to books and plays as well as the press, where any allusion to politics was forbidden. Fouché's spies were everywhere; all at court were required to report on each other, with suspects promptly arrested. Seeing the change in him, and sensing that the strength of his passion for Walewska was undiminished, Josephine herself was plunged into despondency. There were long, silent evenings.

There were moments of farce in Napoleon's new pursuit of

Imperial grandeur. With so much of his spare time spent hunting and shooting, on one occasion he charged Berthier, the administrator *par excellence*, with laying on an immense rabbit-shoot. Out of his depth, Berthier ordered up masses of tame rabbits to supplement the wild ones. When Napoleon took his position in the firing line, the unfortunate creatures rushed towards him, mistaking him for the keeper who fed them. Taking flight from this humiliating battlefield reverse, Napoleon found even his carriage invaded by fearless and hungry rabbits. Berthier was never quite forgiven, and when, on another occasion, the Emperor peppered Marshal Masséna with shot, Berthier was blamed.

The trouble was that, for all his new, consolidated power, Napoleon had to go on. If only he could stop. As it was with Hitler after him, his career was like the flight of an aeroplane: the instant forward momentum was ceased, he would crash to the ground in smithereens. As he himself had written as a youth, 'Ambition is never content, even on the summit of greatness.' Or in the ageless words of Tacitus some eighteen centuries earlier: 'Desire for glory is the last thing even the wise can give up'.

No one realized this, and the terrible dangers into which it would lead both France and European civilization, better than Talleyrand. Shortly after Tilsit, France was stunned by the news that the arch-opportunist Minister of Foreign Affairs, made Grand Chamberlain of the Empire and (after Austerlitz) Duke of Benevento, had resigned. Napoleon would later claim, on St Helena, that Talleyrand had been dismissed for making rapacious demands on the kings of Bavaria and Württemberg; yet he had promoted him to Vice-Grand Elector, the third highest rank in the land.

Talleyrand's disillusion with Napoleon's Grand Strategy had been mounting since before the Austerlitz campaign. Now, with a suppleness which only the former Bishop of Autun could achieve, and yet survive, he went still further, beyond the

GILLRAY, 'The Valley of the Shadow of Death';
Napoleon surrounded by enemies, from 1808 onwards

frontiers of protest; he defected to Tsar Alexander. By modern
standards, this was clear treason. Talleyrand, however, had his
own early-nineteenth-century definition – treason was, after all,
only 'a question of dates'. In his remarkable 'last testament' of
1836, he was explicit:

> I therefore served Bonaparte when emperor as I had served him
> when consul: I served him with devotion so long as I could
> believe that he himself was completely devoted to France. But
> when I saw the beginning of those revolutionary enterprises
> which ruined him I left the ministry, for which he never forgave
> me. . . .[3]

Opportunist, but ever the supreme pragmatist, Talleyrand had
profoundly disapproved of the humiliating terms Napoleon had
insisted on exacting after each of his recent triumphs. Generous
treatment of the defeated Austrians after Austerlitz would, in his
view, have made them a bulwark against Russia, and ensured a

European balance of power. Tilsit was the last straw. With alarm he noted the growth of Napoleon's megalomania, and with it his capacity for self-delusion. Especially did he fear that the excessive humiliation of defeated Prussia would bring forth a rekindling of German nationalism – and history was to prove him correct in his prediction. Convinced that Napoleon could only inflict more, and endless, war on France, from now on began Talleyrand's active opposition to his Emperor. On his resignation, a nonentity, a loyal chief-clerk called Champagny, took over at the Foreign Ministry. Talleyrand's defection marked a major turning point in Napoleon's fortunes.

IN MARCH 1807, George Canning, Pitt's Under Secretary for Foreign Affairs from 1796 to 1799, became Foreign Secretary in the Portland Government, and immediately proved himself a doughty successor to Pitt in his determination to continue the fight against Napoleon. Tilsit, once again, had aroused earnest fears in England that the arch-enemy would now re-energize his plans of three years previously to 'jump the ditch' (though, perhaps fortunately for a Britain deprived of Nelson, most of the invasion barges of 1805 had been left to rot in harbour and were now unseaworthy). Thus Canning's first action, that August, was to send a raiding fleet to Copenhagen, seizing fifteen ships-of-the-line of neutral Denmark, to keep them out of French hands. It may have saved Britain from invasion in 1807, but the raid was counter-productive insofar as it provoked Denmark to declare war on Britain, and Tsar Alexander to honour Tilsit by closing Russian ports to British shipping. Thus all northern Europe now came under the Continental System; but the Copenhagen raid also helped push Napoleon into his greatest strategic error to date.

The only hole in the System now lay at the other extremity of Europe, in the shape of little Portugal – Britain's oldest ally – where Lisbon, under cover of the Royal Navy, remained her last foothold on the continent. Napoleon determined to put an end to this; but in between Portugal and the Pyrenees lay the rugged, inhospitable and politically questionable mass of backward Spain. On 2 August, an Imperial Decree brought into being the Gironde Army of Observation under General Jean Andoche Junot, who had served with Napoleon in Egypt. The following month the Emperor launched an almost hysterical tirade against the Portuguese ruling family, the Braganzas, in the presence of their Minister:

> If Portugal does not do as I wish the House of Braganza will not be reigning in two months' time. I will no longer tolerate a single English envoy in Europe; I will declare war on any power that has one two months from now. I have 300,000 Russians at my back, and with this powerful ally I can do anything. The English declare that they will no longer respect neutrals at sea; I will no longer recognize them on land.

The unfortunate Portuguese wavered, but finally defied Napoleon by rejecting the least of his demands – to confiscate and hand over all British property.

On 17 September Junot marched into Spain – with the blessing of her viciously corrupt and hated dictator Manuel de Godoy, who had ascended from being a private in the Royal Guard to become lover of Queen Maria Luisa.* In October the two governments concluded in secrecy the Treaty of Fontainebleau, whereby Portugal was partitioned, with Spain promised the southern regions and Napoleon securing Lisbon. On 13 November the official *Moniteur* declared that the House of Braganza had been deposed; it was 'new proof of how inevitable is the ruin of all who attach themselves to England'. The invasion of Portugal was reckoned to be no more than 'an armed parade and not a

---

* Godoy had forced Spain into alliance with France in 1795, for which he gained the ironic title of 'Prince of Peace', on which Napoleon poured constant scorn after 1807.

war'. By the end of the month, Junot had reached Lisbon after a remarkable march through desolate country. But, of his original 25,000 troops, only 2,000 exhausted men remained. 'We found not a single peasant in his hut,' recorded Nicolas-Joseph Desjardin of the 58th Regiment. 'Many men met their deaths through sheer misery – or at the hands of the peasantry. We received our rations only when we reached Lisbon.'

It was a warning of what the 'scorched earth' that was to follow, in Spain as in Russia, would signify. Meanwhile, the Royal Navy had forestalled the Emperor by evacuating the Portuguese royal family and its fleet. In command was Admiral Sir Sidney Smith of Toulon and Acre fame, once again demonstrating to Napoleon the meaning of British command of the seas. Britain's loss of Lisbon, however, meant that by the beginning of 1808 Napoleon's Continental System now reigned unchallenged, without seam or hole, over virtually all Europe – in theory, and briefly.

Reckoning his western marches to be secure, Napoleon now turned his thoughts to Turkey and the Near East. He would march to the Euphrates, via Constantinople (which he held to be 'the centre of world empire'), with the connivance of his new friend, Tsar Alexander, thus completing the ruin of the British Empire in the country where he had been thwarted – Egypt – ten years previously. But Spain would upset all his plans.

Spain had been an unenthusiastic ally during the War of the Third Coalition, and had then lost all her fleet at Trafalgar. The once proud Empire which had so alarmed Elizabethan Britain was in the terminal stages of decay, its imperial decline symbolized by the royal family, whose inbred debility and unfortunate ugliness were so ruthlessly portrayed in the canvases of Goya. Fearful that Napoleon was intending a complete take-over of their country, the weak King Charles IV and Queen Maria Luisa allowed themselves to be persuaded by Godoy to follow the Portuguese royals into exile, only to be caught up in a revolution and forced to abdicate in favour of the heir to the throne, their son Ferdinand. The King then revoked his abdication as soon as it seemed safe to do so, creating a state of confusion which admirably suited Napoleon. The pathetic King and Queen ended their days like birds in a gilded cage, and in universal contempt, first in Compiègne, then in Italy – accompanied by the sinister Godoy. Ferdinand was kept in a state of house arrest at Valençay, ironically the château of Talleyrand, who had profoundly disapproved of the whole Iberian operation. 'The old dynasty is worn out,' Napoleon declared. 'It is necessary for me to refashion the work of Louis XIV.' It looked like one more brilliant coup for Napoleon. Spain now became another puppet-state, with Napoleon its *de facto* ruler, appointing his own elder brother, Joseph, king in June 1808.

In early 1808, Napoleon had exploited the confusion in Spain by pouring in over 100,000 troops, under the command of Marshal Murat, who was styled the Emperor's Lieutenant in Spain. Napoleon, however, reckoned without the feelings of the Spanish populace – the proudest people in Europe, fierce to a fault. They detested Godoy and the feeble royal family, and as fervent Catholics were inspired to oppose Napoleon with even greater ferocity because of his breach with the Vatican. They were, moreover, natural guerrillas inhabiting a primitive and desolate country which was ideal for such warfare. Napoleon also underestimated the British card. Though he reckoned he could hold Spain for a net cost of 'no more than' 12,000 men, over the next seven years the 'Spanish Ulcer' would in fact cost him an average of a hundred French lives a day, 40,000 a year, or almost 240,000 in all; it was to prove one of the major factors in his ultimate collapse. Following French orders to arrest the remaining members of the royal family, on 2 May, the famous *Dos de Mayo* immortalized by Goya, a spontaneous uprising exploded in Madrid: 'In an instant the mob rushed to arms and began to massacre all isolated Frenchmen throughout the city.' By the end of the day, 150 French soldiers were counted dead, and a savage martial law had been imposed by Murat. Napoleon swiftly asserted that 'Opinion in Spain is taking the direction I wish; law and order is everywhere restored.' It was far from the truth; within days insurrection had spread through the rest of the country, with the pro-French, 'Quisling' governors of Badajoz, Cartagena and Cádiz assassinated, and provincial juntas raising armies of patriots to combat Napoleon.

By the end of June the British Government, pressed by Canning and the Secretary of War Viscount Castlereagh, had taken the historic decision to despatch an expeditionary force to assist the Spanish patriots. It was commanded by Sir Arthur Wellesley, of Indian fame (he had gone to India in 1796, the year of Napoleon's triumphs in Italy), newly promoted to lieutenant-general in his fortieth year, the same age as Napoleon, and it represented the first time since 1794 that Britain had decided to commit a considerable force to a campaign in continental Europe, as opposed to raiding actions on the periphery, as in the West Indies. It would lead eventually to the supreme challenge of Waterloo, a historic milestone on the road of continental involvement from Marlborough to Haig and Montgomery in the twentieth century. Napoleon now had a serious 'Second Front' on his hands, his forces compelled at the same time to fight against a fanatically Francophobe resistance in Spain in unsuitable terrain.

On 19 July, General Castaños and his 30,000-strong Army of Andalucia, powerfully supported by the peasantry, inflicted a remarkable defeat on the French at Bailén, north of Granada. General Dupont and 18,000 men were forced to lay down their arms, the first such surrender since Napoleon had taken over. Dupont, though wounded, was never forgiven, and on his return to France was condemned to imprisonment for the rest of the war. Much of the fault for this strategic defeat in fact lay with Napoleon, and his belief in the divinity of his star, which had grown so over-inflated since Tilsit. In August Wellesley and his force of 9,000 men – a tiny complement by Napoleonic standards – landed in Portugal, and the success of Bailén was swiftly

SPAIN AND PORTUGAL 1807-14

followed by the rout of Junot and his 13,000 men at Vimeiro.
Junot asked for an armistice; rashly, Wellesley's seniors, two
elderly but inexperienced generals, granted the French highly
favourable terms at the Convention of Cintra (22 August)*
whereby Junot and his 26,000 troops, plus all their baggage and
booty, were repatriated to France.† But Vimeiro proved that a

---

* After Cintra, Wellesley was summoned back to London to face an enquiry
with the two generals, Burrard (who had served under Cornwallis in America)
and Dalrymple (nicknamed 'the Dowager'); both generals never again received
an active command, but Wellesley emerged with his reputation untarnished.
† In contrast to the unfortunate Dupont, Junot immediately returned to Spain
in command of a corps, was badly wounded, and then fought through the

British force, if properly led, could defeat French veterans. By requisitioning every available bullock-cart to assure his supply system, it also showed that Wellesley possibly understood the imposing problems of war in Iberia rather better than the master of warfare himself.

Napoleon, with his brother Joseph now humiliatingly evicted from Madrid, suddenly realized that the Iberian peninsula could now be secured only by substantial reinforcements from Germany, and by his own personal intervention. Meanwhile, at his back he was increasingly aware that Austria, humiliated but not broken at Austerlitz, was creating formidable new armies – as indeed the fallen Talleyrand had warned him. The Tsar now seemed to be his one reliable ally; but how reliable was he? To find out, at the end of September 1808, Napoleon convoked an imposing successor conference to Tilsit. He chose Erfurt, a charming old medieval city in Saxony. In the fifteen months which had ensued since that halcyon encounter on the Niemen, however, things had changed, chiefly because of Napoleon's difficulties in Spain. Alexander had ceased to be the defeated client; it was Napoleon who was asking for favours – notably that Russia keep Austria on the leash.

At this date, the active French Army numbered 350,000 men. But of this total Napoleon was intending to send another 100,000 to Spain, which would leave him in effect with no more than 150,000 men to watch over the totality of his far-flung territories east of the Rhine. In consequence, all the vassal kings, dukes and princes of the German states were ordered up to Erfurt, as proof that all Europe, save only Britain (and now Spain), owed Napoleon allegiance. No expense was spared in the magnificent trappings of the Russian suite, furnished with paintings and tapestries sent from Paris. The Comédie Française, headed by Talma no less, was in attendance. All the pomp and circumstance

---

Russian Campaign of 1812. After a brief spell as Governor of Venice he went mad and committed suicide in 1813.

that Napoleon could muster was deployed to seduce the Tsar, of whom he had written to Josephine the previous year, a trifle bizarrely, 'If Alexander were a woman, I would make him my mistress.' There were banquets and receptions, and shoots. On one occasion, Napoleon in his new-found love for *la Chasse* organized a mass slaughter of hares and partridges on the neighbouring battlefield of Jena, to mark the second anniversary of his triumph there. Though rather more efficiently mounted than Berthier's unfortunate rabbit-shoot, it seemed hardly tactful to a conquered nation that chafed increasingly for revenge, given that so many thousands of Prussians had died on that same field almost exactly two years previously.

None of this, however, seems likely to have impressed the Tsar as much as the openly treasonable *démarche* made to him by Talleyrand early in the proceedings at Erfurt, on the eve of which the latter had written, 'I cannot think of it without fear and hope: the fate of Europe and the world, the future of political power and perhaps of European civilization depends on it.' Although Talleyrand had ceased to be his Minister for Foreign Affairs, Napoleon reckoned that his presence at Erfurt might be useful, in case unforeseen diplomatic difficulties arose. As he scathingly explained, 'I don't employ the Prince of Benevento when I want a thing done, but only when I want to have the appearance of wanting to do it.' But, almost certainly, it was a serious error to invite a disaffected Talleyrand to Erfurt. It was there that Napoleon's former Foreign Minister, still the third man in the French constellation, made this remarkable plea to the Tsar:

> Sire, it is in your power to save Europe, and you will only do so by refusing to give way to Napoleon. The French people are civilized, their sovereign is not. The sovereign of Russia is civilized and his people are not: the sovereign of Russia should therefore be the ally of the French people.[4]

Henceforth, every evening of the conference Alexander would inform Talleyrand of the course of the negotiations that day. In return, Talleyrand would then fortify him with fresh arguments for the morrow. In the words of Talleyrand's biographer, Duff Cooper, the Tsar 'came near to taking down instructions at the dictation of the French diplomatist. This was treachery, but it was treachery upon a magnificent scale.'

As always Talleyrand's conviction of the importance of a strong Austria could be seen at the back of his overture to the Tsar. On his side, Alexander was aware of widespread discontent in Russia with the economic consequences of adhering to the Continental System. The blockade's interruption of the timber trade with Britain had been particularly damaging, while his own mother, the forceful Dowager Empress, was articulate in her anti-French sentiments. What was more, the terms of the Treaty of Tilsit still rankled with many of the leading Russian military. High on the list of grievances was, of course, Napoleon's creation of the Grand Duchy of Warsaw, at Russia's expense. The Tsar, who had arrived on the throne after the murder of his own father, mad Paul, and knew that there were still accusing fingers that pointed at him, hardly needed Talleyrand to drop hints that, after Napoleon's almost casual overthrow of the Bourbons in Spain, no sovereign could feel entirely secure on his throne.

So, with Alexander's resolve fortified by Talleyrand's secret information, Erfurt ended in October with no clear advantage to Napoleon. Russia was permitted to grab territory in Finland and Moldavia, while not challenging France's interests in Spain. On the main issue of Austria, Napoleon was able to extract nothing more than a noncommittal undertaking to support France in the event of an Austrian attack on her. But, in tangible terms, it was from Erfurt that relations between the Tsar and Napoleon began to run swiftly downhill, until the final crunch of 1812, with Russia progressively breaching the Continental System from 1810 on.

Meanwhile, Austria pressed on with the reorganization of her armies.

On a personal level, relations were not aided at Erfurt when

Napoleon, evidently in a state of high agitation, rashly revealed to Talleyrand that he was thinking of a divorce from the (apparently) barren Josephine. With a view to producing the heir deemed essential to the preservation of the dynasty, he had in mind a marriage with one of Alexander's sisters. Talleyrand tarried little before passing the information to Alexander. The Tsar slipped out of an awkward dilemma by explaining that, while he personally was not opposed to such a match, it would be necessary to obtain the consent of the francophobe Dowager Empress. But he remained manifestly horrified by the idea. Instead, as a *douceur* for his services at Erfurt, so cynics might see it, Talleyrand persuaded the Tsar to allow him to have, for his nephew and heir, Edmond de Périgord, the hand of Dorothea, the fifteen-year-old Duchess of Courland.

From Erfurt, though hardly reassured as Austria's armies strengthened by the day, Napoleon sped to Spain, reaching Vitoria in the north on 5 November, to take personal control of his forces there, now 190,000 strong but low in morale. On the way, he spent only ten days in Paris. It was not long enough. Obviously uneasy in her presence, in the light of his deceitful proposition to the Tsar, Napoleon refused to take Josephine with him. Bitterly disappointed, she made a classic plea: 'Will you never stop making war?' To this he replied, with total untruth, 'It is not I who direct the course of events, I only obey them.' The following month there took place an ominous rapprochement between the two arch-enemies, Talleyrand and the sinister Fouché, representing the most powerful aggregate of power in France. Paris gasped when, at a sumptuous reception in his new house in the Rue de Varennes, Talleyrand:

limped eagerly forward to extend the warmest of welcomes to the new arrival, and linking arms with him proceeded to pace up and down through the series of lofty apartments engaged in long and eager conversation, while the rest of Paris gazed and pointed, whispered and wondered.

The object of their talks was nothing less than a coup against Napoleon, to replace him with his ambitious brother-in-law, Murat.

When Pauline heard of the conspiracy against her brother and of his departure for Spain she wrung her hands in alarm, predicting that all the Bonapartes would be massacred. Receiving in Spain the dark news of the Talleyrand–Fouché alliance, Napoleon at once saw it as an even more menacing threat to his rear than the rearming of his fellow Emperor, Joseph. He was, however, then on the verge of administering a shattering defeat to the Spanish–British armies.

THIRTEEN

Sir John Moore's Retreat

1808—1809

I should never have started this adventure.

Napoleon

AGED FORTY-SEVEN, Lieutenant-General Sir John Moore had been sent to Portugal to take over from Wellesley. Sometimes described as 'the father of modern British infantry', Moore was possibly just as able a commander as his predecessor. He had a very modern view of soldiers as individuals capable of constant self-improvement; he had revolutionized discipline by relying more on co-operation than the brutal coercion of the past. As the trainer of a modern British army, he bore comparison with Bernard Montgomery in the Second World War (certainly it was a parallel to which Monty never objected). He had spent the past few years training up a new Light Division at Shorncliffe Camp to the highest and most up-to-date standards, teaching the troops especially to excel at musketry. His career cut short, Moore's most enduring fame was as supplier of the infantry with which Wellington won his victories. But in 1808 he had under his command only 20,000 troops, with which in mid-October he set off painfully from Lisbon to join up with the Spaniards, leaving another 10,000 to defend Portugal. It was, he was constantly reminded, not just an expeditionary force, but Britain's *only* field army — and he was not to lose it. There were certain parallels with French's 'contemptible little army' of 1914 and with Gort's BEF in 1940. Not unlike the French of 1940, Moore's Spanish allies, although the Central Junta now disposed of 125,000 regular troops, were in a state of discord, hopelessly divided in command and disposition. It was a scene calling for the kind of disaster Napoleon was so adept at contriving. His strategy, beautiful in its simplicity, was to thrust on Madrid, splitting the Spanish armies in two, followed by two simultaneous *manoeuvres sur les derrières* (double envelopments) to engulf the isolated Spanish wings.

The campaign opened on 7 November with a reverse being inflicted on Marshals Lefebvre and Victor (only recently ennobled respectively as Dukes of Danzig and Belluno) at Valmaceda, at the hands of General Blake, of Irish descent and one of the most impressive Spanish generals. Napoleon was infuriated that his marshals should suffer even a minor set-back at the hands of 'the worst army in Europe', and administered stinging rebukes. By 10 November, he had won three substantial victories, shattering the Spanish line. Only Moore's approaching force remained still intact, its movements unknown to Napoleon. Meanwhile, however, a most ruthless guerrilla war was launched on Napoleon's lines of communication, as the Castilian peasantry took to the mountains by the thousand. No French detachment was safe, and heavy escort had to be provided. 'Each day saw the murder of several Frenchmen, and I travelled over this assassins' countryside as warily as if it were a volcano,' recounted General Matthieu Dumas, the French Assistant Quartermaster-General, after the war. The ever present perils of ambush and the need to be constantly on the alert, even miles behind the front, imposed a heavy strain on all the troops. 'In such a theatre of war, there is no front or rear,' Napoleon himself admitted. During her very first days with her husband in Spain, Laure Junot herself discovered what it meant:

I saw in front of me an oak of a strange form and aspect. Its branches appeared to me broken and to move heavily in the wind which, at this spot on the mountain, blew more violently. My sight, which is very short, did not allow me to distinguish completely the appearance of this tree. . . . I advanced my head in order to see better and, in the movement, my forehead received a kick from the foot of a horrible corpse, naked, bleeding, mangled and hanging from the tree as a warning of French justice. Nor was it alone; there were three more!'[1]

A few days after this horror worthy of Goya, her escort came across a corpse that had been hacked to pieces among the rocks; it bore the remnants of a French uniform. And so this most brutal of all Napoleon's campaigns went on, year after grisly year.

Nevertheless, by 23 November 1808 Napoleon was poised to take over the leadership of some 130,000 men, breaking through the bleak Guadarrama Mountains, the last natural line of defence to Madrid. Carried astride a cannon (a somewhat absurd spectacle), it was, he complained, a *'Foutu métier.* . . . "Forced labour would be preferable to *this*," murmured some of our veteran soldiers. . . .' His nerves too were on edge, not least because he had added Ney to those in extreme Imperial disfavour – quite unfairly – for the failure of his exhausted troops, operating over impossible country, to close the trap around the Spaniards.

Held up, in glacial conditions, by some 9,000 Spaniards and well-sited artillery at the Somosierra Pass, the key to Madrid and a natural defensive position, Napoleon ordered the Pass to be taken at all costs. Berthier, his ever loyal Chief-of-Staff, backed up by other commanders, claimed that it was an impossible undertaking, whatever the casualties. Napoleon lost his temper, and is reported to have barked, 'Impossible? I don't know the meaning of that word. *Laissez faire les Polonais* – now!' He then turned to his personal escort of Polish Light Horse, and ordered them to charge the Spanish guns 'at a gallop!' It was a callous order, leading to a suicidal action. With a gallantry typical of that nation which Napoleon was already preparing to traduce, and in a style evocative of the British Light Brigade at Balaclava half a century later, his Poles charged, twice, up the steep pass: 'four abreast, gathering speed as we went, unsheathed sabres in one hand, pistol held in the other, reins gathered between the teeth . . . shouting "Vive l'Empereur!", oblivious of the murderous enemy fire from above,' wrote Captain Niegelowski.[2] When the Polish cavalry came to a halt, only thirty yards from the smoking Spanish guns, sixty out of the original eighty-seven had fallen, without a single officer left to command the survivors. Napoleon told them they were 'as brave as my old regiments of the Guard, I salute you', which allegedly caused the fanatically loyal Poles to weep with joy. Shortly afterwards he ordered a carefully co-ordinated infantry and cavalry attack, which seized the Pass. The sacrifice of the Poles was proved totally unnecessary, revealing not only stress, but perhaps a new unsteadiness in Napoleon's personal command.

The Spanish defenders turned and fled. At midday on 4 December, the French entered the sullen and deserted streets of Madrid. Napoleon reinstated his brother, King Joseph, on the throne. The Inquisition was abolished, and new, radical reforms were immediately introduced into the creaky, feudal system of Spain. Many of them were long overdue, but, imposed at bayonet point, they were bitterly offensive to both Spanish pride and Spanish religion. Meanwhile, Moore was still as far away as Salamanca and, aware of the breakdown of the Spanish forces, prepared to play a cautiously bold hand. Discovering from despatches intercepted by Spanish guerrillas that Soult's II Corps had exposed itself beyond its strength, he launched a sudden attack, taking the French totally by surprise at Sahagún, north of Salamanca. It was only partially effective, but it acted as an inspired 'red herring' which persuaded Napoleon to suspend the advance on Lisbon to concentrate all his forces on rounding up Moore. He was, he declared, 'the only general now fit to contend with me. I shall advance against him in person.' The Emperor himself personally took charge, whipping on his tired troops to pursue the 'perfidious islanders'. At one point, he was the first man to enter a village the English had left only two hours previously, causing a concerned Ney to issue a mild rebuke: 'Sire, I thank Your Majesty for acting as my advance guard!' On 27 December, Napoleon wrote to his brother King Joseph in Madrid, 'If the English are not already in full retreat, they are lost; and if they retire, they will be pursued right up to their embarkation and at least half of them will not get away.'

Moore, however, had warning that Napoleon was intending to recross the wintry Guadarramas so as to take him from the rear, and, aided by a two-day snowstorm, escaped precipitately with his army into the Cantabrian Mountains, heading for the small port of Corunna at the top left-hand corner of Spain.

Convinced that the campaign was all but over, and deeply concerned by the news from Paris, on 2 January 1809 Napoleon sped back there to deal with his multitudinous problems at home, leaving Soult to mop up Moore. He had been away from France for a crucial eighty-seven days, and would never return to Spain. News of his departure provoked a considerable stir in the army left behind in Spain, as well as bitter jealousies among the marshals, which were to help Moore in his retreat. There followed a dramatic pursuit, and one of the most heroic retreats in the history of the British Army, with fatigue, hunger and the atrocious winter conditions in the Cantabrian Mountains threatening to break morale and reduce the British forces to an undisciplined rabble. Possibly only a Moore could have achieved it.

On the night of 11 January, three of Moore's four divisions reached Corunna; but there was no sign of the Royal Navy and the promised transports. Yet, with Napoleon's hand off the wheel, Soult advanced circumspectly and Ney lagged behind, so that Moore was given four precious days in which to organize a Dunkirk-style defence of the embarkation perimeter. On the 14th, the long-awaited sails appeared, and Moore began his evacuation. He had lost 5,000 men of his small army on the bitter retreat. The following day Soult, now Duke of Dalmatia,

LIEUTENANT-GENERAL SIR JOHN MOORE
Wounded at Corunna, 1809

decided to attack before waiting for Ney to arrive. Having blown up their gunpowder reserves and evacuated all but 15,000 infantry with nine cannon, the British put up the kind of dogged defence that distinguishes them when in adversity, with backs to a friendly sea. But, in the afternoon of the 16th, tragedy struck when Moore was mortally wounded by a cannon-ball, which tore away his left shoulder, leaving the lungs exposed. Carried off the field in a blanket, he repeatedly urged his bearers to leave him and return to the battle, but had the satisfaction of seeing Soult's assault repelled. Before dawn the following morning he was buried secretly and silently by lantern in an unmarked grave.

> Not a drum was heard, not a funeral note,
>   As his corse to the rampart we hurried;

went the lines (by Charles Wolfe) which immortalized Moore for generations of British schoolchildren. His last words were: 'I hope the people will be satisfied. I hope my country will do me justice.'

In fact, reviling him for failing to hold Spain (an impossible task), Moore's countrymen did not, initially anyway, do him justice.

> Slowly and sadly we laid him down,
>> From the field of his fame fresh and gory;
> We carved not a line, and we raised not a stone,
>> But we left him alone with his glory.

It was his adversary, Soult, who chivalrously erected a monument to his memory on the ramparts of Corunna. Yet of Sir John Moore's small army, safely evacuated by 18 January, 27,000 safely reached Britain, despite severe gales at sea. Beyond that, the achievements of his three-month campaign proved to be immense; the 'red herring' managed to disrupt completely Napoleon's plans, and distract him from pressing on to capture Seville and Lisbon; and he had averted, just in time, what might well have been the greatest military disaster in British history to date. Moore had in effect gained a whole year's respite that would eventually save both Portugal and Spain. If nothing else, it showed once more how crucial the naval supremacy won at Trafalgar would eventually prove against all the massive advantage that Napoleon, with his interior lines, could wield on land. It was a lesson that would be repeated a century later, in both world wars.

After three months had passed, Wellesley, transported by the navy now dominant on the seas, was back in Lisbon at the head of 40,000 men.

SO ENDED 1808, a year Napoleon would always rue. 'I should never have started this adventure,' was his reflection in St

Helena about the Iberian sideshow. By the end of the following year, 1809, no less than 270,000 of his best troops would be committed to the Peninsular War – nearly three-fifths of his total forces. Of them, by the time of the evacuation of Corunna, instead of the 12,000 he had originally allowed for, he had already lost something approaching 75,000 men. Possibly it could all have been avoided, had he endeavoured to control Spain through a Bourbon puppet, like Ferdinand, as he had done with the German states, instead of insisting on the installation of one of his own clan. But he had been carried away by belief in his own star, by sheer hubris following the great triumphs of 1805–7. As with Hitler after his triumphant 1940 campaign in France, the shortcomings of his field commanders filled Napoleon with a mounting conviction of his own divine indispensability, which in turn made it increasingly difficult for him to delegate responsibility. It was a fault that would prove fatal to both. For the first time the lesson was brought home to Napoleon – or at least it should have been, just as it should have been learnt by Hitler after 1940: military supremacy and conquest cannot of themselves buy political success. If only Bonaparte had listened to Talleyrand . . .

FOURTEEN

The Last Victory: Wagram

1809

I expect no good from this battle, but however it ends it
will be my last.

Marshal Lannes

NAPOLEON REACHED PARIS at the end of January 1809
to find that morale was disquietingly low. The economy was in
far poorer shape than when he had launched his Spanish enterprise. The costs of war continued unremitting, on top of the ever
expanding expense of maintaining Napoleon's new Imperial
splendour. It was a consequence notably of the British blockade;
once again there was *Perfide Albion* obstructing his ambitions at
every turn. There was growing resistance to conscription for the
Spanish campaign, the first venture that had lacked the excuse of
a foreign, royalist coalition united against Revolutionary France.
One in ten new recruits were deserting, or mutilating themselves. Yet Napoleon was determined to call up another half-
million. Fouché warned him no longer to count on 'spontaneous'
public enthusiasm. The Imperial family had also become less
popular than ever before, as their mounting greed added to the
overheads of the Empire. Napoleon at least recognized the truth
of some of this, admitting brutally to Fouché that 'This year is an
inopportune time to shock public opinion by repudiating the
popular Empress. . . . she is responsible for attaching a part of
Paris society to me which would then leave me.' He would have
to wait until another triumph could be achieved on the battlefield.

The improbable *entente* between Talleyrand and Fouché,

unpalatable as it was, filled Napoleon with alarm. Perfectly aware of the extent to which these two all-powerful figures had been plotting his downfall while he was away in Spain, Napoleon would have been well within his rights, as an autocrat, if he had proceeded severely against both. That he did not, when he possessed all the power to do so, is remarkable and not easily explained. It is said that Napoleon was the more fearful of Fouché, because, as one of the few survivors from the days of the Terror, he knew how to bring down a regime – and probably had too much on the Emperor personally from the police files at his disposal. But the fact that he never moved against either of the plotters indicates that Napoleon was not a despot of the ilk of a Hitler or a Stalin – or even of a Henri IV or Louis XIV, neither of whom would have hesitated to liquidate two such disloyal ministers. (Fouché himself lasted another two years, until Napoleon discovered he had been intriguing with both the House of Bourbon in exile and the English; yet, even then, he remained in Napoleon's service, on missions to Italy and Dalmatia, and was reinstated as Minister of Police during the 'Hundred Days'.)

On his return to Paris, Napoleon limited himself to a terrible tirade of abuse in an audience to which he summoned Talleyrand, who was now actively conniving with the Austrians, just as he had with the Tsar the previous year. In a half-hour of uninterrupted invective, there was, wrote Duff Cooper, 'hardly a crime omitted from the indictment, hardly a word of abuse that was not applied. Talleyrand was called a thief, a coward and a traitor.'[1] Napoleon accused him of being responsible for the death of the Duc d'Enghien, and – even more unfairly – for the Peninsular War. Talleyrand took it all with impassivity, which provoked Napoleon to lose all control and fly into a daemonic, Corsican rage, taunting Talleyrand with his physical deformity and his wife's infidelity. Finally, when he seemed to be on the point of striking his former Foreign Minister, he dismissed him as being 'nothing but shit in a silk stocking'. Witnesses were horrified, no low-born corporal of the *Grande Armée* would have been allowed to get away with addressing even a recruit like this. As Talleyrand limped down the corridor, he remarked to one of them calmly, 'What a pity such a great man should be so ill-bred!' He then took himself at once to the Austrian Embassy, where in anticipation of services to be rendered he received one million francs from the Austrian Ambassador, a Count Metternich, who had spent his three years in Paris working hard for a rapprochement with France.*

In addition to the appalling tongue-lashing, Talleyrand was deposed from his post as Grand Chamberlain. His role as an adviser to Napoleon was over; he would now be in open opposition. As Duff Cooper remarks, 'During the next five years Talleyrand remained at the Court of Napoleon in a position with which it is difficult to find any parallel.'² He had forfeited in perpetuity the confidence Napoleon once had in him, and was constantly giving him fresh proof of treachery. Yet he was allowed to continue to hold the sinecure honour of Vice-Grand Elector.

NAPOLEON NOW TURNED his back resolutely on the Iberian Peninsula, to face – once again – Central Europe, where the Austrians were proceeding apace with their preparations for war. Giving support to the old adage about the deadlier of the species, at this time three of Napoleon's most unrelenting enemies on the continent were women, all crowned heads: the Dowager Empress Marie of Russia, Queen Louise of Prussia, always chafing at the humiliation of her country and of her rather spineless husband, and now Empress Ludovica of Austria, who lent her considerable weight to the 'Schönbrunn War Party'. Napoleon's defeat at Bailén had decided Austria's hawks that the time was ripe for their country to fight again. The question was,

---

* Metternich returned to Austria later that year, to become – aged thirty-six – Chancellor and Minister of Foreign Affairs.

when? Still only thirty-eight, Austria's ablest military leader, Archduke Charles, currently Emperor Francis's Commander-in-Chief, was a dove in favour of delay. Charles was the younger brother of Emperor Francis, and first fought against the French at Jemappes in 1792. In the Italian Campaign of 1796–7, he was defeated by Napoleon but conducted a distinguished rearguard action, which kept his army together. For this he was promoted Field-Marshal. He gave up his military career, temporarily, to become Governor of Bohemia and then Minister of War. But during the 1805 (Austerlitz) Campaign, he was again back in Italy, summoned to command the Austrian armies there, and checking Masséna at Caldiero. After Austerlitz, he masterminded the successful reconstruction of the Habsburg army. Better than anyone, however, he realized that his army needed more time in which to mobilize and, if possible, to find allies. Better than anyone he knew the state of the army. Under his tutelage, it had since Austerlitz come an impressively long way, despite the perennial difficulties imposed by instilling pro-Habsburg enthusiasm among the various Hungarian, Polish and Balkan non-German-speaking members of the amorphous Empire. The Austrian Army's weakest points remained its staff organization and its communications – defects that were, yet again, to have a baneful influence on the forthcoming campaign. Compared with the reservoir of 200,000 regular soldiers available in 1805, Charles had succeeded in raising a total of 340,000; after the experience on the field of Austerlitz, he had also successfully adapted Napoleon's *corps d'armée* system. His forces were now, in relation to those of Austerlitz, an infinitely superior weapon, deserving far better than Napoleon's contemptuous sobriquet, '*cette canaille*'. Because of Spain, Charles reckoned that Napoleon would be able to concentrate no more than 200,000 men in Germany by the spring of 1809, but he personally would have liked to field a weightier army of 700,000 well-trained men before committing Austria irrevocably to a new war. Yet reports from Talleyrand, via Metternich, stressing French war-weariness, encouraged the hawks of the War Party to act. On 9 February 1809, the Austrian Government committed itself to war.

The raising of 180,000 *Landwehr* reservists in 1808 had already given Napoleon advance warning of what to expect. To pre-empt an Austrian attack he planned to mobilize 260,000 troops in Germany (of whom 100,000 would be produced by his German allies), and another 150,000 to threaten Austria from her Italian 'underbelly'. His 29,000-strong cavalry maintained its deterringly high standards, but the years of attrition had distinctly lowered the quality of the French infantry. 'The worse the troops are,' he told his Minister of War, 'the more guns they require.' With only 311 cannon available, it was not till the last, decisive battle at Wagram that he would be strong enough in artillery, the arm which, he once declared, 'forms the veritable destiny of people'.

Nevertheless, it was imperative for him to strike against the Austrians before the Tsar could be induced, by pressure from his fellow Emperor, Francis, to descend from his perch of now scarcely benevolent neutrality. The 'Spirit of Tilsit' had run very thin indeed. As a subsidiary objective, Napoleon deemed it timely to thwart the growth of resurgent pan-German nationalism. Once again, he found himself forced by his own policies into a pre-emptive war; once again, he moved with consummate speed; once again, as in 1805, he decided to make the Danube the principal theatre. Ratisbon (now Regensburg, in Bavaria), on the Upper Danube, close to the border of what is now the Czech Republic, became his focus of operations. As in 1805, he hoped that a feint in Italy, mounted by his stepson Eugène de Beauharnais and Marmont, would induce the Austrians to split their forces. But this time Archduke Charles was too smart to take the bait.

The Austrians attacked first, on 9 April, well ahead of Napoleon's expectations. In London on the same day their new alliance with Britain came into being, creating the Fifth Coalition against Napoleon. Apart from the old enticement of London gold

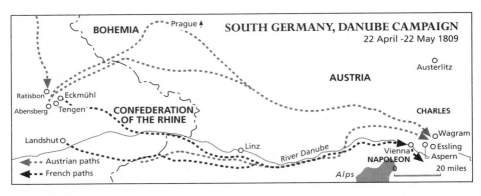

SOUTH GERMANY, DANUBE CAMPAIGN
22 April -22 May 1809

BOHEMIA
Prague
AUSTRIA
Austerlitz
Ratisbon
Eckmühl
CHARLES
Abensberg
Tengen
CONFEDERATION
OF THE RHINE
Wagram
Landshut
Linz
River Danube
Essling
Vienna
Aspern
NAPOLEON
Austrian paths
20 miles
French paths
Alps

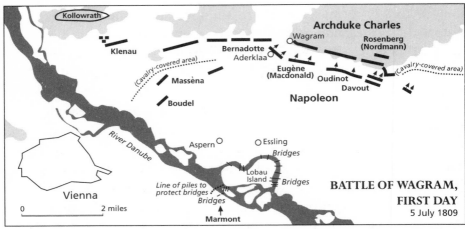

BATTLE OF WAGRAM,
FIRST DAY
5 July 1809

Kollowrath
Archduke Charles
Klenau
Wagram
Rosenberg
(Nordmann)
Bernadotte
Aderklaa
(Cavalry-covered area)
Eugène
(Macdonald)
Oudinot
(Cavalry-covered area)
Massèna
Davout
Boudel
Napoleon
River Danube
Aspern
Essling
Bridges
Lobau
Island
Bridges
Line of piles to
protect bridges
Bridges
Vienna
2 miles
Marmont
0

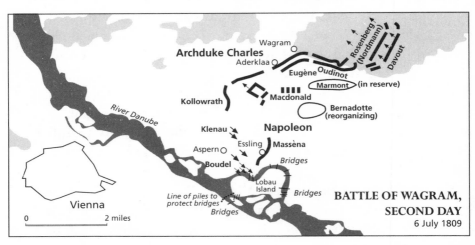

BATTLE OF WAGRAM,
SECOND DAY
6 July 1809

Wagram
Archduke Charles
Rosenberg
(Nordmann)
Davout
Aderklaa
Eugène
Oudinot
Marmont (in reserve)
Kollowrath
Macdonald
Bernadotte
(reorganizing)
River Danube
Klenau
Essling
Massèna
Aspern
Napoleon
Boudel
Bridges
Lobau
Island
Bridges
Line of piles to
protect bridges
Vienna
Bridges
2 miles
0

('St George's Cavalry', as it had come unflatteringly to be called), new British expeditionary forces were promised for landings in Italy and the Low Countries, the latter under the brother of the late William Pitt, Lord Chatham. Moving swiftly, Archduke Charles came within an inch of catching the *Grande Armée* before it could concentrate. Napoleon had committed a cardinal error by placing all the forces in Germany under command of Berthier. Like many a brilliant staff officer, the impeccable Berthier was no commander. Due to a rare confusion of orders between him and Napoleon, a gap of seventy-five miles opened up between the two wings in Bavaria, with the indispensable Davout kept fruitlessly marching and counter-marching.

To meet the emergency, Napoleon left Paris in top haste on the 13th. According to his faithful valet, Constant, he tried to leave before dawn, without telling Josephine. However, she flew out of bed and rushed down to the courtyard in her bedroom slippers. 'Crying like a child, she threw herself into his carriage; she was so lightly dressed that His Majesty threw his fur-lined coat over her shoulders and then issued orders for her luggage to be sent on to her.'[3] There followed another desperate journey in pursuit of war together; for Josephine it would be the last. Meanwhile, in a thoroughly gloom-bound Paris the stock exchange plunged. It was all too clear that the fate of the Empire, and of the Emperor, depended on the course of a single battle, 'more so than at any time since Marengo'.

Once again moving at his usual lightning speed, Napoleon reached Bavaria four days later, on the 17th, just in time, to discover Davout threatened by no fewer than 80,000 Austrians. This was partly due to Napoleon's own miscalculations. Acting with all his old verve, he ordered up Masséna to launch a diversionary attack on Charles's flank. 'Activity! Activity! Speed! I greet you,' he scribbled on the orders to Masséna. Napoleon always remained proud of the five battles fought over the next few days, between Ratisbon and Landshut, in which he restored the situation. In fact, though they inflicted heavy casualties on the Austrians, the engagements were inconclusive, with Charles managing to escape with the bulk of his army intact from a typical Napoleonic trap. The *Grande Armée* was too exhausted to pursue. Meanwhile, during the siege of Ratisbon and its key bridge across the Danube, something terrible occurred. For the first time, the seemingly invulnerable Emperor was slightly wounded in the foot by a spent cannon-ball. It was an alarmingly close shave, and the demoralizing news spread like wildfire through the fatigued army. In considerable pain, Napoleon insisted on riding up and down the lines, as if to prove he was still immortal – if not untouchable. Though a notable local victory, the third in three days, was won by an outnumbered Davout at Eckmühl,* where Charles lost 7,000 in killed and wounded, and 5,000 prisoners against a total of 6,000 French casualties, this first phase of the campaign ended indecisively. Napoleon had achieved no swift knock-out blow, as he had done in 1805 and 1806, though he congratulated Davout for having executed 'another Jena'.

Nevertheless, the Bavarian preliminaries had opened the way to Vienna, and left Charles licking his wounds. He wrote a thoroughly pessimistic note to Emperor Francis: 'If we have another engagement such as this [Eckmühl], I shall have no army left. I am awaiting negotiations.' Certainly it was a remarkable achievement for the *Grande Armée*, when one considers that, with the Guard absent, most of the fighting was done by comparatively raw conscripts. The *esprit* and *élan* of Napoleon's forces were still in evidence; and the outcome of the initial fighting sufficed to deter the Tsar and the wobbling princelings of the Confederation of the Rhine from making common cause with Austria – this time. So in this new war of the Fifth Coalition, Austria, still awaiting the elusive 'St George's Cavalry', found herself alone.

---

* For which he was subsequently rewarded with the title of Prince of Eckmühl, to add to Duke of Auerstädt, gained at Jena.

The Last Victory: Wagram

THE DANUBE AT THE ISLAND OF LOBAU, 1995
David Mynett

Instead of pursuing Charles north-eastwards into Bohemia, Napoleon chose to move on Vienna – drawn, perhaps irrationally, in much the same way as Murat had been in 1805. By 10 May he was at its gates, and three days later the capital surrendered, under threat of bombardment. In marked contrast to his entry of four years previously, he found the people sullen and bitter. There were a number of outbreaks of violence against the French, and the imposition of the oppressive measures which followed indicates how anxious the conquerors were. Contrary to popular legend, Vienna lies not on the main waters of the Danube but on a branch of that great river slightly to the south; thus its occupation left Napoleon on the wrong side of the mighty river. Unlike 1805, its few vital bridges had been destroyed, with the powerful bulk of the Austrian forces re-forming for battle under Archduke Charles to the north. Once again Napoleon's intelligence let him down in a way that it never had in 1805, and he was taken aback to discover that Charles with 115,000 men was bearing rapidly down on the city, where the French had only 82,000 men. He had allowed his effectives to become scattered in a manner quite untypical of the master. If he was to strike tellingly against Charles, he had somehow to get back across the Danube; otherwise he might find himself in a trap. It seemed as if a miracle were needed.

Napoleon's engineers, to whom history has probably never given sufficient credit, provided one. Just four miles downstream from Vienna, there is a cluster of small islands in the river, the largest being Lobau.* The water there was shallow, the current slower, and, as it lay only 100 yards from the north bank, the island's approaches were reasonably protected from enemy gunfire. While Napoleon's chief engineer, General Count Bertrand (who was later to accompany him on his return from Elba), distracted the Austrians by constructing another bridge at Nussdorf, nearer Vienna, bridging materials were floated secretly down the river. It was a major undertaking; there was a distance of 825 yards, half a mile, between the south bank and Lobau, requiring sixty-eight pontoons and nine rafts to span it. It had to be strong enough to support the whole army, with its cannon and baggage trains; and by 16 May Charles was within a few miles of the river. By midday on the 20th, the southern stretch of the bridge was ready, and Masséna's IV Corps and the cavalry began to move on to the island. By 6 p.m. the critical second section of the bridge was in place, amazingly enough unspotted apparently by the enemy (the crossing would have been helped by woods of aspen and willow, and thick undergrowth), and the

---

* Today Lobau is a densely wooded nudist colony. To prevent its recurrent flooding, at the end of the nineteenth century under Emperor Franz Joseph, works on a staggering scale were undertaken to recanalize the Danube. As a result, Lobau and the chain of small islands have now been swallowed by the mainland, but their shapes can just be identified by the elongated lakes that are left.

French began swiftly to occupy the undefended villages of Aspern and Essling on the north bank of the Danube.

It was a most remarkable undertaking, though it was nearly overtaken by disaster when a large Austrian hulk, floating down on the current, smashed the main pontoon bridge. This seriously delayed the build-up of forces on Lobau, while the French light cavalry for once disappointed Napoleon by being unable to provide any clear reconnaissance reports on the position of Charles's main force. In fact, Charles was now fully aware of what was afoot, and was preparing to attack Napoleon with four corps along a six-mile front between Aspern and Essling. Had Napoleon in his heyday been presented with such an opportunity as now lay within the reach of Charles, a foe inferior in numbers backed up against a huge river, it would almost certainly have led to a decisive victory. Charles, however, limited his objective to pushing the French back on to Lobau, rather than attempting a battle of annihilation. At midday on the 21st, the tenuous life-line of the Lobau bridge was breached yet again, interrupting the flow of troops a second time. Napoleon contemplated aborting the whole operation. By this time however, his troops were already heavily engaged at Aspern, where they had been taken completely by surprise, and there was no question of withdrawal.

By dusk on the 21st, only 31,000 men of the *Grande Armée* had been deployed – though it reflected a staggering feat of organization to get so many across the one pontoon bridge. But facing them were over 100,000 Austrians, with at least 260 cannon. The bitter fighting is described by an Austrian eyewitness;

> Both sides, seeing the value of the village, continued to contest the battle here. In every street the fight raged; in every house, in every ditch. Carriages and carts were obliterated by musket fire before the battle was fought hand to hand. Every wall was of strategic importance. . . . [4]

The Austrians came perilously close to driving General Molitor's division back on the river at Aspern on Napoleon's left flank. But that evening a brilliant counter-attack led by Marshal Lannes and General St Hilaire, both heroes of Austerlitz, partly restored the situation by pushing the Austrians out of Aspern. Lannes, the dyer's apprentice and former sergeant who had fought under Lafayette in America, a hero of Austerlitz who had been wounded more times than almost any of his peers, was fearless that day: 'nothing could stand in his way,' recorded the Baron de Marbot, guilty of possibly only a little hyperbole:

> in one instance he captured a complete battalion, a standard and five guns. The Austrians fell back with regularity, but their centre, being compelled to extend as we advanced further, finished by breaking! Disorder set in among the enemy troops to such a degree that we could see the officers and sergeants beating their men with sticks without being able to keep them in their ranks. . . .[5]

In the battle, however, St Hilaire was mortally wounded, his left foot shot away. He died in Vienna two weeks later. A short while later, Lannes had both legs smashed by a cannon-ball. A young French regimental apothecary endeavouring to watch the battle from the Gloriette folly above Schönbrunn saw nothing, on account of the thick smoke from the guns and the burning houses, but he recalled 'how the Duke of Montebello [Marshal Lannes] had felt uneasy about the battle. "We have hurried too much, gentlemen. I expect no good from this battle, but however it ends it will be my last."' The young cadet continued, 'The Viennese spirit is egregious. They curse our wounded even in hospital.'[6]

Then a wounded general brought news that Lannes was dead. Surgeon-General Larrey had amputated his right leg, and at first it had seemed he might survive, but Lannes succumbed to the ubiquitous scourge of gangrene on 31 May. Both his and St Hilaire's death were grievous losses to Napoleon, but Lannes's especially so. He was the first of the marshalcy to die in action, one of the commanders most trusted by Napoleon, and also one of his few true friends. Napoleon wept openly at his death: 'He was a swordsman when I found him, and a paladin when I lost him,' he declared. Meanwhile, himself already wounded so recently, Napoleon had come in such close proximity to the enemy artillery fire that the Guard ordered him out of range, threatening to lay down their arms '*si l'Empereur ne se retire pas*'.

AFTER TWO DAYS' bitter fighting, on the 22nd, under cover of darkness, Napoleon withdrew the whole army back across the Danube on to Lobau, cutting the northern section of the bridge as they retired. Masséna, whose IV Corps had saved the day and who was subsequently given the title Prince of Essling for his distinction there, was almost the last man to cross in safety on to the island. Austrian losses totalled another 23,340, but they lost only six guns; Napoleon, blatantly saving face, claimed only to have lost three guns and 4,100 men, but in fact the total was reckoned to have added up to over 20,000. The plight of the thousands of wounded, left out on the battlefield for two days and nights, was particularly grievous. For once Napoleon showed marked concern, commandeering and slaughtering the horses of even his senior officers to provide broth for the wounded, and ensuring their evacuation to the hospitals of Vienna. For his achievements, his overworked Surgeon-General Larrey was made a baron.

Napoleon had also lost two of his best commanders. Much more seriously, though hard to quantify in terms of divisions and army corps, his reputation had suffered immeasurably. News of the check at Aspern–Essling sped around the world; Europe bubbled with rumours that Napoleon was trapped on the Island of Lobau, that his army had suffered such crippling losses that he was now at the mercy of Archduke Charles. Very probably, had he then possessed in reserve the troops detached to face Wellesley in the Peninsula, Napoleon would have won the day at

ASPERN CHURCH, 1995
David Mynett

Essling. As it was, the news of his setback was particularly cheering for Wellesley and his embattled men in Portugal, and for the shaky Government in London. It was one thing to wrest victory from his subordinates like Dupont at Bailén, but something totally different to administer such a harsh rebuff to forces commanded by Napoleon himself, and on ground he knew personally so well from 1805. One of his least impressive performances, it also suggested a new Napoleon, inflated with conceit from the victories of 1805–7, resting on his laurels and carelessly contemptuous of the *canaille* of the Austrians opposing him. He had acted precipitately, without thorough preparation, in a way that he had never done before. He remained for thirty-six hours after the battle in a state of dazed indecision, evidence of the shock that had been inflicted upon his own morale and self-esteem.

But the engagement, following on the costly earlier fighting around Ratisbon, had shaken Archduke Charles even more. Although his new armies had fought so well, he now lapsed back into that deadly old Habsburg sin of lethargy. Still a dove at heart, he mistakenly believed that Napoleon would now accept a negotiated peace. He half hoped for a general German uprising, for help from the Tsar and for the arrival of Archduke John from the south-east. None of these eventualities occurred: the Germans remained sullenly inactive; Tsar Alexander busied himself in Polish Galicia, at Austria's expense; while John proved himself a busted flush. Just as he had done in 1805, John allowed himself to be defeated, this time by Italian troops commanded by Eugène de Beauharnais and Macdonald, the son of a Scottish Jacobite exile, on 14 June, the anniversary of Marengo. His forces had been driven back into Hungary. Meanwhile, curiously passive, Charles regrouped his army, still over 130,000 strong, around the small town of Wagram. Some six miles back from the Danube at Aspern–Essling, Wagram sits on a flat, alluvial plain, with virtually no features. Unlike Austerlitz, there seems no good reason whatsoever for a battle to be fought there. To the east, the ground (now heavily populated by the 'nodding donkeys' of Austria's oilfields) rises towards the Carpathian foothills just visible in the distance. Wagram lies, rather ominously, only some fifty miles southwards from Austerlitz. Inexplicably, the Austrian commander did little to fortify his unimposing position. In contrast, during the six weeks before the next engagement, Napoleon moved vigorously to redress the improvidence which had caused him to suffer such a reverse at Aspern–Essling. All available forces were summoned to the Vienna area; Davout from Pressburg (now Bratislava) and Eugène from Raab to the south-east, Marmont from Graz and Bernadotte from the north-west, with Vandamme holding Vienna and its approaches. Their convergence was to support Masséna already in position again south of the Danube and on Lobau Island. Altogether, by the beginning of July, Napoleon had managed to muster over

160,000 men, backed this time by a powerful concentration of artillery.

As a new confrontation approached, Napoleon appeared contritely to have absorbed the lessons of Aspern–Essling. He laid his plans most carefully. He had ordered his engineers to drive in a line of piles across the southern reach of the Danube to protect the main bridge across to Lobau Island. This was still the key to, and the jumping-off point for, his next move. The Aspern–Essling sector where he had crossed previously was, however, closely watched by the Austrians, and the two villages were now heavily fortified. According to Baron Marbot, during the period of inaction Napoleon and Marshal Masséna disguised themselves in sergeants' greatcoats, so as to be able to reconnoitre, personally and at their leisure, the riparian stretches of the island within a hundred yards of the Austrian outposts: 'The Austrians were so used to seeing small groups of our soldiers swimming in the area that they stayed peacefully lying in the grass.'[7] Such was the essential gentlemanliness of warfare even by the time of Napoleon. As a result he appreciated that he could erect a series of pontoons across the eastern end of the island, where there was a string of tiny islets, out of sight of the Austrians. From here he could outflank Charles's army to the east. The main crossing would be via the islet appropriately christened Île Alexandre, after Chief-of-Staff Berthier, now forgiven his earlier shortcomings in Bavaria.

On the night of 3/4 July, the bulk of the *Grande Armée* was ready. A diversionary bridge was run across the old route in the direction of Aspern–Essling, and Charles prepared for a renewed attack from that quarter. Archduke John was summoned up from Pressburg to join the main army, but, characteristically, he did not begin to move until midnight on the 5th/6th, by which time the battle would have been fought, and lost.

Early on the night of the 4th, Oudinot, the brewer's son who had taken over II Corps from the dead Lannes, despite being wounded himself at Aspern, swiftly occupied the empty south-east corner of Lobau. He then pushed a brigade across the Danube to seize a bridgehead on the lightly held opposite bank, near Mühlleuten. An impressive array of pontoons, rafts, portable bridges and special landing-craft – all fabricated locally – was assembled for the second river crossing. A new trestle bridge had been built alongside the existing pontoon bridge connecting Lobau to the south bank, both protected from fireships and floating hulks by a line of protective piles driven into the bed of the Danube. At Île Alexandre, where Masséna's main assault force was to cross over to the north bank, a prefabricated bridge, consisting of fourteen pontoons, was swung into position in one piece over a distance of 178 yards – all within a space of five minutes, and despite violent storms. It was another remarkable feat of military engineering; and not a bridge gave way. By dawn on the 5th, Napoleon had got three corps across the Danube, Masséna's, Oudinot's and Davout's, followed closely by Marmont's, and in attack formation. To have moved the best part of 100,000 men in the dark, across two sets of pontoon bridges, then to have mustered them on an island two miles across, in close proximity to a supposedly vigilant enemy, all with virtually no loss of life, was a feat that would have been difficult to rival even in the Second World War, with all its modern mechanization and communications. It showed Napoleon, his commanders and above all General Bertrand and his Corps of Engineers at their very best. By 6 p.m., with 188,900 men and 488 guns, the French were in a good position to attack the Wagram position. Napoleon had skilfully placed his army centrally between the two enemy wings, and with his legendary *coup d'oeil* he could now see that the main Austrian position there had been hastily occupied. A shock frontal attack might break it up. Once again, he seems to have been thinking of Soult's famous assault on the Pratzen Heights at Austerlitz. But the first efforts, in the twilight, were beaten back, with the French attackers firing at each other.

Charles now drew up his own ambitious plan to envelop

Napoleon on his left flank, northwards from the Danube. If it succeeded, it could be another Cannae; but failure would cut Charles off from Hungary, and the armies there. However, as one of the leading American authorities, Brigadier-General Esposito of West Point, notes, 'Its weaknesses were Charles's failure to assemble all available troops, John's proven stupidity, and the innate inefficiency of the Austrian staff and corps commanders.'[8] The two principal Austrian corps commanders, Klenau and Kollowrath (of Austerlitz), failed to leave their bivouacs until 0400 hours on the 6th, while Napoleon was already up and bullying his commanders forward. From the Austrian point of view, it was depressingly the mixture as before, proving that Charles had been right in his belief that – for all his reforms – his army was still not up to facing Napoleon in a major pitched battle.

During the first phase of the Battle of Wagram, there were in the heat of that Central European midsummer mistakes committed on the French side, more attributable to the rawness of many of the rank and file and their commanders than to Napoleon's meticulously laid plans. Something which had certainly never been seen at Austerlitz or Jena occurred when Italian units fighting under Macdonald broke and fled, not stopping until they ran on to the bayonets of the Imperial Guard, standing – as usual – in reserve. Davout on the right was slow to move, having once more received his orders too late, while *Belle Jambe* Bernadotte once again failed to obtain his objective and was pushed back. He committed the serious error of boasting that it was all Napoleon's fault, and that had he been in command he could, by means of a 'telling manoeuvre', have routed the Austrians 'almost without combat'. Promptly relayed to Napoleon, the remark was received with cold anger.

Meanwhile, for a moment it looked as if Charles might succeed in his strategy to roll back the French along the bank of the Danube, where Napoleon's rear areas in their narrow bridgeheads across the river were distinctly vulnerable. The hard-pressed

Masséna in the centre of the line was forced to detach troops to regain a key village, Aderklaa, which had been abandoned by Bernadotte, who then had the misfortune to run into the Emperor. Having grabbed only a few hours' sleep under a pile of drums over the past three nights, Napoleon's temper was more than usually short. Not for the first nor for the last time, he was thoroughly fed up with *Belle Jambe*'s boastfulness, so little matched by his actual performance on the battlefield. 'Is this the kind of "telling manoeuvre" with which you will force Archduke Charles to lay down his arms?' he demanded, according to Marbot. 'I hereby remove you from command of the corps which you have handled so consistently badly.' Bernadotte was flabbergasted as Napoleon continued, 'Leave my presence immediately and quit the *Grande Armée* within twenty-four hours. . . .'[9] This was a uniquely rough judgement on one of his original marshals. Bernadotte would one day soon exact his revenge, in treason and revolt.

Fortunately for Napoleon, the slow-moving Austrians (somewhere about this time Archduke Charles had himself been slightly but painfully wounded) failed to take advantage of the hole left by Bernadotte's default. It was noteworthy that the troops on which Napoleon had to rely to plug the hole were Saxon and Italian levies, which held steady only through the massive artillery support of 112 guns that Napoleon was able to bring to bear; and at this critical phase in the battle it was clear to him that the soldiers he now led were far from being of the calibre of the men of Austerlitz. If he took any risks they might well lead to collapse, if not complete panic. Meanwhile, on the left of the line Boudet's anchor division on the Danube had been forced back dangerously by Charles's enveloping move, into the Aspern–Essling bridgehead. Again, the Austrian advance was checked only by massed artillery fire from French batteries on Lobau Island. On the extreme right, the situation by mid-morning on the 6th looked equally uncertain. The ever reliable Davout, his horse killed under him, was having to fight fiercely for every yard in his advance to Markgrafneusiedl, an important bastion in the Austrian line which was now assuming the shape of the letter Z. Anxiously Davout looked over his right shoulder to see if there was any sign of Archduke John's army approaching. But John with his 12,500 fresh troops was still on his way from Pressburg, some twenty miles away, and was moving with little sense of urgency. Had he marched with the kind of speed which was Davout's hallmark, the result at Wagram might well have been different. In the centre, too, Masséna was suffering from injuries sustained in a fall from his horse on 1 July, and he now moved about the battlefield ponderously in an elaborate coach drawn by four white horses.

Napoleon's cavalry spies informed him that John was still several hours' march away from the battlefield, while Davout – thrusting uphill – was breaking through Rosenberg's corps, which in turn was falling back at right angles to the Austrians anchored on Wagram. Jubilantly Napoleon ordered Masséna to launch his attack with all force through the centre of the line, left of Wagram; as the Emperor explained, 'The battle is won since the Archduke John has not appeared.' In the kind of complicated move that only a Napoleonic formation could achieve in the heat of battle, the breakthrough was spearheaded by Macdonald, with three divisions totalling now no more than 8,000 men. These he formed up in a large hollow oblong, capable of fighting in three different directions as it penetrated the Austrian centre. It was a manoeuvre for which Murat's heavy cavalry would have been ideally suited; but Murat, ill and in semi-disgrace, was not there, nor were reserves available. Instead Macdonald's men charged under a barrage of artillery heavier than any seen in Napoleon's previous battles. It was a pale reflection of Soult on the Pratzen; nevertheless, unlike the earlier engagements of the Wagram campaign, this was where the old style of Napoleonic preparation paid off. The midsummer heat was appalling – and so were Macdonald's casualties. Conspicuous on his white horse and, despite his recent experience, oblivious to the cannon-balls falling barely out of range, Napoleon anxiously watched the course of the battle from a knoll only 2,000 yards behind the front.

By 1300 hours, it was clear the battle was won as Archduke Charles began to prepare an orderly withdrawal. This was no Austerlitz, or Jena, however. With the great heat accentuating the exhaustion of the *Grande Armée*, there was no question of immediate pursuit. Napoleon had won what was to be his last victory, but it was a close-run thing, achieved only at terrible cost. Added to the deaths previously of Lannes and St Hilaire was that of General Lasalle, the genius of the light cavalry, shot dead while leading a charge. What the boastful bulletins could not disguise was that Napoleon had lost nearly a quarter of his effectives engaged in the battle, or at least 32,500. They included forty generals, and a further 7,000 prisoners left in Austrian hands. By comparison, the Austrians had lost something like 40,000 men;* but their armies had not been destroyed, as they had been at Austerlitz.

For his role in the victory at Wagram, Macdonald joined the marshalcy, the only one to receive his baton on the battlefield, and later received the dukedom of Taranto – plus a valuable annuity. Despite his earlier disasters in the campaign, Berthier was made Prince of Wagram and given François Premier's great Château de Chambord. Apothecary Cadet de Gassicourt acidly recalled the scenes at Schönbrunn after the victory: Berthier and the military staff 'spent much of the day giving each other decorations to adorn uniforms which have seen little of the battle. None of the soldiers on duty here shows them much respect; not surprisingly, as they have demonstrated so little courage.' He also noted a subtle change of mood among the locals: 'The Austrians have a really splendid character. I am

---

* Perhaps Wagram's most illustrious casualty was the composer Joseph Haydn, who never recovered from the shock of Napoleon's occupation of Vienna and died, aged seventy-seven, two weeks later.

greeted everywhere I go and treated so courteously, as if I were bringing THEM news of THEIR army's victory.'

Although Napoleon's tactical handling at Wagram had been superb, revealing all his old flair, what was as hard to conceal as the French casualty list was the fact that, during the three-month campaign, he had probably committed more errors of judgement than in all his previous campaigns combined. The cost to his reputation was to prove immense. Almost equally damaging was the realization that the quality of troops he commanded had declined. All too many of them were no longer Frenchmen, but Bavarians, Saxons and Italians whose reliability could not be counted on indefinitely — that is, not beyond the first intimations that Napoleon's grip was faltering. For the first time the *Grande Armée* had to create travelling court-martial teams to carry out on-the-spot executions of stragglers and looters.

IN THE AUSTRIAN TYROL, the brave uprising of local patriots led by the innkeeper Andreas Hofer was ruthlessly crushed. Hofer himself was captured and executed in Mantua; he remains to this day a hero in the Tyrol. And what of the British diversionary efforts to support the Austrians in Italy and Walcheren? In a style which would become familiar to students of the Second World War, it was a sad story of too little, too late. At Messina in Sicily, the childishly vain Lieutenant-General Sir John Stuart, who had been under orders to sail for the Italian mainland, was still dawdling and fretting in his quarters with 15,000 unused troops when Napoleon entered Vienna.

The Walcheren expedition to seize Antwerp opened with high expectations, and ended with proportionate disappointment. Long regarded as the strategic key to British hopes in Europe, Antwerp itself was to be a dark name among British military failures in three great wars. In 1914 an attempt to hold it, by amphibious forces under orders of Winston Churchill at the Admiralty, operating with close similarity to the 1809 blueprint,

WAGRAM, 1809
Napoleon defeats Archduke Charles

collapsed dismally. In September 1944, the British failure to take it, in logical follow-through after the euphoric sweep to Paris and Brussels, prolonged the war in Europe into 1945, and led to a bitter winter campaign by Canadians and British Commandos on the same soggy and insalubrious island of Walcheren where Chatham's forces had landed in July 1809.

The appointment of the second Earl of Chatham had been made on political rather than military grounds; aged fifty-two he was totally lacking in the resoluteness of his brother, Pitt the Younger, and was an incompetent commander. To succeed it needed a leader capable of moving with the speed of a Wellington. It was no mean feat in the age of sail to transport a landing force 12,000 strong across the North Sea to land on hostile territory. But, to the accompaniment of military bands, the expedition did not take off until 20 July — by which time the

Austrian ally whom it was designed to assist had already been beaten by Napoleon. In a mistake which was to be repeated in the nearby Arnhem airborne venture of September 1944, the British landed too far from their immediate objective, the port of Flushing. By the time they reached the port, which was under command of the egregious Fouché (who, in Napoleon's absence grabbed the opportunity to pose as the saviour of France)* the French had dug themselves in, effectively barring the tenuous approaches to Antwerp.

> Great Chatham with his sabre drawn
> Stood waiting for Sir Richard Strachan;
> Sir Richard, longing to be at 'em,
> Stood waiting for the Earl of Chatham,

ran an anonymous contemporary jingle. Though the French were initially taken by surprise, the leisurely way in which Chatham's force moved once ashore would be painfully repeated just over a hundred years later at Gallipoli; it would in fact take over 130 years, together with an infusion of American material strength and zip, to achieve the kind of major amphibious success for which Nelson's victory at Trafalgar so befitted British power. After a bombardment which destroyed half the town of Dutch Flushing, the port was captured. By this time Chatham's force had suffered only 700 casualties, while capturing ten times as many prisoners – a sure indication of the possible advantages of sea-power. But now disease – dysentery, malaria (known as 'Walcheren Fever'), typhoid and typhus – took its toll.

Within weeks the troops among the dank dykes and polders of Walcheren were reduced to a fraction of their strength. Medical conditions were deplorable. 'Something must be done,' wrote Lieutenant-General Sir Eyre Coote,† left in charge after

---

* For his enterprise, he was rewarded with the dukedom of Otranto.

† Coote, who had previously been Governor of Jamaica where he had had a liaison with a slave-girl, is now reckoned, by no less an authority than Debretts, to have been a bar-sinister ancestor of America's General Colin Powell.

Chatham had returned home, 'or the British nation will lose the British Army – far more valuable than the island of Walcheren.'[10] Meanwhile King Louis, the puppet Bonaparte King of Holland, and Bernadotte (still smarting from his disgrace at Wagram) had arrived with 26,000 men to block definitively any British threat to Antwerp and Belgium. By the end of September Walcheren had been evacuated; 4,000 had died of disease. As an epilogue to the military disaster, Canning fought his famed duel with Castlereagh, while the ensuing Walcheren Enquiry implicated the royal family with the details it produced of the Duke of York's involvement in the sale of commissions through his mistress, Mary Anne Clarke.*

At the other end of Europe, in Portugal, where Wellesley had arrived with his new army in April, things had initially gone better. Moving from his bridgehead in Portugal with characteristic energy, and extraordinary speed – though he despised his force as a 'rabble' – Wellesley thrust into Spain, halfway to Madrid. He caught Napoleon's two quarrelling marshals, Soult and Victor, their forces depleted by the demands of the Austrian campaign. Splitting them in a manner drawn from the Master's book, on 28 July Wellesley inflicted a serious defeat on Soult at Talavera, which was to become a famous battle-honour of many British regiments. After so many defeats, in Britain he suddenly became the hero of the hour, when the country most needed one, and was ennobled as Viscount Wellington of Talavera. But it was a short-lived triumph – too late, like Walcheren, to take the pressure off Austria. Immediately after his victory at Wagram, utilizing the advantage of his interior lines of communication, Napoleon sped reinforcements to Spain. Their commander was Masséna, one of the ablest of his marshals. Masséna, who pursued women as relentlessly as he did the enemy, caused

---

* The Duke was the second son of George III, and the 'Grand Old Duke of York' of the nursery jingle. He was C.-in-C. of the British Army up till 1809, when he resigned because of the commission scandals.

WELLINGTON
in Spain, 1810

himself difficulties by arriving in Spain with his mistress, Madame Leberton, disguised as a young officer of the dragoons. But he was a formidable general; Wellington himself remarked that he 'never slept comfortably' when Masséna was opposite him. At odds with his allied commander, the elderly and hopeless Spanish General Cuesta, Wellington was forced to fall back from Talavera. It was probably the worst moment of his career. With his wounded suffering appallingly and with hunger exacting a heavy toll on both sides, the new Viscount now had to fight his way back to the last-ditch defensive which he had carefully prepared, guarding Lisbon – the famous Lines of Torres Vedras.

So ended the Fifth Coalition. In Britain the administration of the elderly Duke of Portland fell – to be replaced in October by that of Spencer Perceval, a modest little lawyer and a forty-six-year-old nonentity whom no one in Westminster reckoned would survive a single session. By the Treaty of Schönbrunn, signed by a humiliated Austria on 14 October, the fourth demeaning treaty imposed by the victorious French, Emperor Francis was forced to pay a gigantic war indemnity of eighty-five million francs, and was deprived of vast tracts of territory, together with some three million people, in addition to those he lost after Pressburg. Salzburg was handed to Napoleon's Bavarian allies and part of Galicia to the Duchy of Warsaw, to placate Marie Walewska's countrymen, while France grabbed Trieste and a large strip of the Dalmatian coast for herself – all fairly worthless to Napoleon. The Austrian army was required never again to exceed a total of 150,000 men. Plagued by epilepsy, the so nearly successful Archduke Charles retired, effectively handing over command to Prince Schwarzenberg. He died in 1847. Napoleon demonstrated his displeasure with the Tsar for not keeping Austria in check, as he had undertaken to do at Erfurt, by refusing to support his claims to Austrian Galicia; this was to leave a niggling sore. And Britain, but for her precarious toe-hold in Portugal, was virtually removed from Europe.

Talleyrand groaned in despair. Once again, Napoleon seemed invincible – once more truly the Master of Europe. He was just forty. But unobtrusively his capital was running down. France was desperately war-weary; and Wagram had been won only by the mobilization of foreign levies – among whom the Italians and the Saxons had proved disquietingly unreliable.

FIFTEEN

Love and Marriage

1809–1810

I must look for ways to further the interests of France
through my next union.

Napoleon

AS 1809 DREW TO AN END, two events took place which
were unconnected, but which together were to have a profound
influence on Napoleon's future, and thereby on world history.
Once Vienna had been captured, Napoleon set himself up in
Imperial splendour in the glorious Habsburg castle of Schönbrunn, just outside Vienna. Josephine – by this time in despair,
and having lost all hope with Napoleon – had accompanied him
only as far as Strasbourg, after her precipitate departure from
Paris. She returned to Paris shortly after receiving news of
Napoleon's reverse at Aspern–Essling. It had clearly not been a
happy time for her. The love affair between Napoleon and Marie
Walewska resumed, apparently undiminished in strength; by
spring of 1807 the eighteen-year-old Pole was confessing to a
friend, Elizabeth Sobolewski, 'I really felt I was married to him,'
and in 1808 he had brought her to Paris, her first visit. Then,
from Schönbrunn, as early as 18 May the following year –
therefore little more than a month after his and Josephine's
departure from Paris – Napoleon wrote to her in Poland, urging
her,

Come to Vienna. I want to see you and give you new proofs of
the tender affection I have for you. . . .

> Many tender kisses on your lovely hands and just one on your
> beautiful mouth.

Until the Austrians who stood in her way had been defeated, she
was unable to reach Vienna, but she arrived after Wagram,
having travelled along roads clogged with the debris of a beaten
Austrian army. She was then set up, discreetly (though hardly
invisible to Josephine), in a villa in the park near Schönbrunn.

By September Marie had indeed received ample 'proof' of
Napoleon's affection: she discovered she was pregnant. For once
there could be no question that Napoleon was the father; at last
it was the proof he needed that he was not sterile, and that he
could found a dynasty. But it was to avail the tragic Pole little.
'Generous by nature and suffused with selfless love as she was,'
observes her biographer, Christine Sutherland, 'she probably
never stopped to think where it left her.'[1] Almost immediately
after Marie had revealed her pregnancy, he was writing to his
brother Joseph in Madrid, 'Yes, I am in love,' but 'I must look
for ways to further the interests of France through my next
union' – that is, he planned a dynastic marriage. By modern
standards, or perhaps by any standard, this was not a gallant way
to treat either his adoring, newly pregnant mistress, or his long-
suffering and sad Empress, now forty-six and back at lonely
Malmaison, far more in love with Napoleon than she had ever
been in those giddy, early days when she had made him so jealous
during the Italian campaign.

Then, the following month, Napoleon was suddenly confronted by the prospect of death more closely than ever before.
Just ten days after the signing of the Treaty of Schönbrunn, an
eighteen-year-old German patriot called Friedrich Stapps very
nearly succeeded in assassinating him. At a military review,
Stapps approached as if intent on presenting a petition. A yard
from Napoleon, he pulled a knife, but was prevented from using
it by one of Napoleon's aides, General Jean Rapp (who, at
Austerlitz, had captured Prince Repnin). Napoleon interrogated

the young man at length, trying to discover his motives, and, in a display of magnanimity possibly designed for German consumption, offered Stapps his life if he would express regret for his attempt. Stapps steadfastly refused, declaring: 'I want no pardon. I only regret having failed.' Against his will, Napoleon had no alternative but to have Stapps condemned. The youth was shot a few days later. General Rapp in his memoirs claimed, 'I never saw Napoleon look so confounded,' and he recorded the Emperor as remarking:

> This is the result of the secret societies which infest Germany. This is the effect of fine principles and the light of reason. They make young men assassins. But what can be done against illuminism? A sect cannot be destroyed by cannon-balls.[2]

The remark showed Napoleon aware of how a battle won would not suffice to suppress the new flames of German nationalism. These would help defeat him within four years and would later plunge France three times within seventy years into even worse misery than that which affected Stapps's splintered nation in 1809. But, more immediately, this warning of his mortality, coming so soon on top of the confirmation that he could sire an heir, goaded him on with renewed urgency to perpetuate the dynasty. 'I want to marry a womb,' he declared.

As has been noted, Napoleon had already toyed with the idea of a dynastic marriage to one of the Tsar's sisters, Russian Grand Duchess Catherine, though he had been seen off by the Dowager Empress Marie. He tried again, unsuccessfully, with her sister Anna, but was rejected once more; then, with offensive brusqueness, he switched his attack. In his new position of strength vis-à-vis the humbled Austrians (in Vienna the wags now nicknamed the Emperor 'Francis *Nul*'), his intentions fell upon a Habsburg princess, nineteen-year-old Archduchess Marie Louise, daughter of Emperor Francis and great-niece of Marie Antoinette. His suit was ably assisted by Count Metternich, promoted Austrian Foreign Minister after the Treaty of Schönbrunn. Even in that age of arranged marriages, it represented a stunning *volte face* and was executed with almost indecent speed. When told, at the time of the signature of the Treaty in October 1809, that Napoleon might be visiting the Imperial family, the young Archduchess wrote in her diary, 'To see the man would be the worst form of torture.' Six months later she was married to him.

Both Josephine and Marie Walewska were devastated by news of Napoleon's intention. Marie returned to an icy Warsaw in December. On the 18th, she received a letter from Napoleon, couched in the formal language he had used when pursuing her in Warsaw three long years previously, and so very different in tone from his passionate exhortations of May:

> Madame,
>
> . . . I note with pleasure that you have safely arrived in Warsaw. Take care of your health, which is very precious to me; chase away the black thoughts – you must not worry about the future. . . .

Two months later he was writing even more stiffly: 'I received news of you with great pleasure, but I regret the black mood you seem to be in; it does not suit you at all.'

On 4 May 1810, she gave birth to a boy, whom the old nobleman Anastase Walewski accepted with dignity as his own and to whom he gave his name. Even before he knew the sex of the unborn child, Napoleon declared, '*L'enfant de Wagram* will one day be King of Poland.' Thanks not least to Napoleon, by the time Alexandre Walewski grew up there would be no Poland, though he was to live to become a distinguished Minister of Foreign Affairs under Napoleon's nephew, Louis Napoleon – and to enjoy a longer and far happier life than the legitimate heir with which Marie Louise would shortly present the Emperor.

As for Josephine, we know from the recent study by Evangeline Bruce that she was distraught about losing Napoleon after nearly fourteen years of storm-tossed marriage, but she nonetheless behaved with admirable decorum. Earlier that year she had

had a premonition of what lay ahead, admitting miserably to her friend Laure Junot, Duchess of Abrantès, who was visiting Malmaison, 'I know I will be shamefully dismissed from the bed of the man who crowned me, but God is my witness that I love him more than my life, and much more than the throne. . . .'[3] Having already heard glumly of Marie Walewska's pregnancy, her first definite warning of the impending divorce came on reaching Fontainebleau at the end of October 1809. There she discovered that builders had sealed the door between her apartment and Napoleon's – on direct orders, she was told, from the Emperor in Vienna. According to Bruce, the next few weeks following Napoleon's return were the most painful of Josephine's life. They dined in silence together, meals of fifteen minutes' duration. In their apartments across the courtyard the other members of the Bonaparte clan, who had always hated her, were visibly gloating over her misery. It was not until the end of November that Napoleon actually told her of his intention; afterwards a courtier found the Empress 'stretched out on the carpet, weeping and moaning'. She was to be allowed to keep beloved Malmaison, the title of Queen and Empress, and to receive an allowance of three million francs a year, while all her (numerous) current debts would be paid. Two weeks later, the divorce ceremony, transmuted into a grand social occasion by Napoleon, took place in the Throne Room of the Tuileries. With dignity, Josephine declared, 'I proudly offer him the greatest proof of attachment and devotion ever given a husband on this earth. . . .' Then she broke down. Napoleon himself was in tears; in the weeks to come he seemed plunged in depression and could think only of Josephine.

In happier times, he was said to have frequently told her, superstitiously, that she was 'one of the rays of his star'. The departure of Josephine was to mark quite definitively the downward trajectory of that star. She had earned great popularity throughout France, and devout Catholics would never forgive Napoleon his divorce and remarriage, which compounded his break with the Pope, Pius VII (he had excommunicated the French Emperor after his occupation of Rome in 1808). On 11 March 1810 Marie Louise was married by proxy in Vienna, and arrived at Compiègne on the 27th. In the best Corsican tradition, Napoleon intercepted her there before she could reach Paris, bedding her well in advance of the official ceremony in the Tuileries. With parallel lack of tact, he planned that that ceremony should follow every detail of that of Louis XVI and Marie Antoinette, with the young bride escorted across the very spot where seventeen years previously her aunt had mounted the scaffold. As Arthur Bryant remarks, 'The guillotine had been legitimized.'[4] That July, a hideous disaster took place at the Austrian Embassy, during a ball given to celebrate the marriage. As the dancing began, a fierce storm sprang up, blowing the curtains on to a cluster of candles. Flames ran up the wall, and in seconds there was pandemonium, with the hostess, Princess Schwarzenberg, and many others burnt to a cinder. Benjamin Constant's wife Charlotte, who was there, wrote to him:

> . . . I swear to you that I still think I'm living in a nightmare – a bare seven minutes covered the whole time from the moment we all started for the doors. . . . the flames reached out into the garden after us. . . . we heard the big mirrors cracking and the chandeliers crashing down . . . and through it the screams of the wretched beings who were still inside.[5]

It was hardly an auspicious omen for the Imperial marriage of Austria and France.

In Spain, Wellington greeted the marriage as 'a terrible event'; the new alliance it created between France and her Austrian foe did indeed look terrifying – on paper. But it was not given Wellington to foresee how, in fact, within the short space of two years, the marriage would help bring about the final Coalition which would ultimately topple Napoleon and his whole dynastic ambition.

SIXTEEN

The British Blockade

1810–1812

When I show myself beyond the Pyrenees, the terrified
Leopard [England] will seek the Ocean in order to avoid
shame, defeat and death. The triumph of my arms will be
the triumph of the spirit of good over that of evil.

Napoleon

WITH THE CONCLUSION of the peace treaty at Schönbrunn, as 1809 ended it looked – once again – as if Europe
might find a new period of relative tranquillity. Napoleon's
extended honeymoon with Marie Louise lasted for the best part
of 1810. Metternich reported back to his new father-in-law and
recent enemy in Vienna:

> The Emperor is much taken with his wife. . . . if the Empress
> continues to dominate him, she could render very great services
> to herself and to all of Europe. He is so evidently in love with
> her that all his habits are subordinated to her wishes. . . .[1]

In his best barrack-room manner, Napoleon revealed to his
cronies that his new bride was so pleased with him in the
bedroom that she would beg him for more. Meanwhile, he spent
more and more time in the pursuit of unwarlike pleasures, at
balls, at elaborate hunts – and even at the opera. Snobbery
(always his Achilles' heel), fulfilled by entry into the grand
Habsburg dynasty, intoxicated him. He arrived late for council
meetings, and left the only extant battle-front, Spain, to Masséna
instead of going to finish off Wellington himself. The new
Empress, however, never conquered the hearts of the French as
had Josephine; she was herself manifestly ill at ease in the city

which had murdered her aunt. On the morning of 20 March 1811, a young Stendhal abed with Angéline in Paris recorded the sudden, repeated booming of the cannon:

> We counted up to nineteen, when mad cheering broke out in the streets. We then realized that we had missed the first three salvoes. . . . the cannon went on booming. It was a boy all right. . . . a young prince had been born. All around us people went wild with joy. . . .

Marie Louise had produced an heir, Napoleon II, the unhappy and short-lived *l'Aiglon*. His father named him King of Rome, possibly in cynical remembrance of the defunct Holy Roman Empire which he had liquidated after Austerlitz. To Josephine he duly reported, 'My son is plump and well. He has my chest, my mouth and my eyes. . . . I hope he will fulfil his destiny. . . .' Napoleon had achieved his dynasty, but assured his fall. And soon he would be slipping back to the transient infidelities which he needed to bolster the sexual inferiority complex that never ceased to fret him. Meanwhile Marie Walewska and infant son were also set up in Paris.

YET AGAIN ONLY BRITAIN was left in the war against Napoleon. After fifteen years of almost incessant conflict, and with constant defeats relieved by only a few minor victories, how much longer could she go on? All Europe, weary of war and starved of commerce, asked the same question. As of the winter of 1809–10, it seemed most likely that France, triumphant against Austria, would now concentrate on finishing off Wellington's 'contemptible little army' in the Peninsula. 'When I show myself beyond the Pyrenees,' Napoleon had boasted to the *Corps Législatif* at the end of 1809, 'the terrified Leopard [England] will seek the Ocean in order to avoid shame, defeat and death. The triumph of my arms will be the triumph of the spirit of good over that of evil.'

But he sent Masséna instead. Wellington fought on, from his bastion in the Lines of Torres Vedras. At Bussaco in northern Portugal, Wellington's Anglo-Portuguese forces turned and administered a severe check to the pursuing French, thereby proving that they were disciplined enough to stand up in line against the French columns, since they could bring to bear at least four times as much firepower. The grim war raged back and forth, as attackers were forced to retire more from hunger in the scorched landscape than from enemy action. It had perhaps been morally reprehensible of Britain to bombard neutral Copenhagen (for a second time) in 1807, after Tilsit, but — not unlike Churchill's desperate attack on the Vichy French fleet at Oran in 1940 to prevent it falling into German hands — it showed that she had no intention of giving in.

The continent went short of coffee, sugar and spices, Russia's trade in the Baltic was paralysed; but in Britain, too, factories closed down as trade withered. In *Vanity Fair* Thackeray tells us how the unfortunate Mr Sedley was bankrupted by the blockade — but another city merchant, old Osborne, thrived as a profiteer. There were unemployment, low wages and periodic starvation in the industrial areas of Yorkshire and Lancashire. There was a crop failure, in 1811, which drove up the price of wheat, and warehouses were crammed with goods which could reach no market. In America pro-French President James Madison broke off trade with Britain, causing angry deputations from manufacturing cities to besiege Westminster, while that same year Luddites smashed up mill machinery. But these social upheavals were due more to the industrial than to the French Revolution, or to Napoleon. The poor suffered, but the war scarcely entered into the lives of the landed gentry. As G. M. Trevelyan remarks of that perennial mystery, why Jane Austen's novels never mention the war: 'No young lady of Miss Austen's acquaintance, waiting eagerly for the appearance of Scott's or Byron's next volume of verse, seems ever to have asked what Mr. Thorpe or Mr. Tom Bertram was going to do to serve their country in time of danger.'² By and large Britain basked, sublimely insouciant, behind the perfect shield which Nelson had won for her at Trafalgar.

In 1810 Admiral Collingwood died, a hero second only to Nelson. The seven long years he had spent at sea (for one fifteen-month stretch he never dropped anchor), enforcing the blockade, epitomized the spirit which lay behind the supremacy attained by the Royal Navy. 'My family are actually strangers to me,' he once remarked to a fellow officer: 'how little do the people of England know the sacrifices we make for them'. Yet 'the first wish of my life', as he wrote to his lonely wife, was 'To stand a barrier between the ambition of France and the independence of England'.

Now 130,000-men strong, nearly 150 ships-of-the-line, 200 frigates and 500 sloops and brigs, that vital 'barrier' represented one of the most powerful war machines ever deployed, imposing its unseen influence on states within Napoleon's vast Continental System, while it armed and sustained the deadly *guerrilleros* who assisted Wellington by their merciless disruption of French supply lines in Catalonia. Trevelyan notes the essential paradox of the navy's splendid performance in action, and the fact that 'the common sailors who saved Britain at St Vincent, Camperdown and the Nile were many of them mutineers in the intervals'. Conditions were slowly improving, yet 'The contrast between their grievances and their indiscipline on the one hand and their splendid spirit in action and on the blockade service may seem unaccountable.' What still mattered – as it had at Trafalgar – was that, chiefly because of its savage discipline, the Royal Navy of 'Jarvie' and Nelson could stay at sea longer than could the French. Morale was also sustained by the rich prizes that occasionally fell into the hands of the watchful 'storm-battered ships'. Yet it was a vigilance which would provoke a war with the United States.

Though Wellington's successes in Spain brought the army to an unprecedented peak of popularity, it remained basically a

part-time occupation for members of the upper classes commanding 'the scum of the earth', as Wellington cheerfully designated
the men who fought his battles, who were indeed drawn from
the dregs of society. The long arm of conscription never reached
out, in a Britain only part-mobilized, as it did across the length
and breadth of Europe. In the latter part of the eighteenth
century, before Wellington took over, the army was so corrupt
that William Cobbett, who had enlisted in the ranks and rose to
be a sergeant-major, had been outraged to discover that the
Quartermaster of his regiment 'who had the issuing of the men's
provisions to them kept about a fourth part of it to himself'.
Despite all Wellington's efforts (such as imposing a strict death
sentence on looters), British soldiers in the Peninsula were prone
to plunder the wretched inhabitants – though never quite as
outrageously as the French did.

Wellington's views on his senior commanders were often only
marginally more flattering than what he had to say about the
rank and file: 'When I reflect on the character and attainments
of some the general officers of this army, and consider that these
are the persons upon whom I am to rely to lead columns against
the French, I tremble. . .' (One is reminded of Churchill's
acerbic Chief of the Imperial General Staff, Field-Marshal Alan
Brooke, who in 1942 declared that half his corps and divisional
commanders were unfit, but that there was no way of replacing
them.) Nevertheless, slowly under Wellington, Abercromby, and
previously Moore, with that meticulous attention to detail which
Wellington shared with Napoleon, the army reformed itself,
producing its redoubtable Light Divisions which would beat
Napoleon at Waterloo, and building up discipline and self-respect
so that, when at last they entered France, they were 'a credit to
the odd social system on which the British Army was based'.[3]

In October 1810, George III began his last descent into
madness, and the following February the Prince Regent assumed
responsibility. In the words of a French historian not unfriendly
to Britain, André Maurois: 'her King was mad, her Regent

frivolous, her ministers second rate; it mattered little, for her instincts and her virtues sustained her'.[4] But Britain was also immensely rich, quite able to go on financing coalition after coalition. In fact, she was getting richer as, with Napoleon locked up in Europe, she was able to mop up the outlying jewels of the French Empire in India and the Caribbean, and to exploit them for her own benefit. In turn, capture of the last French islands in the Caribbean released some seventeen British garrisons to reinforce Wellington. For cheapness and quality, her goods could beat anything produced anywhere else. Like later European despots, Napoleon, unable to defeat her,* resorted to fantasy, rather hoping that Britain would just go away. Even though, in the Peninsula, Wellington was fielding more and more troops with the express objective of overthrowing Napoleon and all his works, as of the end of 1810 militarily the prospects of victory on land by British arms looked about as bleak as they were to do in 1940–1, before Hitler made his disastrous error of invading Russia. Napoleon was about to show him the way.

For Europe under Napoleon's Continental System, things grew worse with every year that the Royal Navy's blockade extended and perfected itself, tightening its grip. German factories were brought to ruin; by 1810, only 3 out of 400 of Hamburg's sugar factories remained in business. Many leading banks collapsed, including a Belgian house in which Talleyrand personally lost a large sum of money. Unable to meet his creditors, he approached (unsuccessfully) the Tsar – with questionable ethics, given that he was still a high functionary of France. (Eventually Napoleon himself bailed him out.) In order to provide the *Grande Armée* with greatcoats and boots, Napoleon's own quartermasters had covertly to breach the British blockade. The black market and profiteers thrived. Increasingly Napoleon alienated those who

---

* Like Hitler perhaps he never seriously wanted to: he once remarked, 'If the English constitution were destroyed, the civilization of the world would be shaken to its foundations. . . .'

should have been his natural allies. The Papal Nuncio declared that the whole of Europe had become 'a prison house'. Reckoning that it was his duty to keep contact with Catholics throughout the world, Pope Pius VII courageously breached the Continental System; for this he was arrested and deported, and Rome subjected to a French military occupation. Napoleon was excommunicated, and throughout Europe Catholics muttered, fuelling further angry opposition against Napoleon in Spain.

Yet, most notably, it was Russia that was hurt by the blockade. At first, Alexander had been faithful to the terms of Tilsit in implementing the Continental System, even to the extent of finding himself formally at war with Britain and promulgating schemes to introduce administrative reforms emulating the *Code Napoléon*. But as Russia's lucrative trade with Britain ground to a halt, so the hawks among the merchants and nobles had become increasingly articulate in their opposition to the 'Little Father'. Indignation about the slight inflicted on the Tsar by Napoleon's abrupt abandonment of the proposed match with the Grand Duchess Anna (even though it had been rejected in St Petersburg) was compounded when the French Emperor handed to the despised, Polish, Grand Duchy of Warsaw the Galician provinces grabbed from Austria after Wagram. From mid-1810, relations began to deteriorate swiftly. The following May the Swedes suddenly offered their throne (which lacked an heir) to Marshal Bernadotte,* still thoroughly disaffected as a result of Napoleon's insult at Wagram, the Swedes hoping that this might both ensure their territories against Russian encroachment and permit some relaxation of the blockade that was ruining their commerce. Ignoring the fact that Bernadotte was Napoleon's least trusted Marshal, Alexander viewed this as a new attempt by Napoleon to 'encircle' Russia.† Gradually more and more 'neutral' ships

---

* Thanks to his conspicuous kindness to Swedish prisoners of war during the Jena campaign.
† Bernadotte was crowned King Charles IV in 1818; ironically, it was to render

were allowed to slip into Russian ports; in the summer of 1811 they included 150 British vessels flying the American flag. Such defiance of his System was intolerable to Napoleon; the war clouds gathered.

IN FRANCE, MORALE HAD only temporarily been raised by the victory at Wagram and by the apparent bid for peace of his dynastic marriage to Marie Louise. The brilliant life of Court balls continued. That was where 'all the eligible men were to be found', recorded de Ségur. 'The unfortunate young girls', daughters of the handful of *ancien régime* families of Faubourg St Germain still in opposition to Napoleon, 'to whom attendance at the Emperor's Court balls was forbidden because of their parents' prejudice, led a very dull life. . . . How were the poor girls ever to find husbands?'[5] In honour of Marie Walewska, Paris danced the mazurka, which had become all the rage. But beneath the glitter there was deep disquiet. The deposed Josephine was greatly missed for her unfailing gaiety, and there was now no one to temper the Emperor's lack of basic humanity. Napoleon's grandiose schemes for the reconstruction of the city had slowed down since 1805. He had begun work on the Arc de Triomphe at the Carrousel (in 1806), modelled on Roman imperial triumphs; but the great edifice on the Étoile remained unfinished – as indeed it would until the reign of Louis-Philippe, after Napoleon's death. He had numbered the streets as they are today, and had provided the city with an adequate supply of water for the first time (which was perhaps the greatest debt Paris owed to him), but still the main thoroughfares remained filthy and insalubrious. Les Halles had been opened, and undoubt-

---

him one of the few legitimate kings in Europe, in contrast to all Napoleon's dynastic creations, while the marriage of the eldest daughter of Eugène de Beauharnais, Josephine, to Bernadotte's son was to make the deposed Empress and the misprized Bernadotte ancestors of virtually every royal house in Europe – with the exception of the British.

edly the most outstanding project of the period was the Musée Napoléon, as the Louvre was then called, where from the looted collections* of Europe the most splendid concentration of treasures of art the world had ever seen was assembled under one roof, under the aegis of Napoleon's 'cultural Tsar', Vivant Denon. But time and pressure of events had not enabled him to make any progress in his plans to build a great new city west of the Champs Élysées.

There were signs, too, that the Imperial family seemed to be falling apart at the seams. In 1810, Lucien, always at odds with his brother and alone in refusing to share in the spoils of the clan, decided to flee his retreat in Italy and make off for America. But, captured by one of the ever watchful British cruisers, he was to spend the remaining years of the war living the life of a country gentleman in England. In July that same year, King Louis of Holland, infuriated by his elder brother's constant memos on how to conduct his family life (his wife, Queen Hortense, daughter of Josephine, was having an affair with Talleyrand's illegitimate son, the Comte de Flahaut) abdicated; his immediate motive was refusal to ruin his subjects by enforcement of the Continental System. He removed himself to Bohemia, beyond the Imperial remit, inflicting a grievous personal wound. 'Should I have expected', Méneval records the Emperor as weeping, 'such an outrage on the part of someone to whom I have been a father? I brought him up on the scant resources of my pay as a lieutenant of artillery; I have shared my bread and the mattress on my bed with him. . . .'[6] Meanwhile the beleaguered Joseph in Spain, constantly in fear of brutal assassination, as well as the Murats in Naples, felt no more secure on their thrones.

The extent to which Napoleon's secret police now busied

---

* After Napoleon's defeat, the victorious Allies ordered some 5,000 works of art to be restored to their rightful owners – a task exceeded only by that which followed the collapse of Hitler's Third Reich in 1945.

themselves in the affairs of his close entourage, and even his family, was an unfavourable comment on the pettiness of his tyranny. In 1811 spies unearthed a treasonable conspiracy between his brother-in-law, Murat, and Vienna and St Petersburg to circumvent the Continental Decrees. Growing ever more unpopular, these had brought about a year of terrible scarcity in France itself, in 1811. Despite constantly raising the level of taxation, Napoleon's national revenues were in deficit to the tune of fifty million francs by the end of the year. It forced him to pass an Imperial Decree cancelling the arrears of pay owed to the soldiers who had died for him, thereby – in effect – cheating even the dead.

As is the way of military dictators, a new foreign campaign presented itself as the only way of distracting domestic discontent. In the autumn of 1811, there was a renewed pretence made at invading England; 80,000 men were concentrated once more at Boulogne, and two million francs spent on renovating the decayed cross-Channel flotilla. But, as with Hitler at the close of 1940, that was not where Napoleon's next move would take place. In any event, an invasion had about as much prospect of success then as Wellington might have had if he had launched a campaign in Central Europe. Possibly Napoleon hoped thereby to draw off the British commitment in Spain; it only seemed to be further indication that he was losing his grip on reality. There was also a limit to how long the French nation, drawing on its Revolutionary capital, could go on glorifying war for its own sake. Outside the army itself, always devoted to Napoleon, there was now little enough love for him in the country at large. Increasingly he had to rely on the terror of the ubiquitous secret police, headed since 1810 by Fouché's even more thorough successor, General Savary, Duke of Rovigo, the kidnapper of the Duke d'Enghien, who had so efficiently spied out the ground, and the Tsar's intentions, before Austerlitz in those halcyon days of five years before. Soon after assuming office, Savary had imposed his stamp by executing two clerks in the Ministry of War, shot for passing information to the Russians.

IN THE SUMMER OF 1812, as Wellington was advancing through Spain and Napoleon was on the brink of launching his fatal plunge into Russia, to the west there suddenly occurred for France two unexpected, heaven-sent distractions. First, on 11 May the British Prime Minister, Spencer Perceval, was assassinated by a bankrupt in the lobby of the House of Commons. Then, on 18 June, the United States Congress declared war on Britain. The two events were interconnected to the extent that Perceval, when killed, had been about to revoke the Orders in Council of 1806. Bitterly resented in America, these arbitrary rules empowered the Royal Navy to board neutral shipping, force it to unload its cargo in British ports, and press-gang any British citizens aboard.

But what disastrous chain of events had brought Britain to war once again with her former colonies, with whom she had signed peace less than thirty years previously? As has been recounted in Chapter 3, following all the goodwill left behind by Lafayette and his countrymen in the young republic, the principles of the French Revolution had aroused the liveliest sympathies. The undiplomatic activities of Citizen Genet and of French privateers, as well as Napoleon's acquisition of the Louisiana Territory, sacrificed most of that accrued goodwill. But in 1803, as we have seen, France sold Louisiana to the US for the bargain price of $15 million. From Napoleon's point of view, the sale was designed to keep America quiet, and tilt her once again towards hostility against Britain. Certainly relations grew progressively worse following Britain's naval triumph at Trafalgar and her consequent attainment of supremacy at sea, because it was at her hands that American shipping now suffered most. Everything turned on the persistence of Napoleon's Continental System and the British blockade. Imposed in retaliation for Napoleon's Berlin

Decrees, which set up the continental blockade of Britain, London's Orders in Council of 1806 imposed the most severe restrictions on all neutral trade with France and her allies. US commerce was particularly hard hit. In 1807, mounting public opinion forced Jefferson to enact an Embargo Act.

That same year, Britain and the US had come close to war over the affray between the uss *Chesapeake* and the British *Leopard*, infamous in American history. *Leopard* had stopped *Chesapeake* ten miles off the US coast, demanding to impress some British deserters on board. When the Americans refused, the British poured three broadsides into *Chesapeake*, rendering her helpless. This insult to the flag had brought about the first united expression of American feeling since the Napoleonic Wars had begun. In December, under mounting public pressure, President Jefferson passed the Embargo Act, not dissimilar to that with which the US protected herself in the initial stages of the Second World War, which forbade American ships to sail for foreign waters at all. In fact, it proved far more damaging to US commerce than either of the belligerent factions, and was deeply unpopular with American shipowners of the Atlantic coast ports, who thrived on old-established, reciprocal trade. The embargo lasted fourteen months, to be repealed in 1809 by the newly elected Madison, heralded as the great peacemaker, and replaced by a Non-Intercourse Act aimed even-handedly at both Britain and France. But this was inexplicably, and rather brutally, rejected by Canning. Relations had lapsed into, mutual recrimination.

Meanwhile, Napoleon had since 1807, in the words of that great American naval historian, Samuel Eliot Morison, in fact been treating American shipping 'harshly and arbitrarily'. He even contemplated using US legislation as a means of bringing her within his Continental System (which Morison describes as being 'strikingly similar to Hitler's scheme for bringing England to her knees without winning control of the sea').[7]

Madison, Jefferson's successor in 1809, had, in the words of

Churchill, 'a stubborn side to his nature, and his practical skill and judgement were not always equal to that of his predecessor'. His advisers warned him that Napoleon's blandishments were entirely designed 'to catch us into a war with England', but he disregarded them. At the same time, he gradually came under fierce pressure from the War Party, formed of frontiersmen and fiery speakers like Henry Clay and John C. Calhoun from Kentucky and South Carolina. Extending the principle of 'Manifest Destiny' into which the Louisiana Purchase had breathed life, their object was to seize British Canada and establish American sovereignty throughout the northern continent.

By the beginning of 1812, the United States population numbered 7,250,000, while Canada's was only 500,000 — most of them French Canadians, subjected only half a century previously and feeling little sense of allegiance to Britain. Except for the presence of 5,000 trained British troops there, to the American War Party Canada must have looked ripe for plucking. On 11 May 1812, little more than a month before Napoleon launched his attack on Russia, worsening relations between Britain and the new republic had been brought to a head by a fight between a US frigate and a British corvette, in which the American had been worsted. That was the same day as Prime Minister Perceval's assassination. A fatal delay then took place in the British Government's intended repeal of the offending Orders in Council. The conciliatory Lord Castlereagh announced on 16 June that the Orders would be suspended immediately. Had there been modern communications, war could have been avoided, despite Perceval's death. As it was, the British change of heart came too late: Madison and the British caretaker Government both obligingly fell into Napoleon's trap, and the two countries blundered into what many historians consider to have been one of the silliest and most incomprehensible wars of all time, the War of 1812.

Certainly it was a war nobody, except Napoleon, wanted. Madison, though far from being George Washington's brightest successor, was — if anything — pro-British. The merchants and seafarers of New England, who were most affected by hostilities, were dead against a breach with Britain, all the way through. But the South and the West wanted war. So too did the hawks in Washington, who, disgusted with Madison, felt that 'national honor demanded a fight'. They also saw improved prospects of conquering Canada — and of resolving once and for all the 'Indian question', posed by Britain's dubious indigenous allies in America's backyard. Contemptuously the British dismissed the infant US Navy as 'a few fir-built frigates, manned by a handful of bastards and outlaws'. But in the war at sea (brilliantly described by, among others, C. S. Forester and, more recently, Patrick O'Brian), with the Royal Navy so deeply engaged in blockading France that it could spare only one ship-of-the-line, the skill of the fast American frigates made an immediate mark. Within the year they had won more successes over the British than the French or the Spaniards had managed over two decades of warfare. Their successes were epitomized in American annals when the USS *Constitution* knocked out the superior HMS *Guerrière*, and when, to the stunned outrage of Nelson's navy, Captain Stephen Decatur sailed into New London with a British frigate as prize — thereby making himself a national hero to succeeding generations of American schoolboys.

The actual strategic value of all these American naval triumphs, however, was slight. On land, the war surged inconclusively back and forth. At Tippecanoe Governor William Henry Harrison defeated Britain's principal Indian ally, 'The Prophet' Tecumseh, thereby assuring his election as president thirty years later; the Americans invaded Canada and sacked York (later Toronto), and were then repelled; in revenge, a British force landed in Washington and burnt the White House,* eating the dinner prepared for the President and Mrs Madison. In 1814, the heroic defence of Baltimore's Fort Henry gave the US her rousing

---

* It was supposedly painted white to cover up the humiliating traces of fire.

national anthem; at Plattsburg, New York, a decisive naval victory was won by the Americans, repelling a serious British invasion from Canada. Much as Washington might deny it, the aim of the American hawks remained the conquest of Canada, and by 1814 that looked distinctly realizable. In January 1815, a last humiliation was suffered by the British Army at the Battle of New Orleans, where General Andrew Jackson imposed a bloody defeat, indeed a massacre, on a particularly incompetent British general, Pakenham, kinsman of Wellington. New Orleans thereby produced the war's second US president in years to come. But the victory was in fact of no consequence, as a stalemate peace had already been signed in Ghent on Christmas Eve, 1814.

It was just as well for both sides. With Napoleon temporarily disposed of, and tucked away in Elba in 1814, a major British effort on land could easily have raised havoc in America. Reinforcements from the Peninsula were already on their way there. On the other hand, had Congress been better prepared for war, and the American conduct of the war more efficient, it could have been ended in one swift blow by capturing Quebec – as Wolfe had done in the previous century. Most dangerous of all for the future of the Anglo-Saxon world as a whole, in November 1814, because of the perceived threat to Canada, Wellington had been invited to take over King George's unsuccessful armies there. Fortunately for Britain, he disapproved strongly of Government policy towards America, and forcefully refused: 'I think you have no right from the state of the war to demand any concession of territory from America.' His views were widely supported in the army; when news of the peace reached it in the New World, one veteran was to comment, 'we are all happy enough, for we Peninsula soldiers saw that neither fame nor any other military distinction could be acquired by this type of milito-nautico-guerrilla-plundering warfare'. But had Wellington taken a different view, or had the Americans seriously threatened Canada, then Britain's best general would, in all probability, have been away fighting in America at the time of Waterloo — with predictable consequences. As it was, some of his badly needed regiments were only just reaching Belgium from across the Atlantic on the very eve of that battle.

'So ended a futile and unnecessary war which might have been prevented by a little more imagination on the one side, and a broader vision on the other. At least it was a cheap one,' observed Samuel Eliot Morison.'[8] In appearance no more than a sideshow, it was nonetheless an integral part of the great global conflict, of enormous potential significance. In America it served to breed a legend that the conflict had in effect been a second War of Independence against British tyranny. Yet it could have ended in dark tragedy for both countries. Happily, there now followed between Britain and the US what American historians describe as the 'Era of Good Feelings'.

Napoleon was the loser.

SEVENTEEN

'Don't March on Moscow'

1812

There is only one step from the sublime to the ridiculous.

Napoleon to de Pradt, Polish Ambassador, after the retreat from Moscow

ON 22 JUNE 1812, the very date on which — courting similar disaster — Hitler was to attack the Soviet Union in 1941, Napoleon proclaimed: 'Soldiers — the second Polish war has opened; the first ended at Friedland and Tilsit.' The proclamation came as little surprise to either side, given how bad relations had become between Napoleon and the ruler whom he had once joked he would like to make his mistress.

Gradually the advantages of the Continental System had been shifting in Russia's favour, to the fury of Napoleon. More and more British vessels were being permitted to enter Russian ports under American flags, 150 in the summer of 1811, and Napoleon could not tolerate this defiance of his system. Meanwhile, having observed the campaigns of Wellington in the Peninsula, the Tsar no longer held the French Emperor in awe.

So started the war that was to be enshrined in history, on the Russian side, by Tolstoy and Tchaikovsky, on the French by the paintings of the terrible retreat from Moscow by Verezhagin and others. There would be technical and costly victories, but none of the great battles of annihilation which Napoleon (and Hitler after him) planned as he crossed the Niemen. And the end would bring only irreparable, strategic and decisive defeat for the *Grande*

Armée. 'Don't march on Moscow' was consistently one of Field-Marshal Montgomery's 'basic rules of war' (Hitler, he notes simply in *A History of Warfare*, 'broke that rule and lived to regret it').[1] Like many other students of military history, he 'never understood Napoleon's reasoning'.*

As the French prepared to invade his country, Tsar Alexander was supremely, prophetically, self-confident. 'We shall take no risks,' he declared to Caulaincourt (who had been sent as an envoy). 'We have plenty of space; and our standing army is well organized. . . . Your Frenchman is brave, but long sufferings and a hard time wear down his resistance. Our climate, our winter, will fight on our side.'[2] Since 1810, the Minister of War Barclay de Tolly, at fifty-one an experienced soldier (of Scottish descent, though ironically it was his French name that was to bring him down), had efficiently been reforming the Russian Army – much of it along Napoleonic lines. It now counted 211,000 front-line troops, including 15,000 of the fearsome Cossacks, who were eventually to be doubled in number. Barclay was also Commander-in-Chief of the key First Army, with Prince Bagration (who had fought so bravely on the northern flank at Austerlitz) leading the Second Army. Massively in the background, however, was old Kutuzov, whose reputation had survived the catastrophe at Austerlitz seven years previously – though, at sixty-seven, he was considered too old for field command.

Was it the Russians' deliberate strategy, as historians often tell us, to fight Napoleon (any more than Stalin fought Hitler) with a 'scorched earth' retreat? Tolstoy, in *War and Peace*, disputes this; on the contrary, he says, 'every effort was made to hinder' the French advance. 'During the whole period of the War not only was there no wish on the Russian side to draw the French into the heart of the country, but from their first entry into Russia,

---

* It is interesting to note, *en passant*, that when he relinquished his role as Allied land commander in September 1944 Montgomery had under his nominal command more troops than Napoleon ever had.

everything was done to stop them . . .'[3] But the Russian armies were simply not strong enough. He continues:

> The luring of Napoleon into the depths of the country was not the result of any plan, and no one believed it to be possible; it resulted from a most complex interplay of intrigues, aims and wishes, among those who took part in the War and had no perception whatever of the inevitable, or of the one way of saving Russia. *Everything came about fortuitously. . . .*'

This last sentence (author's italics) always strikes one as perhaps being more realistic of the true facts of that campaign than the accepted view of what happened.

On the French side, with Talleyrand gone, Napoleon was surrounded by sycophants, such as Foreign Minister Champagny. With Wellington growing ever stronger in Spain, he was – as Hitler was to be – confronted with a war on two fronts. Each year Spain went on draining him of 40,000 men. Yet, miraculously once again, he had managed to assemble a new army over 600,000 strong (of whom slightly less than half were native-born Frenchmen), the main body – under his own direct command – divided into three *corps d'armée* under Davout, Oudinot and Ney, with Murat heading two cavalry corps. The flanks of the main thrust were to be guarded by units comprised, more than half of them, of allied forces (including almost 100,000 Poles), some of whom had not shone at Wagram. Again, parallels present themselves, and one thinks of the vulnerability of some of Hitler's Axis allies, such as the Romanians, at Stalingrad. The *Grande Armée* that headed for Moscow was the largest army Europe had seen in modern times, but in quality it did not compare to the much smaller *Grande Armée* that had last defeated the Russians at Austerlitz. Like Hitler's invading force of 1941, it was not equipped with winter clothing. In May 1812, Napoleon had told Davout that his aim was to be able to 'concentrate 400,000 men at a single point'. He recognized that in backward Russia 'we can hope for nothing from the countryside', obliging his troops to rely on the vast and imposing French commissariat, whose supply vehicles numbered some 25,000. The need to feed, on the hoof, 200,000 animals (of which 80,000 were Murat's cavalry mounts)* forced Napoleon to delay the invasion until the grasses of the Russian steppes had reached their peak.

In 1941, Hitler was delayed by his spring sideshow in the Balkans, and so with striking similarity Napoleon started critically late in the season, losing precious time on the road to Moscow. For the superstitious, it began with a bad omen – when a hare getting up under his horse's hoofs caused Napoleon to be thrown (though not hurt) close to the Niemen. Like Hitler, too, he directed his main effort towards Moscow, on the northern front, reckoning that capture of that city would end the war. Anticipating that the campaign would be over in twenty days – that is, by mid-July – he hoped to defeat the Russians (as he had Mack in 1805) in a vast battle of envelopment.† But the Russians would not oblige. Napoleon captured Vilna, and then Vitebsk, without a struggle – only to discover, to his intense fury, that the Russians had escaped the net. By the end of July, his forces were strung out over 500 miles; some 100,000 men had already fallen by the way from sickness or straggling. The devastating summer heat was proving far more lethal to the unfortunate horses of the cavalry than ever the winter would. Parallels with the first campaigning season of Hitler's *Barbarossa* continue to be hard to resist.‡ In 1941, by the time the *Wehrmacht* was approaching

---

* Only 15,000 of these horses were to return alive from Russia.

† Such, indeed, as Hitler was to achieve in the Ukraine in the early days of his campaign, which resulted in the greatest battle of encirclement of all time – but it did not win him the war.

‡ Moving like lightning from the Polish frontier of 1940, Hitler's Panzers in fact reached Smolensk by 16 July; then, on Hitler's orders, and to the rage of generals like Guderian, they paused on the Central Front while the main effort was switched southwards to the Ukraine. Having failed, like Napoleon, twice to envelop the main enemy forces, Hitler was lured away from decisive strategical success by the temptation of an immense tactical triumph. Heat exhaustion in August too played its vital role in slowing down the attackers.

Moscow, it was not 'General Winter' that had blunted the edge of the Panzers but the dust and heat, multiplied by distance, of the fierce Russian summer. Unprotected by the cavalry, Napoleon's straggling infantry columns began to suffer increasingly from nerves as the Cossacks would suddenly attack out of nowhere. With the growing enfeeblement of his light cavalry arm, both Napoleon's supply of up-to-date intelligence and his remarkable intuition based on it likewise deteriorated. In contrast, Alexander now had the intelligence advantage over him (or so he boasted after Napoleon's fall), by being able to read the code of captured French despatches. This could help explain why the Russians refused to concede defeat, ultimately forcing upon the French Emperor his catastrophic retreat.

From an early stage Napoleon's genius for taking lightning decisions, such as had stood him in such good stead in early encounters with the Russian enemy at Austerlitz, also seemed dulled. On three separate occasions the cumbersome Russian armies were allowed to elude his pincer movements through time inexplicably wasted. One of these was on his forty-third birthday, when he spent the day, 15 August, unnecessarily reviewing the *Grande Armée*. It cost him the opportunity of capturing by surprise Smolensk, the last major centre before Moscow, some 280 miles distant.

Fortunately for Napoleon, this lack of drive was matched by

Often forgotten is the fact that, just like Napoleon's *Grande Armée*, Hitler's vast mechanized force was also extensively dependent for transportation on its unfortunate horses and mules. At Kiev, in September, the Germans won one of the great battles of encirclement of history, killing or capturing upwards of 600,000 Soviet troops. But the diversion, parallel to Napoleon's pusillanimity in August and September, was to cost him the main objective of Moscow. In September 1941, the Russian Central Front remained static; when the Germans moved forward again in October, rains and accompanying mud halted the advance. Then, in November, came the snow – and the freeze-up, for which, like Napoleon's *Grande Armée*, the thinly clad *Wehrmacht*, hoping for early summer victory, was unprepared. As in 1812, time lost in the summer of 1941 was never to be regained, although – unlike 1812 – the campaign was to continue for another four grim years.

RUSSIAN CAMPAIGN OF 1812

EST

LIV

Baltic Sea

Riga

COURLAND

Memel
Shavli O
Jacobstadt O

KOVNO

Dünab

Tauroggen O
Rossieny
Dünab

Tilsit
River Niemen
Keidany

Königsberg
Vilkomir

Danzig
Neustadt
Kovno

To Stettin
Insterburg O
Stallupohnen
Sve

Elbing
Vilkomir

Marienburg
Gumbinnen
Piloni

Marienwerder
Ponarskaia O
Vilna

To Posen
EAST PRUSSIA
Smorgo
Ochmiana

GRAND DUCHY OF WARSAW
Molodetchna

To Thorn
LITHUANIA

R. Narew
Grodno O
Lida

R. Bug
Bialystok
River Niemen

R. Vistula
Vilkavischi O

Slonim
Nesviz

Warsaw O
To Lublin
To Brest-Litovsk

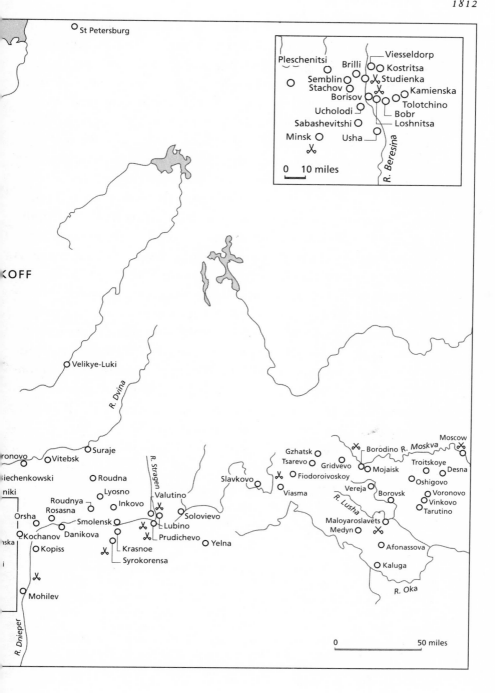

St Petersburg

Pleschenitsi
Brilli
Viesseldorp
Kostritsa
Semblin
Studienka
Stachov
Kamienska
Borisov
Tolotchino
Ucholodi
Bobr
Sabashevitshi
Loshnitsa
Minsk
Usha
R. Beresina

0 10 miles

KOFF

Velikye-Luki

R. Dvina

Suraje

ronovo
Vitebsk
Moscow

iechenkowski
Roudna
Borodino R. Moskva

niki
Lyosno
Gzhatsk
R. Stragen
Valutino
Troitskoye
Tsarevo Gridvevo
Mojaisk
Desna
Slavkovo
Fiodoroivoskoy
Oshigovo
Roudnya
Inkovo
Viasma
Vereja Borovsk
Voronovo
Rosasna
Vinkovo
Orsha
Solovievo
R. Lusha
Tarutino
Smolensk
Lubino
Maloyaroslavets
Kochanov Danikova
Prudichevo Yelna
Medyn
nska
Kopiss
Krasnoe
Afonassova
Syrokorensa
Kaluga
Mohilev
R. Oka

R. Dnieper

0   50 miles

bitter divisions on the Russian side. As reverses mounted and the retreat continued, xenophobic lynch mobs brought about the downfall of the enlightened but much abused commander with the 'outlandish name' Barclay de Tolly – who suffered from having a French-sounding name,* a Baltic accent and a faith which was not Orthodox. He was replaced as supreme commander by the semi-retired veteran of Austerlitz, old one-eyed Kutuzov. In the words of Clausewitz, 'Kutusov was approaching seventy years of age and no longer possessed either the activity of mind or body which one sometimes finds in soldiers of that age. However, he knew the Russians, and how to handle them. . . .'[4] This last was what was to count in the forthcoming, desperate struggle. At the same time, a mystical, semi-religious passion for Holy Russia began to incite the battered Russian forces into new heights of resistance against the invader. Something very similar happened in the Soviet Union in the darkest days of the Second World War, forcing Stalin to suspend, temporarily, his war against the Orthodox Church, and funnel its patriotic fervour into a crusade against the German invader. The famous 'Black Virgin of Smolensk', renowned for its miraculous properties, was brought out and pressed into service with the army, whose simple peasant soldiers marched into battle chanting ''Tis the Will of God!' Meanwhile the *Grande Armée* found itself reduced to little more than 150,000 battle-worthy effectives.

On 6 September, the Black Virgin was paraded past a kneeling Russian Army as Kutuzov prepared to fight its first major battle at Borodino, a village close to the Moscow River, and less than

---

* In fact Barclay was a third-generation Russian, of unquestionable patriotism, whose Scottish forebears had settled in Lutheran Livonia early in the seventeenth century, and he had served loyally in the Russian Army since the age of fifteen. His reputation suffered much at the hands of Tolstoy in *War and Peace* (in contrast with that of Tolstoy's hero, the all-Russian Kutuzov – which was tarnished by Austerlitz, but perhaps excessively refurbished by 1812). It was not till Pushkin nobly tried to rehabilitate him in the early 1830s in his epic poem, *The Commander*, that there was any attempt at revisionism. The duel that killed him took place while the controversy was still raging.

THE BATTLE FOR SMOLENSK, 1812

eighty miles from the city itself. In broken country, it offered promising conditions for a defensive action. The following day, Napoleon's advancing forces encountered Kutuzov's main force digging in for battle. His old opponent from Austerlitz showed little subtlety, committing the error of over-extending his forces.* But, unlike his old self, Napoleon resisted the temptation to turn

---

* Tolstoy, in his brilliant description of the battle in which Prince Andrei was mortally wounded, is critical of the choice of the battleground, by either side: 'There was not the least sense in it for either the French or the Russians. Its immediate result for the Russians was — was bound to be — that we were brought nearer to the destruction of Moscow, which we feared more than anything in the world; and for the French its immediate result was that they were brought nearer to the destruction of the whole army, which they feared more than anything in the world . . . What the result must be was quite obvious, and yet Napoleon offered and Kutuzov accepted that battle.' [*War and Peace*, p. 833–61] Kutuzov, for his part, had not chosen the best ground on which to stand.

the Russian flank, telling Davout, 'It is too dangerous a manoeuvre!' He appealed to his troops to conduct themselves as they had at Austerlitz. There was a fleeting reminder of that heady day when the French stormed into the outskirts of Borodino under cover of thick morning fog; but, unlike Austerlitz, Borodino was a slogging, frontal attack, a battle of brutal attrition. This time the Russian gunners were presented with a superb target as the inferior quality of his troops forced Napoleon to manoeuvre in dense columns. On the 8th, Kutuzov disengaged, much as he had done in the run-up to Austerlitz. Almost one in three of the participants were left dead or wounded, the Russians losing an estimated 44,000 men. These they could replace; Napoleon could not readily make good his losses. More serious for the Russians had been the death of Prince Bagration, the loss of this legendary hero provoking serious demoralization among the defenders.

It was a Pyrrhic victory for Napoleon. He had lost many irreplaceable senior officers – fourteen lieutenant-generals and thirty-three major-generals. Among the wounded were Ney and Davout. The unfortunate Junot, whom Napoleon had (unfairly) accused of 'losing the campaign for me' by allowing the Russians to escape at Smolensk, had succumbed to one of the bouts of madness which was to lead to his death the following year. The French artillery alone had fired 90,000 rounds, in itself an astonishing feat for Napoleon's over-stretched supply lines, but one which could not readily be repeated. According to Ségur, 'seven to eight hundred prisoners and twenty broken cannon were all the trophies of this imperfect victory'.[5] His staff were shocked to find the Emperor, during the battle, listless and apathetic – suffering from a bladder complaint and possibly also from the stomach pains that were to plague him to the end.* It seems to have made him both cautious and indecisive.

---

* A curious historico-medical fact: when his nephew, Napoleon III, marched to defeat against the Prussians in 1870, he too was suffering agonies from a stone in the bladder.

Meanwhile, amid disquieting rumours of fresh conspiracies in Paris, there came reports from Spain that, six weeks earlier, in late June, Wellington had defeated Marmont at Salamanca. It was devastating news, for France's position in the Peninsula had seemed full of promise. Eighteen months before, in March 1811, Masséna had been forced to recoil back to Spain with his starving army from Wellington's last-ditch position in the Lines of Torres Vedras round Lisbon. In May of that year, Masséna had been defeated again at Fuentes d'Oñoro, just across the Spanish frontier. This had cost him his command, and he had been replaced by Marmont. Bitter siege warfare led to the taking and retaking of the frontier fortresses of Badajoz and Ciudad Rodrigo. Once more French numbers began to tell, and it looked as if Wellington and his Spanish allies might be in trouble yet again. Then, with Napoleon beginning to concentrate his mind, and his armies, on Russia in 1812, relief had come. French troop levels in the Peninsula dropped below the 200,000 mark, and Wellington with his now well-trained and experienced Anglo-Portuguese forces was at last to take the offensive. Methodically, he captured Ciudad Rodrigo in January 1812, followed by Badajoz after a bloody assault in April. Now Spain was open to him. The steady, slow advance up through Spain began. With 48,000 men he moved on Salamanca; then after a hard-fought battle there, one of his most successful, he was soon threatening Madrid itself.

AS THE RUSSIANS FELL back from Borodino, Miloradevich, a name from Austerlitz, was placed in command of the rearguard. But Napoleon's losses and Murat's shortage of cavalry meant that there could be no effective pursuit; consequently Miloradevich was able to extract from Borodino 90,000 troops in good fighting order. Just as the Soviets managed to create fresh armies behind Moscow in the winter of 1941, so Alexander gained a breathing space to reconstitute his forces from the vast reserves of Russian manpower. On 14 September, Kutuzov gave the fateful order to abandon Moscow, withdrawing to the south-east. Napoleon stood 75 miles from the capital, and 200 west of Smolensk – roughly the point Hitler had reached by that same date in 1941. But only 100,000 fit men now remained in the once proud army that had crossed the Niemen not three months previously.

After Borodino, Napoleon's faithful valet, Constant, describes him as 'overcome with fatigue. Every now and then he clasped his hands, and with a sort of convulsive movement kept exclaiming, "Moscow, Moscow!"'[6] He now faced a terrible decision, similar to that which confronted Hitler in the autumn of 1941: should he risk all by pushing on to Moscow, or should he fall back on Smolensk, and go into winter quarters? Jomini, the Swiss military historian who accompanied Napoleon on many of his campaigns, saw it through his eyes as follows:

> To force the Russians to a battle, and to dictate peace . . . such was the only means of safety that now remained. My marshals were divided in opinion. Murat, who had at first accused the Russians of pusillanimity, now trembled at the danger of penetrating so far into the interior. Others conceded that we could hope for no repose till we had gained *one decisive battle*.*
> I was also of this opinion. But how were we to obtain this battle? Certainly not by remaining at Smolensk, without provisions or other resources. . . .[7]

If he could have 'holed up' for the winter at Smolensk, he might have been able to make good his losses. On the other hand, just as in 1941, the Russians would then have been much better placed to raise new armies. Napoleon finally made the fatal decision every schoolboy knows: he decided to push on, in the hope that, within a matter of weeks, the Tsar would make peace. But the Russians' scorched-earth policy had deprived the *Grande*

---

* Italics added. The words 'one decisive battle' appear, significantly, at various times in Hitler's *Mein Kampf*. Such a battle was to elude him just as it did Napoleon.

Armée of its habitual resource of living off the land; there was neither shelter nor food – and Moscow itself would burn.

The week after Borodino, the invading army (unlike Hitler) reached Moscow – with Murat, in a swashbucklingly magnificent uniform, one of the first to enter. Few Muscovites were left to admire him. To Tolstoy,[8] Moscow resembled a 'Queenless Hive'. Napoleon waited, in a state of semi-paralysis, day after day, for the overture from the Tsar which never came; 'moody and taciturn', so Constant described him, it seemed as if he were dreaming that somehow another Tilsit was just around the corner. Extending all the way from Poland, the *Grande Armée* was stretched in a long, vulnerable salient 550 miles deep. At its base, Prussia was rearming as the news from Russia grew worse. Shocked, officers of his staff such as Ségur watched Napoleon passing 'whole hours half reclined, as if torpid, and awaiting, with a novel in his hand, the catastrophe of his terrible history . . .'; and Caulaincourt later recorded that the French Emperor 'could not admit that Fortune, which had so often smiled upon him, had quite abandoned his cause'.[9] In a state of self-delusion, not dissimilar to Hitler's at this same point in the campaign, Napoleon ordered fleece-lined coats, but he had no idea how they could be produced. It was the same with the horses: he ordered that 20,000 be purchased locally, though none was to be had within a hundred miles. Days of deceptively balmy autumn weather intervened as Napoleon dallied.

Moscow was incendiarized; the Kremlin blew up with a shattering explosion. What was left was disgracefully plundered by the French soldiers, lighting their camp fires from the extravagant furniture of wealthy Muscovites. In the burnt city, the troops and their officers were quartered on litters of damp straw, surrounded by worthless loot. There was nothing 'more melancholy', wrote Constant,

> than to see the soldiers' squalid tents bestrewn with costly furniture, flung here and there in confusion; silken couches,

valuable Siberian furs, Cashmere shawls, silver dishes, and princely plate on which black bread and bloody horse-meat lay in gruesome lumps. . . . Later on, no horse-meat was to be got for love or money.

Morale plummeted with the first signs of winter. Meanwhile, Tsar Alexander is said to have declared gleefully, 'This is the moment when my campaign begins.'

After the failure of a second peace mission despatched to the Tsar, on 18 October Napoleon decided to leave Moscow. The terrible retreat began, on the 120th day of the campaign which was supposed to have lasted twenty. Furnished with intelligence from a plentiful cavalry, a resource in which Napoleon was now largely deficient, from the beginning Cossacks harried the French. At one point Napoleon himself for the second time narrowly escaped being taken prisoner by Cossacks, one of whom actually reached within twenty yards of him. From this moment on, apparently, appalled by the prospect of captivity, he carried around his neck a small pouch containing poison. Soon the retreating army was crossing the recent battlefield of Borodino, its morale further shaken by the sight of the ground still 'covered with the debris of helmets, cuirasses, wheels, weapons, rags of uniforms – and 30,000 corpses half eaten by wolves . . . this immense tomb'.[10]

November brought the first snow, and with it the disturbing news of an abortive coup that had taken place in Paris on 22 October. General Malet, escaped from a mental asylum, had made an attempt to seize power and restore republican government, proclaiming that Napoleon had been killed in Russia. The whole plot lasted barely a day, and Malet and fourteen others were executed the following week. But what caused serious concern was the number of influential and responsible figures also implicated in the plot.* Napoleon quickened his homeward steps.

---

* In July 1944, while Hitler's gaze was fixed on the crumbling Russian front,

Despite the reforms initiated by Barclay de Tolly, the Russian Army under Kutuzov, wary after its repeated worstings by the *Grande Armée*, still showed little capacity for reacting swiftly. Insofar as such comparisons are valid, it still resembled the Tsarist 'steamroller' of 1914–18 rather than the hard-hitting Red Army, oblivious to its losses, of 1941–5. Any other force should, on paper, have been able to cut off and destroy completely Napoleon's hungry and depleted army as it straggled back westwards. But by now the Russians had already lost 50,000 in sick or stragglers alone, with half the men falling out without a battle; thus Kutuzov was in no state to take advantage of the French plight. The town of Maloyaroslavets, eighty miles to the south-west of Moscow, and scene of one of the grimmest battles of 1941, changed hands seven times on 24 October. Kutuzov was driven off, but he succeeded in forcing Napoleon to give up his intention of retreating via the fertile regions of Kaluga, and instead take the sinister and much ravaged route of his advance through Smolensk. By the time the *Grande Armée* reached Smolensk again, on 13 November, it numbered only 41,500 – less than half of the effectives that had reached Moscow two months previously. One fresh division of reinforcements was surprised south-west of Smolensk and forced to surrender. Vitebsk fell, and, still further to the French rear, Minsk fell too – together with its vast depots holding two million rations. But, under old Kutuzov, decisive victory would be left largely to 'General Winter' and the cruel distances of Mother Russia. Perhaps, for the Russians, it was the sensible thing to do.

Only one serious attempt was made by Kutuzov to seal the French escape route – at the crossing of the Beresina, midway between Vitebsk and Minsk, between 25 and 29 November. In a ferocious battle intended by Kutuzov to be his masterstroke,

a group of army conspirators under the courageous, badly wounded veteran Colonel von Stauffenberg tried – unsuccessfully – to blow him up at his Wolf's Lair headquarters in East Prussia.

140,000 Russians closed in with General Tchitshakov and Wittgenstein* standing athwart the crossings of the Beresina River.
Once again, Kutuzov lagged behind; fortunately for Napoleon his
main force was still twenty-six miles east of the Beresina when
the battle began. Oudinot and Victor (with relatively fresh
reinforcements which perhaps brought Napoleon's forces on the
Beresina to around 49,000 men, as against the Russian total of
some 75,000 within striking distance) fought brilliant actions;
but, as in the battles of Aspern–Essling of 1809, the day was
saved by Napoleon's engineers, under fifty-four-year-old General
Eblé. Working shoulder-deep in freezing water, Eblé himself led
the construction of two 105-yard pontoon bridges, one for
infantry and cavalry, the other for supply vehicles. Twice the
bridges collapsed, under the weight of artillery, but each time
Eblé managed to rouse his exhausted men to repair them. On
the 28th, terrible scenes of panic and carnage took place when
the last men struggled to get across the single surviving bridge as
it collapsed. Ségur described what he saw:

> The column, entangled in this narrow passage, in vain attempted
> to turn back. The crowds of men who came behind, unaware of
> the calamity, not hearing the cries of those before them, pushed
> them on and threw them into the gulf, into which they were
> precipitated in their turn.[11]

On the Beresina the French suffered some 20,000 to 30,000
casualties – possibly as much as a third of these lost during the
river crossing. The river was allegedly blocked with frozen
corpses for weeks to come. Constant claims that a tearful
Napoleon, paler than usual, appealed to Berthier, 'Well, Berthier, how are we going to get out of this?' But, miraculously,
Napoleon on the Beresina had indeed 'snatched an outstanding

---

* Another Russian leader of foreign extraction, like Barclay de Tolly,
Wittgenstein was the son of a Prussian general but had fought for the Tsar at
Austerlitz. He succeeded Kutusov during the 1813 Campaign.

victory out of his worst defeat', as the West Point authors
Esposito and Elting aptly remark:

> The Grande Armee might be dying on its feet, but neither
> winter, hunger, rivers, nor overwhelming odds in men and guns
> could halt it. It trampled them underfoot, and went on. And
> with it, borne above disaster, marched Napoleon's prestige and
> the traditions of the French Revolution. 'You should never
> despair while brave men remain with the colours.'[12]

As much as anything, it was Kutuzov's failure to move faster
that allowed elements of the *Grande Armée* to escape from Russia
at all — for the reasons we have already seen. It would have
required considerably greater forces than Kutusov then possessed.
Though the Beresina was trumpeted as a great Russian victory,
with Kutuzov able to hand over a hundred captured French
colours to the Tsar, in fact it marked the end of his long career.
The following April he was replaced by Wittgenstein, and he
died a few weeks later. Yet it could be argued that he had
defeated Napoleon — and saved Russia. Certainly, nothing but a
defeated and all but demoralized fragment of the *Grande Armée*
straggled into the safety of Poland, its true plight revealed in an
order from Berthier issued before the Beresina to Marshal Victor:
'every day's delay can mean a calamity. The army's cavalry is on
foot because the cold has killed all the horses. March at once — it
is the order of the Emperor and of sheer necessity.'

On 5 December, at Smorgonie, midway between the Beresina
and the Niemen, whence the whole fated expedition had been
launched less than six months before, Napoleon summoned his
marshals. He had, according to Constant, recently been 'harping
upon the necessity of his presence in Paris', and he now told
them that he intended to hasten back there. Though it meant his
abandoning the army to its fate, they agreed. The retreat out of
Russia had been more or less completed, and nothing was to be
gained by the Emperor risking his person. If anything was to be
saved, it was imperative for him to be in France to rally public

opinion, suppress any fresh revolt and raise new armies. Murat would remain behind in command; so brave and dashing on the attack, he proved hardly the best choice to lead a defeated army in retreat. With the dependable Duroc and Caulaincourt, and only a small escort of cavalry, Napoleon hastened westwards, incognito. According to Constant, many of the soldiers left behind 'cursed the Emperor, upbraiding him for having abandoned them thus; there was one universal cry of malediction'.

Napoleon passed Warsaw, barely pausing to see Marie Walewska – whose country now lay in mortal danger from the advancing and vengeful Russians. A bulletin attempting to gloss over the disaster was despatched ahead of him, ending on a bizarre, if not ironic, note: 'His Majesty's health has never been better.' It can hardly have brought much comfort to the abandoned survivors stumbling out of Russia, or to the widows and families of those left behind. As far as his own star was concerned, it was all too plain as 1812 ended that its final setting was only a matter of time. In modern phraseology, from now on it was downhill all the way.

EIGHTEEN

The Battle of the Nations

1813

A people who have been brought up on victories often do
not know how to accept defeat.

Napoleon

THE PROSPECT OF the coming campaign in Russia had 'cast
a gloom over society in general', wrote Laure Junot, the frivolous
Duchess of Abrantès, in her *Mémoires*.

> It was in vain that the emperor ordered balls, fêtes and quadrilles.
> Marie Louise was surrounded by young and beautiful women
> who were commanded by Napoleon to exert every nerve to
> render her gay; but these ladies had brothers, fathers, husbands
> and lovers, so that the joys of the court were forced pleasures,
> and not joys springing from the heart. . . .

As the campaign got under way, Paris had:

> presented a curious but melancholy spectacle. Husbands, sons,
> brothers and lovers were departing to join the army; while
> wives, mothers, sisters and mistresses, either remained at home
> to weep, or sought amusement in Italy, Switzerland or the
> various watering-places of France.[1]

Laure herself had taken off to Aix-en-Savoie, with her four-
year-old son (christened Napoleon), to be diverted by boating
with Talma on Lac Bourget, by listening to the great actor
recite from *The Tempest* in the midst of a storm, drenched with
water, then by embarking on an affair with the Marquis de

Balincourt as her husband struggled with the Russians and increasing madness. On 20 December 1812, she recalled, 'the cannon of the Invalides announced to the city of Paris that the Emperor had returned'. Three days later, lovesick and now abandoned by Balincourt, she tried to take an overdose of laudanum. In January, Junot returned; instead of the dashing, handsome young Governor of Paris who had left her a few months previously, 'there appeared a coarsened, aged man, walking with difficulty, bent and supported by a stick, dressed carelessly in a shabby greatcoat'. He was 'in a strange state,' Laure found; 'often in a condition of somnolence during the day, the night brought him no sleep. He so strong, so much master of himself, wept like a child.'

During the brief time he spent in Paris that grim winter, one colonel found his family and friends:

> in general terror-stricken. The famous 29th Bulletin had informed France abruptly that the *Grande Armée* had been destroyed. The Emperor was invincible no longer. The campaign of 1813 was about to open. . . . people were shocked to see the Emperor entertaining at the Tuileries. It was an insult to public grief and revealed a cruel sensitivity to the victims. I shall always remember one of those dismal balls, at which I felt as if I were dancing on graves. [2]

It spoke volumes for the mood in Paris, in the army and in France as a whole as the full horror of the Russian débâcle was brought home by survivors like Junot. One is reminded, in a different context, of the mood of Berlin as the Soviet colossus began to close in on the city in 1944. In the words of Mademoiselle Avrillon, who was in charge of the Empress's jewellery, 'we were all the more terrified . . . because for 20 years so many uninterrupted successes made us think reverses impossible'. The consternation produced by Napoleon's Bulletin reporting the destruction of the *Grande Armée* in Russia was 'impossible to describe'. [3] Constant recorded that it was:

The first time that Paris saw him come back from a campaign without bringing with him a fresh peace which the glory of his arms had won. On this occasion, all those persons who looked upon Josephine as the Emperor's talisman and the guardian of his fortunes, did not fail to note that the Russian campaign was the first which had been undertaken by the Emperor since his marriage with Marie Louise.

There was a strong, unvoiced sense that Moscow heralded, as Talleyrand expressed it, 'the beginning of the end, and . . . the end itself could not be far distant'. As soon as Napoleon showed himself in Paris, however, in the words of Duff Cooper, 'Once more and for the last time treason hung its head, criticism sank to a whisper, and conspiracy crept underground.'[4] In despair, Napoleon called on Talleyrand yet again. Coldly, he was rejected with the words, 'I am not acquainted with your affairs.' Enraged, Napoleon threatened to have him shot, or hanged. Talleyrand riposted in his usual restrained, whimsical manner, 'The Emperor is charming this morning.' Then he despatched a secret letter to Louis XVIII, who was waiting patiently in the wings in England for the summons that seemed bound to come, now sooner rather than later.

Napoleon deliberately took to appearing more and more frequently in public, taking part in shoots even more often than before. To Duroc he remarked,

It behoves me to bestir myself and show myself everywhere. So that the papers may mention this, since those stupid English newspapers say every day that I am ill and can't move. . . . Wait a bit! I will soon show them that I am as sound in body as I am in mind.

Despite his grave occupations, he never lost sight of his dream to make Paris the handsomest city in the world. Now he talked about building an embassy for the Italian Minister and a palace for the infant King of Rome on the Heights of Chaillot. In one of his few political successes, he began 1813 by attempting to make peace with the Pope with a new *Concordat*.

The balance sheet that confronted the Emperor as 1813 began could hardly have been more discouraging. He had inflicted an estimated 250,000 casualties on the Russians; but, out of the more than 600,000 troops that had crossed the Niemen in June 1812, only a broken 93,000 straggled home; out of 1,300 cannon, only 250 had returned. Even more serious, and irreplaceable in the long run, was his loss of some 180,000 horses. They provided the eyes and ears of his intelligence, the superb cutting edge of his heavy cavalry* — as well as the prime movers of his artillery and supplies. In this one disastrous campaign, seven years of efforts since the joint triumphs of Austerlitz and Jena had been thrown away. The limits of the French Empire returned to what they had been before Tilsit. And now the Russian success was emboldening vanquished nations like Austria and Prussia (nominal, but unwilling, allies of Napoleon during the Russian Campaign) to raise their heads above the parapet once again. Already, under leaders like Yorck, Blücher, Scharnhorst and Gneisenau, Prussia had undergone a miraculous, and historic, transformation, of its army and of its whole society, which in the ensuing century the world at large would come to rue. Other more or less unwilling allies like Bavaria and Saxony, and neutrals like Sweden, were just waiting for the right moment to align themselves against France.

Many historians have analysed the causes of Napoleon's decisive defeat in Russia: he should never have left the war in Spain unsettled at his rear (as Hitler, in 1941, had turned his back on an undefeated Britain); he had not prepared for a winter campaign (but it was the summer heat as much as the winter cold that had defeated him); and of course he should never have

---

* Perhaps the equivalent in terms of the Second World War would be the loss of his Panzer force suffered by Hitler after the failed Kursk offensive of summer 1943, or in Normandy the following August.

gone to Moscow. As Hitler in his turn found out, the unending spaces of Russia were just too great for one man to exercise control over the massive armies involved — even with the vastly more sophisticated communications of the mid-twentieth century. Finally, Napoleon's conduct of the campaign, the indecisions and procrastinations, the retreat from reality, suggested that he was no longer the man of Austerlitz and Jena, or even of Wagram. Almost certainly he had been saved by the ineptitude and the lethargy of the Russian commanders.

By early spring of 1813, the Russian juggernaut in the east had moved steadily westwards until it was approaching Prussian territory and menacing the German provinces allied to France. The Duchy of Warsaw, the tragic dream of a free Poland for which Marie Walewska and so many heroic Polish soldiers had given themselves since 1806, disappeared once again into the Tsarist maw* — not to reappear for more than a century. Marie herself once again took the road to Paris. During the Russian Campaign, Prussia's Frederick William III had been bullied into supplying a corps of 20,000 men to join the *Grande Armée*; barely two-thirds of them survived. In the last days of 1812 General Yorck had signed a secret treaty with Russia, the famous (or infamous, from Napoleon's point of view) Convention of Tauroggen, whereby the Prussian forces moved from a state of nominal alliance with France to one of hostile neutrality — which would soon enough lead to war. The weak Prussian King, whom Napoleon had so humiliated at Tilsit in 1807, hesitated before plunging his country into another contest with Napoleon. But he was carried away by the groundswell of nationalism among young Germans, who, fired by secret societies like the *Tugendbund* (literally the 'League of Virtue'), were sick of being overrun by the French, as the German states had been since the wars of Louis xiv. Frederick William was further galvanized by his hawkish Queen, and by Generals Yorck, Bülow and Blücher

---

* Warsaw itself was actually evacuated by the French on 4–8 February 1813.

(now recovered from the mental breakdown that had afflicted him six years previously). On the edge of revolt, in late February of 1813 Prussia in secrecy signed the Convention of Kalitsch with Russia, promising to enter the war, and being promised in return the restoration of her 1806 frontiers. For the forthcoming campaign, the Russians guaranteed to deploy a force 150,000 strong. Although, after Jena, Prussia had agreed to limit her forces to only 42,000 men, the work of secret rearmament in fact enabled her eventually to send 80,000 to join the Allies in 1813.

Tauroggen* was to herald the German War of Liberation, otherwise known as the Battle of the Nations, which by the end of 1813 would inflict decisive defeat on Napoleon, as well as letting out of the bottle the genie of German nationalism. (Yet, without those liberated Prussians at Waterloo, Wellington would never have won.)

As the New Year dawned, about all that stood in the way of the resurgent Allied forces were a few scattered French-held fortresses like Danzig, Stettin and Glogau-on-the-Oder and a miscellany of fewer than 50,000 troops under Eugène de Beauharnais, the admirable son of Josephine, and Napoleon's stepson, who had taken over command from his rather less admirable brother-in-law, Murat. (Murat had hastened back to the pleasanter climate of his Neapolitan kingdom as soon as he decently could after the retreat from Moscow.) Nevertheless, reworking the miracle which only he could achieve, Napoleon somehow managed to create a brilliant new army out of the wreckage of 1812, and a new strategy. In fact, three more times, in each successive year and after each major defeat, Napoleon would repeat that miracle. Only he, backed by the residual

---

* In July 1944, when Colonel von Stauffenberg, leader of the German opposition to Hitler, was pleading – unsuccessfully – with Field-Marshal von Manstein to help with the Resistance, he made his final plea in one word: 'Tauroggen!'.

fervour of France's revolutionary mystique, could have done it.* Setting himself a staggering target of 656,000 men, he mustered 120,000 half-trained conscripts, drew 80,000 from the National Guard and called up 100,000 more who had escaped service between 1809 and 1812. Troops were pulled out of Spain (although the 'Spanish Ulcer' still continued to eat up over 175,000 of his most seasoned troops in a losing struggle). 'France is one vast workship,' recorded Caulaincourt.

> The entire French nation overlooked his reverses and vied with one another in displaying zeal and devotion . . . It was a personal triumph for the Emperor, who with amazing energy directed all the resources of which his genius was capable into organizing the great national endeavour. Things seemed to come into existence as if by magic. . . .[5]

What a man!

Where his enemies (Britain in particular) erred in their failure to standardize, Napoleon's achievement in the earlier years of settling on standard calibres of field gun had greatly aided him. By mid-August, he would be able to count on the support of no fewer than 1,300 cannon, replenishing the losses of the Russian Campaign. Yet it could never be the same *Grande Armée*. It was gravely deficient in trained officers; even more seriously, the cavalry would never recover from its shortage of horses.

*

---

* Hitler, too, was in effect to reconstitute three new armies following strategic disasters: once after the loss of Paulus' Sixth Army, wiped out at Stalingrad in the winter of 1942–3; then, in 1943, after the loss of all von Arnim's and Rommel's forces in North Africa; and, finally, after the overwhelming German defeat in Normandy in 1944. That winter the reconstituted *Wehrmacht*, even though mortally wounded, was still able to strike a vicious and telling blow against the Americans in the Battle of the Bulge. Unlike Hitler, however, Napoleon was not driven on by having the terrible sword of 'Unconditional Surrender' hanging over his – and his country's – head.

THE ALLIED PLAN FOR 1813 was to advance on a broad front, with widely separated columns, clearing Prussia of the French and striking for Dresden, the capital of Napoleon's principal remaining German ally, Saxony. In the north, an embittered Bernadotte – never forgetting his public humiliation by Napoleon at Wagram – had thrown in his lot with the Allies, and was building up a force in Swedish Pomerania, preparing (cautiously, as always) to move southwards. Meanwhile false threats of a British landing lured the French into abandoning the useful port of Hamburg. With his forces concentrating in the Magdeburg area, Napoleon's plan – grandiose and highly ambitious – was to push the Allies back over the Elbe and strike for Berlin, then to relieve his beleaguered fortresses still holding out east of the Oder and on the Vistula. In his aim of seizing an enemy capital and dividing the Allied armies before they could concentrate, there were echoes of Austerlitz. Once again, Napoleon showed himself capable of moving with astonishing speed; once again, he was aided by procrastinatory squabbles among the Allies. (Old Kutuzov, too, demoted from supreme command but still at the head of the main Russian army directed on Dresden, was a dying man.) He was in any case sorely limited by his lack of effectives. By April they were still far below the figure of 300,000, the minimum he reckoned essential to carrying out his objectives. In cavalry, he could muster only 8,000 against the Allies' 24,000. He was also to prove over-optimistic in his reliance on his Saxon and Bavarian allies.

Characteristically, however, he decided to press an attack in mid-April before the Allies could concentrate on the Elbe. At 4 a.m. on 15 April 1813, he left St Cloud; the next day, at midnight, he was at Mainz on the other side of the Rhine. Disagreements over command in the Allied camp after the death of Kutuzov (he had died three weeks before) were offset by the handicap inflicted on Napoleon by virtue of the tactical intelligence denied him by his acute shortage of light cavalry. Nevertheless, at Lützen near Leipzig, west of the Elbe, he won a costly

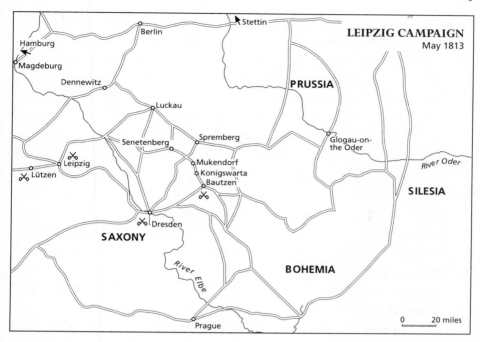

LEIPZIG CAMPAIGN
May 1813

Stettin

Berlin

Hamburg

Magdeburg

Dennewitz

PRUSSIA

Luckau

Senetenberg

Spremberg

Glogau-on-the Oder

River Oder

Leipzig

Mukendorf

Konigswarta

Bautzen

SILESIA

Lützen

Dresden

SAXONY

River Elbe

BOHEMIA

0   20 miles

Prague

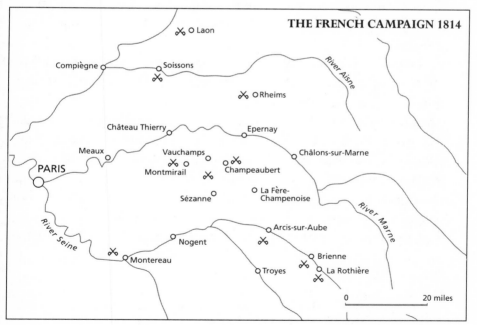

THE FRENCH CAMPAIGN 1814

O Laon

Compiègne

Soissons

River Aisne

O Rheims

Château Thierry

Epernay

Meaux

Vauchamps

Montmirail

Champeaubert

Châlons-sur-Marne

PARIS

Sézanne

O La Fère-Champenoise

River Marne

River Seine

Nogent

Arcis-sur-Aube

Montereau

Brienne

Troyes

La Rothière

0   20 miles

minor victory on 2 May – a Wagram rather than an Austerlitz. To his deep sorrow, there he lost Marshal Bessières, the son of a surgeon, who had been with him ever since Rivoli in 1796, the genius of the Guard who had led the famous charge at Austerlitz, and who had proved both one of his most dependable supporters and one of his few genuine friends. 'Bessières lived like Bayard; he died like Turenne,'* pronounced Napoleon. According to Marmont, 'This was probably the day, of his whole career, on which Napoleon incurred the greatest personal danger on the field of battle. . . . He exposed himself constantly, leading the defeated men of [Ney's] III Corps back to the charge.'⁶ Both sides lost about 20,000 men; on the Allied side, Blücher's Chief-of-Staff, Scharnhorst – the reformer of the Prussian Army, and often regarded as the epitome of German nationalism – was mortally wounded; Blücher himself was wounded, and the less tenacious Yorck took over the Prussian forces. The ferocity of the fighting at Lützen caused Napoleon to remark gloomily, 'These animals have learnt something.' The most valuable thing they had learnt was not to be taken by surprise by Napoleonic tactics.

Given Napoleon's crippling shortage of cavalry, there could be no serious pursuit of the defeated enemy. This was unfortunate for Napoleon; the squabbling Allies were in far worse disarray than he could see, the Prussians wanting to withdraw northwards, to cover Berlin, the Russians eastwards towards Breslau and Warsaw. Tsar Alexander had nominated Wittgenstein to succeed Kutuzov as supreme commander. Aged forty-four, he was the youngest of the Allied commanders – and not 100 per cent Russian. Blücher, the Prussian, had agreed to his appointment, but the Russian, Miloradevich, the veteran of Austerlitz and the

---

* Pierre Bayard (1476–1524), the original 'Chevalier sans peur et sans reproche', was a soldier of exemplary courage; the Vicomte de Turenne (1611–75), Marshal-General of France, was killed on a reconnoitring mission.

THE NARROW ESCAPE, or BONEY'S GRAND LEAP 'a la GRIMALDI'!_____"No sooner had Napoleon alighted & entred a miserable house for refreshment, then a party of Cossacks rushed in after him... Never was Miss Platoff so near Matrimony!! Had not the Emperor been very alert at Vaulting, and leapt through the Window, with the nimbleness of an Harlequin, while his faithfull

CRUICKSHANK, 'The Narrow Escape . . . 1813

Napoleon pursued by Cossacks, 1813

1812 campaign, objected. As a result Alexander himself assumed nominal command, with disastrous results.

Napoleon advanced across the Elbe, on 21 May winning at Bautzen, east of Dresden, another battle of furious intensity. By this time he had managed to concentrate 115,000 men to Wittgenstein's 96,000. Soult was charged with attempting a repeat of his historic success at Austerlitz's Pratzen Heights, breaking through the enemy centre while Ney enveloped them from the left. Ney, however, partly as a result of confusing orders from Napoleon, made a dismal mess of things, robbing the French of what might otherwise have been a copybook Napoleonic victory. Again, each side lost approximately 20,000 men, Napoleon's only trophies a few wrecked cannon and wounded prisoners. As well as the shortage of cavalry (Ney's excuse for failing to pursue), defeat at Bautzen reflected sorely the absence of his better commanders – especially Lannes, killed at Aspern–Essling in 1809; Davout, who had been sent off on a worthless diversion towards Hamburg; and Masséna, battling Wellington in Spain.

Napoleon had suffered another particularly grievous personal loss. Duroc – who had recently predicted his own end – died in agony in his Emperor's arms, after being disembowelled by a cannon-ball. Napoleon had rushed to his bedside, afterwards sitting for an hour with his head bowed in misery. 'Poor fellow!' an old Guardsman was heard to remark; 'he's lost one of his children.' For a while, demoralizing rumours were rife that it was the Emperor, not Duroc, transported in the coffin.

What might have resulted in a decisive victory, which would deter Austria from entering the war, ended yet again in only a modest one, bringing the spring campaign to a close with both sides in a state of exhaustion. With 90,000 of his men – in addition to battle casualties – listed sick, time was now emphatically not on Napoleon's side. He had outrun his supply system, and his lines of communication were constantly menaced by Cossacks and German partisans. On 2 June, he was forced to agree to an armistice – explaining it in terms of 'my shortage of cavalry, which prevents me from striking great blows, and the hostile attitude of Austria'. On 15 June, the British paymaster gave Russia and Prussia £2 million to carry on the war, and Austria £500,000 to join it. Six days later came news of Wellington's victory at Vitoria in Spain. It brought to an end brother Joseph's kingship and took the British uncomfortably close to France's own back-door at Bayonne – less than a hundred miles' distant. On 7 July, Bernadotte finally came off his fence and began moving with 100,000 men towards Berlin. Playing for time in a cunning game of diplomacy, and exploiting France's growing urge for peace, the wily Metternich offered Napoleon peace terms that he would be quite unable to accept. According to Metternich, this provoked 'a series of professions of friendship alternating with the most violent of outbursts'.[7] A furious Napoleon declared, 'You want nothing else but the dismemberment of the French Empire,' refusing – as Hitler was to do once forced on to the defensive – to cede 'an inch of land'.

Meanwhile, lapsing into his final bout of madness, Junot died, clamouring for peace. His death seemed somehow symbolic of how time was running out. Now, during the seven weeks' armistice, Austria was assembling an army, the Army of Bohemia, under Prince Schwarzenberg,* some 200,000 strong, marching northwards from Prague to join the Allies. In vain, and mistakenly, had Napoleon hoped that his dynastic marriage to the Austrian Marie Louise might have neutralized his new father-in-law. On 12 August a self-righteous Austria declared war. By mid-August a terrifying, and unprecedented grand total of 800,000 Allied troops faced Napoleon far from his base, on the upper reaches of the Elbe. By scraping every depot for reserves, the French Emperor was able astonishingly to confront this massive force with 700,000 of his own, though many were conscripts of poor quality.

Now, for the first time, Napoleon had to fight simultaneously the armies of Russia, Austria and Prussia – and the Swedish forces of the renegade Bernadotte, with Wellington closing in on the Pyrenees. Still unable to agree on any joint strategy, the Allies – respectful of Napoleon's menace in a pitched battle – fell back on the next best thing: the 'Trachtenberg Plan', whereby any army attacked by Napoleon would retire, refusing battle, while the others closed in on his flank and communications, like a pack of hounds bringing down a powerful stag. This was designed to prevent any army being destroyed in detail. As always, however, Napoleon moved his formations so fast as to threaten to negate the Trachtenberg compact; yet it was a form of attrition which, at last, was to prove successful.

---

* Schwarzenberg had nominally, and unenthusiastically, been an ally of Napoleon on the Russian Campaign of the previous year. His change of sides perhaps says something about the volatility of alliances in the Napoleonic Wars – as well as about the fickleness of Austrian motivations.

Trying to retrieve his original blueprint of April, Napoleon's plan was to strike for Berlin, capture the Prussian capital and head off Bernadotte's approaching army before it could link up with the Allies in the south. But logistics and the political considerations of keeping in the fight his chief surviving German ally, war-ravaged Saxony, forced him into an essentially defensive battle, with his main force fortifying an armed camp around the old and beautiful Saxon capital of Dresden. His marshals were increasingly restive about his scheme to advance on Berlin. At about this time, he suffered yet another personal blow in the defection of the brilliant Swiss strategist and (later) military historian, Baron Jomini — the *éminence grise* of Ney, who was often rash when left on his own. Reputedly the last officer to leave Russian soil, for his heroic conduct during the retreat from Moscow the previous year Ney had received from Napoleon the sobriquet 'the bravest of the brave' and had been proclaimed Prince of Moscow. But the strains of the Russian campaign, and wounds both there and at Lützen — followed by the defection of Jomini — progressively told on him. His battle conduct would henceforth suffer greatly (notably at Waterloo), and within a matter of days he would blunder clumsily, and foolishly, into a trap laid for him by his former colleague, Bernadotte.

At Dresden, on 26 and 27 August, though prey to an unusual degree of vacillation, Napoleon won yet another victory — this time at the expense of Schwarzenberg. He was aided by a fortuitous cannon-ball, which narrowly missed the Tsar but mortally wounded another renegade French General, Jean-Victor Moreau,* standing at his side. The French camp took heart from this, as a sign of divine retribution; the Allies were discouraged in proportion. During the battle, the valet, Constant,

---

* After Napoleon had come to power, Moreau had misguidedly set himself up as a rival. Becoming involved in a royalist intrigue, he was imprisoned, then exiled. Between 1804 and 1813 he lived quietly at Morrisville, on the Delaware River, USA, but was then enticed to return by the Tsar, as his military adviser — only to be killed almost immediately.

found Napoleon 'in a most deplorable state. He had been in the saddle since 6 that morning. It had rained incessantly and he was drenched through. Even his top boots were full of water, which must have dripped off his great coat. . . .'[8] But, once again, in the thick of the battle he seemed to be untouchable. Murat, back from Naples, struck a brilliant cavalry blow at the Austrians, but was not strong enough to pursue and trap them in retreat. In fact, by overreaching themselves the French suffered an unprecedented disaster. On 30 August, Vandamme, a bold commander keen to win his marshal's baton, allowed himself to be cut off unexpectedly at Kulm, twenty-five miles south of Dresden, by the Prussian Kleist, who suddenly appeared out of the hills behind him. After a fierce fight, Vandamme, outnumbered in a proportion of 3:5, was forced to surrender together with 13,000 men.* In the north, Macdonald of Wagram fame, through mishandling of his corps, had been badly mauled by Blücher.

With only 120,000 French facing 170,000 of the enemy, Napoleon had triumphed at Dresden with losses (apart from Vandamme) of barely 10,000 to the Allies' 38,000. His handling of the battle showed him at the top of his old form, but he was, disquietingly, let down badly by the failure of his subordinates (such as Vandamme) elsewhere. Here the Trachtenberg compact had borne fruit. Thus Dresden, observes David Chandler, 'joined Lützen and Bautzen on the growing list of practically valueless French victories'.[9] Now the big test, the Allies' great opportunity, was about to come.

DRESDEN HAD GONE SOME way to re-establishing the myth of Napoleonic invincibility, but the surrender of Vandamme

---

* Taken to the Tsar, Vandamme was accused of looting, but is alleged to have riposted impudently, 'At least I have never been accused of killing my father!' He was returned to France in 1814, only to be exiled by the returning Bourbons, but he rejoined Napoleon during the Hundred Days to fight in the Waterloo Campaign.

gave the Allies a much needed emotional uplift. Shortage of supplies was rapidly reducing the French forces to starvation level, with the basic bread ration cut from twenty-eight ounces to eight, as the ravages of war in Saxony (once the richest of the German states) rendered foraging unprofitable, if not impossible. By the beginning of September, Napoleon could count on no more than 260,000 tired and hungry men, and about half the number of cannon he had at the beginning of the campaign in the spring. His plan to drive on Berlin was once more aborted, this time by the hole in his ranks caused by Vandamme's and Macdonald's débâcles and by the general reluctance of his commanders. Instead, in breach of his fundamental principle of concentration, he despatched Ney towards Berlin with an under-strength detachment of 60,000 men, while keeping his main force at Dresden. On 6 September, Ney suffering from the loss of his genius, Jomini, and from the shortage of cavalry intelligence that now increasingly beset the whole *Grande Armée*, blundered foolishly into a trap laid for him by Bernadotte, at Dennewitz, less than fifty miles south-west of Berlin. He suffered 10,000 casualties, to 7,000 of the former fellow general whom he had never held in high esteem.

Meanwhile, at Dresden Napoleon was in a serious dilemma. To stay there, with the Allied armies converging, would place him in great jeopardy, but to quit the city would almost certainly mean the defection of his last remaining German ally, the King of Saxony. Weighing up the military against the political, he dithered disastrously for several days. With Blücher continuing to evade all attempts to bring him to battle, on 7 October Napoleon set off north-westwards for what he considered to be the safer stronghold of Leipzig, leaving behind in Dresden two of his best corps, under St Cyr and Lobau. It was a decision that has been rated 'probably the most fateful one of the entire campaign'. His attempts to threaten the enemy capital, Berlin, and to manoeuvre against his rear, had both failed. On 13 October, Blücher, the stubborn old Prussian who detested retreat, Napoleon and Bernadotte in about equal measure, wrote to the Tsar that the three armies were now so close together 'that a simultaneous attack, against the point where the enemy has concentrated its forces, might be undertaken'.[10]

Three days later, in the greatest concentration of force ever seen in the Napoleonic Wars, the Allies – moving in from every direction, the Russians from the south-east, Schwarzenberg's Austrians from the south-west and Blücher's Prussians (plus, more slowly, Bernadotte's Swedes) from the north – finally cornered Napoleon outside the city of Leipzig. It was barely a day's march from the battlefield of Jena, where the French Emperor had scored his crushing victory over the Prussians just seven years previously to the day. Later, with hindsight, Marmont described the French position as being 'at the bottom of a funnel'. In what justly came to be called the Battle of the Nations, 200,000 hungry and battle-weary French with 900 cannon faced well over 300,000 Allied troops and 1,500 guns. Such numbers had never been seen before on a European battlefield. There ensued two days of a grim slogging battle, of an unprecedented intensity. At one point on the first day Murat's heavy cavalry broke through, all but reaching the Tsar's command post – which could have won the day for Napoleon. But, without the reserves to follow up, the exhausted *cuirassiers* were driven off by the Tsar's 'heavies'.

The battle ended roughly in a draw, with Napoleon having sustained some 25,000 casualties to approximately 30,000 of the Allies. But, as more and more Allied reinforcements approached, the odds became heavily loaded against the French. Instead of beating an orderly retreat from Leipzig on 17 October, whereby he could have saved at least part of his army, Napoleon, hoping for some heaven-sent miracle such as had bailed him out so often in the past, made the fatal mistake of delaying to the 18th. On the 17th, the allies moved in in what the American historians Esposito and Elting have described as 'a heads-down, go-and-get-killed, concentric attack'. By nightfall, total, irretrievable defeat faced Napoleon. The only thing which was to save him from annihilation was the leisurely performance of Bernadotte, anxious to spare his own raw Swedes and behaving much as he had when fighting for Napoleon.

At this last, and finally decisive, battle of the brutal 1813 campaign, the French artillery fired off some 200,000 rounds; the Allies lost probably as many as 54,000 killed and wounded, while French battle casualties approached 40,000, with a further 30,000 captured during the retreat on the 19th. Many were drowned when panicky engineers prematurely blew a bridge, crowded with troops, over the River Elster. Among those tragically lost was the brave Prince Poniatowski. He and his fellow Poles had fought magnificently during the battle, and he had just been made a marshal, the first of his countrymen to receive his baton.* He tried to swim the river on his horse, but, exhausted from four wounds, he failed to make it.

The death of the much loved Poniatowski marked the end of Poland's brave hopes in Napoleon. Leipzig equally marked the end of Napoleon's empire east of the Rhine. The Bavarians had already changed sides, and were supplying the victorious Allies with a force under General Wrede (who had fought alongside Napoleon at Wagram). Now the Saxons, deserted by Napoleon, their country ravaged by war, left his camp; not much more than half-a-century later, in a war of revenge for all the humiliations inflicted by the French, they would be invading France hand in hand with the Prussians, whose triumph at Leipzig would herald their emergence as the leading power in Germany.

In this second bitter winter of defeat, the French retreat across Germany was hardly less grim than that of 1812. 'The numbers of corpses and dead horses increased every day,' recorded an Allied observer:

---

* His descendants became Ministers of the Republic, under both Napoleon III and, later, Giscard d'Estaing.

Thousands of soldiers, sinking from hunger and fatigue, remained behind, unable to reach a hospital. The woods for several miles round were full of stragglers and worn-out and sick soldiers. Guns, wagons were found everywhere. . . .[11]

It could have been an account of the German retreat from the Falaise Gap in August 1944. Almost 400,000 of Napoleon's troops had been lost, or cut off in isolated garrisons from Danzig to Dresden; only about 80,000 effectives, plus some 40,000 stragglers, limped back across the Rhine. That Napoleon escaped at all was probably thanks to Bernadotte's dismal failure to reach Leipzig in time, and to the Allies' own exhaustion. By November, Schwarzenberg's command was reduced to only 150,000 men – 'ragged, worn out, wracked by typhus and dysentery'[12] – their lines of communication impossibly extended. Only their enfeeblement staved off an immediate invasion of France.

Less than three weeks after the catastrophe at Leipzig, Napoleon was back at St Cloud, once again leaving his defeated troops behind, to ask for fresh armies. He had been absent from Paris 209 days, compared with 224 in 1812, and only 124 for the Ulm–Austerlitz Campaign of 1905. If it had not been plain after Moscow, the writing on the wall should have been crystal clear after Leipzig. From the capture of Allied correspondence just before the battle was engaged, Napoleon had learnt enough about enemy intentions to realize that only a decisive military victory could save him. Yet France, after twenty-five years of almost constant war, was physically, financially and emotionally drained. Back in Paris, hatred for Napoleon was spreading, as many subversive groups – Royalists, Jacobins and 'liberals' – conspired with increasing impunity. The 1813 campaign had revealed that many of the leading marshals (not unlike Hermann Goering after 1940) had grown soft after being showered with titles and riches; Clarke, the Minister of War, had made such a muddle as to suggest something worse than mere incompetence; Berthier, the once indispensable 'Emperor's wife', was very sick;

in a grave waste of talent, Davout had been left behind, out of the Battle of the Nations, and stuck in Hamburg. Repeated failures in 1813 proved that the cavalry, the key to so many past battles and campaigns, had still not recovered from its losses in Russia – indeed, it would barely do so by Waterloo. Though only the inefficiency of the Allies had saved Napoleon in 1813, and would come close to doing so in 1814, he failed to understand that the driving impulse of nationalism was now no longer an exclusively French asset. In the words of General J. F. C. Fuller, for Napoleon the battle of Leipzig had been 'a second Trafalgar, this time on land; his initiative had gone'.[13]

NINETEEN

'La Patrie en Danger!'

1814

I am still the man I was at Wagram and Austerlitz.

Napoleon

IN THE SUMMER of 1813, Talleyrand, now filled with bitterness towards his former chief and all his works, saw him as 'a man who is ready to hide under a bed'. Yet by the end of the year, with that ineffable ebullience, Napoleon had made one more astonishing recovery. To anyone but the most irrepressible optimist – or a Bonaparte – the situation at the beginning of 1814 would have seemed quite hopeless. France was now at least as divided over the war as America during the last days of Vietnam. Against Napoleon's shaky 80,000 survivors, more than 300,000 Allied troops were mustering along the Rhine; Switzerland had been compelled by *force majeure* to permit passage of Schwarzenberg's army so as to turn the French flank; while in the far south Wellington was across the Pyrenees at Narbonne with 125,000 men. In Italy, Eugène, whose Piedmontese levies were becoming increasingly unreliable, had 50,000 men with whom to face 74,000 under Bellegarde. Yet still Napoleon was far from finished; he called up or alerted 936,000 men (though barely one in eight of these ever saw active service), and supplemented these 'Marie Louises' – as the new, pubescent conscripts were called – by drafting gendarmes, forest guards (mostly discharged veterans) and even customs officers. Regular officers were sent home to organize partisan units. In a minor diplomatic coup, he attempted to clear his flanks by permitting the Pope, under house arrest in France, to return to Rome; and he offered to hand back Spain to the hopeless Ferdinand of the Asturias. Exploiting a sense of 'backs to the wall' and the slogan 'La Patrie en Danger!' Napoleon could still draw on his daemonic will to succeed. He even dreamed of a great new offensive led by Murat and Eugène south of the Alps to threaten Vienna.

Moving with all the self-confidence that the scent of victory throws up, the Allies gave Napoleon little time to gather his forces. By the beginning of January 1814, Blücher and Schwarzenberg were across the Rhine and into France. The cities of eastern France surrendered swiftly to handfuls of Allied cavalry, their inhabitants seduced by Metternich's skilful psychological warfare: he claimed (not unlike the Anglo-American allies from 1943 onwards) that the Allies came in peace and friendship, to liberate France from a tyrant. Then came the Cossacks and the Prussian infantry, and the full horror of what an occupying army signifies* – something which France had been spared since Valmy in 1792. Napoleon was also let down by his marshals: Ney did nothing; Macdonald dithered; Victor withdrew swiftly behind the Vosges, abandoning Strasbourg. Only Mortier fought hard, delaying Schwarzenberg in his advance from Langres. But by 26 January Schwarzenberg was already at Bar-sur-Aube, on one of the tributaries of the Seine, and Blücher was at St Dizier. Both armies were little more than a hundred miles from Paris, which Napoleon had left virtually unfortified, rather than risk adding fuel to the smoulderings of revolt by any suggestion that the highly nervous capital might be endangered. Leaving his throne-less elder brother Joseph in charge of Paris, that day Napoleon

---

* In outrage, Louis Constant wrote of the Cossacks, 'These hideous savages would break into houses, lay hands on everything, load their horses with plunder, destroying what they could not steal. . . . They would smash doors, ceilings, windows, furniture, everything, and then make of the fragments that remained a huge bonfire.' He had evidently forgotten what he had written about the French plundering of Moscow!

reached Châlons-sur-Marne, taking over the reins of battle himself.

There now followed what has been dubbed the 'Campaign of Miracles', in which the Emperor, hopelessly outnumbered but goaded on by despair, his back to the wall, but aided by interior – and short – lines, fought some of the most brilliant defensive–offensive actions of his entire career, worthy of the campaigns of 1796 and 1805.

His situation was not unlike Hitler's by the autumn of 1944, but his guiding principle was what it had been at Ulm and Austerlitz: to catch the enemy armies and defeat them separately, as each overextended itself in the race to reach Paris first. At Brienne, where Napoleon had received his first military schooling, his unskilled conscripts defeated an equal number of Prussian veterans – narrowly failing to destroy Blücher completely. At neighbouring La Rothière on 1 February he was repulsed. Crowing, the Allied generals invited each other to dinner at the Palais Royal the following week.

Napoleon's already shaky army was further weakened by some 4,000 desertions, and, once again (this was the third time), he almost fell into Cossack hands. Civilian morale was low, with the inhabitants holding back their food from their Emperor's army, in anticipation of Allied depredations. A blizzard of bad news followed him: Brussels had fallen; Paris was in the grip of mounting panic; Caulaincourt, Duke of Vicenza, Foreign Minister since November 1813, had been bluntly told by the Allies that negotiations would be based not on France's 'natural boundaries' but on the pre-Revolutionary frontiers of the *ancien régime*; and news had arrived from Eugène in Italy that Murat, Napoleon's own brother-in-law, had deserted to the British.* Napoleon

---

* Though he had fought brilliantly, again, at Napoleon's side during the Leipzig Campaign, Murat had since the beginning of 1813 been in secret negotiation with the Allies. He now agreed to provide a force to fight against France, in return for the Allies guaranteeing his throne. After his brother-in-law's abdication, he found that they were not prepared to honour their promises, and

was shattered by Murat's defection, declaring, 'It cannot be! Murat, to whom I have given my sister! Murat, to whom I have given a throne! Eugène must be mistaken, it is impossible that Murat should have declared himself against me.'[1]

THEN, FROM 10 FEBRUARY, the tide abruptly – but temporarily – turned in Napoleon's favour. In an excess of confidence, the Allies decided to divide their armies, with Blücher at the head of 50,000 men advancing on Paris from the north-east, and Schwarzenberg with 150,000 from the south-east via Sens. At the heart of this division of forces lay political divisions. The Russians wanted a crushing victory, from which a weakened France would be forced to concede to her all her territorial ambitions in the east – notably the whole of Poland; while the Austrians, traditionally alarmed by Russian ambitions, did not want an emasculated France. Lord Castlereagh, Canning's bitter rival, a coldly arrogant personality but a brilliant negotiator, was now British Foreign Secretary. Playing a vigorous and skilful role at Allied Headquarters, he supported the Austrians in opposing the Tsar. This division of forces provided Napoleon with just the kind of situation he had always excelled in, and he won three copybook victories in a row, within six days. Leaving Victor and Oudinot to cover Schwarzenberg, and marching through deep mud with little more than 30,000 men, he struck hard into Blücher's extended flank at Champaubert – just sixty-five miles due east of Paris.

Here, short of artillery horses, he was aided enthusiastically by the local populace, who had already had a brief taste of Allied 'liberation'. Just as Napoleon himself had done in the past, the Allies lived off the land. The requisitioning methods of Blücher's

---

during the Hundred Days he tried to redeem himself in Napoleon's eyes. But his services were refused, and, returning to Italy after Waterloo, he was captured and shot.

Prussians, with much to avenge, were particularly brutal; Yorck damned his men as 'bandits', but Blücher turned a blind eye on looting — except in Prussia. So Napoleon now found no shortage of local volunteers to help drag his guns through mud 'six feet deep'. Marmont, aided by Ney, caught a weak Russian corps off balance, and devastated it; its commander, General Olssufiev, was rounded up in a wood by a nineteen-year-old conscript with less than six months' service. Next, swinging westwards, Napoleon smote the corps of both the Prussians, Sacken and Yorck, at Montmirail — barely fifty miles from Paris, and lying on that confluent of the River Marne, the Petit Morin, which was to be made famous in September 1914, when once again French armies repelled Prussians at the very gates of Paris. Like his successors of a century later, Blücher was driven northward over the Marne at Château Thierry. Then, in the third battle of this remarkable week, on 14 February, Blücher's advance guard, marching carelessly towards Montmirail, was surprised and put to flight by the Guard at Vauchamps, midway between the scenes of the first two battles. At Vauchamps Blücher lost 7,000 men to only 600 of Napoleon's.

In this remarkable 'Six Days Campaign' of 1814, Napoleon's greatly inferior force had covered eighty miles, won three notable victories and inflicted a total of 20,000 casualties on Blücher — or 40 per cent of his original force, as well as capturing a large number of his guns. Everywhere Napoleon went personally in that desperate, brief week in February, he vanquished. He was seen to be at his very best, reminiscent of the tactical brilliance of his First Italian Campaign in 1796.

In sharp contrast, the Allies were at their very worst, showing all their old failures at joint, co-ordinated leadership; it was as if they had learnt nothing since Austerlitz. As Blücher fell back to lick his wounds, on 16 February Napoleon now turned southwards to push Schwarzenberg back across the Upper Seine, and still further away from Blücher. Schwarzenberg — always impressionable — was severely shaken, conscious both that he was in charge of the last army which his exhausted country could field, and that defeat would now entail ruinous retreat across a vindictively hostile countryside. He saved his army by begging for an armistice. Like a boxer on the ropes, however, it was only a ruse to gain time.

Still the legend of Napoleon's immortality seemed to continue to protect him. At Montereau, when reproved by the Guard for exposing himself too far forward, he retorted, 'Fear not, the bullet that will kill me has not yet been cast!' At Arcis-sur-Aube, one of the last desperate battles a month later, he came even closer to death than he had when wounded by a spent cannonball at Ratisbon in 1809. A smoking howitzer shell fell near by, but, so as to prevent the troops panicking, Napoleon deliberately rode over it. According to one of his generals:

> The shell exploded, the horse, disembowelled, went plunging down, taking the rider with it. The Emperor disappeared in the dust and smoke. But he got up without a scratch, and mounting a new horse rode off to inspect the positions of the other battalions.[2]

Wherever he appeared, the Old Guard, and even the young, conscripted 'Marie Louises' cheered 'Vive l'Empereur!' But time and men were running out. Paris and the marshals conspired; in the south, Wellington's methodical advance had forced Soult to fall back on Toulouse; France was terminally sick of war. Caulaincourt, once one of the most dependable of the Emperor's inner circle, was deeply pessimistic. 'We had nothing left but courage,' he wrote later.

> Power and force were in the enemy's camp . . . but the Emperor doubtless blinded himself to his perils as well as to his resources. . . . Discouragement, the word ran, was universal, not only for the daily risks one took, but because the future promised no end.[3]

On 25 February, the three Allied sovereigns, Alexander, Francis and Frederick William, with Castlereagh again pressing British interests, held a council of war — and of peace — at Bar-sur-Aube. Blücher was once more set on the road to Paris, now reinforced by Winzingerode's* corps, detached from a protesting but paralysed Bernadotte.† He was soon reeling back again, this time as far as the River Aisne. Pursuing him, Napoleon, now increasingly short of effectives, suffered a serious set-back at Laon on 5 March. Here the French lost 6,000 to the Allies' 4,000. To Joseph, nervously holding out in Paris, Napoleon reported on the 11th, 'Unfortunately the Young Guard is melting like snow,' adding even more ominously, 'Orders must be given for the construction of redoubts at Montmartre.' The volatile city suddenly realized the immediacy of its peril; but it was far too late to contemplate any serious fortification of Paris. On the 12th, the Duke of Angoulême, nephew to the exiled Bourbon pretender, landed in anglophile Bordeaux (which had gone over to the British) and proclaimed his uncle King of France as Louis XVIII.

Once again, something like a miracle saved Napoleon. The elderly Blücher, sick and exhausted, suddenly collapsed; his Chief-of-Staff, Gneisenau, then halted the four corps about to pursue Marmont's battered forces; meanwhile Schwarzenberg was laid low with gout. On 13 March Napoleon pulled off his last great coup of a campaign of sheer genius: swinging his forces forty miles across Blücher's front to the east, he suddenly swept the Allies out of Rheims, at a cost of only 700 French to 6,000

---

* Winzingerode was an Austrian, who had been captured at Austerlitz. He transferred to the Tsar's service, fighting at Leipzig in 1813, and was then placed under command of Bernadotte.
† Despite Allied urging (Castlereagh had even threatened to cut him off from the British payroll), *Belle Jambe* had refused to advance further than Belgium — in the apparent hope that such restraint might somehow put him in line to succeed Napoleon as France's ruler; he was unaware of the contempt in which he was held in the army (in fact he was regarded by many Frenchmen as nothing but a traitor). Blücher, indeed, saw Bernadotte more as a threat to his rear than as a reinforcing ally.

Allies. It was a brilliant tactical stroke (bearing a resemblance to what Hitler would attempt in his last-gasp Ardennes Offensive, the Battle of the Bulge, in December 1944). A great wedge was forced between the two Allied armies, placing Napoleon in a position to threaten the rear of both Schwarzenberg and the Prussians. French morale soared; to the shocked Allies it seemed as if there could be no end to the new forces which Napoleon could suddenly conjure up. 'I am still the man I was at Wagram and Austerlitz,' he boasted to a wobbling Fouché on 14 March.

For all these stunning tactical victories, however, the time was now thoroughly out of joint for Napoleon. Politically the props were being pulled out from under him. During the night of 23/24 March, the Allies captured despatches from Paris to Napoleon, showing the city to be undefended, frightened and seething with enemies of the regime. Grasping the possibilities, Alexander immediately bullied Schwarzenberg and the Prussians into a new all-out thrust on the capital. Napoleon's instinctive reaction was to move further eastwards to threaten their rear. But now Caulaincourt and his war-weary generals rebelled. Instead, early on the 28th, Napoleon was forced to head for Paris – from which he had been consistently (and unwisely) absent since the end of January. Warnings that his enemies there were about to hand the city over to the Allies caused him to halt at Fontainebleau. He still had some 60,000 troops with him.

Peace, history often tells us, could almost always have been declared at a better moment than that chosen by the great generals – especially if they are inflated by recent successes. In the summer of 1813, after Napoleon had hammered the Allies in the battles preceding Leipzig, he had been offered France's 'natural frontiers',* and possibly he would then (at least in

---

* These so-called 'natural frontiers', defined under the Revolution as constituting the Pyrenees, the Alps, the Rhine, the Channel and the Mediterranean, would have left France in possession of what is now Belgium; would Wellington's Britain ever have accepted this?

theory) have been able to keep his own throne. Late February of 1814, after the string of French victories, might have been a moment when Austria, humiliated yet again, might have agreed to a 'separate peace', accepting the frontiers of 1792. But Napoleon did not know, had never known, when to stop – and (like Hitler) he would *never* cede ground. 'If only Talleyrand were here – he would get me out of it,' he moaned. The supple Prince of Benevento would certainly have known when to say 'stop' – in fact, had said so after Tilsit those long seven years previously – but he was now committed body and soul to the enemy camp. As J. F. C. Fuller wrote of the Napoleon of that time, in what makes an apt general epitaph, 'Pride ruined his splendid strategy.'[4]

By March it was too late. At Chaumont on the 1st, the Allies – their equilibrium at the front somewhat restored – in a treaty not unlike those concluded between the Allies in the Second World War, pledged not to treat separately with the 'Ogre'. (It cost Britain another £5 million in 'Pitt's Gold'.) Disregarding the pleas of Caulaincourt, Napoleon again rejected their offer of an immediate cease-fire and peace based on the 1792 frontiers. From now on, all that was on offer was virtually 'Unconditional Surrender', with the Allies calling on the French nation to overthrow Napoleon.

On 30 March Paris came under the first cannon-fire. A frozen Joseph Bonaparte, together with brother Jérome (now also minus a throne, the Allies having pushed him out of Westphalia the previous year) watched the battle for the outskirts from the Heights of Montmartre. Joseph then sneaked out of the city, heading south amid a long line of refugees. It was a scene that would be repeated three more times over the next 126 years. After he and Mortier had fought hard at Romainville, Marmont, Duke of Ragusa, finally deserting his master, signed an armistice at 2 a.m. on the morning of the 31st. Cossacks rode down the Champs Élysées, and then camped there, the first time since the Hundred Years War that a foreign army had entered the proud city. '*Mon Dieu!* not Cossacks in the Rue Racine!' exclaimed Madame de Staël from the safety of her Swiss retreat at Coppet. Talleyrand pretended to leave Paris, so that, in the words of his biographer, Duff Cooper, 'He could say that he had endeavoured to do his duty, but had been prevented by force.' Talleyrand, charming the Tsar, then proclaimed a rump government to declare Napoleon dethroned. Alexander responded by saying, 'I have determined to stay in your house because you have my confidence and that of my allies.'[5]

On his way to Paris, Napoleon heard the news that same day, and returned to Fontainebleau. There his valet, Constant, described him as never having 'looked so pale and tired as he did now; he scarcely sought to hide his dejection and discouragement'. He spoke to no one, but 'shut himself up in his study with Caulaincourt and Berthier'. Constant sensed, however, that he was in fact not at all 'vanquished by his ill fortune', 'merely dominated by one fixed idea' – the prospect of a new offensive to relieve Paris. On 6 April, however, after a vain attempt to leave the throne to his three-year-old son, he abdicated unconditionally. Five nights later, Constant found him apparently dying. He had taken the sachet of poison which, ever since he had nearly been taken by Cossacks in 1812, he had carried in a small black bag. After much vomiting, however, he survived; this was ascribed by Constant to the fact that the poison had 'lost its efficacy'.[6] On the 14th, a heavily veiled Marie Walewska arrived at Fontainebleau. Whether because of the after-effects of the poison, or because he was sunk in gloom, or because he was bemused by his own thoughts, Napoleon let her spend the whole night there without seeing her – much as he had done on the retreat through Warsaw, after Moscow in 1812. Rejected once again, she then returned to Paris, battling against the hordes of refugees. According to Constant, Napoleon was mortified: '"Poor woman, she will think I wanted to snub her! Constant, I really am so sorry! . . . But I have so many things here!" And the Emperor tapped his forehead.' Two days later he repaired the damage in a letter of touching warmth:

My feelings for you remain unchanged. Keep well; don't worry.
Think of me with pleasure and never doubt me.

> Yours
>> Napoleon

Ⅿⓐⓓⓡⓘⓓ   Fontainebleau   Ⅿⓞⓢⓚⓐⓤ

GERMAN CARTOON, 'Satire from 1814 on the Abdication of Napoleon'
Contemporary German Cartoon, Nap's Abdication, 1814

That same day, the Allies ratified the Treaty of Fontainebleau,
whereby Napoleon was allowed to retain the title of emperor
and given full sovereignty – over the Isle of Elba. On the 28th,
together with his personal suite and a guard of 600 soldiers
permitted him, Napoleon left aboard HMS *Undaunted* for Elba.
France was exhausted; Europe breathed a sigh of relief.

TWENTY

The Hundred Days

1814—1815

> For every Frenchman with a heart, the moment has come to
> conquer or perish!
>
> Napoleon

FOR THE NEXT ten months Napoleon upon his new 'empire'
of Elba, eighteen miles by twelve in area, an infinitesimal fraction
of the empire larger than Charlemagne's over which he had
recently ruled (wits described it as 'bestowing on Caesar the
Kingdom of Sancho Panza'),[1] strutted, and fretted, as successive
reports of France's distress under the Restoration reached him.
Then he began to plot. The English Commissioner on Elba,
Colonel Campbell, recorded:

> I have never seen a man in any situation in life with so much
> personal activity and restless perseverance. . . . I do not think it
> possible for him to sit down to study, on any pursuits of
> retirement, as proclaimed by him to be his intention, so long as
> his state of health permits corporeal exercise . . .[2]

Madame Mère and his sister Pauline visited him. Then, for a few
idyllic days, Marie Walewska and their infant son joined him.
He imposed the greatest secrecy, for fear of upsetting his now
tenuous relationship with Empress Marie Louise,* with its now

---

* Unbeknown to Napoleon (whom she had not seen since January), she had in
fact already returned to her home in Vienna, together with the King of Rome,
the heir for whom he had sacrificed so much. Despite his entreaties, he never

greatly reduced dynastic significance. For this reason, purportedly, he once again rejected Walewska, sending her off back to Naples. But his mind was also preoccupied elsewhere, with plans for a comeback. According to her biographer, Christine Sutherland, for the long-suffering Pole this fresh rebuff was the last straw: 'He had inflicted a wound more profound than when he married Marie Louise just a month before his "Polish wife" brought his son into the world.'[3] Henceforth, Napoleon was more alone than he had ever been.

In France, initial ecstasy at the Restoration of King Louis XVIII swiftly turned to angry disillusion. Detained, unpromisingly, in England (where he had spent the years since Napoleon had chased his Court out of Verona) by a severe attack of gout, the elderly exile from Hartwell did not land in Calais until 24 April 1814. He was greeted by the versatile Talleyrand at Compiègne, where just four years previously Napoleon had taken possession of Marie Louise. Louis was an uncharismatic figure; he was old for his age of fifty-eight, immensely fat, and because of the gout unable to move without support on either side. To one onlooker, the delirious applause with which Paris greeted him was 'quite incomprehensible': 'here is a man whom only yesterday they did not know, and already they are full of enthusiasm for him!'[4]

No less conspicuous was the welcome accorded the conquering Tsar. *Grandes dames* and *demi-mondaines* like Laure Abrantès, and even ex-Empress Josephine, flocked to meet him (in a later, more brutal age they might have had their heads shaven as *collabos*). Alexander was particularly enchanted by Josephine, who with her great charm and residual popularity was able to act as a kind of 'link between the two Frances'.[5] He took to visiting her daily at Malmaison, which now became 'far more crowded than at any time since the divorce'. Then, one day in May, she caught

---

saw either again; Marie Louise soon embarked upon an affair, which was to last fifteen years, with a dashing Austrian cavalry general, Count Neipperg, who wore a black patch having lost an eye in the wars as a Hussar.

cold after she had been out driving with Alexander. Evidently the cold turned to pneumonia, and a few days later she died in the arms of her son Eugène, 'going', in his elegant words, 'as gently and as sweetly to meet death as she had met life'. All France mourned; Napoleon, when he heard the news on Elba, was devastated. To the superstitious, just as the divorce had seemed to mark an end to his successes, so now the final disappearance of this 'ray' of his star indicated that it was soon to burn up altogether.

King Louis ('Louis the Unavoidable', as he came to be known after Waterloo) swiftly set about disenchanting his subjects, endorsing Talleyrand's quip about the Bourbons having learnt nothing and forgotten nothing. The court of the *ancien régime* which had followed him out of exile was even worse. By many Frenchmen they were seen to have arrived 'in the Allies' baggage-wagons', and they behaved like carpetbaggers. The army was shabbily and foolishly treated; obviously it had to be reduced from the huge size attained by the *Grande Armée*, despite all its losses,* but this was carried out in a brusque and mean-spirited manner. Officers discharged by the thousand saw themselves replaced by Royalists, some of whom had recently served against France. Davout, perhaps most admired of all the marshals, was struck from the active list; Masséna, who had been born in Nice (which then belonged to Sardinia), was insultingly told he was a foreigner and would have to become naturalized to retain his commission. The streets of Paris swarmed with discharged and penniless veterans, while some 12,000 ex-officers on half-pay took to meeting in the cafés, to lament 'the good old days' of the Empire. In the countryside, the peasantry – still the largest class of French society and the backbone of the army – was deeply suspicious that property handed them during the Revolution might now be redistributed among the returning émigrés,

---

* It had been about a million-strong since 1812, in a population of thirty-three million.

who were clamouring for restitution. Rightly or wrongly they still regarded Napoleon as trustee of the Revolution. The economy sagged, as inflation took over to fan the embers of discontent.

In Elba, Napoleon learnt that the Bourbons were refusing to pay his pension and were talking of transferring him to a more remote island. All this presented fertile soil for mischief. Meanwhile the rest of Europe, exhausted, bankrupt and its agriculture ravaged by war, speedily demobilized. In the Anglo-Saxon way of things at the completion of a successful war, Britain (though still immensely rich, her land never plundered by invading armies) led the way, with almost indecent eagerness, in forgetting all about 'Boney', and returning to her more traditional and agreeable preoccupations with scandal and baiting the Prince of Wales and his tiresome Princess. Her military, and naval, thoughts were more concerned with the threat to Canada from those upstart ex-colonials of America. Just as they had during that brief Peace of Amiens a dozen years previously, British tourists swarmed across the Channel, curious to see the continent, from which they had been shut out for so many years. In France, Lady Burghersh was shocked by the terrible poverty she found. Metternich told his wife that packs of wolves had been seen prowling round Langres, no more than 150 miles to the south-east of Paris.

In Vienna, where Metternich's Congress danced interminably over a period of nine months, the shape of Europe for the next hundred years was being hammered out – for better or for worse. Between waltzes, dalliances and intrigues,[6] bitter disagreements among the powers almost brought Europe once more to the threshold of general war. Uninvited, and now aged sixty-one, Talleyrand, Prince of Benevento, the veteran diplomat once more in favour and in a position of power, had arrived in Vienna to find himself allocated humiliating quarters, with curtains in tatters and mattresses full of moths. But, not unlike Charles de Gaulle 130 years later, he spared no expense to establish in his person *la grandeur de la France*. Deliberate in his elegance, he was described thus at a *levée* on his sixty-first birthday: 'Wrapped in a plaited and goffered muslin *peignoir*, the Prince proceeded to attend to his luxuriant hair which he surrendered to two hairdressers. . . .'[7]

Out of all this disarray among the victorious powers, Talley-rand – again like de Gaulle – somehow managed to bring a ruined and defeated France not only to the negotiating table, but miraculously to a new position of international eminence. As in 1945, there were those who wanted France reduced to a secondary power; Talleyrand saw to it that she was not. It was surely remarkable that the Foreign Minister of a recently defeated, and occupied, country, who had been responsible for at least some of Napoleon's earlier conquests, should be there to frame the agenda of a peace conference to which he had not been invited – but he was. He was able to maintain France's position on each of four main points of national interest. Unable to save Poland's independence, he managed to prevent all of that country falling into Russian hands – which meant that, though partitioned again, at least she would not be destroyed for ever.*

When Alexander, referring to the King of Saxony, spoke bitterly of 'those who have betrayed the cause of Europe', Talleyrand came out with his most famous *bon mot*: 'That, Sire, is a question of dates.' It could also perhaps be taken as an apologia for his own life. He warned, fatefully, as of October 1814 that if Prussia got her way she would very shortly form a militarist state that would be very dangerous for her neighbours. At the New Year, 1815, a triumphant Talleyrand was able to report unctuously to his new master:

> The coalition is dissolved. . . . France is no longer isolated in
> Europe. . . . Your Majesty possesses a federal system which fifty

---

* Apart from the brief interval of 1919–39, two further world wars, and a cold war, would have to be fought before the Polish independence, which Napoleon had promised Marie Walewska, became a fact.

years of negotiations might not have constructed. You are acting in concert with two of the greatest Powers and three states of the second rank, and will soon be joined by all the states whose principles and politics are not revolutionary. So great and so fortunate a change can only be attributed to that protection of Providence which has been so plainly visible in the restoration of Your Majesty.

France was pushed back to her frontiers of pre-1792, of the *ancien régime*; Bernadotte was tossed Norway for his adopted Sweden; Castlereagh (who had truly earned his keep) reported back to London, confidently, 'The alarm of war is over.' Napoleon, however, was developing other plans.

Meanwhile, during the Congress, Talleyrand also succeeded in cementing the love affair that would continue for the remainder of his life, with his own nephew's wife, Comtesse Edmond de Périgord (later Duchess of Dino), whose marriage he had himself arranged in 1808. In the words of Duff Cooper:

A woman of great beauty, distinction, and charm, highly educated and of semi-royal birth, she devoted the twenty-four most important years of her life to the man who was her husband's uncle and had been her mother's lover.

And who had once been a bishop too – a prodigious man indeed!

One day early in March 1815, all Talleyrand's (diplomatic) achievements suddenly looked like a house of cards. Amid yet another great ball, a courier arrived with the terrible news: Napoleon had escaped from Elba and landed in France. There was a panicky cry round Vienna, 'Has anyone seen Napoleon?' Talleyrand, with the coolness of a Drake at Plymouth, told his new love, the Comtesse, that she should nevertheless continue with her theatrical rehearsals for the next entertainment.

*

WHEN CAMPBELL, THE British Commissioner and Napoleon's guardian, had last seen his charge, he had noted that he seemed 'unusually dull and reserved'.[8] Then, while the unfortunate Campbell had been away in Florence visiting his mistress, Napoleon had slipped out of Elba on a French brig, *L'Inconstant*, which was disguised as a British man-of-war. On 1 March, accompanied by about a thousand men in seven small boats, he landed in the Golfe Juan near Cannes in the South of France. With the Hundred Days, there now began what the critical Correlli Barnett rightly describes as 'The episode in his adventurer's life which came nearest to pure adventure story',[9] almost a fantasy tale out of the young Napoleon's own romantic novel of 1795, *Clisson et Eugénie*. At Gap, above Grasse in the Alpes Maritimes, the former Emperor proclaimed that 'The eagle will fly from steeple to steeple until it reaches the towers of Notre Dame.'

On 7 March, Napoleon, heading swiftly northwards, was confronted at Laffrey just short of Grenoble with the first opposition from royal troops, giving rise to one of the most famous Napoleonic legends. Stepping forward to the levelled muskets, he opened his grey *redingote* and declared, 'Soldiers, if there is one among you who wishes to kill his Emperor he can do so. Here I am!' He was acclaimed in reply with a shout of 'Vive l'Empereur!' Grenoble opened its gates to give him a rapturous welcome, as dignitaries hastened to hide their Bourbon insignia. 'Before Grenoble I was an adventurer,' he recorded on St Helena; 'at Grenoble I was a ruling prince.' Word spread across Europe: 'The devil is unchained.' From Paris, the fat old King and his Court swiftly decamped to Ghent. Continuing his way northwards, Napoleon encountered snowballing support; even Marshal Ney, who had found favour with Louis XVIII, declaring that he would bring his former master to Paris 'in an iron cage', then went over to him at Auxerre. In the Place Vendôme, a wit posted a large notice addressed to the King: 'My good brother – there is no need to send any more troops – I have enough.'[10] There also appeared more menacing, Jacobin graffiti threatening 'Bourbons to the scaffold'.

On 20 March, borne on the shoulders of his Old Guard, Napoleon returned to the Tuileries, which he had left in January 1814, now hastily abandoned by King and Court. There he found the Bourbon fleur-de-lys had simply been glued over the Napoleonic bees on the carpet.

Though he explained that he was returning because, in breach of the Treaty of Fontainebleau of April 1814, his pension had not been paid and he was running out of funds, it was most unlikely that Napoleon would have undertaken his comeback had he not been encouraged by the Allies' dismal showing during the campaign of 1814 and their equally dismal dissensions at Vienna. Hoping to cash in on their disarray, his first act was to put out peace feelers; but he was immediately rebuffed when the powers at Vienna broke off all relations, pledging half a million men to the downfall, once and for all, of the 'Ogre'. England pledged her usual £5 million, and set to fielding a joint force with Prussia of 150,000 men. As a second disappointment, Napoleon learnt that his brother-in-law, Murat, with typical rashness, had sought to regain favour by launching a precipitate uprising in northern Italy. It was swiftly crushed, and Napoleon, infuriated, refused to employ his services in the forthcoming campaign. Murat would be sorely missed at Waterloo.

For all the portliness of middle age, Napoleon had lost little of his phenomenal energy. All the arsenals of France were ransacked for arms. He inherited the Restoration army of 200,000, of which probably only a quarter were battle-worthy. From this he had to fashion – at frantic speed – a new fighting force. It was substantially stronger than the 90,000 with which he had performed so miraculously well in the 1814 Campaign; nevertheless, by the end of the year enemies would be able to mount against him a staggering total of one million men. He would have to strike a devastating pre-emptive blow, before the Allies could mobilize. Once again, it was the story of his entire military career. Once again, the Allies would tempt disaster through their slowness to coalesce; by late May, the only forces they had in the field would be those of Wellington and of Blücher; the Austrians would not reach the Rhine before July, while the Russians would be later still.

The Waterloo Campaign remains one of the best-known, the most thoroughly explored and re-explored, of the whole Napoleonic Wars. Acting in utmost secrecy, Napoleon headed towards Brussels with his Army of the North of 128,000 men. His aim was to strike for Charleroi on the hinge between Wellington to the west (107,000 men) and Blücher (123,000) to the east, moving up from Liège, before the two could link up. He was forty-five, four months younger than Wellington, now elevated to a dukedom, and twenty-six years younger than Blücher, who, in ill-health again after the 1814 Campaign, had been preparing to retire. In all the long years of struggle against England it was the first (and last) time that he would personally face Wellington and the British Army. It was also to be the last battle either would fight. Described by American military historians as 'a slow-moving, clumsy, odd-lot collection',[11] most of Wellington's force was in fact formed of German, Dutch and Belgian units, some markedly raw and unsteady, and was certainly far less formidable overall than the British army which had fought under him in Spain. Indeed, some of the crack British units from the Peninsula were only just reaching Belgium from North America on the very eve of the battle – baneful sequence to the war of 1812.

In contrast, Napoleon's Army of the North was composed of hardened veterans, now homogeneously French. Though outnumbered by the combined British and Prussian armies, it was probably one of the most impressive he had ever led. Its decisive weakness lay in command. More than half the surviving marshalcy had either defected, like Marmont, Oudinot and Victor, were sick, or, like Murat, were considered unsuitable for one reason or another. Mortier was to be crippled with sciatica when battle was joined. The remaining commanders looked at each other with suspicion; since the Restoration, treason now lurked everywhere. Davout, always Napoleon's most reliable battle commander, was left behind in Paris as Minister of War — probably because his unquestioning loyalty was essential to keeping a firm grip on the neurotic and untrustworthy capital. Perhaps even more critical was the loss of the indispensable Berthier. Refusing to rejoin Napoleon in 1815, he was struck off the register of the marshalate, then fell to his death, in mysterious circumstances, from a window in Bamberg on 1 June.

Berthier was replaced as *Major-Général*, or Chief-of-Staff, by Soult, who was, whatever his qualities as a front-line soldier (which had won him the laurels on the Pratzen Heights) a poor substitute. Indolent and unpopular, Soult's orders at Waterloo arrived confused or not at all. Equally disastrous was Napoleon's choice of Ney as his battle-commander. 'The bravest of the brave' in the Moscow Campaign, the red-haired and hot-tempered Ney seems by now to have been suffering from what in a later age would have been described as battle-fatigue, if not shell-shock. At times in the coming battle he seemed almost de-mented. To command his right wing, Napoleon chose Grouchy, promoted marshal (Napoleon's last such appointment) only on 15 April; in St Helena, he would blame Grouchy in particular for losing the battle. And what of the Emperor himself, whose state of health and mind at Waterloo has oft been questioned? To Baron Ménéval, his talk was now 'stamped with a calm sadness and resignation', and he did not find in him:

> that certainty of success which had made him so confident in the past; it seems as if that faith in his star which had inspired him to venture on the hazardous enterprise of returning from Elba . . . deserted him from the moment he reached Paris. . . .[12]

Moving with utmost speed, Napoleon reached Beaumont on the Belgian frontier with five corps, his approach march concealed by wooded country. It was one of the great feats of military history — perhaps on a par with Hitler's sudden arrival at Sedan, only a few miles away, with the devastating *Sichelschnitt* blueprint of 1940, which after a week's fighting was to encompass the ruin of France.[13] Wellington, watching a cricket match with a lady-friend on the 12 June, was taken by surprise. His immediate appreciation, the instinctive reaction of British commanders down to Gort in 1940, was that Napoleon was aiming to cut him off from the Channel ports, when in fact the objective – predictably typical of Napoleon – was to drive a wedge between him and Blücher. Accordingly, Wellington had made the serious mistake of disposing his forces spread out west of Brussels. 'If ever victory was in the grasp of a commander,' Montgomery (who is generally considered to have been Britain's greatest commander since Wellington) comments rigorously in *A History of Warfare*, 'it lay on a plate to be taken by Napoleon. Wellington had only himself to blame for allowing this situation to develop. To me, such neglect is almost unbelievable in a very great soldier. . . .'[14] Clearly, in the view of this austere general, the British Commander-in-Chief had no business to be out dancing on the night before battle.

That day Napoleon issued a stirring order of the day, reminiscent of Austerlitz and the other great moments of the Empire:

> Soldiers, today is the anniversary of Marengo and Friedland, which twice decided the destinies of Europe. Then, just as after Austerlitz and Wagram, we were too generous, we believed in the oaths and protestations of the princes we left on their thrones! . . . Let us then march to meet them. . . .
>
> For every Frenchman with a heart, the moment has come to conquer or perish!

But French morale was not encouraged by the news that day that General Bourmont, commanding one of the spearhead divisions, had galloped over to the Prussians together with all his staff.

On the 16th, Napoleon struck a devastating blow at the main body of Blücher's army at Ligny, less than twenty-five miles

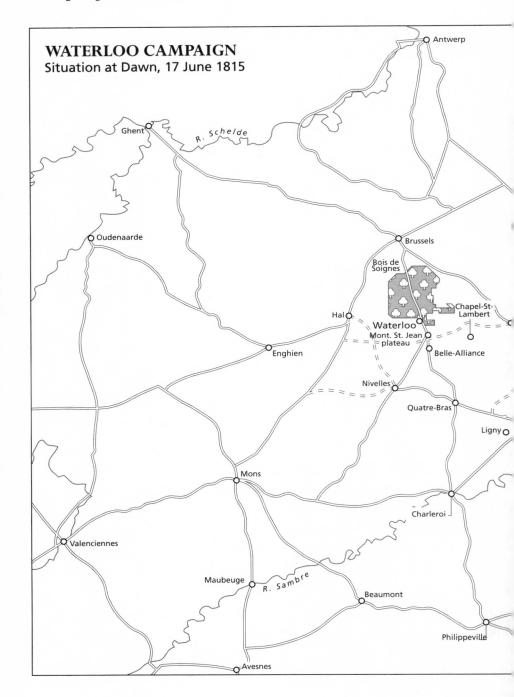

WATERLOO CAMPAIGN
Situation at Dawn, 17 June 1815

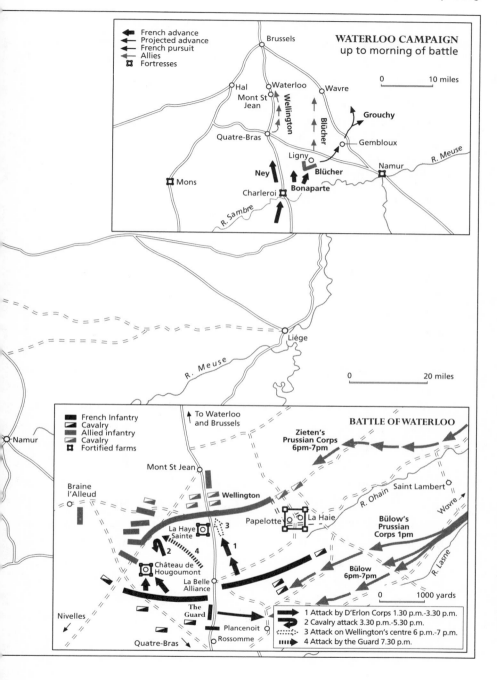

WATERLOO CAMPAIGN
up to morning of battle

French advance
Projected advance
French pursuit
Allies
Fortresses

0   10 miles

Brussels

Hal
Waterloo   Wavre
Mont St
Jean

Wellington   Blücher

Grouchy

Quatre-Bras

Ligny

Ney   **Blücher**

Mons   **Bonaparte**

Charleroi

R. Sambre   Namur

R. Meuse

Liége

R. Meuse   0   20 miles

BATTLE OF WATERLOO

French Infantry
Cavalry
Allied infantry
Cavalry
Fortified farms

To Waterloo
and Brussels

**Zieten's
Prussian Corps
6pm-7pm**

Mont St Jean

Braine
l'Alleud

Wellington

R. Ohain   Saint Lambert

La Haye
Sainte   3   Papelotte   La Haie

2   4   1   **Bülow's
Prussian
Corps 1pm**

Château de
Hougoumont   **Bülow
6pm-7pm**

La Belle
Alliance

Wavre

R. Lasne

Nivelles   0   1000 yards

**The
Guard**   1 Attack by D'Erlon Corps 1.30 p.m.-3.30 p.m.
Plancenoit   2 Cavalry attack 3.30 p.m.-5.30 p.m.
Rossomme   3 Attack on Wellington's centre 6 p.m.-7 p.m.
Quatre-Bras   4 Attack by the Guard 7.30 p.m.

Namur

south of Brussels, outnumbering him with a local superiority of 7 to 5. Wellington had advised Blücher not to stand at Ligny, where he was in an exposed position; but *Alte Vorwärts* ('Old Forward'), as his men affectionately nicknamed him, had had a bellyful of retreating before Napoleon the previous year. Courageously leading a charge against the Imperial Guard, the seventy-two-year-old had his horse shot from under him, was knocked unconscious and narrowly escaped capture. By the end of the day, the Prussians had been badly defeated, losing 34,000 men (including 12,000 who deserted subsequently) to Napoleon's 11,500. A lesser commander than *Alte Vorwärts*, a Schwarzenberg for instance, would have been tempted to fall back eastwards on his lines of communication; but Blücher, unfortunately for Napoleon, in retreating in fact only moved closer to Wellington and Brussels.

Wellington at once comprehended Napoleon's strategy when the messenger came to him in the middle of the famous ball in Brussels on the 15th. To the Duke of Richmond he exclaimed, 'Napoleon has humbugged me, by God! He has gained twenty-four hours' march on me. . . .' He went on to explain: 'I have ordered the army to concentrate at Quatre Bras, but we shall not stop him there and, if so, I must fight him here'[15] – pointing with his thumbnail to Waterloo. Quatre Bras, seven miles as the crow flies to the west of Ligny, lies just over twenty miles down the Charleroi road from Brussels. There Wellington's men in his first ever encounter with Napoleon in fact dealt him a bloody nose. Ney, who lost 4,300 men to Wellington's 4,700, was pushed back almost to his line of departure. Quatre Bras was a minor action, against Wellington's rearguard, compared to the battering the Prussians had received at Ligny, but it kept Ney's detachments from joining the main fight against Blücher and was to have a vital bearing on the great battle two days later. As he had forecast to the Duke of Richmond, Wellington (*Villainton*, as the French called him), now fell back in perfect order to Mont St Jean, a position he had reconnoitred only the previous year and one ideally suited to the kind of 'hard-slogging' defensive battle at which he had proved so adept in the Peninsula. It lay two miles south of the village of Waterloo, and only a short march from Brussels.

A tremendous thunderstorm turned the clay soil into a quagmire, impeding Napoleon's pursuit of Blücher. So on the evening of 17 June the Emperor halted before Wellington's position, on the Mont St Jean plateau. But his own lack of energy in driving after the Prussians, combined with Ney's incompetence, was what really cost him total success at Ligny and Quatre Bras. One whole corps under Ney's command, Comte d'Erlon's with 14,500 men, had been left zigzagging uncontrolled behind the battle-front, without firing a shot. Angrily Napoleon had berated d'Erlon on the afternoon of the 16th, 'France has been ruined. Go, *mon cher général*, and place yourself at the head of the cavalry and pursue the rearguard vigorously.'[16]

Complete victory at Ligny over Blücher could well have ended the campaign there and then. Nevertheless, after the successes of the 16th, French morale was at a high by the morning of the historically decisive 18th. At 1 a.m. on the night of the 17th/18th, just as on the eve of Austerlitz, Napoleon roamed his lines, exhorting his sodden troops. To his commanders, he boasted, 'We shall sleep in Brussels tonight.' Yet it was as if his star, in the shape of the weather, had at last truly deserted him. 'What would I not have given to have had Joshua's power to slow down the sun's movement by two hours!' he remarked in his memoirs, his thoughts as so often harking back unconsciously to the miracle of Austerlitz.[17] The waterlogged ground, however, made it almost impossible for him to manoeuvre his superior artillery; worse still, round shot would not ricochet effectively, thus greatly reducing the deadliness of the cannon-balls, which would bury themselves instead of tearing great holes in the dense British squares.

Napoleon's delays between the 16th and 17th afforded Wellington an invaluable respite in which to dig in on the Mont St

Jean ridge. With his position anchored on the left at the Château de Hougoumont, its six-foot-thick stone walls converted into a bastion of immense strength, and the equally fortified La Haye on the right – a front less than three miles wide – Wellington had chosen his ground well. Old Blücher, too, aided by liberal doses of his favourite medicine, garlic and gin, had recovered and was under way. After meeting Wellington at the farm of the well-named Belle Alliance, on the morning of the historic 18th – dangerously late in the day – he dictated a letter to the British Field-Marshal assuring him that, 'ill as I am, [I will] put myself at the head of my troops and attack the right flank of the enemy immediately Napoleon makes any move against the Duke'. The Prussian decision came dangerously late in the day for Wellington; but Napoleon also committed a delay fatal to his cause by not launching his main attack till 1300 hours, thereby offending against his old maxim, 'space we can recover, time never. . . . I may lose a battle, but I shall never lose a minute.'

SO BEGAN THE DAY, claimed by both sides as a noble triumph.* Most of the 140,000 men about to take part in it were drenched, and exhausted from marching and digging, or from the battles of the previous days. They had passed a miserable night, full of fearsome anticipation. Now, with the sinister whirring of cannon-balls overhead, so well described by Stendhal in *The Charterhouse of Parma*, and beneath the dense fog of smoke that covered the tightly compressed arena of barely three square miles, few can have been aware of the actions that seem so clearly defined in the paintings which adorn the walls of British officers' messes. Like Stendhal's Fabrizio, most would have known little of what was going on. Again and again, Napoleon's attack hung upon the staunch defence, without quarter, of

---

* Certainly the modern diorama at Waterloo gives little enough impression of a British victory.

Hougoumont. There Wellington's Coldstream Guards earned immortal honours. Under Ney's command, the French divisions attacked in clumsy, dense rectangular masses. As Wellington remarked coolly afterwards, Napoleon 'just moved forward in the old style, in columns, and was driven off in the old style' – certainly not in the style of Austerlitz. It was the unfortunate d'Erlon who bore the brunt; on his columns Wellington's deadly musket fire and canister shot exacted a terrible toll.

Early in the afternoon, Napoleon's attention was called to a curious change in appearance of a ridge around St Lambert, beyond his right flank. In the poor visibility, it seemed that the whole area had darkened, as if a large body of troops were massing there. Some of his staff dismissed it as merely the shadow of a passing cloud – but it was the cloud that was to spell final doom for Napoleon. It was the black-clad infantry from Prussia. Blücher was fulfilling his promise. Napoleon refused to contemplate a withdrawal, and with his usual sang-froid he remarked to Soult, 'This morning we had ninety chances in our favour. Even now we have sixty chances, and only forty against us.'

When the concentrated barrage of Napoleon's heavy 12-pounders opened up, with a greater intensity even than that seen at Wagram, Wellington, like a sensible Second World War commander, made his men lie down on the reverse slope of Mont St Jean. His reconnaissance there the previous year was to pay enormous dividends; many valuable lives were saved thereby. In mid-afternoon, Ney, his ginger hair matching his temperament, acted prematurely in the belief that the British were breaking, 'carried away by an excess of ardour', as one French historian put it,[18] and now threw in his main attack on Wellington's centre. 'The French cavalry made some of the boldest charges I ever saw,' recorded Colonel Frazer. 'Never did cavalry behave so nobly, or was received so firmly.'[19] But the impetuous Ney had allowed the cavalry to go in unsupported by infantry. Napoleon was furious: 'He [Ney] is compromising us as he did at Jena.'[20] The British line sagged. Had reserves been available to follow up, it would almost certainly have broken. Through what looked like gathering disaster, Wellington rode with icy nonchalance through the debris of his forward lines, rallying the crumbling defence and showing something of Napoleon's legendary immortality as two aides were killed at his side.

Blücher's Prussians had been slow to move forward, but they were just in time – denying Ney those vital reinforcements. Grouchy, clearly promoted above his level, tarried indecisively, not grasping the initiative to march towards the cannon, as a Murat or a Davout would have done, thus playing no part in the decisive battle against the new menace of Blücher. With its right flank bending inwards at 90 degrees, the French line began to look like the letter S. At 1900 hours, the Guard, led by General Friant of Austerlitz fame, was committed in its famous last attack against Wellington's badly battered but reconstituted centre, which comprised the British Brigade of Guards under General Maitland. Through the smoky haze, to the Grenadiers the advancing *grognards* of the Imperial Guard 'with their high bonnets' looked like 'a corps of giants'. But the British Guards stood firm, and suddenly the French Guard was seen 'to turn and disappear into the smoke from which it had emerged'.[21] The cry, never heard before, and devastating to French ears – 'La Garde recule!' – echoed across the battlefield. The most dreaded formation in the world, perhaps even more redoubtable than Hitler's ss Panzer divisions, was breaking. Once again, as in almost every military disaster from Agincourt onwards, the collapse began – not at the front – but at the rear.

As Thackeray saw the Imperial Guard's advance in *Vanity Fair*,

unscarred by the thunder of the artillery which hurled death from the English line – the dark rolling column pressed on and up the hill. It seemed almost to crest the eminence, when it began to waver and falter. . . .

No more firing was heard at Brussels – the pursuit rolled miles away. Darkness came down on the field and city; and Amelia was praying for George, who was lying on his face, dead, with a bullet through his heart.

It was just after 2000 hours as Waterloo was won for the Allies. Napoleon had fought his last battle. In the grisly epilogue to the ended Napoleonic Wars, the bodies of some 40,000 soldiers, and 10,000 horses, many alive and suffering horribly, were left on the field; among them were 26,000 French. It had been, in the time-honoured words of the 'Iron Duke', 'A damned nice thing – the nearest-run thing you ever saw in your life. . . .' And he had added, 'By God, I don't believe it would have been done if I had not been there. . . .' Nor, indeed, if old Blücher, *Alte Vorwärts*, had not been there. And what if Wellington, as well as an important element of his army, had been in Canada, facing the United States? Yet even if Waterloo had been won by Napoleon, it would almost certainly, in view of the overwhelming forces closing in on him, have been followed sooner or later by the ultimate defeat. The odds were now too great; there was no longer support for him in France.

Abandoning his army in the field a third and last time, Napoleon hurried back to Paris. On 21 June, he summoned Marie Walewska and their son, Alexandre, and said his final farewell. 'The mood was lugubrious,' recorded one of his entourage. 'It was raining, the Emperor was burning state papers, and I was packing his personal effects.'[22] Young Alexandre recalled being taken in the Emperor's arms, and 'a tear ran down his face'. The following day, the third anniversary of the beginning of the march on Moscow, Napoleon abdicated a second time.

Davout, loyal to the last, but disgusted with all the intrigue surrounding him, took the decision to call back Louis XVIII once more – much as he despised him. Just before throwing himself on British mercy, and after riding through his still unfinished Arc de Triomphe, which he had begun after Austerlitz, Napoleon made a final visit to Malmaison, declaring mournfully to his stepdaughter Hortense: 'My poor Josephine! I can see her now, walking along one of the paths and picking the roses she loved so well. . . . We never really had any quarrels except about her debts.'[23] He was now bound for St Helena.

'How far is St Helena from the field of Waterloo?'
A near way – a clear way – the ship will take you soon.
A pleasant place for gentlemen with little left to do. . . .'[24]

Epilogue

One must not be at war with everyone.

Madame de Staël

ON 15 JULY 1815, Napoleon boarded HMS *Bellerophon* at Rochefort. In one of his last delusions, he appealed to the Prince Regent, hoping to be granted asylum in the country of his arch-enemy – from where that restless mind would doubtless contemplate yet another comeback, a new campaign. But the Allies had other, more realistic plans for the 'Ogre'. He would be removed far away from Europe. The choice was an island ('the ugliest and most dismal rock conceivable', in the opinion of the British Army surgeon, 'rising like an enormous black wart from the face of the deep'),[1] whence there could be no return – St Helena, so remote that even now nearly two centuries later no airline lands there, and it can be reached only by the occasional boat service. Guarded by the ubiquitous Royal Navy, not even the loyal and faithful Marie Walewska could possibly join him.

The rest is familiar. The next six years he spent in restless captivity and bucolic boredom at Longwood, an attractive, low-built colonial villa in the middle of the island.* There he lived,

---

* Today, so a recent visitor – judge Sir Stephen Tumim, formerly Britain's Chief Inspector of Prisons – reports, it now contains a portrait of Napoleon with a halo, modelled on Piero della Francesca's *Resurrection*: 'Only the French could have thought of that . . .'

gazing out to sea, writing his memoirs and rewriting history, placing on his colleagues and subordinates the full burden of the blame for his failures. It was there, on 5 May 1821, that he died. When Talleyrand heard the news, at a Parisian salon in the company of the Duke of Wellington, amid the sudden hush somebody remarked, inadequately, 'What an event!' The old diplomatist's riposte was immediate: 'It is no longer an event, it is only a piece of news.'

Cancer of the stomach, which had caused the death of his father as well as of two of his sisters, was diagnosed. But could it possibly have been poison? Some authorities and many Frenchmen still think so. Yet it seems improbable. What motive could there have been? He was safe where he was. There was no prospect of any second Hundred Days. Anyway the French had had enough of war, turmoil, privation – and of Napoleon. And Britain, secure now as the world's only superpower, had no cause to feel menaced. Besides, just as each nation has its Way of Life, so it may be construed to have its own peculiar Way of Death. Poison is distinctly *not* Anglo-Saxon, but it does lie deeply entrenched in the Gallic imagination. The British smother princes, strangle kings and murder them atrociously with red-hot pokers, but they do not poison. In France, on the other hand, by fact or rumour the idea of the poisoning of inconvenient public persons goes back to the Capetian kings in the early fourteenth century, was reintroduced by the Italian Medicis in the sixteenth, and was not unheard of at the Court of Louis XIV.

The Emperor's body was brought back to France in 1840, to lie in perpetual honour in the Invalides – France's greatest son, though not a Frenchman. From then dated the imperishable Napoleonic legend, to be given a new spin (costly to France) by his nephew a few years later.

The death of Marie Walewska four years before Napoleon's own had evidently been kept from him. In 1816 the tragic Pole had married a long-time admirer, General Ornano. The following year, she gave birth to his child but never regained her strength and died, aged only twenty-eight. Very likely she had never recovered from her storm-bound love affair with Napoleon. According to her wishes, her body was returned to Poland but her heart remains interred in the Père Lachaise cemetery in Paris. Their natural son, Alexandre, lived to become ambassador to London under Louis Napoleon, and a distinguished Foreign Minister who did much to improve Anglo-French relations.

Infinitely sadder was the fate of Napoleon's one and only legitimate son, the heir he had sought so ruthlessly, King of Rome, later Duke of Reichstadt, or *l'Aiglon*. A delicate-looking young man, he was kept a virtual prisoner by his Habsburg grandfather, the Emperor Francis, at Schönbrunn, the palace that had witnessed Napoleon's last great triumph against Austria. (He is said to have declared, wistfully, 'Had Josephine been my mother, my father would not be buried at St Helena, and I would not be languishing in Vienna.') Never permitted to communicate with his exiled father, he died at Schönbrunn of tuberculosis in July 1832, aged only twenty-one. Nor did his mother, ex-Empress Marie Louise, communicate with Napoleon – of her own volition. Returning to Vienna shortly after her husband's death, she secretly married her lover, Count Neipperg. She then became progressively swallowed up once more by the Austrian Court, marrying its Master of Ceremonies after Neipperg's death. Much criticized by her contemporaries for her neglect of *l'Aiglon*, she died young in 1846.

With *l'Aiglon*'s death ended the dynastic hopes of Napoleon, only to be resurrected briefly – and disastrously – by his nephew, Louis Napoleon, son of the Emperor's third brother Louis, formerly King of Holland. Louis Napoleon was to take upon himself the title of Napoleon III (*l'Aiglon* had briefly been Napoleon II after his father's first abdication), and was to capitulate at Sedan in 1870 – to those same Prussians who had settled the fate of his uncle at Waterloo.

Of the Bonaparte family, Letizia, *Madame Mère*, lived until 1836, dying comfortably off at the age of eighty-six in Rome, and respected by all who knew her. She had lived up to her favourite saying, 'Just so long as it lasts', having always prudently put away some money in case of a change in fortune. Her daughter Caroline survived Murat until 1839, dying in Florence. Napoleon's elder brother Joseph, the unhappy King of Spain, settled in America (where Lucien had also tried unsuccessfully to immigrate), but, like Lucien, Louis and other members of the family, ended his life in Italy, aged seventy-six. Jérome, King of Westphalia, and the youngest brother (as well as possibly the most talented), became Governor of Les Invalides, Marshal of France (1850) and President of the Senate. He lived until 1860, well into the Second Empire, dying also aged seventy-six. Napoleon's favourite sister, Pauline Borghese, in 1814 sold her sumptuous palace on the Faubourg St Honoré to a victorious Wellington. She received 500,000 francs (plus 300,000 for the furniture), which seemed a remarkably fair deal – given that France was then an occupied and defeated nation, and that she had paid only 300,000 for the property in 1803. In 1824 the building became, and has remained ever since, the British Embassy – the envy of all others in Paris. Pauline moved to Italy, and died there in 1825.

Like the Bonapartes, several of Napoleon's marshals and top generals who survived his war lived to ages remarkable for an age of medicine primitive by our standards – remarkable, that is, if one accepts the notion that stress, not to mention repeated wounds in battle, is the enemy of longevity. Soult, the hero of the Pratzen Heights, lived to eighty-seven; Bernadotte to eighty-one, Grouchy to eighty-one also; Marmont to seventy-eight and Surgeon-General Larrey to seventy-six. At the other extreme, two of the most courageous and flamboyant, Murat and Ney, had their lives cut short by the firing squad. Murat, on receiving the news of Waterloo, had returned by sea to Italy, but was arrested in Calabria. Tried, condemned and shot half an hour after delivery of the sentence, he met his fate with his customary panache. One of the most colourful figures of the Napoleonic era, not always reliable as a commander, but to the end courageous to a fault, Murat in death became a kind of model for many subsequent *beaux sabreurs* of the nineteenth century. Ney, mistakenly chosen to be Napoleon's right hand at Waterloo – and the man who possibly cost him the battle – had hoped to be allowed to retire quietly to Paris. But, traduced by General Bourmont (who had defected to the Allies on the eve of Waterloo), he was arrested in August, tried before a court of peers and condemned to death. It was his seduction by Napoleon at Auxerre during the Hundred Days that ultimately dished him. He was shot on 7 December 1815, but – 'the bravest of the brave' to the end – he was permitted to give the signal for the firing squad to shoot. Aged forty-six, the same as Napoleon, he had fought at almost every battle of his. Made Prince of Moscow and Duke of Elchingen, he was a brilliant front-line commander, but – as Waterloo had so fatefully proved – no strategist.

Grouchy, Napoleon's other disastrous appointment in June 1815, and the last of the marshals, proscribed but not executed by the Second Restoration, took off to Philadelphia – like Talleyrand before him, and other eminent exiles – where he found others of the entourage ensconced. Permitted to return to France in 1820, he had his baton (and his pre-Revolutionary marquisate) restored by Louis-Philippe in 1831. Dying in 1847, he all but lived to see France ruled by his old master's nephew, Louis Napoleon. Marmont, Duke of Ragusa, who had blotted his reputation permanently by deserting Napoleon in 1814 and then voting for the execution of Ney, did live to see the Second Empire (though only from exile, as a result of the equivocal role he had played in the revolution of 1830). Soult, Duke of Dalmatia, retired to Düsseldorf until 1819, when he returned, forgiven and restored in rank. He became Minister of War from 1830 to 1834, and represented France at Queen Victoria's coronation – where for the first time he met his old adversary, Wellington. Minister of Foreign Affairs in 1839, he died in 1851 covered in honours and a marshal-general of France – a distinction hitherto accorded only to Turenne, Villars and Saxe, and to no other Napoleonic general.

Davout, Duke of Auerstädt and Prince of Eckmühl, possibly the most dependable and among the most talented of Napoleon's marshals, died early, of consumption, in 1823. He was only fifty-three. After Waterloo he had been dismissed from all his posts and exiled briefly to Louviers, but was reinstated two years later. Masséna, Prince of Essling and Duke of Rivoli, along with Davout one of the ablest, the foe who had most disturbed Wellington's slumbers in Spain, died quietly in Paris in 1817, aged fifty-nine. The only slur on the reputation of this man of the *midi* was his legendary rapacity for women, his tardy arrival on the battlefield of the Peninsula being blamed on his excessive dalliance with the mistress disguised as a Dragoon, Madame Leberton. Mortier, long-time commander of the Guard who had saved the day at Dürrenstein in 1805 and fought with distinction at Austerlitz, rallied to Napoleon in 1815, but missed Waterloo after being stricken with acute sciatica at Beaumont. He too was pardoned by Louis XVIII after a brief period of disgrace, was sent to St Petersburg as ambassador in 1830, but was killed by a bomb when inspecting the National Guard five years later.

Larrey, the Surgeon-General, who invented the first custom-built field ambulance for evacuation of the wounded, amply deserved a baton for his services to the wounded and sick, but did not receive one, though he served Napoleon steadfastly to the end. Himself wounded at Waterloo, he lived until 1842, having held many distinguished medical posts.

Finally, among the marshals, there is Bernadotte. It was he, perhaps the least deserving of them all, who ended with the greatest spoils, a kingdom that would survive any of those created by his master. Having earned Napoleon's extreme displeasure at Jena, and having been sent off the battlefield at Wagram, he had requited this humiliation by abandoning him to become Crown Prince of Sweden in 1810. He dallied in his leadership of the Swedish forces fighting Napoleon at Leipzig, and never appeared in the Campaign of France of 1814 – evidently in the misguided hopes, as we have noted, that he might be invited to succeed Napoleon following the first abdication. Refusing to join the Seventh Coalition against Napoleon in 1815, he had instead grabbed Norway for his adopted country. In 1818 he succeeded Sweden's childless sovereign to become King Charles xiv, thereby ironically making Napoleon's early love, Désirée Clary, the only legitimate queen among all the ephemeral Napoleonic creations. Having proved himself to be a better monarch than a marshal, Bernadotte died of apoplexy in 1844, aged eighty-one, but his and Désirée's progeny were to become, after the House of Windsor, the only members of a European royal family still to grace thrones by the end of the next century.*

Of Napoleon's two sinister police chiefs, who served him so well, General Savary, made Duke of Rovigo, was sentenced to death under the Restoration, but was pardoned after a brief period in exile. In 1831, Louis-Philippe recalled him to service to command troops in France's newly acquired possession of Algeria. Two years later he died of a hideously disfiguring cancer of the mouth. Though it was probably caused by his incessant cigar smoking, the Arabs insisted that God had so afflicted him on account of his evil character. As for Fouché, Duke of Otranto, that remarkable survivor from the Terror who had voted for the execution of Louis xvi, the Hundred Days had seen him briefly reinstated as Napoleon's Chief of Police; much more surprisingly, he was then given the same post after Waterloo by Louis xviii. (Talleyrand commented, 'One must do him the justice to recognize that he has omitted none of his friends' from the list he drew up of those whose conduct during the Hundred Days

---

* They also bore the blood of Josephine, through the marriage of her granddaughter Josephine (via her son Eugène) to Oscar, Crown Prince of Sweden and son of Bernadotte and Désirée. That the despised *Belle Jambe*, once the dedicated Republican, and the Empress whom Napoleon had divorced, should succeed where Bonaparte failed and leave a dynasty provides, seemingly, a fitting footnote.

could not be forgiven.) The reaction against him from the 'Ultras' around the King became so great that his office was soon under threat. Talleyrand was in at the kill, proposing the dreaded sentence of exile to the United States, as Minister. 'America is such a beautiful country,' he explained with teasing malice:

> I know it, I have travelled through it and lived in it; it is a superb country. There are rivers there such as we have never seen. The Potomac, for instance, nothing more beautiful than the Potomac! And then those magnificent forests full . . . of daturas,

he added, with marvellous botanical inexactitude. But Fouché was instead despatched from Paris to head the French Legation in Dresden. A year later passage of a law against all regicides brought an end to his public career. He spent his last days in Trieste, in great comfort – thanks to the vast fortune he had amassed, one way or another. But, having served in turn the Revolution, the Directory, the Consulate, the Empire and, finally, the Bourbon Restoration, with good reason he remained untrusted by all to the end of his sixty-one years.

It was when Fouché, the regicide and ex-oratory headmaster who had led a vigorous campaign against Christianity under the Revolution, had come piously to kneel before Louis XVIII and kiss hands, with Talleyrand leaning on his arm, that Chateaubriand phrased his devastating remark about 'Vice supported by Crime'. Even more remarkable as a professional survivor, indeed one of the most remarkable men ever produced by France, Talleyrand, former Bishop of Autun, and made Prince of Benevento (as well as immeasurably rich) by Napoleon, was to make some of his most outstanding contributions to France during the Restoration. It was thanks to his skill at the Congress of Vienna, resumed after Waterloo, that a defeated France was able to achieve such favourable terms in the peace settlement. But, inevitably, his days in power as Louis XVIII's 'Minister-Plenipotentiary' were numbered, as were Fouché's. Along the years he had made too many enemies among members of the *ancien régime*. By the end of 1815, he was forced to resign, and was replaced as both Prime Minister and Foreign Minister by the Duke de Richelieu. For once even Talleyrand appears to have been taken by surprise.

Yet even now this did not mark *finis* to Talleyrand's career. For the next fourteen years, up to the age of seventy-six, he spent the winters agreeably in Paris, the summers at his Château of Valençay, writing his five volumes of memoirs and – allegedly – siring a child upon the wife of his nephew, the exquisite Duchess of Dino, who was now his constant companion; and playing whist. ('What a sad old age you are preparing for yourself,' he cautioned a young woman who could not play cards.) After Louis XVIII died in 1824 – the last king of France to die on the throne – Talleyrand, who had been present at the coronation of his brother, Louis XVI, now as Grand Chamberlain played an important role in the crowning of Charles X. Surrounded by the Ultras, and himself a conservative bigot, the new King – Louis XVIII's younger brother, and the former Comte d'Artois, had little use for the old diplomatist. Then, in July 1830, once more the dread tocsins were heard in Paris, and the *tricoleur* flew from Notre Dame. With haughty dignity, Charles X took the familiar path of exile to England, then to Prague, handing over to his grandson, Henri, Comte de Chambord, a king who would never reign, superseded by the liberal Louis-Philippe. 'It is not I who have abandoned the King,' was Talleyrand's comment; 'it is the King who has abandoned us.' Louis-Philippe soon had Talleyrand back in harness. Under his new King, he helped create modern Belgium, assure its independence from France and enthrone its first king, Leopold I. An octogenarian, he ended his career triumphantly as ambassador to London for four years, doing his best to cement a new era of good relations which his former chief had so thoroughly disjointed during two decades of war. Politically, he had even seemed to outlive France's conqueror, Wellington, forced to resign his premiership in 1830.

In May 1838, Talleyrand died, aged eighty-three, and having served no less than eight regimes. After Napoleon himself, he was undoubtedly the most influential Frenchman of that epoch. In a last testament of historic weight, he wrote:

> I therefore served Bonaparte when Emperor as I had served him when Consul: I served him with devotion so long as I could believe that he himself was completely devoted to France. But when I saw the beginning of those revolutionary enterprises which ruined him I left the ministry, for which he never forgave me. . . .

He had never put any interests above those of France — interests which were, he declared in a sentence that might have been written for a future President de Gaulle, 'not in my opinion ever in opposition to the true interests of Europe'.

Of Talleyrand's famous interlocutors with whom he had constructed the New Europe of post-1815, Castlereagh committed suicide in 1822, aged sixty-two, shortly after being made Marquis of Londonderry — there were rumours at the time that he was being blackmailed as a homosexual — his death commemorated by some of Byron's most brutal lines. Second only to Pitt in his opposition to Napoleon, he had masterminded two Coalitions, and had given powerful impetus to the Congress System as a means of reducing international tension. It was he who had selected St Helena as Napoleon's ultimate place of exile. His eminent colleague Metternich after Waterloo went on to become virtual master of Austria, for the next thirty-three years, reinforcing Habsburg absolutism and striving to crush the forces of revolutionary nationalism abroad. Miscalculating the year of revolution, 1848, he resigned, went into exile in Holland in 1851, then lived out the remainder of his life on his estates. He died, aged eighty-six, in 1859 — having seen with disquiet the re-establishment of the Empire in France under Louis Napoleon.

The oldest of all the Coalition commanders, Blücher, *Alte Vorwärts*, died in Silesia in 1819, aged seventy-three. Tsar

Alexander I died ten years after Waterloo, aged only forty-eight. After Waterloo, together with Wellington (who had posted British sentries around the Pont d'Iéna to prevent his Prussian allies from destroying it in revenge for 1806),* he had done much to protect France from the more vindictive actions of Blücher's soldiery. He had played a leading role at the Congress of Vienna, but, with Napoleon despatched, he had become something of a mystic, taking little direct part in the ruling of Russia.

In England, exhausted but triumphant, life returned to normal with notable speed. The unseemly behaviour in public of the Prince Regent and his vulgar, lubricious wife Caroline – worse than anything that even the British press of the end of the twentieth century could dredge up, continued to be a delight to the cartoonists like Rowlandson – and the despair of constitutional monarchists. Yet, despite the succession of yet another uninspiring sovereign, William IV, little more than two decades after Waterloo suddenly from the depths of unpopularity the British monarchy was to burst into its fullest blossom under Victoria, setting its seal on a hundred years of Pax Britannica.

Wellington – the artificer of it all – lived well into it, until 1852, when he died aged eighty-three, and all Britain mourned. Waterloo made him England's most honoured son, whom none could contravene except at their peril. Honours and diplomatic missions were heaped on him. In 1828 he reluctantly agreed to become Prime Minister, but resigned over the issue of constitutional reform in 1830. He returned in 1834, and became a staunch ally and counsellor of the young Queen Victoria. He remained Commander-in-Chief of the army until his death; but his deadening hand on army reform had its injurious impact on the Crimean War. His reputation, following Waterloo, as

---

* Urging him to 'have nothing to do with so foul a transaction', Wellington also had to dissuade Blücher from summarily executing Napoleon, were he to fall into Prussian hands.

Britain's greatest commander of all time eclipsed that of Nelson, dead those ten years. Yet — heresy as it may be to say it — Britain and her allies might ultimately have won without Wellington, but *never* without Nelson. As the commander who did ultimately defeat Napoleon, the culmination to all that hard slogging in the Peninsula, undoubtedly Wellington deserved every scrap of the fame and glory accorded him. Yet, in the longer perspective, Europe probably owed as much to him for his wisdom and moderation as a peace-maker. One could have wished that he, rather than the leaders of a vengeful France bled white by four years of carnage, had been present at Versailles a hundred years later. Just possibly a second terrible world war might then have been averted. Considering the appalling depredations that France under Napoleon had wreaked upon Europe, from Lisbon to Moscow, during the previous twenty years, the peace that followed was (at least by modern standards) an outstandingly generous one. From it a new, prosperous, unhumiliated and unvengeful France was allowed to arise, and for it the world owed a great debt to the men of 1815 — to Metternich, Castlereagh and Talleyrand; and to Wellington the man of peace as much as to Wellington the man of war.

FRANCE IN THE IMMEDIATE aftermath of Waterloo was a sad country indeed. There is no accurate compilation of the global casualties resulting from the Napoleonic wars, but even if they never ascended to the scale of a twentieth-century world war, in terms of those dead from starvation and typhus, as well as battlefield losses, they must have run into millions. Estimates of military dead in France alone range from 430,000 to 2,600,000; when one considers how many Borodino and Leipzig accounted for, it seems likely that a realistic overall figure would be somewhere over a million — out of a total population of approximately thirty-three million. There used to be a popular saying that, before Napoleon, the French were a race of tall men.

Certainly the twenty years of war had wiped out a whole élite of young men. Over the next century the population of France, once the biggest in Europe, became more or less static – and who can say that, in comparison with her new enemy, Germany, France had even recovered by the time of the hideous blood-letting of 1914–18? Clearly she had not by the date of the Franco-Prussian War half a century after Waterloo.

Eighteen-fifteen was a terrible year for France, and 1816 was not much better. Though mild enough by twentieth-century standards, the peace terms were harsh compared with those of 1814; there was an indemnity of £28 million to pay off, an occupation for five years by an Allied force of 150,000 troops; French Savoy was handed over to Sardinia, and the Saar to Prussia (which meant the end of the dream of a frontier on the Rhine, and the beginning of a German presence on its left bank). In Paris the victorious sovereigns held swaggering parades on the Champs de Mars. French pride was devastated. Over the rest of the country, a 'White Terror', comparable to the *épuration* which followed the Liberation of 1944, held sway. Royalist bands plundered and looted and settled old scores; in Nîmes Protestant women were beaten up because of their religion; Napoleonic generals were lynched, and several followed Ney before the firing squad. Louis XVIII seemed powerless, remarking that if the Ultra deputies had their way 'They would purge me too.'

Impotent, homosexual and chair-ridden, his court breech-clad and bewigged in a manner that reminded people disagreeably of his brother, the late Louis XVI, he was hardly an endearing figure. Cold and calculating, he led Chateaubriand to remark of him, 'Without being cruel, the King was hardly human, so insensitive was he to other people's misfortunes.'[2] Seeing the King at the Tuileries in 1821, Madame de Staël's daughter, the Duchess de Broglie, recorded 'a perpetual smile on his lips, but his eyes are hard and unsmiling'. Wits derided the fat old monarch as 'Louis deux fois neuf', referring to his two restorations. (Yet, years later, Léon Gambetta, who didn't always get things right, considered Louis to have been 'the greatest King of France after Henri v'.) Politically the country was bitterly divided between the bigoted Ultras, Liberals and supporters of Napoleon, to the extent that many Frenchmen must have wondered whether a new revolution might not be in the offing. It was commonly said, 'If you have not lived through 1815, you do not know what hatred is.' But France was just too exhausted for more bloodshed. Economically, she was weighed down by crippling taxation, her trade paralysed by the years of British blockade; and on top of this the indemnity to the Allies had to be discharged and the army of occupation paid for. Then, as if all that were not enough, 1816 brought a disastrous harvest coupled with widespread cattle disease. Famine was close at hand.

But France is renowned for her resilience in defeat. Within three years, Talleyrand's successor, the Duke de Richelieu, had managed to persuade the Tsar to reduce the crushing indemnity and the Allies to end their occupation two years ahead of time. In 1817, a big loan was negotiated with an English bank called Barings. Culturally, France blossomed as she had not for many years. It was a time when Balzac, Musset, Dumas, Victor Hugo and Stendhal published their first works, and when painters like Delacroix and Géricault and musicians like Berlioz made their debut. With the heavy hand of Napoleonic police repression of the arts removed, Paris arose phoenix-like as the literary, artistic and musical centre of Europe. The *vie bohème* and the Left Bank made their appearance; and, with the dearth of manhood, it was not altogether a bad time for a young man to grow up in.

Louis died in 1824, to be succeeded by his younger (and far more conservative, and bigoted) brother, the Comte d'Artois, Charles x. Domestic crises proliferated, and in time-honoured fashion he looked around for a foreign cause with which to distract minds. As fortune would have it, in 1830 the Bey of Algiers insulted France by striking the French consul with his fly-whisk. Charles sent an armada under General de Bourmont (the 'traitor' of Beaumont, who had traduced Marshal Ney). France's new colonial empire had begun – and with it a headache which would return to plague her, and bring down a republic, just over 130 years later.[3] But the Algerian diversion could not save the last of the Bourbons. Chateaubriand recorded, 'Yet another government hurling itself down from Notre Dame.' On 2 August 1830, Charles abdicated in favour of Louis-Philippe, son of 'Philippe Égalité', Duke of Orleans, who had played so dubious a role during the Revolution. Under the 'Bourgeois King', prosperity returned to France in a big way. But political instability seemed inbred. France became bored with the *enrichissez-vous* world of Louis-Philippe, and in 1848 another revolution paved the way for a return to imperial dreams of past glory. Louis Napoleon, nicknamed 'the well-intentioned', proved however to be but a tinsel image of his uncle, and was to lead France to a far greater humiliation than 1815 at the hands of Bismarck's resurgent Prussians.[4] Perhaps not until de Gaulle's Fifth Republic of the 1960s was anything resembling the power and glory of the Napoleonic era to be seen again.

THE ADVENT OF LOUIS NAPOLEON brought with it a huge rekindling of interest in the First Empire in France. Books on Napoleon became a new growth industry. But were the lessons learnt? What were they? Following Napoleon's hour of greatest triumph at Tilsit, in 1807, France did undoubtedly experience a period of unprecedented economic prosperity. But it was illusory; as with Hitler's Reich in the halcyon years of 1940–2, it was largely at the cost of subjugated neighbours. As such, inevitably, it built up a massive reservoir of resentment against Napoleon, which in due course would play its role in his downfall. Also, the Continental System never really worked; as late as 1810, embattled Britain would still somehow be receiving over 80 per cent of her wheat imports from France or her allies, while in the long run its failure would turn out to be fatal for France herself.

British experience of the Napoleonic blockade was, a century later, to have a most important influence in the shaping of grand strategy in both world wars. Indeed, in the Second World War the timetable for Britain shows a curious similarity to what happened during the Napoleonic Wars:

- defeat of the First Coalition (1939–40)
- banishment of Britain from Europe (Dunkirk)
- failure of invasion from Europe and triumph of sea power (1940–1)
- formation of new coalitions but continuing enemy land triumphs (1941–2)
- backbone of enemy broken in Russia (1942–4)

Of course, the parallel ends there. In 1815, with Napoleon defeated and the rest of Europe exhausted by war and blockade, the field was left clear for Britain 'to become the workshop and the banker of the world, the very thing Napoleon had sought to prevent';[5] but in 1945 it was Britain that emerged devitalized.

Once the spirit of Tilsit had begun to wear thin, more than any other factor it was the Continental System and its consequences that led Napoleon on the road to Moscow in 1812; just as it was, still, the English dynamo and her treasury that would continue to sustain his enemies. ('Russia was the last resource of England,' Napoleon admitted on St Helena. 'The peace of the world rested with Russia. Alas! English gold proved more powerful than my plans.')

For the *Grande Armée*, Tilsit was a kind of watershed, after which it never seemed quite so good again. First of all, with longed-for peace at hand it was hard to keep up the old revolutionary fervour, let alone the standard of training with which it had marched out of the Camp of Boulogne in 1805. While recruitment grew increasingly inefficient, losses had left their mark, particularly those suffered at Eylau, and particularly among the *cadres*. Then came the 'Spanish Ulcer'. Goering-like, some of the marshals began to wax fat on the fruits (and loots) of peace. They took to quarrelling with each other and disobeying orders. As a result of all this, after 1807 units of the *Grande Armée* were less capable of performing the complex manoeuvres that had brought victory at Austerlitz and Auerstädt, and they indulged more in costly mass tactics – such as were to prove Napoleon's undoing at Waterloo.

Other enemy armies began at last to study and emulate the Napoleonic technique. Soon after 1807 it was discovered that Napoleon's valuable shock weapon, his shield of skirmishers, could no longer shake a prepared enemy line. The Emperor also found himself fighting in countries where, for the first time, the inhabitants would prove virulently hostile. Then, with each succeeding battle, the forces present grew steadily larger. This had a disastrous effect on Napoleon's highly personal style of command. The scale of operations in Russia (as Hitler in his turn was to discover) was simply too great for one man to control. As the armies grew larger, so did the casualty lists, until, at grim Leipzig in 1813, a terrible battle of attrition cost Napoleon five times his losses at Austerlitz. The *Grande Armée* never recovered.

The lessons to be derived from Napoleon's amazing run of victories in 1805–7 are those that have been learnt (or not learnt) by military adventurers through the ages, from Xerxes to Hitler – there is seldom such a thing as a *limited* victory. One conquest only leads on, ineluctably, to another, to protect what has already been won. Napoleon's wars on the continent gained him no real friends (Talleyrand understood this), only crushed enemies: 'Prussia vanquished but fuming, Austria secretly implacable', in the words of Thiers. Resurgent already in 1809, only to be knocked down again at Wagram, Austria nevertheless would be inexorably at Napoleon's throat once more in the Leipzig campaign of 1813. As far as the Russian colossus was concerned, although Napoleon had left Tilsit persuaded that he had effectively seduced the Tsar, it was clearly a seduction requiring constant attention and refurbishment. For it was upon Russia's continuing benevolence that Napoleon's grandiose future schemes had depended. Unlike Austria and Prussia, she alone had not been invaded and subjugated on her own territory; her armies had been defeated in a series of great battles, but all of them on somebody else's soil; and in terms of manpower she still remained the world's most powerful land force. Though Russia was defeated in 1805 and 1807, invaded and desperately mauled in 1812, in 1814 it was the Tsar's armies that would be in Paris, forcing Napoleon to abdicate.

Yet, all the time, it was Britain's gold and her inflexible will to bring Napoleon down which helped breathe life into coalition after coalition. The cost to Britain had been enormous: over the whole twenty years of war, she had paid out in subsidies to her allies nearly £66 million, and almost half of this, disproportionately, in the last three years; between 1793 and 1815 government spending had risen from 6 per cent of the national income to 25 per cent and the national debt had soared from £245m to £834m – equal to £43 per head of every man, woman and child.[6] Figures for overall deaths caused by the twenty years of war are uncertain, though one recent historian, Rory Muir,[7] puts them at between 200,000 and 250,000 (probably most from disease); at total which, from Britain's far smaller population, he equates (strikingly) with the scale of losses (though much more compressed in terms of time) suffered in 1914–18. But what this expenditure bought for Britain, a 'Pax Britannica' enduring over the next century, derived almost entirely from the fact (and a fact that is often overlooked) that although (as in 1939–45) without Russia there could have been no Allied triumph, at Waterloo, the final round of the Napoleonic Wars was won by a *British* – and not a Russian, Austrian, or even Prussian victory. The settlement of 1815 inevitably invites comparisons with that of 1945; but the difference is that the defeat of Nazi Germany left no acceptable regime with which to negotiate, no tame Bourbons waiting in the wings to be restored – and no Talleyrand to negotiate on behalf of the defeated. Yet the statesmen of 1815 surely deserve History's recognition for the moderate and enduring peace which they constructed.

As Victor Hugo remarked, Waterloo was not just a battle: it marked a change in the direction of the world. One of the most formidable changes of that direction lay in the future of Prussia, so deeply humiliated in the Jena Campaign of 1806 ('Don't beat so loud – he's only a king!' the drummers of Napoleon's Guard had been contemptuously ordered when the dejected Frederick William arrived at the raft on the Niemen). Despite Talleyrand's warning, Napoleon had committed his gravest error at Tilsit by imposing the harsh terms which, *inter alia*, deprived Prussia of half her territories and subjected the remainder to a degrading occupation. At Jena he had destroyed a feudal army, as well as the feudal nation to which it belonged. But he would be responsible for the *national* army which, out of the ashes, would arise to smash him at Leipzig, in the War of the Nations of 1813 – and ultimately destroy him at Waterloo. Although Napoleon had defeated every professional army in Europe, it was the sheer numerical weight of the resurgent peoples that finally ground him down. As he himself once confessed, 'Against greatly superior forces, it is possible to win a battle, but hardly a war.' In the long run (as Hitler was to discover), military brilliance is not enough; numbers are what count.

Beyond the context of the Napoleonic Wars, in the longer term Prussia's humiliation at Jena was perhaps to produce the most dire political consequences for successive generations of Napoleon's adopted countrymen, and indeed for all Europe. His attempts to sweep away the medieval structure of the German states and 're-order' it – much as he had done in north Italy – would unwittingly pave the way for German unification. Out of it would emerge a new super-state east of the Rhine: the Prussian-led German Reich. Sixty-five years after Austerlitz, it would inflict upon Napoleon's own nephew as shattering a defeat as any he had ever dealt out. The technique of conscription introduced by Napoleon to create his mass armies was to mark the beginning of the era of total war – 'a backward step for mankind', remarks André Maurois in his *History of France*.[8] Three times in the century that lay ahead, such a mass army would – in the hands of the descendants of Blücher – lay waste to France.

One of the great ironies of Napoleon's years of triumph lies in what he did to the ethos of the French Revolution, the impetus of which had so materially aided him in his conquests. While at home, in France, he had put into reverse many of its principles, he carried those same principles in the baggage-train of the *Grande Armée* to the nations it conquered. Born and bred in Paris, ideals of liberty, egalitarianism and nationalism had been unleashed among all the European peoples, and – long after Napoleon's conquests were forgotten – these would clash resoundingly with the Old Order.

THERE IS AN (APOCRYPHAL) ANECDOTE about a British dignitary interviewing Chairman Mao. He asked him what, in his opinion, might have happened if, instead of President Kennedy, Khrushchev had been assassinated. Mao reflected a while, then replied, 'It's hard to tell. But I don't suppose Mr Onassis would have married Mrs Khrushchev!' Students of history love to play with its 'what ifs'. *If* Napoleon could have hung on to Louisiana, instead of selling it to America, it would have made France ultimately the world's number-one power – but would a Pitt or a Castlereagh have permitted it? *If* Napoleon had not won so resoundingly at Austerlitz, might there have been no Waterloo ten years later? And could he have won at Waterloo? As Wellington had observed, the battle was indeed 'the nearest-run thing you ever saw'. Both sides had made mistakes, but Napoleon had made most; *if* he had had Berthier, instead of Soult, Davout instead of Ney; *if* he, Napoleon, had been, physically as well as mentally, the man he had been at Austerlitz; *if Alte Vorwärts* had not been there? And what *if* Napoleon had won definitively, without a replay?

In a light-hearted article entitled 'Napoleon or the Kaiser: Choose', Norman Stone, Oxford's Professor of Modern History, has speculated exactly thus: Lucien Bonaparte would have been made King of Scotland, Joseph King of England; a guillotine would have been set up in Whitehall; Oxford – Stone's fancy ran free – would have (perhaps rather usefully) been turned into a school of military engineering and medicine, the Dean of Christ Church, protesting, 'bayoneted by Polish troops stabling their horses in the cathedral'. But, marginally, the Professor reckons it would have been better to have been defeated by Napoleon than by the Kaiser. In the long run, it would possibly have been beneficial; at least we would have had good trains, 'sensible property laws and decent schools'.[9] (He makes no mention of the cuisine.)

A yet more distinguished historian from Cambridge, G. M. Trevelyan, tackled exactly the same theme ninety years previously. Then aged thirty-one, the future Master of Trinity won a prize in a competition in the *Westminster Gazette* in July 1907 with an essay entitled 'If Napoleon had won the Battle of Waterloo'. His starting point was the signature of the 'Convention of Brussels' in July 1815, when a defeated Wellington was offered the same generous terms to 'evacuate the seat of war' which the French had been accorded at Cintra seven years previously. Napoleon, exhausted, was overwhelmed by the cries for 'peace' that ran down the ranks of his army, and was persuaded to propose a pact of 'unexpected clemency' to England. His aim – almost Gaullist in its modernity – was simply to remove her 'from the scene of affairs and from the counsels of the continental monarchs'. The result was to be a Europe remarkably akin to the dreams of a Jacques Delors, with France dominant, the Germans remaining 'the quietest and most loyal of all Napoleon's subjects' (remember this was written seven years before the holocaust of 1914), and Britain isolated. In the ensuing years of peace, in a marginalized Britain 'distress grew yearly more intolerable, among both the rural and industrial populations' – until, in 1825, there broke out 'the ill-advised but romantic rebellion of Lord Byron'. Then;

> The savage reprisals of government established the blood feud between one half of England and the other. Byron's execution made as great a noise in the world as any event since the Fall of the Bastille. . . . The writings of Shelley, especially after his long imprisonment, obtained a popularity which was one of the most curious symptoms of the time. . . .

This pleasing fantasy closed with Napoleon dying in 1826 of a kind of Alzheimer-like premature old age, enjoying delusions that Josephine was still alive.

BRITISH 'EUROSCEPTICS' OF THE 1990s might be forgiven, if in their gloomier moments, they were to foresee that by the two hundredth anniversary of Waterloo, in 2015, most of Napoleon's social agenda for Europe will have been achieved (though, more probably, the principal beneficiaries will by then prove to be the heirs to Kaiser Wilhelm). Yet, if the prolonged struggle over Napoleonic hegemony has any lesson, or moral, useful to Britain today, it is perhaps the value of coalitions. Muddled and inefficient as they may be, two world wars and a cold war show that, in the long run, they win wars – and possibly prevent them. Powers, however strong, that exist alone, isolated, are usually doomed.

REFERENCES

Preface

1 Alistair Horne, *The Fall of Paris: The Siege and the Commune, 1870–71* (London, 1965; rev. edn, 1990).
2 Alistair Horne, *A Savage War of Peace: Algeria, 1954–62* (London, 1977; rev. edn, 1996).

ONE: The Rise of the Adventurer

1 Adolphe Thiers, *History of the Consulate and Empire* (London, 1845), vol. VII, pp. 337–8.
2 *Napoléon et Marie Louise: souvenirs historiques de Baron de Ménéval* (Paris, 1844–5), vol. I, p. 186.
3 M. de Bourienne, *Memoirs of Napoleon Bonaparte* (London, 1836), vol. II, p. 18.
4 Henri Beyle (Stendhal), *The Charterhouse of Parma* (London, 1962), p. 21.
5 Comte M.J.E.A.D. de Las Cases, *Mémorial de Ste Hélène* (Paris, 1823).
6 Duc de Raguse, *Mémoires* (Paris, 1857).
7 Ibid., vol. I, p. 78.
8 Quoted in Evangeline Bruce, *Napoleon and Josephine: An Improbable Marriage* (London, 1995), p. 209.
9 Raguse, *Mémoires*.

TWO: An Uneasy Peace

1 Gwynne Lewis, *Life in Revolutionary France* (London, 1972).
2 Bruce, *Napoleon and Josephine*, p. 64.
3 Clarence Crane Brinton, *A Decade of Revolution* (London and New York, 1934).
4 Duff Cooper, *Talleyrand* (London, 1932), p. 272.
5 Ibid., p. 28.
6 Ibid., p. 123.
7 Lewis, *Life in Revolutionary France*, p. 182.
8 André Maurois, *History of France* (London, 1949), p. 327.
9 Quoted in Bruce, *Napoleon and Josephine*, p. 356.

THREE: Partners in Coalition

1 W. S. Churchill, *A History of the English-Speaking Peoples* (London, 1957), vol. III, p. 240.
2 Carola Oman, *Nelson* (London, 1947).

3 Lord David Ce cil, *A Portrait of Jane Austen* (London, 1979), p. 18.
4 G. M. Trevelyan, *English Social History* (London, 1944).
5 S. E. Morison, *The Oxford History of the American People* (New York, 1965).
6 Letter to Lord Shelburne.
7 Cooper, *Talleyrand*, p. 139.

FOUR: **The Army of England**

1 George Canning, '*L'Oracle*, 1803–1804'.
2 Churchill, *History*, pp. 239–40.
3 In the House of Commons, 22 July 1803.
4 Quoted in Evelyn Berckman, *Nelson's Dear Lord: A Portrait of St Vincent* (London, 1962), p. 82.
5 Trevelyan, *English Social History*, p. 503.
6 G. Callender, *Sea Kings of Britain: Keppel to Nelson* (London, 1924), vol. III, pp. 244–7.
7 Quoted in Berckman, *Nelson's Dear Lord*, p. 92.
8 Churchill, *History*, vol. III, p. 241. There is a Churchillian inaccuracy here: the 'Grand Army' had not yet come into being.
9 William Lord Auckland, *Journal and Correspondence* (London, 1862).

FIVE: **Preparing for a New Campaign**

1 Thiers, *Consulate and Empire*, vol. VI, p. 5.
2 Ibid.
3 *La Correspondance de Napoléon 1er* (Paris, 1862), letter 9133.

SIX: **La Grande Armée**

1 John Keegan, *The Face of Battle* (London, 1976), p. 170.
2 D. G. Chandler, *The Campaigns of Napoleon* (London, 1967).
3 Baron de Fain, 'Mémoires', from Col. J. G. Vachée, *Napoleon at Work* (trans. London, 1914).
4 Baron von Odeleben, *A Circumstantial Narrative of the Campaign in Saxony* (London, 1820).
5 I am indebted to Douglas Porch's excellent book *The French Secret Services* (London, 1994).
6 Anthony West, *Mortal Wounds* (London, 1975), pp. 102–4.
7 Porch, *French Secret Service*, p. 7.
8 I am indebted here to Elizabeth Sparrow, 'The Alien Office, 1792–1806', *English*

Historical Review, 33/2 (1990), pp. 361–84, and 'The Swiss and Swabian Agencies, 1795–1801', *English Historical Review*, 35/4 (1992), pp. 861–84.
9 Gen. Comte de Saint-Chamans, *Mémoires* (Paris, 1896).
10 Thiers, *Consulate and Empire*, vol. VI, p. 13.

SEVEN: **Ulm and on to Vienna**

1 Correlli Barnett, *Bonaparte* (London, 1978), p. 109.
2 Quoted in Arthur Bryant, *The Years of Victory* (London, 1944), pp. 179–80.
3 Letter to Czartoryski, 23 September 1805.

EIGHT: **'Le Beau Soleil d'Austerlitz'**

1 Christopher Duffy, *Austerlitz, 1805* (London, 1977).
2 Maj.-Gen. Sir R. Wilson, *Brief Remarks on the Character and Composition of the Russian Army* (London, 1810).
3 Quoted by the British Ambassador, Sir Arthur Paget, in his reports to the Foreign Office.
4 Field-Marshal Montgomery, *A History of Warfare* (London, 1968), p. 354.
5 Alfred de Musset, *Confessions d'un enfant du siècle* (Paris, 1836).
6 Leo Tolstoy, *War and Peace* (London, 1869).
7 Ibid.

NINE: **'Soldiers, I Am Pleased with You'**

1 Gen. P. Comte de Ségur, *Histoire et mémoires* (Paris, 1837), p. 468.
2 A. F. Becke, *An Introduction to the History of Tactics* (London, 1909).
3 From an account by Napoleon's aide, Lejeune.
4 M. Lombarès, 'Devant Austerlitz. Sur les traces de la pensée de l'Empereur', *Revue Historique de l'Armée* (Paris, 1847); Duffy, op. cit.
5 *Memoiren des Königlichen Preussischen Generals der Infantrie Ludwig Freiherrn von Wolzogen* (Leipzig, 1851), p. 28.

TEN: **'Uncheered by Fortune'**

1 Churchill, *History*, vol. III, p. 251.
2 Maj.-Gen. J. F. C. Fuller, *The Decisive Battles of the Western World* (London, 1957), vol. II, p. 418.
3 Ibid., p. 421.
4 Gen. C. von Clausewitz, *On War* (New York, 1962), p. 91.

5 Brig.-Gen. Vincent J. Esposito and Col. John Robert Elting, *A Military History and Atlas of the Napoleonic Wars* (New York, 1963).
6 Chandler, *Campaigns of Napoleon*, p. 494.
7 See Alistair Horne, *To Lose a Battle: France 1940* (London, 1969; rev. edn, 1990).

ELEVEN: **The Raft on the Niemen**

1 L. Madelin, *Le Consulat et l'Empire* (Paris, 1932), p. 307.
2 Churchill, *History*, vol. III, p. 254.
3 Norman Davies, *God's Playground: A History of Poland* (Oxford, 1981), vol. II, p. 267.
4 Christine Sutherland, *Marie Walewska, Napoleon's Great Love* (London, 1979), p. 6.
5 *The Notebooks of Captain Coignet*, ed. L. Larchey (New York, 1890), p. 138.
6 Gen. Comte J. Rapp, *Mémoires* (Paris, 1821), p. 118.
7 Countess Potocka, *Mémoires, 1794–1820* (Paris, 1897).
8 Baron M. de Marbot, *Mémoires* (Paris, 1891).
9 Chandler, *Campaigns of Napoleon*, p. 545.
10 J. de Norvins, *Souvenirs d'une histoire de Napoléon* (Paris, 1897), pp. 204–5.
11 Thiers, *Consulate and Empire*, vol. VII, p. 362.
12 Churchill, *History*, vol. III, p. 254.
13 Davies, op. cit., p. 267

TWELVE: **Talleyrand Defects**

1 Georges Lefebvre, *Napoléon, 1807–1815* (London, 1969), p. 7.
2 Duchess of Abrantès, *Mémoires* (1895), quoted in Peter Gunn, *Napoleon's 'Little Pest': The Duchess of Abrantès, 1784–1838* (London, 1979), p. 106.
3 Cooper, *Talleyrand*, p. 351.
4 Cooper, *Talleyrand*, p. 176.

THIRTEEN: **Sir John Moore's Retreat**

1 Quoted in Gunn, *Napoleon's 'Little Pest'*, pp. 135–6.
2 Quoted in Sutherland, *Marie Walewska*, p. 118.

FOURTEEN: **The Last Victory: Wagram**

1 Cooper, *Talleyrand*, p. 187.
2 Ibid., p. 190.
3 Bruce, *Napoleon and Josephine*, p. 436.
4 Quoted in *Vienna: A Travellers' Companion*, selected by John Lehmann and Richard Bassett (London, 1988), p. 217.

5 Marbot, *Mémoires*, vol. II, p. 194.

6 Cadet de Gassicourt, *Papers of an Army Apothecary*, quoted in *Vienna*, pp. 188–9.

7 Marbot, *Mémoires*, vol. II, pp. 239–40.

8 Esposito and Elting, *Military History*, map 105.

9 Marbot, *Mémoires*, vol. II, p. 273.

10 Quoted in Sir John Fortescue, *History of the British Army* (London, 1899–1930), vol. II, p. 89.

FIFTEEN: Love and Marriage

1 Sutherland, *Marie Walewska*, p. 133.

2 Rapp, *Mémoires*, vol. I, p. 153.

3 Bruce, *Napoleon and Josephine*, p. 439.

4 Bryant, *Years of Victory*, p. 343.

5 Quoted in West, *Mortal Wounds*, p. 186.

SIXTEEN: The British Blockade

1 Quoted in Bruce, *Napoleon and Josephine*, p. 456.

2 Trevelyan, *English Social History*, p. 470.

3 Ibid., p. 505.

4 Maurois, *History of France*, p. 339.

5 Gen. P. Comte de Ségur, *Mémoires: la Campagne de Russie* (1901), quoted in Sutherland, *Marie Walewska*, p. 158.

6 Baron de Ménéval, *Mémoires* (Paris, 1894), vol. I, p. 387.

7 Morison, *Oxford History of the American People*, p. 378.

8 Ibid., p. 398.

SEVENTEEN: 'Don't March on Moscow'

1 Montgomery, *History of Warfare*, p. 365.

2 Gen. A. A. L. de Caulaincourt, *Memoirs* (London, 1950), vol. I, p. 108.

3 Leo Tolstoy, *War and Peace* (London, 1943).

4 Gen. C. von Clausewitz, *The Campaign of 1812* (London, 1843), p. 139.

5 Ségur, *Histoire et mémoires*, vol. I, p. 360.

6 Louis Constant, *Mémoire* (London, 1896), vol. III, p. 320.

7 Gen. Baron A. H. Jomini, *The Art of War* (Philadelphia, 1875), vol. II, pp. 285–7.

8 Tolstoy, *War and Peace*, p. 966.

9 Ségur, *Histoire et mémoires*, vol. II, p. 87; Caulaincourt, *Memoirs*, vol. I, p. 310.

10 Marbot, *Mémoires*, vol. III, p. 150.

11 Ségur, *Histoire et mémoires*, vol. II, p. 313.

12 Esposito and Elting, *Military History*, map 125.

EIGHTEEN: **The Battle of the Nations**

1 Quoted in Gunn, *Napoleon's 'Little Pest'*, pp. 145–6, 157.

2 Quoted in Bruce, *Napoleon and Josephine*, pp. 463–4.

3 Ibid., p. 463.

4 Cooper, *Talleyrand*, pp. 211–12.

5 Caulaincourt, *Memoirs*, vol. II, p. 345.

6 Raguse, *Mémoires*, vol. V, p. 15.

7 Prince C. L. W. Metternich, *Mémoires* (Paris, 1880), vol. II, p. 461.

8 Constant, *Mémoire*, p. 121.

9 Chandler, *Campaigns of Napoleon*, p. 912.

10 C. von Plotho, *Der Krieg in Deutschland und Frankreich* (Berlin, 1818), vol. II, p. 440.

11 Chandler, *Campaigns of Napoleon*, p. 937.

12 Esposito and Elting, *Military History*, introduction to 1814.

13 Fuller, *Decisive Battles*, vol. II, p. 484.

NINETEEN: **'La Patrie en Danger!'**

1 Bourienne, *Memoirs*, vol. III, p. 292.

2 Gen. H. Camon, *La Guerre Napoléonienne: précis des campagnes* (Paris, 1925), vol. II, p. 152n.

3 Caulaincourt, *Memoirs*, vol. III, pp. 11–17.

4 Fuller, *Decisive Battles*, vol. II, p. 489.

5 Quoted in Cooper, *Talleyrand*, pp. 223, 224.

6 Constant, *Mémoire*, vol. IV, p. 259.

TWENTY: **The Hundred Days**

1 Maurois, *History of France*, p. 342.

2 Neil Campbell, *Napoleon at Fontainebleau and Elba* (London, 1869), pp. 243–4.

3 Sutherland, *Marie Walewska*, p. 232.

4 Quoted in Bruce, *Napoleon and Josephine*, p. 475.

5 Ibid., pp. 476–7.

6 Susan-Mary Alsop, *The Congress Dances* (New York, 1984).

7 Quoted in Cooper, *Talleyrand*, p. 247.

8 Campbell, *Napoleon at Fontainebleau*, p. 353.

9 Barnett, *Bonaparte*, p. 200.

10 Quoted in J. Naylor, *Waterloo* (London, 1960), p. 16.

11 Esposito and Elting, *Military History*, map 156.
12 Ménéval, *Mémoires*, vol. II, p. 444.
13 See Horne, *To Lose a Battle*.
14 Montgomery, *History of Warfare*, p. 366.
15 Marquess of Malmesbury, *A Series of Letters* (London, 1870), vol. II, pp. 445–6.
16 Drouet, J. B., Comte d'Erlon, *Mémoires* (Paris, 1884), p. 96.
17 Napoleon, *Commentaires* (Paris, 1867), vol. V, p. 200.
18 Gen. G. Gourgaud, *La Campagne de 1815* (Paris, n.d.), pp. 96–7.
19 Col. Sir A. F. Frazer, *Letters* (London, 1859), p. 547.
20 Gourgaud, *Campagne de 1815*, p. 97.
21 Keegan, *Face of Battle*, p. 127.
22 Quoted in Sutherland, *Marie Walewska*, p. 236.
23 Reine Hortense, *Mémoires* (n.d.), quoted in Bruce, *Napoleon and Josephine*, p. 484.
24 Rudyard Kipling, 'A St Helena Lullaby', from *A Choice of Kipling's Verse Made by T. S. Eliot* (London, 1942).

Epilogue

1 Quoted in Barnett, *Bonaparte*, p. 211.
2 Quoted in Desmond Seward, *The Bourbon Kings of France* (London, 1976), p. 256.
3 See Horne, *Savage War of Peace*.
4 See Horne, *Fall of Paris*.
5 Fuller, *Decisive Battles*, vol. II, p. 441.
6 Figures from Rory Muir, *Britain and the Defeat of Napoleon, 1807–1815* (London 1996), pp. 376–7.
7 Ibid, p. 377.
8 Maurois, *History of France*, p. 353.
9 *Spectator*, 23 March 1996.

SELECT BIBLIOGRAPHY

Alsop, Susan-Mary, *The Congress Dances* (New York, 1984)
Anderson, J. H., *The Napoleonic Campaign of 1805* (London, 1912)
Auckland, William Lord, *Journal and Correspondence* (London, 1862)
Baldet, Marcel, *La Vie Quotidienne dans les Armées de Napoléon* (Paris, 1964)
Barnett, Correlli, *Bonaparte* (London, 1978)
Becke, A. F., *An Introduction to the History of Tactics* (London, 1909)
Berckman, Evelyn, *Nelson's Dear Lord: A Portrait of St Vincent* (London, 1962)
Bidou, Henry, *Paris* (London, 1939)
Bonal, H., *La Manoeuvre de Iéna* (Paris, 1855)
Bourienne, M. de, *Memoirs of Napoleon Bonaparte* (London, 1836)
Bowle, John, *Napoleon* (London, 1973)
Brinton, Clarence Crane, *A Decade of Revolution* (London and New York, 1934)
Britt III, A. S., *Campaign Atlas to Wars of Napoleon* (New York, 1972)
——, *The Wars of Napoleon* (New York, 1977)
Bruce, Evangeline, *Napoleon and Josephine: An Improbable Marriage* (London, 1995)
Bryant, A., *The Years of Endurance* (London, 1942)
——, *The Years of Victory* (London, 1944)
Memoirs of Sergeant Burgogne 1812–1813 Introduction by Richard Partridge (London, 1996)
Burton, Lt-Col. R. G., *From Boulogne to Austerlitz* (London, 1912)
Callender, G., *Sea Kings of Britain: Keppel to Nelson* (London, 1924)
Camon, Gen. H., *La Guerre Napoléonienne: précis des campagnes* (Paris, 1925)
Campbell, Neil, *Napoleon at Fontainebleau and Elba* (London, 1869)
Caulaincourt, Gen. A. A. L. de, *Memoirs* (London, 1950)
Cecil, Lord David, *A Portrait of Jane Austen* (London, 1979)
Chalfont, Lord (ed.), [Seymour, W., Kaulbach, E., Champagne, J.] *Waterloo: the Battle of Three Armies* (London, 1979)
Chandler, D. G., *The Campaigns of Napoleon* (London, 1967)
——, *Dictionary of the Napoleonic Wars* (New York, 1979)
——, *Waterloo: the 100 Days'* (London, 1980)
Christian, R. F., *Tolstoy's War and Peace: A Study* (London, 1962)
Churchill, W. S., *A History of the English Speaking Peoples*, vol. III (London, 1957)
Clausewitz, Gen. C. von, *The Campaign of 1812* (London, 1843)
——, *On War* (London, 1962)
Clunn, Harold, *The Face of Paris* (London, 1933)
Coignet, Capt. J. R., *The Notebooks of Captain Coignet* (London, 1929)
Coles, Harry L., *The War of 1812* (Chicago, 1965)
Colin, Comdt J., *La Campagne de 1805 en Allemagne, Revue Historique de l'Armée* (Paris, 1905–7)

Select Bibliography

Constant, Louis, *Mémoire* (London, 1896)

Cooper, Duff, *Talleyrand* (London, 1932)

Crankshaw, Edward, *The Habsburgs* (London, 1971)

Creevey, Thomas, *The Creevey Papers,* ed. Sir H. Maxwell (London, 1903–5)

Czartoryski, Prince A., *Memoirs* (London, 1888)

Davies, Norman, *God's Playground: A History of Poland* (Oxford, 1981)

Davout, Marshal, *Opérations du 3ᵉ Corps 1806–1807: Rapport du Maréchal Davout, Duc d'Auerstädt* (Paris, 1904)

Dixon, Pierson, *Pauline: Napoleon's Favourite Sister* (London, 1964)

Drouet, J. B., Comte d'Erlon, *Mémoires* (Paris, 1884)

Duffy, Christopher, *Austerlitz, 1805* (London, 1977)

Elting, John R., *Swords around a Throne: Napoleon's Grande Armée* (London, 1986)

Ermolov, A. P., *Zapiski [Memoirs]* (Moscow, 1865)

Esposito, Brig.-Gen. Vincent J., and Elting, Col. John Robert, *A Military History and Atlas of the Napoleonic Wars* (New York, 1963)

Fairon, E., and Heusse, H., *Lettres des Grognards* (Paris, 1936)

Fortescue, Sir John, *History of the British Army* (London, 1899–1930)

Fraser, Antonia, *Love Letters* (London, 1976)

Frazer, Col. Sir A. F., *Letters* (London, 1859)

Fuller, Maj.-Gen. J. F. C., *The Decisive Battles of the Western World,* vol. II (London, 1957)

Gates, David, *The Spanish Alpha: the History of the Peninsular War* (London, 1986)

Goltz, Gen. C. von, *Jena to Eylau: The Disgrace and Redemption of the Old Prussian Army* (New York, 1913)

Gourgaud, Gen. G., *La Campagne de 1815* (Paris, n.d.)

Guedalla, P., *The 100 Days* (London, 1934)

Gunn, Peter, *Napoleon's 'Little Pest': The Duchess of Abrantès, 1784–1838* (London, 1979)

Harvey, P., and Heseltine, J. E., *The Oxford Companion to French Literature* (Oxford, 1959)

Herold, J. C., *The Age of Napoleon* (London, 1963)

——, (ed.) *The Mind of Napoleon* (London, 1955)

Hibbert, Christopher, *Nelson: A Personal History* (London, 1994)

Horne, Alistair, *Napoleon, Master of Europe 1805–1807* (London, 1979)

Janetschek, C., *Die Schlacht bei Austerlitz* (Brünn, 1898)

Jarrett, Derek, *Pitt the Younger* (London, 1974)

Jomini, Gen. Baron Antoine H., *The Art of War* (Philadelphia 1875)

——, *Life of Napoleon* (Kansas City, 1897)

Keegan, John, *The Face of Battle* (London, 1976)

Lachouque, Comdt Henry, *Napoléon à Austerlitz* (Paris, 1960)

Lachouque, Henry, and Brown, Anne S. K., *The Anatomy of Glory: Napoleon and His Guard* (London, 1961)

Las Cases, Comte M.J.E.A.D. de, *Mémorial de Ste Hélène* (Paris, 1823)

Laver, James, *The Age of Illusion* (London, 1972)

Lefebvre, G., *Napoléon, 1807–1815* (London, 1969)

Lejeune, Col. L. F., *Souvenirs d'un Officier sous l'Empire* (Paris, n.d.)

Lewis, Gwynne, *Life in Revolutionary France* (London, 1972)

Lombarès, M., 'Devant Austerlitz. Sur les traces de la pensée de l'Empereur', *Revue Historique de l'Armée* (Paris, 1947)

Madelin, L., *Le Consulat et l'Empire* (Paris, 1932)

Mahan, Admiral A. T., *Influence of Sea Power Upon the French Revolution and Empire* (London, 1982)

Malmesbury, Marquess of, *A Series of Letters* (London, 1870)

Manceron, Claude, *Austerlitz* (London, 1966)

Marbot, Baron M. de, *Mémoires* (Paris, 1891)

Masson, F., *Napoléon et les Femmes* (Paris, 1894)

Maurois, A., *Chateaubriand* (London, 1938)

——, *A History of France* (London, 1949)

Ménéval, Baron C. F., *Mémoires* (Paris, 1894)

——, *Napoléon et Marie Louise: souvenirs historiques* (Paris, 1844–5)

Metternich, Prince C. L. W., *Mémoires* (Paris, 1880)

Mikhailovsky-Danilevsky, Lt-Gen., *Opisanie Pervoi Voiny Imperatora Aleksandra s Napoleonom v 1805-m Godu* (1844)

Montgomery, Field-Marshal, *A History of Warfare* (London, 1968)

Montholon and Gourgaud, *Memoirs of Napoleon*, vols I and II (London, 1823)

Morison, S. E., *The Oxford History of the American Peoples* (New York, 1965)

Muir, Rory, *Britain and the Defeat of Napoleon: 1807–1815* (London, 1996)

Musset, Alfred de, *Confessions d'un enfant du siècle* (Paris, 1836)

Napoleon I, *Commentaires* (Paris, 1867)

——, *La Correspondance de Napoléon 1ᵉʳ*, vols XI–XV (Paris, 1862),

——, *Maximes* (Paris, 1874)

Naylor, J., *Waterloo* (London, 1960)

Norvins, J. de, *Souvenirs d'un histoire de Napoléon* (Paris, 1897)

Odeleben, Baron von, *A Circumstantial Narrative of the Campaign in Saxony* (London, 1820)

Oman, Carola, *Nelson* (London, 1947)

——, *Napoleon at the Channel* (New York, 1942)

Oman, Sir C. W. C., *A History of the Peninsular War*, seven volumes (Oxford, 1902–30)

Parquin, Capt. D. C., *Napoleon's Army* (Camden, Conn., 1969)

Plotho, C. von, *Der Krieg in Deutschland und Frankreich* (Berlin, 1818)

Pocock, Tom, *Remember Nelson* (London, 1977)

Porch, Douglas, *The French Secret Service* (London, 1994)

Potocka, Countess, *Mémoires, 1794–1820* (Paris, 1897)

Quennevat, J.-C., *Atlas de la Grande Armée* (Paris, 1966)

Raguse, Duc de, *Mémoires* (Paris, 1857)

Rapp, Gen. Count J., *Mémoires* (Paris, 1821)

Rémusat, Mme C. de, *Mémoires* (Paris, 1893)

Rogers, Col. H. C. B., *Napoleon's Army* (London, 1974)

Rothenberg, G. E., *The Art of Warfare in the Age of Napoleon* (London, 1977)

Rudé, George, *Revolutionary Europe 1783–1815* (London, 1967)

Saint-Chamans, Gen. Comte de, *Mémoires* (Paris, 1896)

Savary, Gen. A. J. R., *Mémoire sur l'Empire* (Paris, 1828)

Ségur, Gen. P. Comte de, *Histoire et mémoires* (Paris, 1837)

Seward, Desmond, *The Bourbon Kings of France* (London, 1976)

Schama, Simon, *Citizens: A Chronicle of the French Revolution* (London, 1989)

Schom, Alan, *100 Days: Napoleon's Road to Waterloo* (London, 1993)

Sparrow, Elizabeth, 'The Alien Office, 1792–1806', *English Historical Review*, 33/2 (1990), pp. 391–84.

——, 'The Swiss and Swabian Agencies, 1795–1801', *English Historical Review*, 35/4 (1992), pp. 61–84

Stendhal (Henri Beyle), *The Charterhouse of Parma* (London, 1962)

Stutterheim, Maj.-Gen., *A Detailed Account of the Battle of Austerlitz* (London, 1807)

Sutherland, Christine, *Marie Walewska, Napoleon's Great Love* (London, 1979)

Thiébault, Gen. A. C., *Memoirs* (London, 1896)

Thiers, A., *History of the Consulate and Empire*, Books XIX–XXIV, vols VI and VII (London, 1845)

Tolstoy, Leo, *War and Peace* (London, 1869)

Trevelyan, G. M., *English Social History* (London, 1944)

Vachée, Col. J. G., *Napoleon at Work* (trans. London, 1914)

Vienna: A Travellers' Companion, selected by John Lehman and Richard Bassett (London, 1988)

Weber, Eugene, *Peasants into Frenchmen: The Modernisation of Rural France, 1870–1914* (London, 1977)

West, Anthony, *Mortal Wounds* (London, 1975)

Wilson, Maj.-Gen. Sir R., *Brief Remarks on the Character and Composition of the Russian Army* (London, 1810)

——, *Narrative of Events during the Invasion of Russia* (London, 1860)

Wolzogen, Gen. L. von, *Memoiren des Königlichen Preussischen Generals der Infantrie Ludwig Freiherrn von Wolzogen* (Leipzig, 1851)

Yorck von Wartenburg, Gen., *Napoleon as a General* (London, 1902)

Young, Peter, *Napoleon's Marshals* (London, 1973)

INDEX

Abercromby, General Sir John, 14, 295

Aboukir Bay, Battle of (1798), 12, 62

Abrantès, Duke & Duchess of *see* Junot, General Andoche; Junot, Laure

Addington, Henry (1st Viscount Sidmouth): and Cadoudal plot, 26; political jousting, 45; peace policy, 50, 54–5, 60–1; reduces army and naval strength, 50, 59; loses office, 52; in uniform, 65

Aderklaa (village), Austria, 275

Ajaccio, Corsica, 5

Alexander I, Tsar: meets Napoleon at Tilsit (1807), 1–5, 229, 393; reforms, 39; and Enghien murder, 51, 68; Pitt seeks alliance with, 56; reacts to Napoleon's annexation of Ligurian Republic, 69; friendly relations with Britain, 102; and 1805 Potsdam Treaty, 120; and Dolgorukov, 133–4; strategy before Austerlitz, 135; at Austerlitz, 150–1, 155–6, 163, 169, 175, 177, 181–2; withdraws after Austerlitz, 184; informed of 1805 armistice, 185; alliance with Prussia, 197, 213; Talleyrand defects to, 236; alliance with Napoleon, 237, 243; closes ports to Britain, 237, 245, 297; and Napoleon's Near Eastern plans, 239; at Erfurt Congress, 243–5; Talleyrand's plea to, 244–5; and Napoleon's remarriage plans, 246; and Austrian alliance, 261, 271; Napoleon's displeasure with, 283; Talleyrand approaches for financial help, 296; and Napoleon's 1812 campaign against Russia, 307–8, 311, 318–20; appoints Wittgenstein to command, 334; assumes nominal army command, 335; at Bar-sur-Aube meeting with Allies, 351; urges attack on Paris, 352; in occupied Paris, 354, 358; criticizes King of Saxony, 361; death, 387; *see also* Russia

Algeria, 390–1

Alien Office (British), 101–2

Alle, River, 226, 228

American War of Independence (1775–83), 40

Amiens, Peace of (1801), 14–15, 35, 360

Amstetten, Austria, 122

Angoulême, Louis Antoine Bourbon, Duke of, 351

Anna, Grand Duchess of Russia, 287, 297

Ansbach, Bavaria, 112, 120, 198

Antwerp, Belgium, 10, 278–80

Arakcheev, Alexei, 138

Arc de Triomphe, Paris, 298

Ardennes: 1940 offensive, 203, 366; 1944 offensive ('Battle of the Bulge'), 352

Armed Neutrality *see* League of Armed Neutrality

Army of Andalucia (Spanish), 241

Army of Bohemia (Austrian), 337

Army of Boulogne (French), 76

Army of England (French): formed, 11; Napoleon commands, 62; becomes *Grande Armée*, 82

Army of the North (French), 365

Army of the Sambre-and-Meuse (French), 8

Arnhem airborne landing (1944), 280

Arnold, Benedict, 48n

Aspern-Essling, Battle of (1809), 160, 267, 269–72

Auckland, William Eden, 1st Baron, 65, 118

Auersperg, Prince, 126

Auerstädt, Battle of (1806), 207–11

Augereau, Marshal Pierre, Duc de Castiglione, 80, 203, 205–6, 222–3

Augezd (Austerlitz), 175

Augsburg, Bavaria, 113

Augusta, Duchess of Saxe-Coburg-Sallfeld, 166

Augustus III, King of Poland, 215

Aulic Council (Austria), 111–12, 123

Austen, Admiral Francis, 44

Austen, Jane, 41–2, 44, 293

Austerlitz, Battle of (1805): visibility, 84, 142; Davout at, 88; artillery at, 91, 162, 168; site and terrain, 94, 97, 131, 134, 136–7, 140–3; Napoleon's battle plan, 95, 119, 143–5, 163, 228; Allied strategy, 136–7; preparations, 148–50; troop numbers, 150, 165; conduct of battle, 151–7, 159–81; casualties, 163, 178–9, 182, 393; victory bulletin, 183; assessed, 186–9; weapons losses, 203; Russian disgrace at, 216

Austria: 1794 victories, 8; defeats in Italy, 8–9, 121; in Second Coalition, 12; Marengo

Index

Index

Index

Index

Murat, Caroline (*née* Bonaparte; Napoleon's
sister), 114, 380
Murat, Marshal Joachim, King of Naples: at
Tilsit, 2; in 1795 action against Paris rebels,
7; in Austrian campaign, 80−1, 110,
112−15, 122, 124−6, 128−9, 265; as
cavalry leader, 88; spying, 99; character,
113−14; coup at Danube bridge, 125−6;
rebuked by Napoleon, 125, 128, 181; at
Austerlitz, 144, 152, 160, 162−3, 171,
178−81, 188, 210; titles, 194, 232; in
Prussian campaign, 203−4, 207, 210−11;
makes advances to Countess Potocka, 217;
occupies Warsaw, 218; at Eylau, 221, 222,
224; threatens Königsberg, 226; and
Friedland, 227; reaches Niemen, 228;
command in Spain, 240; absent from
Wagram, 276; conspires against Napoleon,
300; and 1812 Russian campaign, 310,
317−18; enters Moscow, 319; commands
army on retreat from Russia, 324; returns
to Naples, 330; defeats Austrians (1813),
339; at Battle of Leipzig, 341; and
Napoleon's 1814 plan to attack Vienna,
346; deserts to British, 347−8; captured
and shot, 348n, 380−1; Italian rising
crushed (1815), 364; absent from Army of
the North, 365
Musset, Alfred de, 390

Nansouty, General Etienne Marie Antoine
Champion, Comte de, 161−2
Naples, Kingdom of, 12, 68−9; *see also* Murat,
Marshal Joachim
Napoleon I (Bonaparte), Emperor of the French:
meets Alexander I at Tilsit, 1−5, 229, 393;
hostility to England, 2, 45−6, 71, 146,
183, 238, 252, 292; background, 5−7;
Italian campaign, 8−9; insults Austrians,
9−10; acclaimed by Directory, 11; and
invasion plans against England, 11−12,
62−4, 67, 71, 76−7, 186−7; Egyptian
campaign, 12, 56; appointed First Consul
after Brumaire, 13; made Consul for life,
14; English visitors, 15−16; appearance and
dress, 16, 27−8, 134, 145; popularity and
ascendancy, 16, 23, 25, 193; civil reforms,
17−20, 23−4, 194−5, 298; attitude to
women, 20, 31; artistic taste, 24−5; and
censorship, 24−5; assassination plots
against, 25−6, 51, 64, 102, 286−7;

autocracy, 25, 233−5, 237; caricatured in
England, 25, 45; succession question, 25;
coronation, 26−7; has Enghien murdered,
26, 51; love-making, 27−8, 31−2;
personality and character, 27−30, 104−5;
relations with Josephine, 28, 31−4, 74−5,
108, 218−19, 234, 285; riding and
hunting, 28, 98, 232−3, 235, 244, 291;
personal relations, 30−1; religious
scepticism, 30; fathers child on Marie
Walewska, 32n, 286, 288; infidelities, 32,
108, 292; on Alexander I, 39; ambitions for
French paramountcy, 47, 49−50, 56, 71,
231−2, 283; rejects 1803 British terms,
50−1; territorial annexations, 50, 68;
declared Emperor, 52; and use of Navy,
61, 71−5; and Third Coalition strategy, 69;
1805 Austrian campaign, 76−82, 110−12,
115−21, 123−31; military science and
organization, 83−96, 98−100, 393;
position at Austerlitz, 84, 131, 134,
142−3; Austerlitz plans, 95, 119, 143−6,
163, 187−8; military staff and HQ, 96−8;
intelligence services, 99−101, 266,
299−300; encourages army morale, 103−5,
145; Bulletins, 104, 326; economic
practices, 107, 300; and Dupont's stand on
Danube, 115; near-escapes, 116; Ulm
victory, 116−17; learns of Trafalgar defeat,
120; rebukes Murat, 125, 128, 181; enters
Vienna, 126−7; Dolgorukov meets, 133;
cheered by troops before Austerlitz,
149−50; conduct of Austerlitz battle, 149,
153−5, 160, 166, 170−5, 177−81; eve-of-
battle practices, 149; post-Austerlitz
actions, 183; receives Emperor Francis after
Austerlitz, 184−6; pride in Austerlitz
victory, 186−7; and Blücher's movements
at Waterloo, 187; refuses magnanimous
peace with Austria, 192; triumphal
monuments, 193−4; largesse, 194; and
1806 Prussian campaign, 199−213; fury at
Bernadotte's behaviour at Auerstädt, 210;
enters Berlin, 211; in Poland, 214−18;
policy on Poland, 215, 220; relations with
Marie Walewska, 219−20, 225, 234, 285,
354−5; 1807 campaign against Russia,
220−1; and Eylau, 222−4; Friedland
victory, 228; triumphal 1807 return to
Paris, 231; Imperial Court, 232;
correspondence, 233−4; driven nature,

Index

Index